WHEREVER
THEY MAY BE!

Translated from the French by
Monroe Stearns and Natalie Gerardi

BEATE KLARSFELD

WHEREVER
THEY MAY BE!

The Vanguard Press   New York

80057

Original title: PARTOUT OU ILS SERONT
© 1972 by J. C. LATTES-EDITION SPECIALE, Paris.
This edition copyright © 1975 by Vanguard Press, Inc.
Published simultaneously in Canada by
Gage Publishing Co., Agincourt, Ontario.
All rights reserved.

Library of Congress Catalogue Card Number: 74–81809
ISBN: 0–8149–0748–2

Designer: Ernst Reichl
Manufactured in the United States of America

CONTENTS

ILLUSTRATIONS

These illustrations follow p. 120

WHEREVER
THEY MAY BE!

1

THE EDUCATION OF
A GERMAN GIRL

Three weeks after I was born, Hitler entered Prague.

In Berlin, my father, Kurt Künzel, quietly put down his pencils, quit his job as an insurance clerk, kissed his wife Helen and his only daughter Beate-Auguste good-by, and left on a long journey. Infantryman Kurt Künzel had rejoined his unit. He spent the summer of 1939 on maneuvers, and the summer of 1940 somewhere in France.

I have a picture of him smiling as he stands guard before a command post in Normandy. In those days he used to send us packages. Then, during the summer of 1941, his regiment was moved to the East. When winter came, a lucky case of double pneumonia got him transferred back to Germany, where he did bookkeeping for the army.

The English quickly set him free in 1945, and he rejoined his little family in the village of Sandau, where we had been grudgingly taken in by a relative after being driven from Berlin by the bombings. It was there that we and a group of terrified old people, women, and children witnessed the arrival of the "Tartars on their shaggy ponies." Polish laborers occupied our cousin's house and took our belongings—doubtless an even exchange, for we had spent several prosperous months in Lodz, then known as Litzmannstadt, with my godfather, a Nazi official.

For the benefit of those who think that childhood experiences determine a person's basic choices in life, let me say that the Soviet Tartars did us no harm. Neither my mother nor her little six-year-old daughter was molested or raped.

Late in 1945, we returned to Berlin, where the three of us lived in one room, first on Uhlandstrasse and then on Holsteinische Strasse, both in Wilmersdorf.

In elementary school I was a conscientious and well-behaved student. The school was so crowded that it was split into two sessions. Added to that, the school closed down completely in winter because of the coal shortage. I would spend whole days playing hide-and-seek with my friends in the acres of rubble, trying to climb to the roofs of the bombed-out houses and searching for hidden treasure.

In those days no one ever spoke of Hitler. Before April 1945, I remember reciting little poems in honor of the Führer in kindergarten. I spent my childhood among the ruins of Berlin, unaware of why the city had been destroyed and divided into four sectors. The only explanation for the world in which I grew up was: "We have lost a war and now we must work." My father didn't talk much and neither did my mother, unless she was heaping abuse on my father, which was not unusual.

When I was at the difficult age of fourteen or so, my parents began to get along better. Then I became the object of their recriminations. Neither of them had learned anything from the tremendous upheaval they had gone through. They were not Nazis, but they had voted for Hitler like everyone else. Still, they felt no responsibility for what had happened under the Nazis. Whenever my mother and her neighbors talked, they ended up whining about the injustice of their lot and recalling the precious things they had lost in the war. There was never a word of pity or understanding for other nations; they bitterly criticized the Russians.

Berlin resounded with the roar of airplanes bringing us food during the blockade. I asked no questions of others nor of myself, but continued along the path that had been set for me. In 1954 I was confirmed in the Evangelical Lutheran Church, but even then I had no faith. To this day I have remained a total stranger to the problem of religion. At that time, however, Providence was good to us: we moved into a two-room apartment on Ahrweilerstrasse, and I finally had my own room.

When I was sixteen, I entered the Schöneberg commercial high school, where I was an average student in the subjects that would prepare me to become a secretary in two years. My father was drinking and beginning to let himself go; my mother was grumbling constantly. I wanted to earn my own living and get away from my parents and that stifling atmosphere.

When I was eighteen, I got a job as a stenographer with Schering, a large drug firm. I would get up at 6:30 and cross Berlin on the S-Bahn to Wedding, where I would spend hour after hour pounding out on my typewriter chemical formulas I could not understand and making sausage sandwiches for my fat young boss. I was so young that my fellow workers had little use for me until I began to act like them and say bad things about the people in other departments. Then they let me share their gossip and tales of sexual adventures.

I seldom breathed the air of Germany, confined as I was in the sealed retort that was Berlin. Sometimes I would go to see an aunt in the "Zone"—East Germany—or visit some other relative in West Germany. I was shy and rarely went out with boys. They did not attract me much anyway. The ones I met reminded me of younger versions of my father. I didn't know any students at all, and I never had a chance to speak a language other than the one I had heard around me for twenty years.

In West Berlin, as in the Federal Republic, most people voted for Konrad Adenauer's Christian Democratic Union (CDU) or for the Social Democrats (SPD). My parents voted CDU. I myself liked the SPD because of Willy Brandt, whose young, open face contrasted with those of the other politicians.

I did not know myself at all and never tried to, but because I was completely unattached, with no change in sight, I felt a certain dissatisfaction. I showed it in a total lack of enthusiasm for the prospects my mother envisioned for me: a bank account, a trousseau, a suitable marriage such as my cousin Christa had made. Soon my family was calling me a bad daughter. But I held firm, and doubtless this is what saved me. I never again took that "straight" road that led, I had found, to anything but happiness.

From the time of my twenty-first birthday on February 13, 1960, I had but one thing in mind: to leave that city for which I nevertheless felt a deep, though inexplicable, fondness. In my many crossings from West to East Berlin, especially on Sundays, I had made the monuments, the museums, and even the streets of the two Berlins my own. For me Berlin did not end at the Brandenburg Gate as it did for those around me; it extended along Under den Linden, which was mine just as the Tiergarten was. I knew nothing of politics or history, but deep down I felt that in spite of all appearances, Berlin was still a single city. I even preferred the charm of the Eastern Zone, as somber and poor as it was, for there I seemed to meet up with a past I had not known. It was doubtless during these wanderings, on which I did nothing but daydream, that I became convinced, contrary to all facts, of the strange unity of my country. I was lonesome, but through the scattered compost of the two Germanys my roots were sinking deep into German soil.

On March 7, 1960, at 7 A.M., I first saw Paris. The sky was gray, the Gare du Nord was gray, my mood was gray. My mother had predicted the worst misfortunes; to her I was not merely ruined, I was already lost. My father had turned his back on me. To him Paris was the whorehouse of Europe, and he saw me consigned to the streets.

I knew only a few words of French, so I immediately enrolled in the Alliance française. Three days later I became an au pair girl, and I remained one for more than a year. I was sorry that in that home and family I was not treated a little like the eldest daughter. Many German girls came to Paris to learn French and to come into contact with French culture and ideas, but few of them really took advantage of all Paris had to offer. They often went back home dissatisfied with the hard life they had led.

On rue de Belvedere, in Boulogne, I slept in a disgusting attic and trembled with fear of the spiders. Twice a day I took the child of the family to school, and twice a day I picked him up again. Seven hours a day I washed, ironed, cooked, and cleaned. As I was a hard worker—and also fond of cleanliness—I had not yet learned to restrain my zeal. So in the evenings I was almost too tired when it came to studying my lessons in the blue Alliance française textbook about a model French couple, Monsieur and Madame Vincent, who surely would not have given so much work to girls who had come to France to love it.

Fortunately I got fired. I had had the nerve to invite a couple of friends over one Sunday, and my employer had returned to catch us watching television—*his* television.

So I moved in with the Fallauds, on rue Darcel at the edge of

the Bois de Boulogne. M. Fallaud tried to make love to me;
Mme. Fallaud took no interest in her home and chatted intermi-
nably on the telephone with her friends. I took care of four-year-old
Dominique and six-year-old Marc. I also learned how to make pies
—and more pies. I ventured to speak French only when I went
shopping, for I met only foreigners at the Alliance and was too
scared to talk to the fellows who came up to me in the Latin
Quarter, attracted by the map of Paris that marked me as a
stranger.

I still hardly knew the city that so enchanted me. What a dis-
covery! How different from those monotonous new apartment
houses of West Berlin. I loved to walk along the old streets of
the Marais or the ones between the Seine and the boulevard Saint-
Germain with my nose in the air, admiring the harmonious façades,
each with its own personality. Here people were animated, with a
thirst for life, each different from the others. A walk along the
boulevard Saint-Germain or the Champs-Elysées was like going
to a play. I had then, and I still have, a feeling that there was a
solid bond between the city and me, and that in Paris I would
blossom.

One May afternoon, I was waiting, as usual, for the Métro at
1:15 P.M. at the Porte-de-Saint-Cloud station. I felt someone staring at me and looked up to see a dark-haired young man in a
checked suit, with a briefcase in his hand.

"Are you English?" he asked.

Of course it was a trap. He was later to tell me that German
girls always say "no" to that question. Afterwards it's too late to
remain silent.

At the Sèvres-Babylone station he got off to go to the School of
Political Science—with my telephone number. Three days later
he called me, and I was happy. We went to see "Never on Sunday"
on the rue du Colisée.

Serge was finishing his education, and he was almost as poor
as I. I liked him at once for his mixture of seriousness and imagina-
tion. On a bench in the Bois I learned that he was Jewish and
that he had lost his father at Auschwitz. I was surprised and
moved, but also in a certain sense shrank back a little. In Berlin
I had hardly heard anything good about the Jews. Why was this
complication befalling me now? But Serge's expression had a
warmth that I have never stopped giving in to; I cuddled up to
him.

He told me about his father, whose example, I sensed, was still a model for him: his father had enlisted in the Foreign Legion in 1939, been one of the few survivors of his regiment in the Battle of the Somme, escaped from prison camp, joined the Resistance in Nice, and been arrested there in September 1943. He had died in the gas chamber at Auschwitz.

Summer vacation on the Côte Basque with my new family in a sad little suburban house surrounded by a garden where only gravel grew. Serge and I wrote to each other regularly. He corrected my mistakes in grammar. I got annoyed and called him "professor." He got irritated and replied:

"You must broaden your experience, read, dip into everything that great men have bequeathed us. Dostoyevsky, Tolstoy, and Stendhal didn't write to make money; they wrote for themselves and for you, too, so that you may become aware of who you are. So you have your work cut out for you."

Sometimes I complained:

"I envy you for not having such commonplace work as I have. You don't know how lucky you are. You know where you're going, but what's ahead for me? I need lots of courage, and you aren't here to give it to me."

In the fall we got back together again, and we stayed together. Serge made Paris, which he knew remarkably well, come alive for me. We never stopped talking. For too long I had been imprisoned within myself; it was like a deliverance. He brought history, art, the whole world of ideas into my life. I had more time: I used to sleep ten hours a night; now I made do with six, as he did.

When he realized how ignorant I was of my own country's history, Serge, who had a history degree from the Sorbonne, undertook to teach me. That was how I came into contact with the terrifying reality of Nazism.

I did not feel at all responsible for it as an individual, but insofar as I was one tiny part of the German nation, I became aware of new obligations. Was I tempted to stop being German? Serge himself had never thought of it. Not for a minute: that would have been too easy, he said. It was exciting as well as difficult to be a German after Nazism.

One day Serge told me how the story of Hans and Sophie Scholl's short life had prevented him from hating the Germans completely. It was a ray of light for me. I felt part of the Scholl family.

Hans and Sophie Scholl were students. At Easter 1943, they and Adrian Probst, Professor Huber, and a few others had written and distributed tracts in Munich condemning Nazism and its crimes. They were not heeded, but were arrested and beheaded. I read what Thomas Mann told the Germans over the American radio on June 27, 1943:

"Now their eyes were opened, and they laid their young heads on the block to testify to their faith and to the honor of Germany . . . after having told the president of the Nazi tribunal to his face: 'Soon you will be where we are now,' and affirmed as they faced death: 'A new faith is being born, a faith in honor and freedom.' Brave, magnificent youths! You shall not have died in vain. Never shall you be forgotten!"

Being on the fringe of ideologies, parties, and organizations, the only thing that made them risk their lives was their conscience as Germans. Although it seemed meaningless and sterile in 1943, the significance of their act has grown with time until it reached Serge and, through him, me. In them I saw myself.

November 1960. Serge was on military duty. The separation brought us still closer together. We went to see each other often, and we wrote every day. In my wretched French I told him:

"Your letters make my feeling for you grow. I don't know myself any more. I read and reread your letters, memorize the phrases that speak of love, and do not hesitate to believe every word. At first I always doubted them a little because I was afraid I might be disillusioned. But during the nights when you made love to me I could feel that you did love me, and now I return that love with all my heart. For the first time I am deliberately putting into writing that I love you."

Almost every evening Serge would telephone me. My employer, Mme. Pontard, a mathematics teacher who had not married off her daughter Monique, kept telling me: "Beate, he won't marry you. He's not serious. Frenchmen never marry foreigners."

What difference did it make? Waiting for Serge took all the burden out of my daily existence. He was on maneuvers at Mormelon in February 1961, when he wrote:

"You must make your life a poem, Beate. You must re-create it and participate in it, not unconsciously by merely existing, but consciously by living it and asserting yourself. Out of a little Greek expedition against Troy, Homer fashioned the *Iliad*. We all have the same power, if not in the realm of art, then at least in that of life. A little courage, a sense of humor, some energy, and some involvement with humanity: that's poetry enough to transform your life and lift it to the level of an exciting experience.

"Darling, all this advice has probably either put you to sleep or made you smile, but it's the best birthday present I can give you. It's also the most sincere and the most enduring. It's not your 'professor' who's writing you now, but your Serge, who loves you."

In June 1961, I met Serge's sister Tanya, who was a teacher of Russian. We spent a marvelous evening with Claude Nedjar, one of Serge's best friends, and Cibulsky, an extraordinary Polish actor who was to die in a train wreck a few years later. We were all so caught up in the Slavic charm of that evening that Tanya and Serge took me to their mother's.

I had both looked forward to and dreaded that first meeting with Raissa.

I had noticed when I was with Serge's Jewish friends that what had happened under Nazism had prejudiced them and their parents against young Germans. So I wondered what was in store for me in the next few minutes. Serge had waited a long time to introduce me to his mother; doubtless I had changed in the last year.

Raissa took my hand. She was distinguished looking, kindly and sincere, with an extraordinarily youthful point of view. In just a few minutes we were getting along well. I helped her make tea, and she reminisced about Berlin, where she had studied chemistry. She told me how she had come to Paris from the Bessarabian region of Rumania at the age of sixteen and had been one of the very few women admitted to study science at the Sorbonne, how she had married a Rumanian student in the Town Hall of the Fifth Arrondissement, and then, in her charming Russian accent, she talked about the war. When she told of the night her husband was arrested, I sensed all the anguish that separates the Jews and the Germans.

RAISSA'S STORY

Everyone has one unforgettable event in his life, something that was either extremely joyful or sorrowful, Raissa began. The night of September 30, 1943, has left its mark on my entire life. I want to tell you about it.

We were living in Nice, having managed to get out of Paris in June 1940, just before the Germans arrived. My husband had a friend, an engineer, who was in the Resistance. This man told us to get a hiding place ready in case the Gestapo came, and he even built us one, working at night. He put a false wall in the back of a closet and painted it white. High up on that wall he put some shelves that I stacked with bed linen, and below he put a pole on which I hung our clothes. There was a door that closed from the inside, and to enter we had to stoop to the floor. We had a hard time explaining to the children, who were usually pretty wild, that they had to be absolutely quiet in there if the Gestapo came after us.

Up until that awful night the Gestapo had raided only hotels and rooming houses. But that day my husband had come home in a gloomy mood. "From now on," he said, "I'm not going out any more. In a few days we'll get out of Nice."

We went to bed. After midnight I heard a truck outside—there was usually no traffic after 8 P.M.—and suddenly our apartment was flooded with light. This was it. I quickly woke my husband, and we grabbed the children and put them in the hiding place. Then I went in. My husband stayed behind for a few moments to straighten up the beds and hide our clothes. Then he joined us.

The hiding place was a tiny triangle of space next to the apartment of some people from Alsace: a mother, a father, a girl the same age as my eleven-year-old, an eighteen-year-old girl, and a twenty-four-year-old son. The father, M. Goetz, had told us they were Protestants who had left Alsace to protect their son. As they were French, they wanted to stay in France. They were really Jews like us, but in those days the Jews mistrusted one another. Fear does strange and horrible things to people.

Their son never slept at home; he probably had a hiding place somewhere else. When the Gestapo banged on their door, the younger girl opened it and asked for identification. (During those troubled times many false policemen would show up at Jewish homes to steal money and jewels.) The only answer she got was that one of the Gestapo broke her nose with his revolver.

I can't describe the poor girl's howls, her parents' shouts, and the Gestapo's threats—all of which we could hear in our hiding place. They were apparently beating the young girl, who was crying and saying: "I don't know where my brother is. Leave me alone." The father was shouting out the window for the French police: "We're French. Protect us. The Gestapo are murdering us!"

My husband was so horrified that he crawled out of our hiding place, saying: "I'm leaving to save you. I can stand a concentration camp. I'm strong." (The poor man was thirty-eight years old, 5'5", and healthy.) "You couldn't take it, and neither could the children." (We didn't know about the gas chambers then.)

I tried to stop him, but he went out. The Germans soon pounded on our door. My husband opened it, and I could hear their first question: "Where are your wife and children?"

Arno, my husband, had the presence of mind to answer that we had gone to the country while the apartment was being disinfected. They began to search it. You can imagine, Beate, how I felt when one of them opened the closet, pushed our clothes aside, and came closer and closer to the false wall of our hiding place. Probably God took pity on us, for he did not touch the wooden wall, which was only inches away from him. My daughter had bronchitis and was coughing a lot, but her instinct for self-preservation was so strong that she stuffed her pajamas into her mouth so she wouldn't cough. Serge almost suffocated, his face was pressed so tight to my breast.

Our neighbors' screams continued. The Gestapo were searching every floor of our building. It was like a horror movie.

Finding no one but my husband in our apartment, the Germans ordered him to get dressed. Then they left. My husband came over to the hiding place and whispered: "Give me the front-door key." He kissed my hand and said, "God help you." Then he left to calm down the neighbors. Alas, they all died in Auschwitz.

Until two in the morning all we could hear was screaming and weeping and people coming and going. Everyone was rounded up and forced into the trucks. Then, suddenly, it was quiet, but the stillness was more terrifying than all the noise had been. I was afraid to move. The children had to go to the bathroom, and they used the floor. It was pitch dark, and the air was stifling.

We stayed in the hiding place until 6 A.M., standing because there was no room to sit. Finally the children couldn't take it any longer, so I summoned all my courage and opened the false door. I told the children not to budge and not to scream if one of the Gestapo happened to catch me. Then I crept out into the apartment and got our clothes. I looked out the window; there was no one on the street. About seven o'clock I heard some neighbors go downstairs.

I was afraid there still might be soldiers on the landings, but at the same time I couldn't stand the fear and uncertainty any more. So I opened the apartment door and when I saw someone I knew go by I asked him if the Germans were still there. He said they were gone. Then he went out and came back to tell me that the street was safe. We fled. The friend who had built our hiding place took us in.

We had been saved, thanks to my husband's self-sacrifice.

2

A NAZI MUST NOT BE CHANCELLOR

That evening I became part of the Klarsfeld family. They were a bit Bohemian, everyone thought more of the others than of himself, and there was no generation gap. The mother had sacrificed for the children, and the children had close ties to the mother without losing one speck of their independence. Tanya and Serge had each seen a good part of the world, more or less as vagabonds. What's more, Serge sent me to Greece and Turkey in 1961, for he had often hitchhiked through those countries. I also went to Bucharest in 1962 to meet Raissa's sister, Lida.

In March 1963, Tanya became engaged to Alik, a Jewish engineer, whom she had met in Bucharest before he left Rumania. In the middle of the engagement party Serge suddenly got up: "I forgot to tell you that we're not just celebrating Tanya and Alik's engagement, but Beate and Serge's too."

We were married on November 7, 1963, in the Town Hall of the Sixteenth Arrondissement. Serge later told me that he had had a raging toothache all that day and was not even aware that we were really married.

That night we boarded a sleeper for our honeymoon. The destination: Munich, the one artistic center in Europe that Serge, my Wandering Jew, had not been to. He had just come out on top in the competitive examination for assistant director of the French National Radio and Television System (ORTF). In July 1964, he was promoted to work with the deputy director of radio broadcasting. And I had left my job with a firm of Lyon silk manufacturers and taken another as a bilingual secretary with the Franco-German Alliance for Youth (OFA), which de Gaulle and Adenauer had just established.

We had set the scene to live a stable, orderly life like that of thousands of other young couples.

I was very enthusiastic about the OFA. I even offered to write a handbook for young German girls working *au pair* in Paris. The book made a big splash in Germany, for it came out just at the right time: a German *au pair* girl had recently been murdered in Neuilly, and the German papers were full of the details.

My handbook was also the beginning of a great deal of friction between me and the OFA, its secretary general, François Altmayer, who was then in the Bonn office, and the director of the French wing, Robert Clément.

Although the OFA had approved of my writing the handbook, and although in the final analysis it subscribed to the line I took in it, it did not like to admit that the ideas of a young stenographer could be important. When I was invited to speak at conferences on Franco-German exchanges as a kind of expert, the OFA directors were quite cool to me, and they would always be careful to make it clear that "Mme. Klarsfeld is expressing only her own opinions. . . ."

An incident with Voggenreiter, the publisher of the German edition of my handbook, further chilled my relations with the OFA by revealing how dependent the German branch was on the Bonn government, even though it was theoretically part of an independent bi-national agency.

I had listed among the cultural associations the Franco-German Exchange, which sponsored seminars in German history at the Sorbonne. Now, this was a French friendship association with the German Democratic Republic [East Germany]. My German publisher, who was hoping to sell a good number of my handbooks to the various state education ministries, had to withdraw all copies to revise the page with the address of the Franco-German Exchange. The Youth Minister, who had planned to distribute the handbook to girls about to go to France, changed his mind at the last minute.

I was severely scolded: "Don't you realize that you have listed an association connected with East Germany? You must be out of your mind!"

We couldn't understand each other, the OFA directors and I. To them, Germany was simply the Federal Republic. To me, Germany was all the German people.

In the spring of 1966 I would wheel Arno, my baby, from the Porte de Saint-Cloud to the poets' garden at the Porte d'Auteuil. We had decided that our son was to be a Jew and bear the name of Serge's father. The OFA had granted me a year's leave of absence without pay. We had taken a three-room apartment on boulevard Murat, a few doors away from my mother-in-law's. I changed Arno's diapers, played with him like a doll, and found every smile a precious moment.

When I could, I would go to the Town Hall of the Fifth Arrondissement, where there was Marguerite Dunand's collection of books on feminism. I was doing research on a subject dear to my heart—The German Woman as the French See Her—which I hoped to turn into a book.

On weekends the three of us would stroll along the *quais* of Paris, and in the bookstalls I would pick up colorful observations by French writers—travelers, prisoners of war, reporters—of the love life of German women. I learned a great deal about my fellow citizens and about their observers. A periodical, *Women in the Twentieth Century,* asked me for an article. I wrote:

I have come to wonder what made me and plenty of other German women leave our homeland. There are many good reasons for doing something specific in another country, such as studying the language or the culture, but I think the efforts we made reveal a more powerful and often unconscious motivation—the desire to be free.

Under Wilhelm II our grandmothers' whole existence could be summed up by the three K's (*Kinder, Kirche, Küche*—children, church, kitchen). For a few years during the Weimar Republic they could breathe more freely, and they took hope. Then Hitler sent them back to the children again, and later to the factories when the need for munitions became pressing. . . .

Since the war, women have made a real contribution to the creation of a new Germany, which has turned out to be not so new after all and in which now, as in the past, they play hardly any role in politics. A political role means participating in the real responsibilities, in the destiny of our country. How many women have done this in the whole history of Germany?

Doubtless this lack of participation by women in politics is one of the basic reasons for the political imbalance of our country and for the ease with which it allows itself to be dragged into disasters.

Public opinion in Germany is now in the process of taking a dangerous turn which will once again lead to a domesticated woman dedicated to providing her husband with the greatest possible comfort and to her natural reproductive function.

I belonged to the German Social Democratic Party. After my book was published, Willy Brandt, who at that time was mayor of West Berlin, received me in his office and told me about his stay in Paris after he had fled his country in 1937. I know many Germans consider him a traitor, but I admire him for not having said, "My country right or wrong."

I was to meet Willy Brandt again later.

When I went back to work at OFA in October 1966, my job in the information division had been eliminated for "budgetary reasons." I found myself back at the typewriter, and sometimes at the switchboard, frustrated by lack of opportunity for creative work.

In December 1966, our whole family rented a spacious six-room apartment in a splendid turn-of-the-century building on rue de l'Alboni overlooking the Seine. My sister-in-law, my brother-in-law, their four-month-old son Maldoror, Raissa, and the three of us all moved in together. It is in this very building and in this very apartment that they filmed, after our departure in 1970, the celebrated movie *The Last Tango in Paris*.

Our pets were also part of the family: Minette, our alley cat; Nikita, Tanya's white cat; Petia, the gentle cocker spaniel; and Kroutch, the hamster. Serge budgeted our expenses: we paid two-fifths of the rent; Tanya and Alik, the same; Raissa, one-fifth.

I was in charge of the food, and two or three times a week I went marketing at Les Halles. We were able to hire a maid and two *au pair* girls—one for the morning, the other for the afternoon —to look after the children. It was a fascinating experience, this family kibbutz in Passy.

Just as we were getting settled there, Kurt-Georg Kiesinger, the prime minister of Württemberg-Baden, began his campaign for the chancellorship of the Federal Republic. A few French newspapers, *Le Figaro* and *Combat* among them, brought up his past work as a propagandist for Nazism. I could not believe my eyes, and dashed out to get some German newspapers. The only protests came from a famous writer and a leading philosopher.

Günter Grass wrote an open letter to Kiesinger:

How can the youth of this country oppose this party of the past, which is now rising from the dead in the form of the National Democratic Party (NPD) [a neo-Nazi party], if you crush the Chancellorship of the Federal Republic under the weight of your past?

And philosopher Karl Jaspers was stunned:

Many Germans, a small minority, perhaps a million, are astonished. The possibility that their nation might be governed by a former Nazi is terrifying to them. . . . What seemed impossible ten years ago is now happening almost without opposition. It was inevitable that former Nazis would succeed in rising to high posts, even in politics. For there were too few non-Nazis to keep the government, the educational system, and the economy running. But if a former Nazi should become chief of state, it would mean that from now on the fact that a man has been a Nazi would be of no importance.

Into my mind flashed Hans and Sophie Scholl's final appeal to each and every one of us:

Once the war is over, those who have been to blame must be severely punished to rid anyone of the idea of repeating a similar adventure. . . . Don't forget the little lieutenants of that regime either. Remember their names so that none of them will get away with what they have done. Don't let them change their tune at the last minute and act as if nothing had happened.

I kept hoping that Kiesinger would not be elected, that the Bonn deputies would realize that they were responsible to Germany. But he did get elected, and became head of the West German government. Immediately there was a conspiracy of silence in the press, especially as a great coalition of Christian Democrats and Social Democrats had been formed. Brandt became foreign minister.

So it was necessary to react—but how? The example of the Scholls told me how. The important thing in the fight against Nazism is to strike right away, even if you are not sure of succeeding. Above all, it is necessary to be brave, follow your conscience, keep your eyes open, and act. Afterwards—well, in my case, my actions would pursue me and drive me onward, and others would draw inspiration from them.

I decided that the first thing I would do would be to take a stand publicly. I wrote an article and took it to two morning dailies. They listened to me politely and advised me to go to *Combat.* I had some trouble finding the old building on rue du Croissant in Montmartre that housed the newspaper that is keeping the spirit of the French Resistance very much alive.

The young editor I talked to, Michel Voirol, seemed surprised to find a German determined to protest Kiesinger's election. The first open discussion appeared on January 14, 1967, the day of Kiesinger's official visit to Paris. I wrote for the opposition:

Official Germany has several faces. Willy Brandt is the only one of whom the French need not be suspicious. At the moment, when Germany seems to want to be identified with the person of Kiesinger, fate has offset that desire with Willy Brandt's installation in high government office.

It was not hatred of Kiesinger, nor a morbid fascination with the past, nor despair that motivated me. A future for Germany was within our grasp. "Why You Should Bet on Willy Brandt" was the title of my second article, which appeared in *Combat* in March 1967.

As a German I deplore Kiesinger's accession to the Chancellorship. The election of this former member of the Nazi Party—even if that was merely opportunism—is practically an exoneration of an era and an attitude. Sociologist Hannah Arendt used the phrase "the banality of evil" in speaking of Eichmann. To me Kiesinger represents the respectability of evil. . . . There is certainly nothing to prevent Kiesinger from feeling at peace with himself and, now that he is in a position of power, from easing the consciences of those few Germans who did have pangs.

Willy Brandt's attitude was the opposite of Kiesinger's. As a young man he was sincerely democratic, and he has never ceased being so. How many others can say as much when it was so easy to swim with the current? . . . The true German democrats who fought Nazism with actual weapons were very few. Paradoxically, they almost became the bad conscience of Germany by furnishing proof that it was possible to become involved on the side of right and morality. . . .

Willy Brandt and his team are the only ones who can set Germany's

political life on a new course because they really want to do so and
because they have shown proof of their political maturity. Attaining
the Foreign Ministry of the Federal Republic is the first step in their
achievement of power. It is in the interest of countries that fear
Germany's ambitions to help Brandt become Chancellor. The countries of the East in particular should welcome him with all the consideration and admiration due a man who was and still is their ally
in the war against Nazism. They should also regard him as the only
true spokesman for Germany, and should refuse to deal with Kiesinger.
Finally, they should do their utmost to help Brandt in his efforts to
solve the German problem by bringing the two Germanys together
in a socialist framework. Thus the German people will, doubtless with
satisfaction, grow accustomed to the prospect of having as their Chancellor not some former minor official in the Nazi regime, but a foreign
minister who is the pride of his country. In that respect the interests
of France, and of all Europe from the Atlantic to the Urals and beyond, are the same.

At that time Brandt was almost unknown in France, and no
one, not even in Germany, dared gamble on his political future.

All of my political stands increased the hostility of my superiors
and colleagues at the OFA. No one ever mentioned my articles
in my presence, but there was a noticeable effort to make my
working conditions more and more unbearable. A confrontation
was at hand.

Though I felt the storm gathering at work, the joys of my home
life absorbed me completely. Our private life was more easygoing
and gay than if each element of our commune had lived apart.
Arno was growing up and he delighted me. Serge had resigned
from ORTF and joined Continental Grains, the leading multinational cereal firm. He was being trained as a specialist in complicated brokerage matters, and so he traveled frequently, especially
in Eastern Europe, where his knowledge of Russian was of great
help to him.

We were so well organized that I could go traveling alone, as
Serge had done ten years earlier. In May I went to the United
States and to Guatemala, where Serge had relatives.

When I returned to Paris, I spent a day with Serge discussing
events in the Middle East. The next day—June 6, 1967—war broke
out. Serge and his constant companion Josy, who also worked for
Continental Grains, enlisted as volunteers at the Israeli Embassy.
They took a leave of absence, bought plane tickets for Tel Aviv,

and took off early one Monday afternoon, leaving me in tears. My brother-in-law Alik had promised Serge that he would look after Arno and me if anything should happen to him. I did not try to discourage Serge from going, for I had visited Israel with him the previous year and knew his devotion to the Jewish cause. I also knew the dangers that threatened Israel.

Serge's plane was delayed in Athens, but twenty-four hours later an El Al plane took on all who wanted to cross the Mediterranean. On Wednesday, he was one of the first to gather at the Wailing Wall.

There was no further need for volunteers, but by using his old ORTF card Serge was able to follow the Israeli troops in their attack on Syria. When the fighting was over on Saturday, he took a plane to Bucharest. The following Monday, Josy and Serge went back to work at Continental Grains.

On August 30, 1967, the OFA fired me.

I telephoned Serge at once, my throat so tight that my voice was barely audible:

"The director has just forwarded me a letter from the Secretary General of the OFA that says I'm about to be disciplined."

"For being late?" was Serge's first thought.

"No. For reasons of policy. Listen to what it says: '. . . I have had to authorize disciplinary action against you with a view toward your dismissal. The reason is that an article entitled "Germany's Troubled Sleep," which appeared over your signature in Combat on July 27, 1967, is a serious infraction of the rules governing OFA employees . . .' "

"Speak more distinctly. I can't understand you."

I went on reading:

" 'To be specific, you wrote as follows: "If the USSR recognized the danger Kiesinger represents to democracy in Germany in the future, and if it truly wanted to get rid of him, there is no doubt that it would be morally justified in the eyes of the whole world. If it did so, the USSR would greatly influence Germany in the direction of democracy and socialism. . . . Kiesinger has been pussyfooting in these early days of his regime, for the man who was able to gain as high a reputation in the ranks of the Brownshirts as he has now attained with the Christian Democrats is well aware of how much his future will depend on the first weeks of his administration."

" 'Your article, therefore, seriously violates the loyalty requirements set forth in Article 3 of Paragraph 2 in the Office Regulations, according to which every employee is obliged to refrain in
his statements, pursuits, and publications, from any behavior likely
to reflect unfavorably on OFA . . .' "

"Come to my office right away," Serge said, "and we'll talk it
over."

The letter upset me completely. To be dismissed without notice
or compensation made me feel that I had committed some crime
that had disgraced the OFA.

I removed my personal possessions from my desk. No one, not
even the girl at the switchboard, dared say good-by to me or shake
my hand.

When I reached the Continental Grains building, Serge's jaw
was clenched, and he shuddered as if he had a high fever every
time he felt his emotions rise. My own feelings didn't show as
much, but each of us had the same lump in his throat.

One of Serge's friends tried to calm us down. "Stop this," he
said. "You can take it all back, since you've been given an opportunity to reply to the charges against you within two weeks."

Another said: "Don't get into a complicated and fruitless lawsuit. Remember, you need the money. Get a better job."

A third said: "Now you can see what it costs to lead a crusade."

That was too much. I didn't want to listen to them any longer.
Serge took me to a bistro on rue des Saussaies, where we sat looking across a table at each other and saying nothing.

"How can I take your being fired without making some protest?" said Serge. "You're the first woman in France since the war
ended to tell the truth about a Nazi. That would be the worst
kind of submission."

He reached for my hand across the table and kissed it. There
flashed into my mind a photograph of a young couple lined up on
the rubble of the Warsaw ghetto with other Jews about to be
massacred. Standing in ranks before them, helmeted and booted
and with machine guns in hand, were their S.S. masters. The man
and the woman were leaning against each other, and he was holding her hand. No, he was not protecting her. It was too late for
that. But their love would survive. They were already at death's
gate, yet their eyes and lips showed something that could not be
destroyed—the look of two people who love each other.

The picture faded, but it was the turning point of our life. We made up our minds to fight, and our fight would take priority over everything else. It was a decision reached in a moment and with scarcely a word spoken. But it was a total commitment. We would fight not to ease our conscience, but to win. We knew that that meant total war. Serge's career, our family life, our material security all would take second place.

3

KIESINGER'S RECORD UNDER HITLER

It was only a step from rue des Saussaies to the Elysée. I went there at once and asked for Secretary General Bernard Tricot. He was astonished to see me, but he did listen. His reserved manner, however, gave me little hope.

On September 13 he wrote: "I must tell you that in my opinion the President's office has no authority to intervene on your behalf. Neither is it up to me to become involved in the proceedings you have already instituted."

So the highest level French authorities were washing their hands of the matter, even though I had been a French citizen for four years.

I now had to fight on two levels: one, for justice by means of a lawsuit; the other, to sway German and French opinion with the revelation of Chancellor Kiesinger's Nazi past.

As a matter of fact, the two became one, for we decided to bring the case before a French court rather than before the OFA arbitration committee, which was composed of two judges appointed by the German and French governments. Such a committee would bury the matter quietly, whereas if the case were heard in the magistrate's court of the Eighth Arrondissement in Paris, it would have a chance of reaching the public through newspaper reports.

Serge reminded me that the earliest newspaper reports about Kiesinger would surely be in the Potsdam archives in East Germany. He had already got the basic data from the Library of Contemporary Jewish Documents (CDJC) in Paris. Then he remembered one of the lecturers he had had at the Sorbonne, Professor George Castellan, a historian of the German army. Serge telephoned him and told him he wanted to do research in the Potsdam archives. Castellan gave him the name of a Herr Heyne, the director of Franco-German Cultural Relations in East Berlin.

In 1967, East Berlin was one of the most mysterious of European cities, and to go there with such a purpose as ours could be compromising. Serge had worked for Martial de la Fournière, a technical adviser to Secretary of the Army Pierre Messmer, and so he wrote him as follows:

"My wife, a French citizen, has been dismissed from her job here in France for publishing an article exposing a German as a former Nazi. France has done nothing to help her, but I myself feel obliged to assist her. We need to collect data on Kiesinger. The papers we need are in East Berlin. I want to make all this clear so that I will not be accused of foolhardiness, espionage, interference with diplomatic relations, etc."

Serge's forthrightness must have had some effect, for we had no trouble whatever.

Serge took several days' leave, and went to East Berlin. He located Heyne in the Volkskammer and explained what he wanted. He was directed to the Ministry of the Interior, where on the following day he explained his intention of collecting data on Kiesinger's past to a committee of seven or eight persons. The committee's response was favorable, and for the next three days Serge took copious notes on the thick files he was given. He returned from East Berlin with a huge folder of photocopies. He had also discovered a book by Raimund Schnabel on radio propaganda under Hitler.

To the papers from East Berlin we added items we had unearthed at the Wiener Library in London, as well as thousands of microfilms we ordered—to the tune of $400—from the United States State Department catalog. A quick survey of these papers enabled me to write and have printed at our expense a pamphlet entitled "The Truth about Kurt-Georg Kiesinger," which appeared before Christmas 1967.

We began to experience the day-to-day hardships produced by

our campaign. It was so expensive that we had to stop paying taxes.
Though we knew they would only increase by such postponement, we at least had cash in the meantime. We reduced our food
budget and sold our old car. We dismissed the nurse and one of
the au pair girls.

The hours I devoted to politics conflicted with the housework,
but I had no trouble switching from one to the other. I was washing our own dirty linen and Germany's at one and the same time.
My mother-in-law worried about what would happen to us, thinking that an undertaking like ours would deprive us of a normal
existence. She kept reminding us of our duty to Arno. Deep in
her heart, however, she approved of what we were doing. She took
care of Arno when I had to be away, and when we needed money,
she or my sister-in-law helped us out. My own mother, however,
who had been a widow for a year, highly disapproved of my campaign. To her it was quite natural for me to have been fired for
criticizing the Chancellor.

Night after night I pored over miles of microfilm looking for
even the tiniest items that might support my argument. Bit by
bit I was able to reconstruct Kiesinger's past. Luck was with me.
In the summer of 1968, I met the historian Joseph Billig, who had
written an extraordinary work, *L'Hitlérisme et le systéme con-
centrationnaire* ("Hitlerism and the Concentration System").

Billig was one of the few persons who truly understood and
could describe the part some German diplomats had played in the
extermination of the Jews under Hitler. He seemed, however, un-
communicative and skeptical when I first told him about Kiesinger.

"What he did is of little interest to me," Billig said. "I doubt
that he did very much."

Nevertheless, he agreed to examine our research, and soon he
admitted that it had convinced him. Thus we were able to prepare
a deeper study. *Kiesinger or Subtle Fascism* contained my direct
accusation and definitely stripped the veil from the true face of
Kurt-Georg Kiesinger.

THE KIESINGER RECORD

Kiesinger joined the Nazi Party on May 1, 1933, when he was
a young lawyer close to thirty years of age—no longer an adolescent.
His membership card, which he kept until the collapse of Nazism,
was No. 2,633,930.

In his student days he belonged to some Catholic organizations, but after 1933 he tried to integrate his militant Catholicism with Hitler's policies as a whole. His conscience as a Christian fitted in with Hitler's anti-Semitism, which proposed to the new Germany the exaltation of German grandeur.

In August 1940, Foreign Minister Joachim von Ribbentrop assigned Kiesinger to the department of radio broadcasting as an assistant scientific aide. In this capacity the thirty-six-year-old lawyer first put his beliefs and his abilities at the service of the Third Reich.

Gradually he advanced to head of programming. His title of assistant scientific aide merely identified him as an employee of the Foreign Ministry, for bureaucratic practice in the Third Reich was so flexible that this designation bore little relation to the actual nature of Kiesinger's work. He rose from the grade of assistant to that of chief officer in the department. A contractual arrangement with the ministry allowed for easy advancement, provided it did not involve a change of title, for there was a quota. Kiesinger's nontitular position in the Foreign Ministry also facilitated his delicate role as intermediary between Ribbentrop's Foreign Ministry and Goebbels' Propaganda Ministry, which were in constant conflict.

Kiesinger owed his job to Under-Secretary for Foreign Affairs Martin Luther, a confirmed Nazi, whom Ribbentrop had hired in order to introduce into the Foreign Ministry the Hitlerian spirit that had been lacking there. Ribbentrop thought he needed to "reconcile his ministry with Hitler's closest disciplines and be the link between them." To accomplish this "all important" end, Ribbentrop organized under Luther's supervision the "Germany Department."

Collaboration with Party members in matters of foreign policy actually meant collaboration with Himmler, who had become the absolute authority on putting Hitler's ideology into practice. Luther's department, therefore, was organized to work in accordance with the demands the Party made on the Third Reich's foreign policy. At the Nuremberg Trials, Secretary for Foreign Affairs Ernst von Weizsäcker said that Luther's department "had tried to get control of other departments. It created its own subdivisions to handle matters that were not at all the province of the Foreign Ministry, such as racial policies, the Jewish problem, police administration, and so on. Luther's job was guaranteed by Ribbentrop, Reinhard Heydrich's Security Service (S.D.), and the Gestapo."

The broadcasting department was dominated by Luther's attitude. It dealt with matters more from an ideological than a diplomatic point of view. Kiesinger was not a traditional diplomat in the Foreign Ministry; he was closer to those who were developing under the alarming shadow of the Party and especially of the S.S.

According to a decree of September 8, 1939, the broadcasting of propaganda over stations in Germany or in occupied countries was entrusted to Ribbentrop. The department was charged above all with influencing or directing foreign radio stations and, should the need arise, acquiring them so that they might also disseminate Nazi ideas.

In July and August 1940, Kiesinger led a foreign newspapermen's tour of France. In his report on August 21, 1940, he wrote:

Their news stories were intended, first, to impress their readers with the invincibility of German arms in the war and, secondly, to show the behavior and attitude of the victor during the war and after the battles. In addition we had to demonstrate clearly to all readers, especially to those in Southeast Asia and Latin America, where France is considered Europe's leading nation in politics and culture, that such an image was false. . . . The news stories on the attitude of the German soldier in France demonstrated what the victors had accomplished, the importance of the reconstruction work they were doing, and the extraordinary achievements of the Nazi welfare administration in meeting the needs of the population and of returning refugees. . . . Once I had the opportunity to deliver a little lecture at Strasbourg on the history of Alsace-Lorraine, which was well received.

Kiesinger's superiors appreciated his efforts right from the start. There was a twelve-point program that all stations under German control were to implement, which Gerhard Rühle, the director of the department, signed on September 26, 1941, before sending it on to Hitler. As a matter of fact, the text was typed on a special large-type machine to spare Hitler the trouble of looking for his glasses. Kiesinger, Hans Schirmer, Markus Timmler, and others of Rühle's associates compiled the program. It was Kiesinger's job to see that each station adapted it in such a way that it would contain authentic Nazi dogma, and also to do what was necessary to correct errors and delete exaggerations that might impair its effectiveness.

1. Germany will win the war.
2. Germany has the best armaments, the best soldiers, and the best leadership.

3. England started the war and is waging it by means of other peoples' money and blood.
4. Churchill is making war on civilians.
5. That Jew Roosevelt aspires to worldwide Jewish supremacy.
6. Roosevelt wants to conquer South America.
7. Roosevelt and Churchill want to impose their tyranny on the high seas that belong to the whole world.
8. Hitler has delivered the world from Bolshevism, humanity's greatest danger.
9. The Archbishop of Canterbury is the apostle of antichrist.
10. Germany is fighting for social justice against Jewish capitalistic exploitation.
11. Germany is creating a new order.
12. Hitler's victory means a thousand years of prosperity, happiness, and peace.

Kiesinger rose very rapidly in the broadcasting department, which had about two hundred employees in Berlin alone, and as many outside the Reich in stations answerable to it located in German embassies and occupied territories.

In 1941, Kiesinger became head of the department's Division B, one of the two bureaus of General Affairs. He was responsible for the preparation and the execution of the line to be taken in propaganda originating in Germany for broadcast to other countries, the restructuring of propaganda as a whole from the point of view of means and methods, proposals for propaganda programs, suggestions for effective subjects and arguments. In addition he had to coordinate the work of the eleven different offices that handled broadcasts to other countries: Western Europe and French-speaking Canada; the British Empire; Spain, Portugal, and Latin America; Italy; Southeast Asia; the USSR; India; the Far East; the United States; Africa; and the office that dealt with the colonial problem.

Kiesinger also supervised the censorship of all programs destined for other countries. Consequently, after 1941 he was directly responsible for the content of Nazi broadcasts to foreign nations.

In 1941, Kiesinger also joined the board of directors of Inter-radio, the gigantic broadcasting company established by Ribbentrop and Goebbels as a vehicle for propaganda on the Nazi war abroad. It used Fifth Column methods, in which Kiesinger was an expert. At that time, in fact, he gave lectures on "basic problems in political propaganda" for the benefit of future specialists.

As a member of that board Kiesinger was, in the name of the Foreign Ministry, a shareholder in the company to the extent of ten million Reichsmarks. He was, furthermore, the liaison officer between the Foreign Ministry and Interradio; if the various departments of Interradio did not follow the directives issued by the regional offices of his department, he had authority to make them do so.

Interradio's policy objectives are clearly set forth in a document dated November 5, 1941:

After our victory in this war, the energies now devoted to fighting can be rechanneled to the construction of a new Europe under German authority. Persistent political and cultural work for several decades to come should root out all forces and ideologies hostile to the German way and to National Socialism. That is why the Reich has always been interested in constructing a network of German-controlled broadcasting stations abroad. . . .

The foreign broadcasting stations that Germany controls or influences will at first be under the supervision of the central departments in Berlin. They will be a means of warfare to bring about in due time a truly forward-looking contribution to German culture, science, and economics, which will thus actively promote the grand design of Germany's policies.

Thus the directors of Interradio were not only citizens fulfilling their duty as combatants in the civilian sector of the Fatherland during the war, but they were also the future builders of a new Europe to be dominated by Hitler.

The following document, issued in March 1942, gives an accurate picture of the extent of Kiesinger's influence at Interradio:

Authority over the political content of the Foreign Ministry's broadcasts is not limited to the text of news programs alone, but extends to all Interradio programs. You are requested to take note of the fact that Herr Kiesinger, director of the department of foreign broadcasts, has been appointed permanent liaison officer between the Foreign Ministry's broadcasting department and Interradio. Herr Kiesinger is in charge of issuing all directives concerning general propaganda broadcasts to other countries and of their execution.

In 1943, Kiesinger was appointed deputy director of the broadcasting department. He also remained director of Bureau B and was made director of the second general division, Bureau A, which was responsible for broadcasts, international radio relations, licensing of broadcasting stations, and technical matters connected with them. In March 1942, he also took over coordination of broadcasts to the East.

Consequently Kiesinger became the moving force of the whole huge, complex, and powerful organization for broadcasting Nazi propaganda. He was the only one who could negotiate the political and bureaucratic complications of this extraordinary spider web. He was behind all programs, owing to his authority to issue explicit directives for adapting propaganda to different geographical regions. Once the programs had been adjusted to the circumstances, their text had to be sent to Kiesinger for his approval.

Kiesinger also held the extremely powerful position of deputy to S.S.-Standartenführer Gerhard Rühle, whose Party card was No. 694. Kiesinger was close to the new chief of the department of cultural policy, S.S.-Brigadeführer Dr. Franz Six after Six returned from Russia, where, in his capacity as chief of Hitler's Einsatzgruppen, he had supervised the liquidation of commissars as well as thousands of Jews.

Kiesinger devoted particular attention to the pivotal point of Hitlerism, namely, the Jewish problem, and apparently he never questioned the Nazi oppression of Jews or the "final solution"— extermination.

Kiesinger's radio propaganda aimed at arousing anti-Semitism throughout the world, a goal that had to be attained without the introduction of manifestly inaccurate statements.

When, in September 1941, the broadcasting department began to develop the twelve topics of the propaganda—especially No. 5: That Jew Roosevelt aspires to worldwide Jewish supremacy— the German Ambassador to Washington, Hans Dieckhoff, commented: "That is a sure way of seriously compromising our other statements, which happen to be accurate, on the domination of the United States by Jews."

Dieckhoff's memorandum outlined how to deal with the matter:

In our counterattack we should avoid calling Americans Jews unless we are completely certain that they are. If we state that an American public figure like Roosevelt is a Jew when every American knows that he is not, we will make our other claims suspect. . . . I recommend taking the following line: Isn't the President continually surrounded by advisers and close friends who are Jews? Isn't Felix Frankfurter, whom the President appointed to the Supreme Court, one of his most trusted advisers? Isn't Judge Rosenman, who writes the President's speeches, a Jew? Isn't Morgenthau a personal friend as well as a neighbor in Hyde Park? Isn't Mrs. Morgenthau one of Mrs. Roosevelt's closest friends, and doesn't she see her every day? Aren't Mr. and Mrs. Morgenthau Jews? . . .

That memorandum must have been entirely to Kiesinger's liking, for he sent the Propaganda Ministry a copy on November 22, 1941. Thus he fulfilled his duty of stirring up anti-Semitism abroad while "the final solution of the Jewish problem" was getting under way in his own country.

The Foreign Ministry's Germany Department shared Kiesinger's concern for the effectiveness of Nazi propaganda, and so did the S.S., as is shown by this example of their agreement as to its character. At the Krummhübel conference of April 1944, attended by the press attachés from the various embassies, Eberhard von Thadden, the head of the division of racial problems in the Germany Department, advised that in anti-Jewish propaganda abroad "we must keep everything we issue within the bounds of reason." Von Thadden, who was to be deeply implicated on the diplomatic level in the Eichmann trial, guaranteed the execution of the "final solution," leaving it to Kiesinger to prepare worldwide opinion to accept the liquidation of the Jews.

In addition to regular broadcasts, Kiesinger's department was responsible for the dissemination abroad of anti-Jewish propaganda programs over the stations of German embassies. On December 1, 1943, for example, Kiesinger's department advised the German Embassy in Lisbon to take the following line in its broadcasts to Latin America:

Give details on the people's attitude toward the Jews, their growing opposition toward Jewish immigrants, information on illegal operations and machinations on the part of Jews. Generalized statements are not enough; cite definite cases. For example, in Brazil, the case of the Jew Itzig Lowenstein, who emigrated from Lodz a year or two ago dressed in rags, yet was able to make a fortune within a short time in foodstuffs or textiles or some other area by finding loopholes in the law or by exacting illegal rates of interest.

Kiesinger even intervened personally to keep a Danish singer named Bendix from getting on the German air waves because he was half Jewish.

One of the duties Kiesinger performed best was circulating evil stories about Jews throughout the world, thus stirring up hatred against them. Kiesinger would later protest that he did not know what was happening to the Jews in the extermination camps, but that is not true. As a director of Interradio he got daily and weekly "secret" bulletins containing all the information his department had gathered. Kiesinger was as well supplied with data on the actual extermination as he had been with information on the preparations for it. The German diplomatic service kept the Foreign Ministry's broadcasting department informed on all "special measures" against the Jews in occupied countries.

And also, starting in January 1942, Kiesinger could read or listen to Thomas Mann's desperate appeals to the German people over the BBC:

January 1942. This news will seem incredible, but my source for it is reliable. Four hundred young Dutch Jews have been deported to Germany, where they were subjected to experiments with poisonous gases. The deadly nature of this essentially Germanic weapon of war, a veritable sword of Siegfried, has been demonstrated on these young men of an inferior race. They are dead . . . victims of the new order and the warlike ingenuity of the master race. For such a vicious purpose they were barely good enough. They were, you see, Jews . . . .

September 1942. The passion for torturing them has not abated. At this very minute it has reached a peak with the insane decision to utterly eradicate Europe's entire Jewish population.

When Kiesinger was a witness at the 1968 trial of two Nazi diplomats, Adolf Beckerle and Fritz von Hahn, all he said about his knowledge of the fate of the Jews was that in 1944 he suspected that "there was something more than mere evacuation going on."

The Final Solution—the physical extermination of the Jews—was fully known to the Foreign Ministry's propaganda department. The only proof necessary is a document from the Krummhübel conference that Ribbentrop organized for April 3 and 4, 1944, which brought together authorities on the Jewish problem from German embassies in Europe and Foreign Ministry authorities on propaganda, including, apparently, Kiesinger's broadcasting department. In his report to the conference, Eberhard von Thadden, the Foreign Ministry diplomat assigned to the Jewish problem, stated that the duty of foreign propaganda on the Jewish problem was "to prepare people everywhere to understand the measures our leaders are taking against the Jews."

Franz Six states: "The part Jews have played in European life has ceased along with their part in European politics. . . . The literal extermination of Judaism in the East has deprived Judaism of living reserves."

In November 1944, Goebbels enthusiastically endorsed Hans Fritzsche's proposal to bring Kiesinger into the Information Ministry and give him an important position. Kiesinger was one of the principal Nazi executives of whom it can be said with absolute certainty that he knew the whole truth about the sufferings and the annihilation of the Jews. He did not resist it actively, or even passively by resigning his incriminating position. Although he knew the truth, he continued to spread anti-Semitic propaganda throughout the world by the craftiest and most effective means. There were, to my mind, few men in Germany whose moral responsibility was so involved.

You may ask whether the sadistic executioners of Auschwitz were not worse than Kiesinger. My answer is that a man who aroused sadism in others, and who spread slanders about a people whose extermination he had sworn to accomplish, was a major participant in a major crime.

In May 1945, Kiesinger was imprisoned by the American forces. After seventeen months he was freed and denazified by a commission, of which his father-in-law was a member, which nonetheless classified him as a Nazi unfit to hold government office. When Kiesinger decided to enter politics he had to be examined once more by his father-in-law. This time he was classified as one of the least important Nazis. His denazification papers have, luckily for him, vanished since then.

I am sure that Kiesinger has not merely changed his colors or become a Christian Democrat without reservations. The fall of the Third Reich was too complete for anyone now to profess sympathy for Hitler. There are many German citizens, however, who retain a conviction that their national superiority as a people imposes on them the obligation to form a Europe totally dedicated to the spread of German civilization. They believe that to accomplish that they must first and foremost stimulate a recognition among the German people of their superiority and preserve and nourish their purity. Their primary objective is to make Germany a power in European politics, from which position she can proceed to realize her destiny.

Kurt-Georg Kiesinger, Chancellor of the Federal Republic of West Germany, has lied.

He has claimed he became a member of the Nazi Party because he hoped, like many other Catholics, to work from within the movement toward the Christian ideal. He has said that after the bloody purge of the Brownshirts in 1934 he became aware of the true nature of Nazism and severed his connection with it. He has specifically stated that he was only a low-ranking scientific aide in the Foreign Ministry and had no real responsibility.

None of those assertions has stood up against a thorough examination of the facts.

4

FIRST POLITICAL
INVOLVEMENTS

Serge had come back from East Germany not only with data on Kiesinger, but also with information that was to further strengthen my resolve to have my case against the OFA heard in a French court and not by the OFA's arbitration committee.

Serge had asked the East Germans to check on the past history of the German member of that committee. We were given official documents to the effect that Walter Hailer, who was to pass upon the legality of my dismissal, was himself a former Nazi and, to complete the irony, had joined the Party on the same day as Kiesinger: May 1, 1933. His card was No. 3,579,848. Hailer, regional orator of the Nazi Party and member of the S.A., was now in 1968 one of the highest magistrates of the Federal Republic of Germany and president of the administrative court of Württemberg-Baden.

I soon had data on Hailer, which I sent to the French President's office as well as to Jacques Rietsch, the judge of the Paris administrative court and the French member of the OFA's arbitration committee. Rietsch admitted to me that he was astonished to learn that his colleague would have a conflict of interest if he sat on the hearing. His surprise was still greater when he learned that Kiesinger had appointed Hailer to that committee.

Enraged by what I knew about Hailer, I wondered whether any

other Nazis had sat or were still sitting on the OFA's board of directors. My research was not in vain. In the CDJC card index, under the heading of German Criminals, I found the name of Fritz Rudolf Arlt, who was an administrator of OFA from 1964 to 1966.

Arlt had had a remarkable S.S. career. He was not only an exponent of theories on the Jews, but also S.S.-Standartenführer and a colonel in the Death's Head Regiment of the S.S., stationed principally in Katowice, a few miles from Auschwitz, as an authority on racial policy. On November 9, 1941, he was posted as lieutenant colonel to the headquarters of Heinrich Himmler, the Reich's commissioner on racial problems. Arlt was adjudged a war criminal in Poland and in the U.S.S.R., where he was convicted by default.

When the OFA was created, Arlt was made one of its directors. Reappointed in December 1965, Arlt shortly thereafter resigned on the publication of an article in *Elan* describing his Nazi past, about which not one word had even been whispered in France or in the OFA. There was no scandal. None of the OFA employees was informed that a Nazi criminal of the worst kind was one of their directors. I could appreciate the difference between the treatment I got and Arlt's. He had been an active participant in atrocious crimes, but to the other OFA directors he was a man to be respected and perhaps even feared.

As the weeks went by, I found that other former Nazis were sitting on the OFA board of directors, notably Foreign Ministry officials: Karl Kuno Overbeck, who was a member of the S.A. and also of the political division of Ribbentrop's ministry; and Luitpold Werz, who had joined the Nazi Party on October 1, 1934, as No. 2,873,248.

There was, therefore, a logic behind my dismissal from OFA. Later I learned that Chancellor Kiesinger's cabinet had put pressure on OFA to get rid of me.

My hearing in the Eighth Arrondissement court took place on February 19, 1968. The night before, I had telephoned about forty reporters who had already been made aware of the case through my pamphlet. The French and the international press came to the hearing in considerable numbers. My message, Kiesinger's Nazi past, and my protestation of innocence reached hundreds of thousands of readers.

On February 19 the court found that it had no jurisdiction, and I took the case to the Paris Court of Appeals. Four months later, on June 18, 1968, that court sustained the lower court's opinion and sent my case back to OFA's arbitration committee. I was in a somewhat Kafkaesque situation, now that appearing before OFA's arbitration committee was the only course open to me.

In order for the committee to challenge Walter Hailer, the German judge, I would have to ask him to disqualify himself. I did so. I also wrote the French judge, the other member of the committee, asking him to declare his German colleague unqualified for this hearing. That desperately wily move ended with Walter Hailer being challenged in September 1968. Consequently the OFA became involved in a slow reorganization of its administrative procedure that resulted in a change in its constitution, for since there was no provision for a substitute judge, one had to be made in my case.

I had involved myself in a very complicated legal battle that set some precedents. *La Gazette du Palais* dealt at length with the case from the point of view of international conventions and jurisdictional immunity. The *French Yearbook of International Law* twice, in 1969 and 1970, reviewed my case and its numerous implications, especially in respect to a civil servant's right to continue in his employment. It turned out that I had to fight on familiar ground. Any evasion or giving up would have meant repudiating my first contentions, and I could not bring myself to do that.

In September 1967, soon after my dismissal, I had written to the German Minister of Justice Gustav Heinemann, who was later to become President of the Federal Republic. Heinemann promised to look into my case. I was to follow his good advice more literally than he thought, for on December 8, 1967, his Secretary of Justice, Horst Ehmke, wrote me:

I have been too busy with other matters to be able to study your case earlier. I do not know the outcome of the suit you brought before the French court on November 27, but I imagine the court will send the case back to the OFA committee in accordance with Article 23 of the OFA constitution. On the other hand, you should not expect much from a plea before an arbitration board in Germany. If, however, you wish to pursue such a course, be very cautious and choose your lawyers with the greatest of care.

My personal opinion is that an attempt to demonstrate the political aspects of this complicated case will assure you a greater likelihood of success than any court decision would. . . .

The Minister of Justice thereby showed me the path I should take. I would make a political issue of the case in Germany rather than get myself involved in long legal actions. My battle was to resume on another front.

February 1968. Reporters keep going in and out in little groups. They go to the nearby Elysée Palace to follow the Franco-German dialogues, then come back to swap data and evaluate the handouts that the government spokesmen or the press secretaries have just issued. The Hotel Bristol bar is a nerve center. Willy Brandt likes to stay at that hotel, whereas Chancellor Kiesinger prefers the ambassador's residence on rue de Lille.

The day is drawing to a close. One by one the ministers who have accompanied Chancellor Kiesinger are taking the temperature of the press. They hang around the bar or the lounges in order to chat in a relaxed atmosphere. Finance Minister Franz Joseph Strauss has just joined the little knot of reporters around me. It is almost 11:30 P.M. We end the long discussion we have been having about my latest disclosures on Kiesinger's past. I step aside, for I cordially dislike Strauss, the strong man of German conservatism, who is almost drunk.

The son of Axel Springer, the German press lord, is keeping me company. He is a photographer.

"This campaign of yours against Kiesinger is absolutely futile," he tells me. "You would be well advised not to talk about it any more, for he got into power by the democratic process. It's too late to protest."

Late in the evening Willy Brandt makes his appearance. The reporters jump up to get to him. He stops in front of the elevators. He is tanned and relaxed and is wearing an elegant pin-striped suit —quite different from the man I had met in the summer of 1966. I take advantage of the occasion to remind him of the interview I had asked him to give me for *Combat*, for which I had sent him a list of questions that dealt, for the most part, with his personal recollections of his stay in France before the war.

"I'll get to work on it soon," he says.

He never did. Later, when my campaign against Kiesinger had become still fiercer, one of Brandt's aides told me of the apprehension on his staff. "You can understand that Brandt, as Chancellor Kiesinger's Foreign Minister and a member of the coalition government, could not give you that interview. If he did, he would seem to be endorsing your campaign."

On February 14, on its page devoted to opinions it did not necessarily endorse, *Combat* published my article entitled: "The CDU-SPD Coalition Is Virtually Doomed." I published articles in *Combat* fairly regularly because of the obligation I felt to make the French know how I felt about developments in German politics. It was by no means a fruitless effort. Since there were very few French correspondents in Bonn, the French got little information about Germany.

I returned to the subject still more forcefully on March 22, 1968:

The reunification of Germany is both right and desirable. Furthermore, it is inevitable. But we want no unification that might endanger the rest of the world. We want a peaceful reunification that will make a non-nuclear-power Germany an indispensable bridge between the East and the West. We want a reunification along socialistic lines because that is the only kind of regime that will be acceptable to the two states that now represent the German nation. The French should beware of being fooled by a new order in Europe. They should, therefore, while there is yet time, help the genuine German socialists mount a true opposition and thereby, let us hope, set up a strong government.

Nine o'clock in the morning, March 20, 1968. I had reached West Berlin after a three-week trip through the German Democratic Republic, which I thought I ought to get to know thoroughly. Timidly I rang the doorbell at Theology Professor Gollwitzer's house, where Rudi Dutschke had taken refuge. The household was still asleep. After several fruitless attempts, and many long waits in the headquarters of Students for a Democratic Society (SDS), I had made up my mind to take him by surprise just as he was getting out of bed.

I wanted the students' help in advancing my campaign against Kiesinger in Germany itself, for I knew it would be hard, if not impossible, to conduct it from Paris. My first meetings with members of the Federation of Socialist Students in Berlin had not been very productive. They were unable to understand, for they thought it natural for a former Nazi to have been elevated by German capitalist interests to the leadership of the Federal Republic. That was only logical in a situation they wanted to attack in its entirety.

I rang several more times. The door finally opened, and the tousled head of a young girl appeared.

"I would like to see Rudi Dutschke."

"He's asleep, but come in anyway."

The girl called out: "Beate Klarsfeld is here."

A few days earlier I had talked with Rudi on the telephone, and so he recognized my name.

"Good. Have her come in."

I went toward the room from which the voice had come. It was really a living room with a sofa-bed in the middle. Since the shutters were still closed, the room was in semi-darkness. I could barely make Rudi out, for he was still in bed. His wife Gretel was beside him, and between them was their baby Che, only a few weeks old. Rudi seemed very fond of his family; he was one of the extremely few SDS leaders who was able to keep both his family life and his political life in hand.

Gretel finished changing the baby and began to give him his bottle. Rudi raised himself on one elbow. He was very simple and frank, much as he was on platforms where I had heard him speak.

I told him that I was planning a conference in Paris on young Germans and young Jews joining forces against neo-Nazism, and that I wanted him to take part.

"I agree with you in principle," he said, "but I'll probably have to go to Prague in the next few days. Things are getting tense there. I'm not sure I can get to Paris in time."

Rudi was a strong contrast to the young SDS abstract talkers I had encountered in the past few days. He was clear and precise, and completely unpretentious. He had the grip of a leader, and could have gone back to ordinary society and provided a comfortable materialistic existence for himself and his family, owing to his intelligence, his skill as a speaker, and his dynamic personality.

But Rudi was not a product of the German consumer class. He had been exiled from East Germany for opposing its excessive dogmatism, and in the West he also attacked the basic faults of society. Through work and talent he had succeeded in making the students of Berlin, and later of all Germany, the most politically aware in Europe. Students in neighboring countries looked up to them.

On April 11, 1968, three weeks after our meeting, the defenseless Rudi Dutschke was shot point blank with three bullets. He was in a coma for weeks, lost the power of speech for a long time, and finally had to withdraw completely from the German political scene. His assailant, it was said, was a mentally deranged loner, but in his rooms were found swastikas, S.S. insignia, and a bust of Hitler. His attack on Rudi was the climax of a hate campaign led by Axel Springer through his newspapers, and by politicians like Kiesinger.

My charges against Kiesinger had not yet made the splash I had hoped for in the principal French and German newspapers. With my bulging file under my arm, I roamed the editorial offices, insisting on being received by editors-in-chief or by special-assignment reporters. Invariably I got the same answer: "That's all very interesting, but what can you do about it? He's already Chancellor."

I had to change my plan of attack.

For the first time I recognized that my exposures would have small impact unless I did something so sensational that the papers would want to report it. If I could settle on something appropriate, and get its meaning across to the public, then the cause for which I was fighting would come to light. For a long time I pondered how to proceed. Then I decided I had to do something right in Kiesinger's presence.

From Paris I telephoned the German Parliament in Bonn: "I should like to attend the Bundestag session on April 1. How do I go about getting in?"

"All you need do is reserve a seat in your name and pick up your ticket ten minutes before the session begins."

I made a reservation under my maiden name; I had learned that Kiesinger would be speaking on that day.

As soon as I got to Bonn on March 30, I went in search of a press photographer. Some students eventually put me in touch with one who worked for the German Press Agency, and I took him into my confidence. We arranged for him to spot me discreetly before I entered the Bundestag.

I was almost late in getting there. I checked my coat, climbed up to the public gallery, and took a seat in a row of benches guarded by a sergeant-at-arms. Soon Kiesinger mounted the rostrum and began to speak. It was the first time I had seen him in the flesh.

I would say merely that he was a handsome sixty-five-year-old who seemed ten years younger. Nearly six feet tall, with silver hair and an intelligent, understanding expression—the very image of a respectable family man—and even a trifle attractive, except that I thought his eyes too small for the size of his face. As for his private life, I couldn't have cared less. I knew that his home life was irreproachable, and that he was so fond of animals that he had once put his rowboat back into the water to rescue a spaniel that was drowning in Lake Constance. He did not appear to be much interested in money. All these dimensions of the man are indeed to be respected, and a consideration of them might have been an obstacle to my campaign if I had paid them any heed, but I didn't. For that matter, Hitler and Himmler had led exemplary private lives.

A man, especially one who plays an important role, is only a sort of rack from which his deeds hang. And in my eyes, his deeds—their significance—are what really count. As much as I would want to describe the physical aspects of Petia our cocker spaniel or our cat, I try, on the contrary, not to be swayed by the physical aspects of persons I meet in my extrafamilial life. I never let myself be impressed by attractions, repulsions, or other personal magnetisms, and I keep a certain balance so as not to lose the thread of my direction.

I had decided to heckle the German Chancellor while he was addressing the full session of Parliament, but I had not realized how hard it is to shout in an orderly assembly. I was afraid I would not have the courage to open my mouth. So I kept looking at the clock, telling myself that I would wait until the minute hand was on the dot of twelve. It was agonizing to keep staring at that hand moving over, closer and closer to the appointed moment. Then, at last, dramatically brandishing my clenched fist, I shouted as loud as I could: "Kiesinger, you Nazi, resign!"

Once I had got the words out, it was easy to repeat them.

The Chancellor stopped his speech. I could sense that he was upset. He looked toward me, as did all the members of Parliament. There, in the presence of the representatives of the people of the Federal Republic, his past had risen before him.

The sergeants-at-arms descended upon me. One put his hand over my mouth and dragged me out of the hall into a tiny office. I refused to give my name, and was hauled off to the nearest police station. Only then did I answer any questions. The police superintendent, who had heard of me, sent for my briefcase from the checkroom where I had left it. He kept me for three hours, then released me.

The next day the German newspapers printed pictures of me brandishing my fists, which pleased the leftists, or being muzzled by the sergeant-at-arms, which signified that truth was being repressed in Germany. All the papers, of course, commented on Kiesinger's Nazi past and on the documentary evidence I had assembled. I had reached my goal. The wall of silence was crumbling.

I knew I had risked a fine or a jail term with a suspended sentence, but there were no penalties. The authorities had apparently decided that it was better not to call any further attention to the incident.

Once or twice a week a few young Germans would attend meetings in an apartment near place de la Contrescarpe in Paris. They had formerly belonged to the Social Democratic Party, but were considered too radical and had been expelled. Consequently, they had joined Dutschke's SDS. They wanted to make contact with French students.

During one of the meetings we learned of the attempt on Rudi Dutschke's life, and late that same evening in April 1968, we decided to organize a protest demonstration in Paris. Alain Krivine and his friends supported us by having pamphlets printed. I made banners in my apartment.

We had agreed to meet at the corner of avenue Montaigne and rue François I, and demonstrate before the German Embassy. I was astonished to find a thousand students there, but also about one dozen vans of the National Security Police. There were lots of red flags. This first large demonstration was to herald the coming explosion in May.

The young people were shouting: "Springer is a murderer!" Some French students were waving signs reading: "Kiesinger is a Nazi." I was amazed. Could my campaign at last be bearing fruit?

After brief speeches by Krivine and Daniel Cohn-Bendit, the demonstration officially broke up, but it was whispered about that it would move over to the Latin Quarter. We took the Metro in small groups. Once we got there, we were surprised to find a large number of security police, helmeted and armed. I had given my banners to a young German student, who stashed them in a basement entrance and took to his heels before violence broke out. There were a few clashes, but to me that was not the main point. Violence served only to make our performance go astray and lose its political significance.

Meanwhile, during an election rally in Württemberg-Baden, the young people of the Extra-Parliamentary Opposition (APO) filled two-thirds of the hall and shouted: "Kiesinger is a Nazi! A Nazi!"

In order to quiet them, Kiesinger said: "You are too young to have known Nazism, and you have a right to know what your Chancellor did during its regime."

He never kept his promise to tell them.

In April, I went to Esslingen where, I had learned, the political parties would debate in public. I took along three enormous suitcases full of pamphlets.

"If you want to make a short speech and distribute your pamphlets," a student told me, "this is a good chance."

I was not known there, and I had prepared nothing to say. Anyone in the audience, however, was allowed to speak. I waited an hour for my turn.

Once behind the microphone, I panicked. The square was huge, full of young people, and I did not know just what to say. I introduced myself, however, and reviewed my campaign. A burst of applause gave me courage, and I went on to rehearse Kiesinger's past. Probably I was too long-winded, for I heard from the crowd: "Make it short! Cut it down!"

That was that. I cut my speech short, and merely announced that I had pamphlets to pass out.

It took four telephone calls for me to reach Günter Grass, who had to leave that day for a writers' conference in Prague.

"I want to ask you to take part in a big meeting we are organizing at the Berlin Polytechnic. I am near your house now and could stop in right away."

He agreed.

The meeting had been organized with the help of Michel Lang, the organizer of the Jewish Work Club of Berlin. It reached a wide audience, for at that time in Federal Germany, any Jewish organization was treated with a certain respect. Considering the guilt complex of the Germans, an attack on Kiesinger from young Jews would certainly carry more weight than all the activity of the young opposition members.

Number 13 Niedstrasse, in Friedenau, was a funny, old-fashioned, ivy-covered house with a small garden between it and the street. The gate was wide open. Günter Grass welcomed me, and took me through the quite modern dining room to a balcony screened from the street by a hedge. It was already growing dark, and so I had trouble distinguishing his features. He let me talk for some time about my plan. Then he said:

"I am not particularly eager to speak at such a gathering. To my mind, the students have been carrying on disgracefully for some time now."

He seemed more amenable after I told him that this would be a gathering of Jewish students. I left with his promise that he would attend the meeting if nothing untoward developed.

I returned to Berlin on May 9, a few hours before the meeting. It had proved quite hard to organize, and out of caution several good speakers had declined to appear. With the help of Serge, who had come with me, I carefully prepared my part.

The young people in Michel Lang's organization were selling our pamphlet about Kiesinger for thirty pfennigs. They had stuck big posters on walls all over the city and distributed gummed badges.

Well before the demonstration began, almost three thousand young persons had jammed into the university auditorium. Long-haired and bearded, they seemed enchantingly romantic. The advertised speakers were Günter Grass, Johannes Agnoli, Ekkebart Krippendorff, Jacob Taubes, and Michel Lang. Günter Grass's speech, in which he boldly attacked Kiesinger as "the heaviest moral mortgage on Germany," set the tone of the meeting. When my turn came to speak, I was propelled to the microphone. I felt dazed by the crowd squeezed together on the rows of benches, squatting on the floor just below the platform, and standing in the aisles. I declared that we must keep escalating our efforts to break the wall of silence surrounding Kiesinger's Nazi past. And I promised:

"I give you my word that I will publicly slap the Chancellor."

There was a spirited response from the audience. From various parts of the hall came shouts of "childish!" or "stupid!" Some even said: "Do it if you've got the guts!" One group kept sneering. "Promises! Nothing but promises!"

A resolution calling upon Kiesinger to resign was passed by three-fourths of the meeting. Both the East and the West German newspapers reported it. I took the risk of publicly announcing my intention to slap Kiesinger because I had to make sure that people knew the symbolic gesture I was planning had been premeditated. I had a feeling that such a gesture would deeply stir the Germans.

The following evening I took a train to Bonn. We planned to descend on the capital the next day to protest the coming vote on the "law of exception" that would give the Chancellor dictatorial power in the event of disorders, and the East German government had put at the disposal of the "Committee for Preserving Democracy" an eight-hundred-seat train. However, the young people showed they were as critical of East Germany's government as of West Germany's. When the train stopped at or passed through East German railway stations, they shouted at the top of their lungs such slogans as "Bureaucracy leads to Fascism and Stalinism," and "Turn communists into good socialists."

The West Germans were stupefied as they watched the train go by. It was the first time since the cold war began that a train bristling with red flags had crossed the Federal Republic to the shouts of "Capitalism means Fascism," and "Citizens, don't watch us, join us," and "SPD and CDU, hands off the Constitution." Also, quite often, "Kiesinger is a Nazi."

There was some concern that our train would wind up on a siding, but the police avoided any clash. About 8 A.M. we pulled into the Bonn station. Forty thousand demonstrators had been expected, but sixty thousand showed up.

The next day barricades sprang up like thorny hedgerows all over Paris. The great conflagration of the "days of May" had begun.

I undertook to organize a Franco-German Action Committee at the Sorbonne and mounted a display of photographs of the demonstrations in Germany and the police repression of them. My purpose was to make the young French understand the battle a minority of young Germans were waging against the resurgence of Nazism and for the rehabilitation of an entire people. I quickly realized, however, that the French students were interested only in their own problems. Nevertheless, it seemed to me that the contest in Germany, not the one in France, was of paramount importance, because the Federal Republic had external problems, such as its relations with East Germany and other Eastern European countries, that would determine the future of Europe. There was at last a good chance for Brandt's Social Democrats to take over in the near future and adopt a foreign policy different from the Christian Democrats'. To me, a bet on that game was much safer than a bet on the one surging through the streets of Paris.

On May 29, half a dozen youths and I occupied the OFA building. From the windows we hung three big banners: *Franco-German Alliance for Youth Occupied—No Emergency Laws for Germany —Solidarity between French and German Students and Workers.*

Robert Clément, the director of the French wing of the OFA, made no objection. General de Gaulle had left Paris, and Clément was not sure whether the government would fall. Those twenty-four hours of peaceful occupation were punctuated by the appearance of numerous youth organization leaders appealing for financial support from the OFA or wanting to hold structured dialogues on the OFA's future and necessary changes in its procedures. My former co-workers were shocked to see me blithely leading the attack on the offices where only a few months earlier I had been pounding a typewriter. They expected me to be arrested, but I wasn't.

During the summer of 1968, I applied myself to publicizing facts about German politics in a series of articles for *Combat*. On September 2, I wrote:

The key to European security and peace and to the liberalization of Eastern Europe is the reunification of Germany into a truly socialistic, democratic, and pacifistic nation. So long as the German people re- • fuse frankly to acknowledge their responsibility for the tragedy that made Europe what it is today, so long as they will not expel from government positions the survivors and the putrescent odors of the Third Reich, and so long as a healthy national attitude continues to be confused with pan-Germanic expansion and the lust for power, so long as the monopolies that rule its economic and intellectual life are not reduced in authority, the status quo in Europe will remain an intangible reality. All this is happening in a world in which disasters far more bloody than Prague's seem barely to rouse the conscience of the good-for-nothings in the capitalist and the communist blocs. These have rigidly assumed an insufferable attitude of defiance toward each other, even though they have duties to perform far more edifying than recourse to arms, as well as responsibilities toward the Third World proportional to its problems. In order to shatter that confrontation, in order to avoid letting Europe relapse into a total cold war as in 1948, reason demands that we begin at the beginning. In the beginning was Germany.

In Germany, where I went that summer of 1968 to give a lecture in Frankfurt on "Kiesinger and the Jews," there would soon begin what the press was to call the "Klarsfeld-Kiesinger duel."

5

THE SLAP

Late in the afternoon of Sunday, November 3, I arrived at the West Berlin railway station. Serge had tried to smile encouragingly when he saw me off the night before, but he could not hide his anxiety. I had left to fulfill my promise.

My mother-in-law had tried to dissuade me, saying: "You are right, but you may get killed. The police will think it an assassination attempt and shoot. You ought to think of your child."

Think of him I did. I had written in German and in French a statement to make clear the meaning of what I was about to do, no matter what happened:

By slapping Chancellor Kiesinger I want to bear witness that a part of the German people—especially the young—is deeply revolted at having as head of the government of the Federal Republic of West Germany a Nazi who was assistant director of Hitler's foreign propaganda effort.

The Third Reich represented a philosophy as stupid as it was cruel. . . . We don't want any more of that again, and we refuse to allow Germans who had any kind of authority under the Third Reich to play any part in Germany's political life. . . . Kiesinger and his colleagues are turning Germany into a revengeful, expansionist nation that ignores the consequences of world war and demands atomic weapons. So long as Kiesinger and his accomplices remain in power,

50

all the people who suffered under Nazism, especially those in the East, will have good reason to be wary of the Germany governed from Bonn.

For the sake of peace, freedom, and socialism in Europe, and for the honor of Germany, Kiesinger and his accomplices must be removed.

I was immediately aware that Berlin was under tight police control with reinforcements from the Federal Republic.

At the Republican Club, the meeting place of the Extra-Parliamentary Opposition (APO), the atmosphere was gloomy. The young people drinking beer and reading political magazines did not hide the fact that they had been expecting huge demonstrations, but the police had mounted too strong a protective front for them to oppose.

So the Congress would be held after all, in spite of the opposition's claim that it would prevent that "illegal" assembly—illegal because West Berlin was politically distinct from the Federal Republic.

I left the huge, imperial-style apartment on Wielandstrasse just off the Kurfürstendamm. I wanted to maintain my determination. The police lines didn't impress me. A young woman can find their weak spots and penetrate them more easily than full battalions. I would get through and I would win simply because I was weak and alone.

"We can't do much for you."

I didn't take that well. I had expected at least some help from the young anti-fascists.

"Not even a ticket to the Congress. The police lines don't give us a chance."

I didn't know where or when the sessions would be held. Or where I would sleep that night. I didn't want to go to my mother's for fear the police would descend on her after my gesture. So I accepted the offer of a young revolutionary:

"I'll lend you my cellar. You can stay as long as you want."

For the first time I would stay in a commune of young people— a two-story house in a residential section near Berlin-Wannsee, surrounded by a large, unplanted garden. Two young couples, one with a child, lived on separate floors. The cellar had been turned into a small apartment. It was well heated, and it had running water. I was satisfied despite the train trip I would have to make every morning and evening.

"You work for *Combat?*"

The young secretary whipped through her card file, but found nothing. Was I going to have to go back empty-handed after getting through three police lines to reach the press office? I insisted politely. I had to have a press card to open doors for me during the sessions.

"If you'll show me your press card, I'll ask my boss."

I could not back down. Serge had given me an expired ORTF pass. I was counting on its red, white, and blue chevron to influence the accrediting officials. I had removed Serge's picture and replaced it with mine.

The secretary returned a few minutes later smiling apologetically: "Unfortunately all the seats are taken this morning. There are too many reporters."

Now what? How was I to get close to Kiesinger?

The night before, a leader of the leftist groups told me to go to the big demonstration in support of Horst Mahler at the Court of Appeals. Mahler, a young lawyer, was to appear before a legal review board for having taken part in a raid on the Springer offices in Berlin. He stood a good chance of being disbarred.

The atmosphere of the Berlin streets grew charged as I got closer to the courthouse. Both camps were seized with excitement. In less than half an hour they clashed. As if by miracle, three thousand young people sprang up around the building. Anti-riot squads were everywhere. Molotov cocktails began exploding.

"Come this way," shouted a girl in a crash helmet hanging on to the rear of a motorcycle that jumped onto the sidewalk.

The clash was one of the most violent there had been between the police and the students. There were over a hundred casualties among the students and as many among the police. I worked my way around the police barriers. Behind me tear-gas bombs were exploding, echoing the bursts of the Molotov cocktails. Police sirens were followed by ambulance sirens. I saw how desperately the young Berliners and their allies, the underprivileged young, could fight for Mahler and how bitter they were over failing to prevent the CDU Congress.

On a street corner a young man turned around and yelled at me. I recognized Reinhard, whom I had invited to Paris a few months earlier to talk about Germany at the Anne Frank Club. He yanked me into a nearby café. I reminded him of the promise I had made six months before to slap the Chancellor, and told him of my problems in getting into the Congress.

"Get a photographer into the act," Reinhard suggested. "In exchange for giving you his pass he can get some good shots of your slap."

He gave me the name of Michael, a free-lance photographer at the big picture magazine *Stern*. I met him that same afternoon in his little apartment-laboratory near the Sportpalast. He listened to my long explanation of what I had in mind.

"I'm with you," he said. "I'll ask my magazine for a pass."

The first event, it turned out, was to be a cocktail party for the Chancellor at the Hilton Hotel.

Back in Paris Serge and I had reasoned that I would have the best chance of success at a public reception when Kiesinger would not be surrounded by his bodyguards.

That evening I felt certain of achieving my purpose.

For the occasion, I had bought a cocktail gown trimmed with gold embroidery. The area around the hotel was as well guarded as the Congress Hall. The invitation that my *Stern* photographer had given me just fifteen minutes before worked wonders. I got through the three checkpoints outside with no trouble, and then through the final one at the entrance to the reception rooms.

Several guests were already there. There was a lavish buffet laden with mountains of caviar and baskets of little sandwiches, but my throat was so tight that I couldn't swallow.

I was afraid—not of what might happen to me, but of failing, missing my chance, spoiling everything I had worked so hard for all these months. You aren't very brave, I kept telling myself over and over. I forced myself not to think of the danger involved. But merely knowing that soon every eye would be on me made me nervous.

For the time being I concentrated on my objective. I always lay my plans on the spot. Circumstances are so impossible to foresee that it is useless to imagine details in advance. I prefer to improvise once I know the situation.

I mixed with a group of reporters, though the thought that one of them might recognize me made me even more tense. Then, out of the din, a phrase leaped out at me: "Isn't it a pity! Kiesinger has the flu and isn't going to come this evening."

My morale was low. The only thing that kept me going was the certain knowledge that if I turned around and went back to Paris without having done my utmost, I would be still more unhappy. I went to the telephone office at the railway station to tell Serge. He has greater confidence in me than I have, and when I am wavering I always turn to him. In his eyes or the tone of his voice I can recognize the person I wish I were.

On Wednesday I went back to Michael's to ask him for another pass. Kiesinger was to speak that evening to his "dear Berliners" at the Neue Welt, a big restaurant in Hasenheide. The place looked as if it were being besieged. Iron gratings fenced off the sidewalks around it, and automobiles moved at a snail's pace through the labyrinthine paths created by rolls of barbed wire. Police, helmeted, armed with long clubs, and wearing bulletproof vests, were stationed at all strategic points. Anti-riot firetrucks waited in the nearby streets. All the buses had been rerouted.

Michael drove me up to the restaurant, and the "Press" sticker on our windshield got us through. My notebook and pen in hand, I mingled with the reporters. One of them worked for East German television and had interviewed me several times. He exclaimed: "So you are really going to keep your promise!"

I asked him not to say anything.

Then, when I saw the platform, my resolution gave way to bitter disappointment. Kiesinger and his party were seated behind a table on a platform that was well over six feet high. The steps at each end were guarded by strapping fellows from the Christian Democratic security force.

For a moment I considered going up on the platform and pretending that I wanted to ask Kiesinger for a statement, but I quickly saw that only photographers were being allowed up there. So I found Michael and asked him for one of his cameras, then hurried back to the platform. Two of the guards cut me off.

"Where's your photographer's pass?"

"I don't have it with me."

They pushed me aside unceremoniously, and I beat a retreat. For two hours I sat through the session in a cold rage.

The room was jammed with Kiesinger's supporters. No Berliners had been admitted. After distributing free tickets in movie and theater box offices, the organizers had realized they were being picked up by young radicals who hoped to fill the hall and then stage a noisy demonstration. At the last minute these tickets had been declared invalid, and whole vanloads of loyal Christian Democrats were imported for the occasion.

The session ended with terrific applause for Kiesinger and shouts of "Down with the Reds! The Reds are all Cohn bandits!"—a pun on the name of the radical leader, Daniel Cohn-Bendit.

To have slapped Kiesinger under these circumstances would have aroused uncontrollable resentment. I could have been lynched or trampled. Now that I look back on it, I admit I was afraid.

There was only one morning session left. I had to grasp my last opportunity during the final session at the Congress Palace.

The day began badly. About 9 A.M. my photographer told me he had not been able to get a pass. However, he did help me to cross the three outside barriers in his car. We could not get any closer, so he left me in the parking lot, lying on the floor of the car, holding my breath every time anyone came near.

We had decided that he should go in to test the admissions officials and sample the atmosphere of the hall. Long minutes passed. My fingers and feet were freezing. Fifteen minutes. Twenty minutes. What if he decided it would be too hard to get me in and didn't come back at all? I was considering leaving the car and trying to get past the checkpoints by myself.

Was I going to be defeated now that my goal was so near? My nerves were taut. Then at last I saw Michael threading his way through the parked cars, his cameras dangling from his neck. The guards who had checked him in and then seen him go out let him in again.

I stuck out just one corner of the green pass. Then I checked my brown coat trimmed with a wide white stripe that made a big Cross of Lorraine. I was wearing a red skirt with a wide belt, and a white turtleneck. I got out my notebook. Back again to playing reporter.

The huge hall was full. Michael took back his pass with relief. Little groups were chatting in the aisles while they waited for the party leaders to arrive.

The chairman of the welfare agencies, Margot Kalinke, was speaking, but no one paid any attention. On the platform sat the presiding officer and important members of the Christian Democratic party machine. Below, on the floor of the hall, was a long table covered with a white cloth. There were flowers everywhere.

Chancellor Kiesinger sat in the center, flanked by former chancellor Ludwig Erhard, Bruno Heck, the secretary general of the party, and Defense Minister Gerhard Schröder. Kiesinger was writing; he appeared to be putting the finishing touches on the speech he would deliver in about an hour.

I walked slowly down the aisle, stopping every five or six yards to listen to the speech and jot something on my pad. When I got to the end I noticed that the table behind which Kiesinger was sitting was much wider than it had seemed from the rear. I would not be able to lean across it and reach his face. I hesitated for a few moments. Two or three security guards stood at either end of the table. I went up to one of them, showing my pad. I had to improvise.

Suddenly I looked up and motioned with my hand, pretending to be waving at someone on the far side of the table. Then, as if it were the most natural thing in the world, I asked the guard: "I should like to get to a friend there. May I pass behind the table?"

He hesitated: "There's no passageway."

I insisted.

"Go around on the outside. You can't go this way."

I stayed where I was and kept smiling toward the far side of the table. He took me gently by the sleeve and whispered: "All right, go ahead, but be quick."

I slipped behind the dignitaries.

As I got behind Kiesinger he sensed my presence and half turned around. My nerves tensed agonizingly. I had won. Shouting "Nazi! Nazi!" at the top of my lungs, I slapped him. I never even saw the expression on his face.

The next thing I remember is that Bruno Heck grabbed me around the waist. Behind me I could hear Kiesinger's voice: "Is it that Klarsfeld woman?"

Before I was hustled out I had time to hear the buzzing that swept through the hall. All the Bundestag members who were there were moving in confusion toward the platform. The reporters were streaming off their benches.

I felt as if I were in a vacuum. I couldn't think. All I could do was keep repeating to myself: "I did it. I did it. All that work was not for nothing."

The procession escorted me along corridors and staircases and everyone stopped to watch. The policeman who was holding me

by the arm and kicking me in the calves kept chanting in an outraged voice: "She slapped the Chancellor."

We went into an office, where a policeman took my identity
card. I followed the subsequent events without interest. The essential thing was behind me. I could still hardly believe I had
done it.

"Ah, so it's you!" he said. "I noticed your pamphlets scattered
along the Kurfürstendamm."

As a matter of fact, from the time the Congress opened, Berlin's
young anti-fascists had turned the intersection of the Kurfürstendamm and Joachimstaler Strasse into a forum, and had distributed
"The Truth about Kurt-Georg Kiesinger" to the crowd.

Old Ernst Lemmer, Kiesinger's Berlin deputy, came into the
office leaning on his stick. For a long time he had been "refugee"
minister. As a member of the 1933 Reichstag, he had voted to give
Hitler full power. As a Nazi propagandist, he had extolled the
Third Reich in over two thousand articles. He stood before me
and delivered a sermon:

"Listen, my dear child, what do you mean by slapping our
Chancellor?"

"I can't stand having a former Nazi as Chancellor. I slapped
him to let the whole world know there are some Germans who will
not be put to shame."

Lemmer started to leave, shaking his head. Then he turned
around and said: "I could be your grandfather."

He was hardly outside the door before he gave the reporters
his personal opinion: "That woman, who could be very pretty if
she were not so sickly looking, is a sexually frustrated female."

Two weeks later *Stern*, which had printed Lemmer's opinion,
published a letter of apology from him: "When I made that remark, I did not know that Frau Klarsfeld is married and has a
child, or that her father-in-law perished in Auschwitz."

The telephone never stopped ringing. Plainclothesmen took me
out by a side door. We went through the enormous basement,
where I was astonished to see an army of policemen in battle
array. We came out and I was shoved into a police car. I caught
a glimpse of Michael making the victory sign.

At police headquarters, two inspectors questioned me exhaustively. Then, after offering me some sausages and potato salad in

the canteen, they allowed me to notify my family that I had been arrested. I called Serge at his office. He was not there. My mother-in-law answered at our apartment:

"Serge is coming home to change his clothes. He's all excited. He told me: 'I knew she'd do it.' He's going to take a plane this afternoon and he'll be in Berlin tonight. What should he bring you in case you have to stay in jail?"

I knew that Serge would come. Nothing bad could happen to me once he was there.

I also telephoned Horst Mahler's office. He was not in, but I left a message. When he arrived, the policemen left us alone together. Mahler's first words were whispered, for he was afraid the room was bugged: "It's marvelous! What you did is absolutely marvelous!"

I found that thereafter my act got wholehearted support from the Extra-Parliamentary Opposition. I was no longer alone.

For about twenty minutes Mahler and I discussed the main lines of my defense. But we did not suspect that my trial would be held that very day.

Meanwhile a tribunal was being assembled in desperate haste. The young prosecutor was made to ride with me in the automobile that took us to the police court in the Tiergarten. After a half-hour's wait, a bailiff came to tell me that in view of the late hour—it was almost 5 p.m.—my hearing had been postponed to the following day. Two policemen took me to a cell. I left my personal belongings at the desk. A policewoman tossed me a nightgown and some sheets. The barred door opened, then shut. I was in jail.

I lowered the hard plank from the wall to which it was hinged and made up a bed on it. Then I lay down and tried to put my thoughts in order and relive every moment of the day. Suddenly the barred door opened.

"Come right away. Your lawyer is waiting for you."

Mahler was indignant: "They're going to try you at once. There are several hundred young people outside. Plainclothesmen are on most of the benches in the courtroom. Only about a dozen of the reporters who came here could get in."

I was scared that at any moment my skirt would fall down, for I had had to leave my belt at the police desk. Shivering with nervousness, I threw my coat over my shoulders.

I was shut into a small cage. Neelsen, the prosecutor, was carrying on in front of me. I guessed him to be no more than thirty-two years old. He diligently related all the facts. Every time he pronounced the words, "Chancellor Kiesinger," I expected to see him genuflect.

I learned that Kiesinger's first reaction had been to minimize the incident. "I don't prosecute women who slap me," he had said. But his entourage had pressured him into lodging a complaint. He had signed the papers in the car taking him to the airport for his plane to Bonn.

The prosecutor called as a witness Commissioner Samtag, who was in charge of the Chancellor's security during the Congress. He stepped to the bar.

"What did you see?"

"I noticed the defendant as soon as she came up to the head table. She was not wearing a delegate's badge, but she had a reporter's notebook in her hand. A few minutes earlier the Chancellor had been signing autographs for persons who had come up to him from all over the hall. Since I had observed the defendant conversing with one of the security men, who let her pass, I was not alarmed when she slipped behind the row of officials.

"The Chancellor was well protected by six armed bodyguards. One of them had already drawn his gun, but he could not fire it because the defendant was shielded by the Chancellor and others."

It would not have taken much for them to have struck me down. At any rate, in order to slap Kiesinger I had taken as great a risk as those who in that year of 1968 had done away with Robert Kennedy, Martin Luther King, and Rudi Dutschke.

My lawyer demanded that Kiesinger be called as a witness since he claimed to have received "blows and wounds."

"That's just a trick of yours to get the trial postponed," Judge Drygalla snapped.

Mahler then challenged the court on the ground that the judge was "partisan."

The court adjourned for a few minutes. The judge said: "The court denies the request of the counsel for the defense, which is designed simply to postpone this trial."

The tribunal upheld the judge's impartiality.

The prosecutor rose:

"It must be taken into consideration that a representative of our nation has been attacked. Therefore we must proceed to judgment without delay. I demand a penalty of one year in prison and a warrant for immediate arrest. Otherwise all this young woman has

to do to escape into the Eastern Zone is buy a ticket on the S-Bahn.
I recall to your attention that the defendant went to Potsdam for
the data she cites in her pamphlet."

Throughout these arguments Judge Drygalla was coolly polite
to me. He allowed me to speak without interruption, even when I
rebuked him by saying, "Your hasty procedure is very reminiscent of the Nazi courts."

My slap had been merely symbolic. I had no intention of doing
the Chancellor any physical harm. The prosecutor, however, tried
to shatter this argument.

"Her act of violence was an attack on the honor of the person
she slapped. Does it have to be explained for a proper legal interpretation of the incident that a slap in the face is an insult? The
court, therefore, has no need of proofs or of witnesses to the
offense for it to be evident that the victim has suffered physical
and psychological harm from being slapped. Furthermore, the
character of the offender is important and must not be overlooked
when you render your decision on the penalty of imprisonment
I am asking."

Before retiring to consider the case, the judge made a statement
that worried me:

"Germany has been the scene of violent political conflicts before, and the history of our times has blamed the Weimar Republic
for not having put a quick end to the disturbances that occurred
during its regime."

The verdict was returned a few minutes later: "One year in
prison. The reasons adduced will be made known to the public
by being published in six mass-circulation national newspapers at
the expense of the defendant."

That would have cost me more than fifty thousand marks.

Even Mahler, who was used to harsh sentences, was astonished.
As for me, I was stunned. I felt a band of iron closing around my
chest. How could I endure a year away from Serge and Arno?

I hardly heard Mahler ask: "Have you anything to say to the
court? Don't worry. Of course we'll appeal."

"You've got to do something. I won't go to jail for anything in
the world."

It was a cry from the depths of my being. Then an almost un-
governable rage overcame me as I addressed the president of the
tribunal.

"I demand that you take into consideration that, owing to my marriage, I am a French citizen. If you put me in jail, I will demand that my lawyer immediately get in touch with the French Commander in Berlin and discuss with him whether I should not be tried by a French court in Berlin. We shall then see whether in West Berlin, which is under international law, my French citizenship is not of greater validity than my West German nationality."

I had touched one of the sore points in the relationship between the Federal Republic and West Berlin. The intervention of one of the occupation powers would definitely not be appreciated in Bonn, especially in so ticklish a case.

My argument struck home dramatically. The judge and his counselors left the courtroom without adjourning the session. The tactics that Serge had devised before I left Paris had had the anticipated effect. When the judge returned, he announced that my sentence was suspended. I was free.

I left the court with Horst Mahler and a reporter. It was after 8 P.M. We went straight to the large auditorium of Berlin's Free University, where several thousand students had been gathered to celebrate the fizzling out of the Christian Democratic Union Congress and Kiesinger's departure from Berlin with a black eye. A tremendous burst of applause greeted us. Mahler's name was chanted over and over again. His prestige among the youth of Germany was very great.

Into a microphone I declared how glad I was that I had kept my word. I asked the young people to take advantage of the extraordinary circumstances I had been able to create in order to intensify the campaign against Kiesinger throughout the whole country.

The radical youth groups took my slap, that victory *in extremis,* as their own. It had released thousands of students from the frustration they had felt during the previous three days when the police suppressed all their demonstrations.

The meeting continued, but I was hauled off to a press conference the Republican Club had called at the last minute. While I was replying to questions, Serge appeared. I was so glad to see him that I didn't care if the press saw me throw myself into his arms.

On the morning of November 8, I was sure that we had won. At breakfast our friends in the Wannsee commune gave us sev-

eral newspapers with blazing headlines. All their front pages were
devoted to the previous day's incident, with many pictures showing the Chancellor with his face behind his hand or, a moment
later, looking disgruntled and with his eyes hidden behind sun-
glasses. There were also pictures of me in my Cross-of-Lorraine
coat, surrounded by policemen, or in the defendant's box leaning
toward Mahler, or challenging Kiesinger in the Bundestag with my
fists upraised.

The insult to the Chancellor eclipsed all other news. The word
"slap" entered the German political vocabulary. All the front-page
headlines featured the word.

In reporting Kiesinger's embarrassed opinion: "That woman
goes around with university hooligans," and that of his spokesman, Günter Diehl: "She is a monomaniac about the Chancellor,"
the press gave even more space to my true motives: "She slapped
the Chancellor because she wanted to reveal to the world his Nazi
past and demonstrate German youth's refusal to have Germany
represented by a former Nazi."

It was impossible to picture me convincingly as a hysterical
woman. The work I had been doing for almost two years was beginning to pay off. I had written too much, spoken too many times,
agitated too frequently for anyone to be able to pretend that I
was just a hothead.

Back in Paris, only a few minutes after the incident, Serge had
distributed to the press agencies a release that emphasized:

"By slapping Chancellor Kiesinger my wife committed an act
long planned and premeditated, which aimed at stressing the
Chancellor's Nazi past for the edification of German youth."

The statement I had recorded before I left Paris was broadcast
over several stations that afternoon.

It became clear that the Germans were wondering how their
Chancellor could have put himself into a position of being slapped
because of his past, especially when he had so solemnly declared:
"German youth has a right to know how their Chancellor stood
during the Third Reich," but had not kept his word.

To the crime of lèse-majesté combined with humiliation—a
unique one in the annals of German history—now was added the
scandal of the sentence: one year of imprisonment. The act itself
and the Berlin court's reaction to it were going to encounter severe
criticism during the weeks to come. Some people approved of my

act and disapproved of the sentence; others condemned both what I had done and the sentence I had gotten. There were plenty of heated arguments among the newspaper editors as well as on street corners. Even children were talking about it, for the slap had called into question the sacrosanct nature of authority: whether one should respect a man because he is Chancellor or because he is a man of integrity.

On the Eastern side of the Wall, there were shouts of joy. My statement was broadcast over both radio and television in the German Democratic Republic. On the day after the slap, a camera crew came to film me in West Berlin.

All of the East German headlines were approximately the same: "In the name of millions of victims, B.K. has symbolically slapped that old Nazi Kiesinger" or "For killing a Jew, one day in jail; for slapping a Chancellor, one year."

On the day of my return to Paris, thirty-six hours after the slap, Interflora delivered a bunch of red roses. The card read: "Thanks—Heinrich Böll." I wanted to laugh and cry at the same time. Böll, the Catholic novelist so sensitive to human passions and so full of genuine and powerful feelings, approved of me.

I did not have to pay for the publication of my sentence in six newspapers, as Judge Drygalla had decreed. It appeared that the Chancellor had no wish whatever to see his career under Hitler spread all over the front pages, and *Der Spiegel* satirically remarked: "Chancellor Kiesinger has saved B.K. 50,000 marks."

I still had a long way to go. Serge called that to my attention:

"You're just like one of those actors who get famous for the character they play in a television serial. You've got to get away from being typed like that by playing other parts just as well, if not better. Not everyone can do that."

It was a question not only of my future, but of our battle. I resolved to go on.

6

KIESINGER'S FALL

For eleven months after the slap—until Kiesinger's defeat in the September 1969 elections—I was to be constantly on the move.

The hardest part for me was to be away when Arno was sick with the flu, the mumps, or the measles. Raissa kept lecturing me and pretending she did not want to take care of Arno so that I would stay home. But I had to leave. If I were to give in and cancel a demonstration or a speech, I might lose momentum. So I would kiss Arno's fevered brow and, with a heavy heart, leave on the night trains that would save me precious time.

How many times Serge and I would part at the Gare du Nord or the Gare de l'Est with a tender kiss that gave me the strength to go on! How many times I would wake up dry-mouthed in a train compartment as another gray German morning was breaking. How many times I would feel almost physical exhaustion when I thought of how vast the country was and when I looked at the gigantic factories, the innumerable cars, and all those strange men and women whose political awareness I was trying to arouse. At those moments what I wanted to achieve seemed so unreal, so unattainable, that I would ask myself whether it was worth sacrificing so much energy and so many of the comforts of home for it.

64

At those times Nazism seemed to belong entirely to the past; the dead to be definitely dead; and all suffering soothed by time. I thought of myself as alone and very small. Then I would count up all the personal benefits I was deriving from my efforts. I would cling to Serge's love, which had never ceased to grow, and to the trust that so many unknown persons had in me. I was getting letters from all over the world—from Jews, non-Jews, Germans, Frenchmen.

The reason people who did not know me as I actually was kept writing me with such complete confidence was that what I was doing was an incarnation of anti-Hitlerian Germany, a Germany that was acknowledging the burden of its past in order the better to combat it. That was why there was sometimes such enthusiasm for me. It sprang from the deepest feelings of men and women who still could not face up to what Germany had done. The German people had caused such terrible destruction that the scars on the flesh of Europe were still tender. Distrust of Germans in general was so great that, by a kind of backlash, individual Germans who rightly or wrongly were thought exemplary were trusted as one would have liked to trust the German people as a whole.

In the countryside and in the towns of Germany, I conscientiously pursued the task I had set myself. I went from the speaking platform to leadership of a demonstration. I thought up attention-provoking exploits. I wrote exhaustive reports. I clung like a mongrel to Kiesinger's trouser cuffs. I barked, and sometimes I also bit.

November 7, 1968. I slapped Chancellor Kiesinger.

November 11. Brussels. Raissa and I arrived two days ahead of Kiesinger, who was to speak to the Belgian NATO officials.

I had asked the help of Belgium's Jewish Students' Union and of Michel Lang's Jewish Club in Berlin. We made plans for a conference to take place at the Free University of Brussels a few hours before Kiesinger's address. I paid for the Berliners' trip with the two thousand marks I had received for an article in *Horizont*, an East German magazine of international politics. The students' suitcases, stuffed with copies of "The Truth about Kurt-Georg Kiesinger," went astray at the Berlin air terminal but turned up on the next plane.

November 13. 7 A.M. Persistent rapping on our hotel room door. "Police! Identity check." My mother-in-law opened the door a crack and thrust our passports through it to two plainclothesmen.

"That's not enough. You'll have to come to headquarters with us. You have fifteen minutes to get dressed."

Once the door was shut, I rushed to the telephone and called one of Serge's best friends, Philippe Lemaitre, the Brussels correspondent of *Le Monde*, as well as Michel Lang, whose room was on the floor below us. My mother-in-law roused Serge in Paris, and he promised he would immediately call Hubert Halin, the secretary-general of the International Resistance Union. Halin notified his friends in the inner circles of the Belgian government, and especially those in the Ministry of Justice.

More knocking on the door. "Hurry up!"

My mother-in-law replied: "We're ladies. We need time to get dressed properly."

Presently we had to leave. Michel Lang was also under arrest. We were taken straight to Belgian police headquarters, where we had to wait a long time. I was ushered into a small office. Two police officials questioned me and recorded my statements. I was convinced that the purpose of this arrest was to keep me from speaking, hold me in custody until evening, and then put me on a train for Paris. At first I was in a fury. I looked at my watch every five minutes to see whether I was already late. Then I began to use my head. It couldn't be helped. If they did not let me speak, they would have trouble with the students and the scandal would be all the greater. The officials had a lot to type up. I listed Kiesinger's official positions and his duties, and also described the trip he made in 1940 with foreign correspondents into occupied Belgium and France. Then, looking straight at the officials, I added:

"You must have lived through the Nazi occupation of Belgium. You know what that was like."

They told me that they had been in the Resistance, but "an order is an order." The German ambassador to Brussels had asked the Belgian authorities to prevent any incidents during Kiesinger's visit. Troublemaker Number One was me.

About 12:45 P.M. an inspector came in, handed me a sheet of paper, and asked me to sign a pledge to leave Brussels immediately after my speech. He added: "Some VIP's have interceded for you."

My mother-in-law and Michel Lang had been released a few minutes before.

I jumped into a taxi and headed straight for the Free University, where the conference had just begun. Michel Lang was reading the text of my speech. I was greeted with a frantic ovation.

"We won't let Beate leave!" the students shouted.

Some of them suggested blocking the campus gates at 4 P.M. so that I would be protected from the police, but I refused to let them. Once I had finished speaking, a delegation of students got the police to extend my stay until 6 P.M., which gave me time to talk at length with *Der Spiegel*'s correspondent.

Kiesinger delivered his speech that evening. The Belgian students staged a demonstration that I learned about from the newspapers the next morning in Paris. Kiesinger had been deeply humiliated before the Belgian government, Prime Minister Gaston Eyskens, Foreign Minister Pierre Harmel, NATO Secretary-General Manlio Brosio and other officials, the Common Market directors, and the entire diplomatic corps—all of which, of course, was reported in Germany, where the press emphasized that it was the second time in less than a week that Kiesinger had been insulted at my instigation.

The following day, the Munich *Süddeutsche Zeitung* ran a cartoon that summed up the situation: an airplane in flight and below it a witch on a broomstick trailing a streamer that read "Beate Klarsfeld." The cartoon was captioned, "The Chancellor's Advance Guard." The Germans were beginning to realize the embarrassment to which they were exposed by keeping on as Chancellor a man whose reputation was being assailed not only in Germany but outside of Germany as well. The influential weekly *Die Zeit* emphasized this by stressing that Kiesinger's stock and his image were in a decline, and that a crisis had just occurred. It attributed this in a large degree to the Berlin and Brussels incidents. According to some reporters who had access to the Chancellor at that time, the Belgian ordeal had been much more painful to him than the one in Berlin.

November 15. Paris. German reporters stormed our apartment in order to see how "that hysterical young woman who goes around with university hooligans," as Kiesinger had described me, lived. They seemed to think they would find the place in a mess, but everything was impeccable. As soon as they came in they were impressed by our large foyer and our three rooms overlooking the Seine; in fact, they were so amazed that they mistook the reproductions on the wall for originals. For the occasion, I had bought myself a wool dress with a red bodice and steel gray cuffs. It had cost me plenty, but it had the desired effect, especially since I was wearing Dior patent-leather pumps.

They took pictures of me preparing a meal in my spotless kitchen, and thereafter I became in their eyes a real middle-class housewife who was driven by an irresistible impulse to leave a well-ordered existence and a well-to-do home to which she was much attached. Kiesinger's idea that I was a professional revolutionary fell flat.

November 18. The Ilyushin-18 took off for a rough flight from Le Bourget to Schönefeld. The visibility was so poor that we could not land in East Berlin. We headed for Warsaw, then Prague. Finally we had to spend the night in the Budapest terminal, along with eight hundred other stranded passengers.

November 19. We reached East Berlin, were I was welcomed with flowers left over from the night before and a big black Ziss car. I stayed at the Unter-den-Linden luxury hotel, where two young people came over to my table and asked for my autograph—the first time in my life—which I wrote on a menu.

November 20. I caused a small panic in East Berlin. Although I had been invited only to do an interview on East German television, I had told the East German Press Agency in Paris that I would hold a press conference on Kiesinger's Nazi past in the Potsdam Archives building. My East German hosts were dumfounded. They did not like having their hand forced. Since no foreigner has a right to invite Western reporters into a government agency, the press conference was forbidden.

So far as I could observe, the incident did not diminish the general enthusiasm. An album of hundreds of press clippings and cartoons that had appeared in East Germany since my "exploit" was ceremoniously presented to me. I found the East German papers quite favorable. How could such a rigidly communist state bestow so much praise on a single sensational act—and one that undermined authority to boot?

November 22. Michel Lang joined me, and we left for Dortmund to attend a meeting of young socialists at which Günter Grass and the singer Dieter Süverkrupp were to share the stage. Grass was none too pleased at having to play second fiddle to me.

Probably he was a little envious of all the publicity my slap had gotten. Kiesinger had not replied to his open letters and his reproofs, whereas my behavior had had far more practical effect.

November 23. I made a 33-r.p.m. record in Dortmund, titled "The K. Affair—The Story of a Slap." Actors read items from my data, and I myself explained the meaning of my act and recited a poem I had written about it. Pläne-Verlag issued it as an item on its list of socialist and revolutionary songs.

THE SLAP GERMANY NEEDED

Germany needed it
> in order for the cruel, greedy, cowardly, sheeplike
> generations to be seen as culprits
> who thought they could conceal from us forever
> the German people's true sense of honor;

Germany needed it
> for the Russians who died defending
> their homeland at Stalingrad
> or the betrayed German youths
> whose tears froze on their eyelids
> when they thought of those whom they would see no more;

Germany needed it
> for the smoke of Auschwitz
> that will cease wafting the stench of the ovens
> into the nostrils of Germans
> only when that day comes when all Germans will sense their
>   unity
> with those who suffered behind the barbed wire;

Germany needed it
> for all the monuments of the world
> defaced by the swastika flag
> and for all the Manolis Glezios
> who ripped them up;

Germany needed it
> for the thoughts of Hans and Sophie Scholl
> while, their necks on the block,
> they waited for the head of our true Germany
> to fall into the basket;

Germany needed it
    for the reconciliation
    of Jews and Germans
    who would not see the dawn of brotherhood break
    except in a common struggle against fascism;

Germany needed it
    for a Germany free of desire for revenge,
    for a Germany now divided
    yet someday surely one again when
    through socialism we shall win peace and the world's respect;

Germany needed it
    so that many may put on the magic spectacles
    of Günter Grass
    and again see men as they were
    in that dark night,
    and so that Kurt-Georg Kiesinger
    may hide behind a false blindman's dark glasses
    eyes that he has closed to all that.

And Germany needed
    the hand of a woman to deliver it,
    for no one asked the women
    who were consumed in the gas ovens
    and who died in the bombings
    and who shrieked under torture
    whether they were women;

And still the mother
who smiles at the smile of her infant
cannot conceive that he may be murdered
or that he may become a murderer

That is why
impelled by fifty million corpses
and by all generations yet to come,
my hand struck the face of ten million Nazis,
and why
the same insult and the same bruise
has marked their forehead.

November 29. In Paris I gave a speech on the meaning of my crusade to the International League Against Racism and Anti-Semitism. I had made up my mind that I would accept every invitation to speak, whatever it was, so that I could make the facts about Kiesinger known to all.

December 1. I had hardly gotten off the train in Munich when a basset hound came up to me followed by a man holding a bunch of flowers. He introduced himself as a Mr. Koenig, a journalist. It was he who had invited me to Munich and had organized a meeting in the Rationaltheater. He suggested that I spend that Sunday with him and his family. His wife's greeting, however, was far from cordial. Lunch ended in a quarrel because Koenig did not want to help with the dishes.

It was not until I was leaving that I grasped what that man had in mind. He wanted to be my manager and organize a lecture tour through Germany—to put me on display as though I were the woman who gets shot out of a cannon in the circus. He would pay all expenses and keep half of the ticket sales. He was flabbergasted when I turned him down.

December 2. The audience at the Rationaltheater, Munich's political cabaret, was composed of all the city's journalistic and literary figures, who had come to inspect me as if I were some strange animal. They were expecting some kind of sensational show, but were disappointed. So was my would-be manager, who had suggested that I jazz up my story. Poor fellow! I never saw him again.

December 3. I felt much more comfortable at the teach-in at Munich University. That evening I announced that I was going to run for election against Chancellor Kiesinger in September 1969. I thought I might thereby escape the prison sentence that awaited me when my case was heard at the Court of Appeals. Also, I could wage my own campaign with greater effect. All I had to do was find a political organization that would support me against Kiesinger.

December 7. In Dortmund I spoke to the communist youth of the Federal Republic. Also finished my recording.

December 10. The Jewish Students' Movement had set up a debate in the Edmond Fleg Center in Paris on the topic, "Was It Necessary to Slap Chancellor Kiesinger?" There were heated discussions. I had summoned from Bonn some French-speaking Opposition students who described the difficulty of their struggle against fascism. A new dialogue began between the young Jews and the young Germans, but it remained within the framework of joint action.

A motion I made was carried with the help of the Society of Former Deported Jews. An important item in it was "the need for the Jewish people not to let German democrats fight alone against the same forces that had destroyed over six million Jews and that were trying to reconcile Germany with its Nazi past."

One of the directors of the Jewish Students' Movement decided to accompany me back to Berlin with a flag bearing the Star of David, to protest the recent acquittal of the Nazi judge, Hans-Joachim Rehse, who had been sentenced to five years in prison for "aiding criminal acts." The Supreme Court of Appeals had upset that verdict in April 1968, despite the fact that a judge assumes full responsibility for his actions.

Judge Oske, who presided over the trial, adduced that "every state, even a totalitarian state, is obliged to assert its authority." Therefore it was impossible to "blame a government for having recourse in a critical period to extraordinary methods of intimidation." Proof of that was "the recent adoption of emergency laws in the Federal Republic."

As might be expected, that opinion caused a considerable stir in the courtroom. The audience interrupted the reading of the opinion several times, and a former prisoner of the Gestapo succeeded in striking Rehse as he was leaving the courtroom a free man.

I had paid for the militant Jew's trip, for he would have been unable to raise the fare in forty-eight hours. I thought it essential to show the Germans that Jews would come even from another country to protest the rehabilitation of Rehse.

December 14. Ten thousand persons gathered before the Berlin-Schöneberg Town Hall shouting, "Rehse is a murderer" and "Get the Nazis out of the courts."

I spoke emphatically: "The leaders in Bonn have acted as if Germany had merely taken a wrong turn during the twelve years of the Nazi regime. They stand for work, family, prosperity, and above all, no political conscience. And thanks to apolitical citizens, they have quickly re-established and reinforced a prosperous capitalist system. Germany is going along fine, but in what direction?

. . . The objective now—make no mistake—is to bring the country under political control again. To accomplish this, they have to go beyond the piddling sentences that have managed to persuade the masses that the crimes of Hitler's Reich were the work of only a few sadistic individuals. That notion has spared the most morally and effectually guilty: the men in politics, law, and administration who masterminded the crimes.

"Now the system is going even further by rehabilitating them. If things go on like this, they will wind up rehabilitating Hitler. When that day comes, we who are here in such numbers will be quite alone, everyone for himself. When Kiesinger became Chancellor, I could see the beginning of a real reconciliation between Germany and her Nazi past, and that therein lay Kiesinger's place in history. I wanted my acting as an individual to check him, but his total defeat must be the result of collective action."

East German observers were there. Their newspapers focused on my appeal. I could see that all was going well for my eventual candidacy. Long articles had made me well known in the German Democratic Republic and in the communist press of West German and the socialist countries.

January 22, 1969. Two soldiers were found with their throats cut in Lebach, near Saarbrucken. The conservative press exploded and attributed the crime to the Extra-Parliamentary Opposition. It seemed clear to me that no militants who call themselves idealists would have cut the throats of sleeping soldiers—who were actually civilians in uniform—just to get their hands on some weapons. There had to be a quick reaction.

I went to Bonn at once and wrote a pamphlet, had several hundred copies printed, and circulated them by putting them into the mail boxes of all the newspapers in the Press Building. In the pamphlet, I announced the formation of a committee of inquiry headed by the Extra-Parliamentary Opposition. Of course I had no one to conduct such an inquiry, but it would be enough for the reporters to write that the Saar police have received support from the Opposition committee.

Later the murderers were caught—young conservatives who did it to get the weapons.

Early in January the Düsseldorf DVZ, a pro-communist weekly, asked me to be its Paris correspondent. My weekly articles for it brought me 800 marks a month. I figured that this was a clandes-

tine subsidy from East Germany, but the DVZ editors denied that
they had been pressured into hiring me.

January 30. Cologne. My talk on imprisonment while awaiting
trial helped warm up the audience. Other speakers dwelt on the
fascism that exists in Greece, Spain, and Portugal, for there were
immigrant workers in the hall. The young people wanted to go into
action, but unfortunately they had no program for doing so. The
meeting broke up early. A first division descended on the Greek and
Portuguese consulates; windows and doors were broken at the
United States Information Agency; the Spanish Railway Office was
damaged, as well as a Spanish community center and the Greek
Club. Police sirens shrieked throughout the city.

In Frankfurt hundreds of protesters answered the call of the
Students for a Democratic Society, which wanted to celebrate in
its own way the thirty-sixth anniversary of Hitler's rise to power.
There was a gala performance at the opera for the benefit of the
Foundation for the Aid of German Sport. The cream of the German establishment was there expecting to have a pleasant evening,
even though they could hardly fail to remember the historical
event it commemorated. It was a real provocation for the anti-
fascists. Students greeted the Chancellor with shouts of "*Sieg heil!
Kiesinger is a Nazi! Slap Kiesinger!*" They blocked traffic and overturned automobiles. Violence erupted all over West Germany.

January 31. I spoke in the largest auditorium of the University
of Hamburg. Two thousand in attendance, and an impressive number of police.

February 1. Duisburg. And freezing cold! I spoke in the Town
Hall Square. Fortunately my speech was short, for I had to turn the
pages with my glove off and I was getting numb. In the evening I
left by car for Dortmund. There I took the night train to Berlin
for a meeting at the Free University.

February 3. Serge joined me to help me prepare for the hearing
before the Court of Appeals. The election of the President of the
Federal Republic took place today. Heinrich Lübke, the former
President, had been unseated by Germans from the East and by
his own behavior. He had had to resign his position prematurely
after having been accused of designing huts for concentration
camps. He denied drawing the plans, but handwriting analyses
convicted him.

We hardly dared believe it when we heard that Gustav Heinemann had been elected President of the Federal Republic—a smashing defeat for the Christian Democrats whose candidate, Gerhard Schröder, a former stormtrooper, had been backed by the neo-Nazis. I ran into Heinemann in the lobby of his hotel. A reporter dashed up to get a picture of him, and suggested that Heinemann shake my hand. A picture of the President-elect shaking the hand of the woman who had slapped the Chancellor would have been a gross insult to the head of the government. Heinemann was annoyed at having to refuse, for he knew how much I respected him and what a moral lesson the Germans could derive from seeing him grasp my hand. He got out of the situation gracefully: "If I were still only the Minister of Justice," he told the reporters around him, "I would have shaken Mrs. Klarsfeld's hand, but now the responsibilities I am about to assume do not permit me to."

February 4. I took an early-morning plane from Berlin to Nuremberg. In the afternoon I spoke at the Normal School. In the evening I led a demonstration through the streets to police headquarters. Young people carrying banners decrying fascism formed a hedge around me and booed Kiesinger. I felt almost drunk as I heard my voice in the night air of the very city in which Hitler, thirty years earlier, had prepared to mobilize the German people for his satanic projects. I had the impression my voice was that of another Germany; I was not alone, there were many with me.

February 14. Last night Arno, who had come with me to Oldenburg, stayed up late listening to his mother. Today I was speaking in Bonn for the first time, addressing the fighting wing of the Party for Democratic Action and Progress (ADF), which had nominated me in Kiesinger's electoral district—No. 188, of Waldheim in the Black Forest—one of the most solidly Christian Democratic in Germany. I was also No. 2 on the Württemberg-Baden list of candidates. That was a giant step forward for me. I had taken precedence over many hard-core communists, and I could sense their cautiously concealed hostility toward me. I had been imposed on them for my newsworthiness and for having the backing of East German leaders.

The press kept me in the limelight. As a matter of fact, I had become the ADF's chief vote-getter, even though I was not receiving the concrete support I had a right to expect from the party organization. Its political concerns were far from compatible with my objectives, but at least I was to be reimbursed for all the trips I made for them, and that made me freer to travel.

I could see how far I had come since the OFA had fired me. Single-handed, my fist my only weapon, I had taken by storm the smallest of the five West German political organizations. I could, therefore, press on toward a moral goal that might have been neglected by political forces that were by no means negligible.

My first speech in Bonn that evening certainly bore no resemblance to the kind of speeches the extreme leftists were accustomed to hearing. They must have wondered what kind of high protection I had in East Berlin if I talked there as I did to them.

"Whenever I am asked to speak, even to audiences not of the left, I appeal to ethics, for I believe in morality in politics. I believe that every German, whether of the East or the West, has inherited the good and the bad that Germany has bequeathed him. Every German has a duty to assume that honor and that liability, and I do not call him a good citizen who thinks he need not be concerned with his country's past because he was born too late. . . . We Germans have duties and moral obligations in respect to our past. . . . The task incumbent on all who want a new Germany, a peaceful Germany, and a Germany deserving of the respect of other nations, is to create a genuinely socialist state.

"In the forthcoming elections my role will be to say all over Germany, and face-to-face with Kiesinger, what healthy Germans think of him and of what he stands for. This is not going to be a battle for a certain percentage of the votes in my district, but open defiance on a national scale."

The meeting was at the full and the audience was listening attentively to the ADF president when suddenly the door flew open and in burst Arno, his pants down to his ankles, shouting at the top of his lungs: "Mama, I've got to do poopoo!" I had to leave the Congress to attend to much more urgent business.

February 20. I was off to the Congress of the National Democratic Party (NPD) of neo-Nazis in Bayreuth.

If that party were to get five percent of the votes in the coming September elections, it could win a seat in the Bundestag. The anti-fascists had only one means of blocking them: compelling them to strip off the veil of respectability behind which they were trying to conceal their true nature.

When I reached Bayreuth late in the evening, I learned that the city government had refused to issue a permit for the Congress, not out of any political convictions, but out of fear that foreign tourists might stay away from the Wagner Festival. The 650 delegates, therefore, had moved a few miles away to Schwabach, where they were being protected by a helmeted security force armed with clubs and chains.

By showing my DVZ press card, I got into the auditorium, where I was soon noticed by two stalwarts who tailed me closely. As I came in, Adolf von Thadden was proposing to safeguard democracy in Germany by putting an end to the "Reds" and to swiftly suppress student riots by replacing the police posted around the universities with a militia of tax-paying workingmen.

I got to my feet and strode to the platform, shouting as loudly as I could: "Von Thadden, you keep talking about democracy all the time. Now let some true democrats have a say."

The security men leaped on me, but von Thadden stopped them by shouting into the microphone: "Gentlemen, gentlemen, don't you know how to treat a lady? I can thank my lucky stars that my cheek is farther away from that lady's hand than the Chancellor's was."

The audience roared. After *Deutschland Über Alles* was fervently chanted, the demonstration came to an end. Once outside, I found I was unhurt and relieved.

February 27. After Augsburg I went to Waldshut, on the edge of the Black Forest near Switzerland, a rural region but with an up-to-date look. Some of the militant radicals were coming to give me some advice about the elections, such as where my rallies should be held and how I should talk to the local people.

Was the extreme left going to waste its energy getting a few votes here while the Social Democrats were in the process of replacing the Christian Democratic Union with a well-planned platform? I explained to them that I had no intention of shutting myself up in empty rooms, that my campaign was on a national scale, and that I was going to appear everywhere Kiesinger held a rally. I was going to harass him in the street in front of his hotel even if I had nothing but a handful of young people tirelessly shouting "*Sieg heil!*" The reporters who followed Kiesinger would repeat and expand my protest, and thus it would reach all Germans. By weakening Kiesinger I would be supporting the Social Democratic campaign and giving Brandt a bigger chance.

March 12. Kiesinger was paying an official visit to Paris. I had invited four friends to come from Berlin. Along with me they were to address the Sorbonne students on Thursday, the 13th.

On Wednesday evening, as the five of us were going out into rue de l'Alboni, a dozen or so plainclothesmen descended upon us and took us away in three automobiles. I was booked at the La Muette police station and set free around midnight, but my friends were taken to General Intelligence. On the following day they were put into their car and escorted to the frontier.

All day long Serge and I were accompanied by policemen stationed outside our apartment house in two cars, one on avenue President Kennedy, the other on rue de l'Alboni. We engaged them in conversation and they showed us our pictures, which many Paris policemen had, doubtless out of fear that we would commit some outrage against the Chancellor.

In the evening, still followed, I spoke at a conference organized by leftist groups at the Hotel Moderne on two general topics: Kiesinger and S.S.-General Heinz Lammerding.

The reporters for German papers who were in Kiesinger's party attended the meeting and took note of the hostility of the French toward the Chancellor.

After speaking in Waldshut on March 22, and in Constance on the 23rd, I began the Easter marches on the 28th. Easter is the traditional time for protesting the issue of nuclear armament for Germany, and I spoke in Hamburg, Duisberg, and Essen.

April. We had been working like truckhorses. For over forty-eight hours I had had almost no sleep, and for ten days I had been typing the German text of *Kiesinger or Crafty Fascism*. *Extradienst*, a news service whose premises served as a meeting place for West Berlin radicals, undertook the printing of this 100-page pamphlet, three thousand copies of which were circulated on the eve of my hearing before the Court of Appeals.

It was the weapon I needed for that trial. The press promised to give it a lot of space and to indicate in editorials that Kiesinger had not yet published the documentation on his Nazi past that he had promised on April 22, 1968. On the other hand, I, the slapper, had spoken out and demonstrated just what that past of his was, and I had not been sued for slander. Nothing in our book could be refuted. I have never stated anything I could not prove.

April 15. My hearing began. Once again I appeared before judges for having slapped the Chancellor of the Federal Republic of West Germany.

The criminal court was a big, gloomy, massive, prewar building. It was surrounded by thirty police cars so that no one could park there. Over a thousand policemen were there, ready for war. Even the reporters had to pass four checkpoints. But anyone hoping for an incident was disappointed. A demonstration by anti-fascists that the police—but not the young people—were expecting did not materialize. Under the circumstances, as I had decided to be Kiesinger's prosecutor during the hearing, I had to fight my battle with documentation that proved Kiesinger's Nazi activities, not with incidents that would be ineffectual anyway. Arno, Serge, and Joseph Billig (the historian who had helped me with my report) were there, along with thirty photographers and dozens of reporters.

The following morning, the press gave detailed descriptions of my hairdo, my knitted dress, and my spike-heeled shoes. I had taken particular care to present my best Paris image as proof of my comfortable financial situation and my middle-class lifestyle.

The arguments opened with a request that the president of the tribunal, Taegener, disqualify himself. My lawyer made the most of the fact that Taegener had publicly stated to a reporter with whom he was having coffee in the court canteen that my trial would be "over in three hours." After a short deliberation the court denied the request.

I was questioned exhaustively. The president of the tribunal, in his icily polite way, tried to trip me up in my story. I gave him direct answers and, I think, managed to stay out of his traps. One of my replies was repeated in the papers and on the radio. It had come to me spontaneously, but as if a strange voice had uttered it, the voice of all who, in my person, were standing before German justice.

"Frau Klarsfeld, how did you happen to decide to use violence against the Chancellor of our country?"

"Violence, your honor, is the imposition of a Nazi Chancellor on German youth."

I talked so much about Kiesinger's Nazi past that Taegener grew

impatient and stopped me with a remark that delighted the commentators: "That will do. You have already shown that Kiesinger
was one of the activists of the Nazi regime."

Very quickly the arguments got on to the political level. I explained the meaning of my act. Serge, who had been admitted as
an assistant to my lawyers, testified that inasmuch as he was a Jew
he was completely behind me. When Billig was called as a witness,
the court concentrated entirely on Kiesinger's record.

President Taegener asked whether the witness could verify his
statement that Kiesinger knew what was going on in the concentration camps. In due time, therefore, the Chancellor himself became the defendant.

Billig, who was born in St. Petersburg, had become a French
citizen and had received his doctorate from the University of
Berlin. He was an embarrassing witness. Not only did he speak
perfect German, but he also had a formidable accuracy that delighted the audience. He gave Taegener a real education on the
organization of the Foreign Ministry under Hitler.

It became clear that the court wanted to get the business over
with in a hurry. Early in the afternoon the hearing was adjourned
to the following day.

Then, surprise of surprises! The next morning my lawyers had
not even gotten their papers out when the president of the tribunal
announced that the trial was postponed to a distant date on the
grounds that the court had little time at the moment and that
Kiesinger could not appear to testify in person.

Before we could react, the judge and his associates vanished
through a little door. The hearing ended like a farce, with a great
burst of laughter, but it had achieved its purpose. The press now
had plenty of material for long stories: "Beate's Slap Shakes Chancellor," and "Kiesinger Retreats Before Beate Klarsfeld," and "The
Slap that Caused a Political Crisis." They would have an effect, I
hoped, on some voters' consciences.

April 29. I faced my Württemberg-Baden constituency for the
first time in the little town of Rheinfelden. Gunnar Matthiessen,
an ADF official from Bonn headquarters, was with me. He was a
very good speaker and very cautious in his political selections.
There were only a few people in the back room of the restaurant,
which was generally used for wedding banquets and political rallies.

They were on my side, but they irritated me with all their patronizing, tried-and-true bits of advice.

I settled with Matthiessen that I would be in my electoral district whenever Kiesinger was there. The ADF would help me carry on my campaign.

On May 10 I took the night train, by myself as usual, and stretched out on yet another banquette for the trip to Stuttgart, where a NPD Congress of neo-Nazis was to meet over the weekend. Serge, who was going to demonstrate with me, had already arrived. Our first disappointment was to find that the Social Democrats and the union leaders had taken off for the weekend. The NPD's rabid security force had transformed the Congress hall into a fortress. They had barricaded the entrance with wooden boards, and turned themselves into a human barrier by linking hands and spreading their *lederhosen*-clad legs. I shuddered at the thought of having to tangle with those giants, and the young demonstrators apparently did too, for there were no hand-to-hand encounters.

It was extremely important that our protest against the NPD get full attention so that it could not be said that the neo-Nazis met with no opposition. We decided to make the most of our ridiculously pitiful resistance. The press would be looking for something sensational to report. If nothing happened, they would merely print a picture of Adolf von Thadden speaking. So why shouldn't we give them a chance for a picture that would reflect our line and not the NPD's?

I proposed that we hang a huge Nazi flag in the main square and solemnly proclaim Stuttgart the foremost Nazi city in Germany. Getting the material for the flag was no cinch. Sewing it up was no cinch either, not to mention painting a swastika on it. But finally we produced a reasonably good flag.

Luck was with us. We made such an impression right in the center of the city that the picture of our flag and of us haranguing the good citizens of Stuttgart appeared in the papers of Germany and the rest of the world with the caption: "Germans Protest Neo-Nazi Congress."

May 28. Back in East Berlin, I assembled photographs of documents to illustrate the book on Kiesinger that the Heinrich Heine Publishing Company of Frankfurt had commissioned. It was to have a much more controversial tone than the previous one, for I wanted to use it in my election campaign. From Berlin I went to Frankfurt, then to two rallies in Lebenstadt and Hanover, before returning to Paris on the 30th. How could I keep all this up until October?

June 21. I put the finishing touches on my manuscript in the Potsdam Archives. When I got back to Paris, I learned that the twentieth session of the World Peace Congress in East Berlin had awarded me the Gregory Lambrakis Medal. Not being completely informed about the true situation in Germany, the authors of the citation accompanying the medal—which shows the hero of "Z"— inscribed it: "For her courage and the fight she has made for national independence." I was nonetheless much moved to be so honored as a German woman.

June 30. Bremerhaven. The ADF leaders here had given my arrival a great deal of publicity: posters and pamphlets. We drove to Bremen with Arno, arriving with an hour to spare. We wanted to inspect the sound equipment in the Nordseehotel, which the ADF had hired. Herr Naber, one of the hotel owners, met us at the door and announced: "I have cancelled the rental of the hall. B.K. shall not enter my hotel."

He had not shut his doors to the other parties, as the papers pointed out, and had even admitted Admiral Karl Doenitz, Hitler's successor, when that Nazi recently attended a Navy reunion in Bremerhaven.

After four rallies in small towns in the region, we reached Oldenburg, where Kiesinger was to speak at a big rally restricted to members of the Christian Democratic Union. I managed to gather about three hundred young people of the city, which is inhabited mainly by retired officials. There were not enough policemen to stop us from blockading the main door of the Weser-Ems-Hall.

The Chancellor's helicopter landed in an empty lot behind the building surrounded by a high iron fence. Kiesinger got out of it smiling, doubtless under the impression that we were cheering him, and waved to us. In a moment, however, he recognized his mistake, but he seemed determined not to be embarrassed and so continued to smile and wave.

Serge and I were hoisted to the top of a car parked up against the fence and so could see everything that was going on. The booing increased as Kiesinger came nearer. Suddenly there he was, right in front of me. He recognized me at once. His jaw tightened and his smile vanished. My arm was raised and, like the others, I was shouting what once I was the only one to shout: "*Sieg heil!*" and "Kiesinger is a Nazi." Now these taunts were harassing the Chancellor, even in so reactionary a city as Oldenburg. Kiesinger looked at me as if he wanted to say something, then made a feeble gesture of dismissal. He shook his head and went toward the hotel kitchens, obliged to use the service entrance.

A journalist accredited to Bonn told me: "Kiesinger's friends have advised him on several occasions to arrange a meeting with 'that woman' so that he might reach an understanding with her. But Kiesinger always replied: 'There's no possibility of an understanding with her.'"

July 24. I went to Baden-Baden, then to Frankfurt, where I witnessed the fiercest clash yet between the shock troops of the neo-Nazi NPD and the young APO members. I got out of it safely, but others were not so lucky. Everywhere stretchers were carrying away anti-fascists in particular, their noses or jaws broken by bicycle chains or loaded clubs. *Stern*, which supported Brandt, made no bones about publishing pictures of the smashed faces of these young German citizens. Confronted by Hitler's direct descendants, they have done what all Germans ought to have done. I drew strength from their example.

In Frankfurt, I also had to straighten out the mess over my book. The publisher was in a tough financial bind. One of his editors told me that there had been a lot of argument over my manuscript, and that it might well not be published by the date we had counted on —which would be a blow to my campaign—or else might not be published as I had written it. I had not received any proofs in spite of several requests for them. Then a young Israeli, Abraham Melzer, who had taken over his father's publishing firm in Darmstadt, wired me that he knew about Heinrich Heine's financial difficulties and offered to buy the manuscript and publish it himself as soon as possible. He, too, could not bear the thought of a Nazi being returned as Chancellor.

Herr Bingel, Heine's manager, refused to give me the proofs, although they were ready. I left his office in a rage and went to the local SDS headquarters, where I explained the situation to some young men and persuaded them to follow me.

We marched on Bingel's office and refused to leave until we got the proofs. I needed only to read the first page to see that my anti-

Kiesinger work had been turned into a pro-Kiesinger tract. Doors
slammed. There was no further discussion, only shouting. I telephoned Melzer, who came with a lawyer, but he turned out to be
so soft that we got rid of him. We dangled a carrot on a stick
before Bingel in the form of threats and a check for two thousand
marks. He gave in. The book was rescued.

August 14. With Arno, I started on a three-day tour of my electoral district, for Kiesinger was going to campaign there over the
weekend.

I had telephoned from Paris for a group with a car in which I
could follow Kiesinger's procession. We got five young men and
an Opel-Kapitän, and later a Volkswagen bus lent by a sympathetic
dairyman to carry six young people, pamphlets, posters, and the
tomatoes and eggs we intended to throw. Our first stop was
Uhlingen.

The little village was touching in its simplicity, set in a smiling
valley with rows of red-roofed cottages framed by dark pines. The
platform that had been set up in the little square was hung with
evergreen boughs, flags, and garlands of flowers. It was a real holiday for the seven hundred fifty inhabitants.

The border patrol's big helicopter almost turned over when it
landed on the meadow next to the Hotel Alte Post. Kiesinger's
appearance was the cue for a fanfare and for girls in local costume
to march up to him with armfuls of flowers.

We parked our cars. When we got out of them with our ammunition and our shabbily dressed, bearded youngsters, people looked
at us as though we were visitors from another planet. Arno had to
go to the bathroom, so I took him into the hotel. There I found
some ten persons talking together. When they turned around, I
saw that they were reporters. "Ah," they exclaimed. "So Frau
Klarsfeld has kept her word. This will be an interesting stop."

The better to interrupt the rally, we stood on a bench. As soon
as Kiesinger began to speak, we shouted in chorus: "Nazi!" Arno,
teetering on his perch, joined in gleefully. Suddenly some myr-
midons of the law who had sneaked up behind us tipped over the
bench on which we were standing. Kiesinger lost patience at this
interruption and shouted angrily: "It's always the same faces.
Point them out clearly so that everyone can see who they are. I
have nothing against my opponents, but if those people want to
destroy the State, we are not going to let them do it."

We stopped on the way to Waldshut, where the last rally of the day was to be held, replenished our supply of elderly eggs, and got a crate of damaged fruit. The town had been painstakingly decorated. The country people were all in their best clothes, and the mayor and his colleagues were in a dither. The Chancellor's arrival was to be the climax of the local festival—the Chilibi—which was being celebrated that day.

We had already notified the young locals to meet in the hall at 8 P.M. We went there separately and had to take seats where we could find them, for the hall was almost full. The security force got nervous as soon as they saw us, and the rally began slowly. Finally the mayor announced that the Chancellor could make only a brief appearance because he was very tired after so full a day.

The moment Kiesinger began speaking, about forty young people stood up, raised their arms, and booed him. The embarrassed Kiesinger thought he could wait out the storm, though he was surprised at the number of agitators. The dumfounded public made no reaction; it was the first time something like this had ever happened in the traditionally conservative village.

Kiesinger tried a flash of humor, but it was lost in the continuous booing and shouting. He stammered a few sentences that no one could hear. Then, red-faced, he left the platform and sat down.

When the rally broke up, the townspeople heckled me. "It's shameful," said one woman, "to bring up a child a fanatic. The poor kid ought to be in bed at this hour. He's dead tired."

Quite a crowd gathered around us.

"It's strange," I said, "that during the war you didn't have any such pity for the Jewish children they jammed into cattle cars before burning them up in Auschwitz."

The woman did not answer, but moved away and disappeared. The others slowly did likewise.

"Did anyone in Waldshut," I continued, "protest against the crimes committed in Vietnam? Did anyone come to the defense of children burned with napalm?"

One man raged at me: "Oh, these Jews! It's a pity they weren't all exterminated."

The newspapers gave a lot of coverage to incidents like these, which cropped up every day. *Publik* wrote: "B.K. is giving Kiesinger nightmares. He breaks out in a rash whenever he sees her or even hears her. Socialist Karl Schiller himself never succeeded in upsetting Kiesinger's aplomb, but the young people of the APO, who can be counted on the fingers of one hand, are doing so."

August 19. With Arno beside me I held a press conference in Berlin. My book, *Kiesinger, a Documentation,* had just been published—six days before my second trial before the Court of Appeals. I emphasized this coincidence. I had on several occasions met Karl Gerold, the publisher of the *Frankfurter Rundschau,* who was a good friend of Brandt and a former anti-Nazi emigré. Now he was convinced, and he gave me a whole page in his courageous and popular newspaper. I used it for an exhaustive article on "Kiesinger and the 'Final Solution.'" Gerold himself, who was very influential, added a resounding editorial on the same topic, entitled "Kiesinger Never Again." It was the strongest in the entire campaign.

Many reporters came to that Berlin press conference and also to the one I held in Frankfurt on August 23, and many reviews of my book appeared. There was considerable emphasis on the fact that it was a weapon for the elections, not a commercial book. And as a weapon it was effective. Heinrich Böll had written a strong preface.

August 25. My second trial began. The first point to be settled was whether Kiesinger would testify, since he was the plaintiff and it would be his last chance to reply publicly to my charges.

President Taegener ordered read to the court a letter in which Kiesinger replied to the court's summons by protesting that his electoral campaign gave him no free time. The judge concluded: "As a result, Chancellor Kiesinger, so far as we are concerned, is not present. . . ."

I noticed that the trial was taking a favorable turn, for the court did not appear aggressive—quite the countrary. My judges could not send the Chancellor's opponent in the election to prison, for that would create a scandal, and so they were going to appear generous in order to take the wind out of my sails. To guard against this, I decided not to prolong a trial that could bring me no advantage other than Kiesinger's significant absence. I therefore declared that in the absence of the Chancellor, who was discrediting himself by his cowardice, I would not answer any questions: "I am not going on with this farce. So far as I am concerned, the trial is over."

My lawyers also refused to plead. Then everything happened very quickly. The court adjourned to deliberate, and returned with the verdict everyone expected—except Prosecutor Neelsen, who still demanded a year's imprisonment—four months in jail, sentence suspended. (I was later to be pardoned by Brandt when he came to power.) The court explained its leniency by the fact that I had acted "out of conviction."

Serge spent a week of his vacation going back and forth to Hamburg to oversee the printing of a pamphlet with a red cover: *Kiesinger or Subtle Fascism,* the French edition of my earliest research. We published it ourselves under our rights as authors of the German edition.

On September 8, President Pompidou was paying an official visit to Bonn, an occasion on which Kiesinger's Nazi past once more had to be revealed. On September 5, Serge brought home a big suitcase full of copies that still smelled of the binder's glue. We made the rounds of the ministries, the legislative assemblies, the Elysée Palace, and the government offices to give them to the top politicians in France and to the men who would be going to Bonn with Pompidou. The German correspondents in Paris also received copies, and they wired Bonn that the French officials would be reading B.K.'s book on Kiesinger on the flight to the German capital.

September 7. I reached Bonn. I had asked the Hamburg printer to send me, under my maiden name, a whole carton of the red booklets, and I found it waiting for me at the Bonn railway station. With the help of two young ADF members, I set out to distribute them at the press conference that was to follow the Franco-German talks. Laden with the heavy packages, we arrived at the Press Building a little late.

The guard stopped us. "Where are you going?"

"Günter Diehl, the government spokesman, has instructed us to deliver these books."

We went up to the second floor. About a hundred German and foreign reporters were already in the large conference room. No one paid any attention to us. We slipped in and methodically handed out the booklets, beginning at the rear of the room. The reporters began to get excited. By the time the guards noticed that it was not an official document we were handing out, it was too late. Most of the reporters were already reading it. We were expelled, followed by several correspondents who snatched the last few copies out of our hands.

As we were going down the stairs, Günter Diehl was just coming up. Flushed with success, I handed him a copy that he brushed aside.

"Diehl is a Nazi!"

He spun around and for a moment couldn't find words. Then he shouted: "Communists! Bolsheviks!"

Günter Diehl had been one of Kiesinger's closest associates during the war. When he became Chancellor, Kiesinger made Diehl director of information. Diehl was also one of the Nazi experts on psychological warfare and subversive propaganda and, in December 1939, liaison officer between the Foreign Ministry and the "Bureau Concordia" of the Propaganda Ministry. Along with Otto Abetz, who was to be the German ambassador to Occupied France, Diehl set up a propaganda program directed against France over secret French-language stations that represented the various French political tendencies. These broadcast, as if absolutely true, information designed to create panic in French communities. In November 1940, Diehl was a radio executive in Brussels, and until March 1943 he held a similar position in Vichy. He finally returned to Germany as an adviser to Struve's legation, which supervised the bands of French fascists that Jacques Doriot directed.

What I did in Bonn made the Germans smile—and think a little. They now knew that French officials were well aware of their Chancellor's work for the Nazis.

Berlin-Hamburg. I remember the ADF rally in Hamburg on September 16 as the largest in the whole campaign. The speakers were unrealistically hopeful and kept talking about getting 8 percent of the vote, but when it came my turn to speak I stated my opinion frankly: "We will not even get 2 percent."

September 20. Karlsruhe. With hundreds of young people, we besieged the Gartenhalle, where Kiesinger was speaking. I could no longer sneak into halls to speak against him, for someone would always recognize me and I would be unceremoniously escorted out.

Ravensburg, Waldshut, Rheinfelden, Esslingen . . .

September 26. Serge met me with Petia, our cocker spaniel, to be my bodyguard during the hectic final two days before the election. Petia proved to be a help, for at one of the last rallies, in Waldshut on September 27, when Serge, two friends, and I were handing out pamphlets in the crowd that had come to hear Kiesinger, a woman with an ice cream cone ran up and threw the ice cream in my face, temporarily blinding me. Then she started hitting me with her fists. Petia began to jump and bark, attracting Serge's attention. Serge dropped his pamphlets and pulled the woman off me.

Albruck, Waldshut, Dorgezn, Unterbruckringen, Trangen, Sackingen, Gorwihl, Hochsal . . . all day long the names of the villages where Kiesinger stopped and where we staged demonstrations and passed out our pamphlets flew past.

Sometimes Serge and I were the only ones of our party in the front rows where, of course, we kept interrupting Kiesinger. When we shouted "Willy Brandt for Chancellor," together with the socialists who took the risk of coming to Christian Democratic rallies, the reporters were astonished and the Christian Democrats were very angry.

"You're ADF people. You have no right to campaign for Brandt."

"Better to give your votes to Brandt's SPD than to waste them on the ADF."

September 28. Election day. The results will soon be in. I went straight from Waldshut to Bonn with Serge and Petia, for as a candidate I was entitled to be present in the Assembly for the vote counting. I got in, but not without some trouble, and two or three of the security men stuck right beside me for fear of a disturbance.

Reporters also stuck close by, asking for my predictions. I told them frankly that my party, the ADF, would not get more than one percent of the vote.

The ADF officials were cool. They had not expected to see me there. They were still optimistic, so when the first returns were announced, they left without even saying good-by.

That night the television coverage began with a shot of the Bundestag, and the newscaster pointed me out as: "Beate Klarsfeld, this evening's guest of honor."

I felt a hand on my shoulder. It was the Bonn police chief, who apologized that he couldn't share my politics but offered his "personal congratulations" for my "courage." Several Christian Democratic officials said the same thing to me that evening. I have often remarked on the almost exaggerated respect conservative Germans—policemen included—have for a woman who can take a stand.

The ADF got only .7 percent of the national vote, but that made no difference. It meant the NPD did not get the fateful 5 percent, and so there would be no neo-Nazis in the Bundestag. The numerical requirements for the coalition of socialists and liberals were met. Brandt would be Chancellor. Kiesinger was held responsible for the CDU-CSU defeat and surrendered his leadership of the CDU to Rainer Barzel, his younger rival.

Willy Brandt's success made me serenely happy and gave me a satisfaction that nothing could ever erase. It was confirmation that I had not fought in vain, that my cause had not been backward-looking, and that I had not been motivated by spite. My battle had looked toward the future. Once defeated, Kiesinger was immediately forgotten. A new leaf had been turned.

I am convinced that I played a modest but tangible role in this victory of the forces of progress. I have not stopped rejoicing over Kiesinger's fall. Would I have had the strength to go on if hundreds of thousands of votes had kept Kiesinger in office? I doubt it. I would soon have tired of fighting the same battle over and over again, and my ability to spring back would have crumbled.

Once again I was deliciously anonymous. I could become a real mother and a real wife again. Two or three times a week Serge and I would devour a double feature at the neighborhood movie. I felt young again every time I thought of the important job I had done so well, of the fight I had led, of the blows I had so recklessly delivered on my sizable adversary.

How I relished that memorable handshake between Kiesinger and Brandt after power had passed to the new Chancellor! That grim smile on the face of the defeated Nazi as he tried to be gracious to that other German who had been his opponent.

Throughout my campaign I had felt myself gradually becoming what I now call myself—"a reunified German." My activities showed me as a German woman of neither East nor West, trying to preserve values that both German states, regardless of ideology, should share. The struggle for the moral rehabilitation of the German people will put an end to the divisiveness that has long separated Germans from Germany. I extracted from it a keener sense of my duty. Even though I was called a model for the youth of the East, even though in the West I have succeeded in building a narrow but solid bridge between the Jewish people and the German people across the deep gully of the six million victims they have in common, there was still plenty of work for the little "private politician," which was soon to be my nickname in the Federal Republic.

7

BLOCKING
A NAZI FROM THE
COMMON MARKET

On March 30, 1970, the *Süddeutsche Zeitung*, Munich's big independent daily, reported that Ernst Achenbach was the candidate to succeed Fritz Hellwig as the German member of the
Committee of the European Economic Community (EEC) in
Brussels. The paper went on to say that Achenbach, a Free Democratic Party (FDP) member of the Bundestag, would soon be
appointed by the federal government.

I had come across Achenbach several times during my research
into Kiesinger's past. Out of my files I drew a memorandum dated
June 28, 1940, from Schlottman of the Cultural Division of the
Foreign Ministry, radio section, to Otto Abetz, the German ambassador to Paris. The memorandum stated that the embassy
secretary, Dr. Ernst Achenbach, was to set the political policy of
the department handling German broadcasts in Occupied France.

Well, well, well. Here was another familiar name: Dr. Gustav
Sonnenhol was the head of that department. Just a few weeks ago,
the President of the Federal Republic, Gustav Heinemann, had
personally opposed his nomination as Secretary of State for Foreign
Affairs because of the role he had played in 1943–44. Perhaps it

would be just as possible to force Achenbach to give up his international ambitions. Wouldn't appointing a former Nazi diplomat contribute to the restoration of Nazism and put the Europe of 1970 under the aegis of the swastika that aimed at enlisting Europe in a crusade against bolshevism, Anglo-Saxons, democracy, Jews, freedom?

The newsweekly *Der Spiegel* wrote that Achenbach's candidacy was the result of a bargain made the day after the September 1969 elections between FDP president Walter Scheel and the right wing of his party. Achenbach represented important industrial interests—he was the Essen lawyer for the big industrial interests of the Ruhr—and his appointment to Brussels was one of the conditions the right wing of the party had made for helping Brandt become Chancellor. *Der Spiegel* reported that Scheel, who had become Foreign Minister, had sent an emissary to Paris in March 1970 to allay any French reservations. "If the French will agree, the Dutch and the rest will follow suit," Scheel is supposed to have said.

That very day Serge and I went to the Library of Contemporary Jewish Documents (CDJC). Every time I cross the square in which stands the monument to the Unknown Jewish Martyr, I am inspired anew by the words of Edmond Fleg inscribed on that white monument that points skyward in the old section of Paris: "Before the Unknown Jewish Martyr bow your head in tribute to all martyrs, and march with them along their sorrowful way, for it will lead you to the mountaintop of justice and truth."

The CDJC was our first recourse, for we knew that it had several boxes of source material from the German Embassy. There were, however, only a few odds and ends about Achenbach. We'd be sunk if now in 1970 we could not show what this Nazi diplomat's real job had been in 1943. We had to collect convincing data quickly and make it public.

Fifteen hours of work at the CDJC and the Library of Contemporary International Information gave us enough material to allow us to spend the night of April 1 compiling a six-page memorandum in French and German. This became the basis for my open letter to Achenbach published in the *Frankfurter Rundschau* on April 4, and in *Combat* on April 8:

> Your actions during the Third Reich, your beliefs at that time, and the part you played at Nuremberg and in the Naumann case do not recommend you as a representative of the Federal Republic . . . .

I continued by exposing the true nature of Achenbach's career in France that was unknown until our research had brought it to light.

Achenbach had been a member of the Nazi Party since 1937. He was appointed to the staff of the German Embassy in Paris shortly before the war, and he later returned with Otto Abetz, whose political adviser, if not inspirer, he was. When Abetz was being cross-examined in November 1945, he stated: "The most important part of the embassy was the political section, which was under the direction of Ernst Achenbach."

Schleier, who was second-in-command in the embassy, admitted at Nuremberg that the most important political questions—particularly the directives for Franco-German collaboration—were handled by Abetz and Achenbach together. Another diplomat, Ambassador Karl Ritter, said at Nuremberg: "Achenbach was a man of great capacities; he had a reputation for being very efficient. . . . The ambassador was considered to be putty in his hands, and it was really Achenbach who called the tune."

It was Achenbach who, on August 13, 1940, stressed the importance of complete German control over French newspapers, radio, motion pictures, theater, and book publishing. It was also Achenbach who played a prominent part in the fateful meeting between Hitler and Pétain at Montoire. One of Pétain's ministers, du Moulin de la Barthète, gives a striking picture of Achenbach in his memoirs of the Vichy government, *Les temps des illusions* ("The Years of Illusion"):

> In a soft, almost obsequious voice, Achenbach told me how pleased the ambassador was over the initial conference with Laval the previous evening. Laval had been superbly witty, modest, and alert, and had completely charmed the Führer. France was lucky to have two such men [Pétain and Laval] at the helm. So far as Germany was concerned, there was no antagonism whatever toward France, just a little embarrassment over the necessity of the military occupation of so beautiful a country. "If only your allies had not let you down! But everything can still be fixed."

Du Moulin saw Achenbach again when Otto Abetz and his staff crossed the demarcation line on December 16, 1940, to come to the aid of their vassal Pierre Laval, whom Pétain had disgraced and who was being kept under close surveillance at Châteldon.

Laval was waiting for us on the steps with a pedigreed dog on either side of him. He had got himself up like a gentleman-farmer, in heavy shoes and athletic socks. He shook Abetz's and Achenbach's hands cordially, and was introduced to Sonnenhol and Gontard, the two Germans on the staff. I discreetly withdrew, but I heard the beginning of their conversation: "You are true friends to have come all this way to see a friend in trouble. I shall never forget it. It was really first-rate of you to pay me this visit." He shook hands with them again.

That very evening Laval's "true friends" took him back to Paris with them.

One of Laval's friends, Julien Clermont, also shows Achenbach in an extraordinary situation in a meeting with Laval:

It was on June 21, 1942. Laval was to speak on the following day, and was putting the finishing touches on his address. The contents had been weighed, he said, on a pharmacist's scale.

While all this was going on Cornet, the attendant, announced the arrival of Achenbach, the head counselor of the German embassy in Paris.

"Have him come in," said Laval.

Then, as was his custom, he asked his visitor to take a seat with him and his associates.

"I'm just finishing dictating my speech for tomorrow," he said quite casually. "Wait a minute and I'll be through."

He turned to his secretaries and proceeded to dictate a few insignificant remarks. Then, as if he had suddenly had a glorious inspiration, he exclaimed loudly: "After all, I want everyone to know how I feel, and this shall be my concluding thought: *I want Germany to be victorious because otherwise Bolshevism will overrun Europe. Okay?*" he finished easily, turning toward Achenbach.

Achenbach's pale cheeks flushed with pleasure.

Through Abetz, Achenbach, and Theo Zeitschel, the embassy was behind the earliest measures for racial discrimination. It put continuous pressure on Vichy for Laval or Darlan to enact legislation more and more in accordance with the Nuremberg laws. It was distinctly in favor of total liquidation through deportation to the East, was wholly behind the S.D. [the S.S. Security Service] in the conception and execution of anti-Jewish measures in France, was particularly influential in raising diplomatic obstacles in Berlin to prevent the Gestapo's Bureau for Jewish Affairs from interning or deporting various categories of Jews of foreign nationality or origin, and helped break down the Italians' disinclination to persecute the Jews in their zone of occupation.

After the Wannsee Conference on January 20, 1942, when the dreadful "Final Solution of the Jewish Problem" was adopted, S.S. Martin Luther, an Under-Secretary in the Foreign Ministry, got the consent of Reinhard Heydrich, the head of the Reich's central Security Department (RSHA), for his ministry to be consulted on all matters pertaining to anti-Jewish measures outside the Fatherland. The liquidation of the Jews resulted, on the whole, from the collaboration between Himmler's and Ribbentrop's ministries. That collaboration between the German ministries was what was effected in France.

On March 1, 1941, Theo Zeitschel, Achenbach's subordinate, sent his superior valuable data on anti-Jewish operations, including a report on what was said at a conference concerning the Central Jewish Office in Paris. This quickly led to the creation of the efficient General Commission for Jewish Affairs, which was to do the work the Germans wanted. That conference took place at the embassy on February 28, 1941. Present were Abetz, Achenbach, Zeitschel, and Theodor Dannecker, the head of the S.D.'s Department IV-J.

"On that occasion it was noted that thanks to the previous accomplishments of the S.D. under the management of Dannecker, a master file was almost completed in which all Jews in France were listed under four different headings. The S.D., in addition, had taken pains to make a very thorough census."

Theo Zeitschel, the embassy's specialist on Jewish matters, claimed to be the illegitimate son of Emperor Wilhelm II. In 1940, when he was twenty-seven years old, he was an S.S. colonel and a counselor in the embassy, under the supervision of Achenbach, responsible for relations with the S.D. On November 19, 1941, he was also put in charge of relations with Count Fernand de Brinon, the Vichy government's general representative in Paris. One communication to Abetz, dated August 21, 1941, is enough to give a picture of Zeitschel:

An appeal for help has appeared in the Jewish newspapers in Palestine. It is directed to the ten million Jews who live in America to remind them that in the areas we now occupy in Russia are six million Jews, or a third of all the Jews in the world, who have been designated for extermination. My opinion is that there is only one response to be made . . . .

He then recommended that the ambassador propose to Hitler and Ribbentrop the sterilization of all Jews.

Zeitschel's suggestion, insane though it may seem to us, was to be surpassed six months later by the decision to physically exterminate the Jewish people.

The hostility of the embassy's political division, under Achenbach, toward Jews was constant. It was evident from the time of the first deportation: a convoy of a thousand French Jews had been arrested in a reprisal move. Foreign Ministry Under-Secretary Martin Luther wired the embassy on March 11, 1942, that Heydrich had informed him of a plan to "transfer to the Auschwitz concentration camp in Upper Silesia the one thousand Jews arrested in Paris on December 12, 1941, in reprisal for attacks on Wehrmacht soldiers. It is a matter of only Jews of French nationality. The shipment by special train of those one thousand Jews has been set for March 23, 1942. I will be obliged for a reply indicating that there is no objection to putting this plan into effect."

Achenbach's political division, through his subordinate Von Nostitz, on the same day sent the laconic and fateful reply marked "Secret": "No objection to the proposed action against the Jews."

On March 18, 1942, the German Embassy's political division expressed its satisfaction at the appointment of a high-ranking member of the S.S. as chief of the German police in France, which would "bring the results we want in the Final Solution of the Jewish Problem."

A short time later, after Jews had been ordered to wear the yellow star, pamphlets and posters began appearing everywhere, and the embassy printed an enormous number of posters that read: "Jews kill in the dark. Learn how to identify them so that you can beware of them."

On August 26, 1942, a member of the Gestapo's Bureau for Jewish Affairs wrote a memorandum after receiving a telephone call from S.S.-Sturmbannführer Herbert Hagen, a close associate of S.S. Karl Oberg, "the butcher of Paris." Hagen said that Achenbach had called to inform him about the current situation in respect to the deportation of stateless Jews. As a matter of fact, Achenbach had to make a report on its progress to the Foreign Ministry in Berlin. Added to that proof of direct communication between Achenbach and Hagen is a memorandum dated February 4, 1943, dictated and signed by Hagen, about the difficulties presented by the Italians in the anti-Jewish program. He indicated that the German Embassy—that is, Achenbach—had been informed about it so that it might help induce the Italians to stop protecting Jews.

Right after that memorandum Achenbach signed and sent one of his own to Heinz Röthke, the chief of the Gestapo's Bureau for Jewish Affairs, that contained the embassy's report on the matter.

Today Achenbach is Herbert Hagen's lawyer. The two are linked by their complicity in the anti-Jewish campaign.

In 1943, Achenbach returned to the Foreign Ministry in Berlin where, under the supervision of S.S. Professor Franz Six, he directed two branches of the Political and Cultural Division. That is when Achenbach got to know the deputy director of the closely related Department of Political Broadcasting. Like his own, that department was famous for the number of young Nazis in it, all of whom were intelligent and efficient employees rather than career diplomats. Its deputy director was Kurt-Georg Kiesinger.

In 1953, he was involved in the Naumann conspiracy, in which he was active as liaison between the former Secretary of Goebbels' Propaganda Ministry and the big industrialists of the Ruhr. His intention, which the British thwarted, was to slip Nazis into all West German political parties in order to get them back into power through free elections.

In 1953, Achenbach wrote a preface to a book by Abetz, who was then a prisoner in France:

Can a Franco-German entente be seriously discussed when one of the most dedicated front-rank fighters for such an understanding, the German ambassador to Paris during the war, is still in prison? There is no better evidence of that man's integrity than, in spite of the injustice he has suffered, his continuous requests to his German friends to keep a Franco-German entente in mind.

An example of the "integrity" of the Nazi diplomats is this excerpt from a memo Abetz wrote on July 2, 1942:

In principle, the embassy has no objection to the deportation of forty thousand Jews to Auschwitz. Nevertheless, the following relevant facts should be considered. The embassy has always been of the opinion that anti-Jewish measures should be executed in such a way that they will continue to increase the strong anti-Jewish sentiment in France, which is growing even stronger. . . . From the psychological point of view, the majority of the French people will be more impressed if deportation measures affect only non-French Jews and are not applied to French Jews, unless the number of foreign Jews is insufficient for the required quota. Such a proviso should not be taken to mean that French Jews should have any privileged status; in the course of eliminating the Jews of all European countries, the French Jews will also be exterminated. And, to reassure you, you can count on a certain number of French Jews being included in the quota you have indicated.

Of course I received no reply to my open letter. It had to be written, however, so that anyone whose attitude had changed might have a chance to prove it. It ended as follows:

Now the Federal Republic under Gustav Heinemann deserves some respect, especially since Willy Brandt, whom I myself have seen acclaimed in The Hague, London, Paris, Erfurt—in the West as well as in the East—is its Chancellor. Now German youth, even that part of it that was in revolt until October 1969, has some respect for the government's programs, for the youth helped Brandt into power. Your possible appointment, the result of an election deal, will serve only to stir up a controversy we had hoped was settled, and at the same time it will bring dishonor upon the government and on the reputation of the Federal Republic.

Western Europeans have given the committees the responsibility for important economic, social, and political questions, and your presence in Brussels can only affect them adversely.

The choice is even simpler for the French. To them, approving Achenbach is equivalent to approving Abetz and everything he stood for. I myself have already furnished the French government with a report I compiled as soon as I got the astonishing news of your candidacy, and in a few days all the other members of the EEC will have a copy of it.

That is why, sir, I appeal to your sense of public duty, and assure you that you will do yourself great honor by abandoning your candidacy. You may be sure that if you do, in spite of the differences between us, I will feel personally indebted to you.

Photocopies of all the documents quoted above were already in my possession. Serge had quit his job at Continental Grains three months before, and we were living on his separation allowance. It kept shrinking as we engaged in distributing our report and the papers that supported it. Every time I heard the whir of the Xerox machine at the post office, I thought of it as an infernal monster devouring our food and rent money.

What drove us to do it was the conviction that we were the only persons—and we felt desperately lonely—to rise to the demands of the occasion. No government, no political party, no individual had protested up until then simply because they lacked the energy.

Once we had the basic data ready, I undertook to circulate it. I took it first to the politicians, sending a copy to the president of the EEC; to the Foreign Ministries of The Netherlands, Italy, and Luxemburg; to Willy Brandt; to the Prime Ministers of Belgium and Great Britain. In Paris I went to the Elysée Palace, where a deputy took my report and promised to give it the "careful examination it deserved." I also went to the Quai d'Orsay, and there is no doubt that Foreign Minister Maurice Schumann studied the documents I left there for his attention. Some months later, on June 23, he replied to the letter in which I had asked him to take action for the exclusion of Achenbach from the Franco-German parliamentary group: "I will seize the first opportunity available to me for making known our joint feelings."

But the politicians will budge only if the press creates a stir. So, to get the press moving, I had to meet several conditions: first, see that they had copies of the report; second, create a situation that would give reporters and commentators a reason for expressing their opinion. One writer on foreign affairs told me: "You push Achenbach out a window, and I'll print your report."

I spent all of April 4 going to the international press services, the big French dailies, and representatives of the most important European papers. I did not just leave my report with them, but discussed it and tried to get them to accept my interpretation of Achenbach's possible appointment.

I made long telephone calls to two friends in Brussels: Philippe Lemaître, who covered the Common Market for *Le Monde*, and a young German woman who was an executive in its inner circles. Some of her associates had reacted violently when they learned that Achenbach was about to represent the Federal Republic.

Wilhelm Haferkamp, the other German commissioner in Brussels, took advantage of a mission to Jerusalem to look for documents that were more compromising to Achenbach in the Yad Vashem archives, a center of information on victims of Nazism. Unfortunately he found none, and so he sent a young member of his staff to Paris. The young man got in touch with Serge and returned to Brussels with a briefcase bulging with documents. These so convinced Haferkamp that on April 15 he went to work in earnest against Achenbach.

But to return to the situation in Brussels on April 4, during the course of some fierce arguments with my friends we reached a decision. There was an "association of EEC officials who had been deported to concentration camps or had been in the Resistance," and we made good use of it. Its leaders were not content to send letters of protest to the papers; they went in person, evidence in hand.

The mission was successful. On April 6, Agence France Presse (AFP) broadcast the association's protest, emphasizing that it was well-founded and that it contained a document in which "the German deputy advocated the arrest and deportation of 2,000 Jews." On April 7, *Le Figaro* published a short piece entitled, "Sharp Reaction to the German EEC Candidate." The influential *Le Monde* printed an article that became the basis for the whole campaign. It emanated, so far as documentation was concerned, from the release I had sent P. J. Franceschini, who ended by saying:

A brilliant lawyer and an eloquent defender of war criminals and persecutors of the Jews, Achenbach attracted further attention in 1953 in the Naumann case. As the liberal representative in the North Rhine-Westphalia Diet and putative Minister of Commerce, his name was mentioned in connection with the attempts Dr. Werner Naumann (former secretary in the Propaganda Ministry) made to procure a following and a political career for former Nazis, notably through "calls" in the Free Democratic Party. "In a few weeks there won't be any more talk about denazification," he said to Naumann, who replied: "I'm not so sure the French have such short memories."

After the *Le Monde* article, I put into operation the plan that we had mapped out for bringing the matter to international notice. Only a scandal about something as big as the Common Market could make the German government back down.

But it was a touchy situation. The Social-Liberal coalition had only a small majority of the votes. Now members of Achenbach's party were about to defect and go over to the Christian Democrats: Erich Mende, the former leader of the FDP, and Siegfried Zoglmann, another conservative. Achenbach might well follow them if the government did not support his Brussels ambitions. I was ready with an answer for people who claimed that my program might injure Brandt: "If Brandt has a sufficiently convincing report on Achenbach's Nazi career, he can put pressure on him, for a statement from the Chancellor on this matter is as good as keeping Achenbach out of German politics."

The communists did nothing. The Düsseldorf *Deutsche Volks-zeitung*, for which I wrote regularly, did not publish my piece on Achenbach. East Germany kept silent. And although I paid a call on the Tass Agency in Paris, I found it equally unenthusiastic. Achenbach, a prominent big-business lawyer, represented powerful outlets in the East. Once again governmental interests were in conflict with morality.

How was I to break so many dikes that this affair would overflow onto the international scene? What had been published in Paris on April 7 was sufficient reason for going into action. In Bonn, Walter Scheel stated: "The press will probably make a big fuss about this affair for a couple of weeks, and then no one will hear any more about it." The single AFP dispatch was not enough. Consequently we substituted wide geographical coverage for further news releases. I telegraphed for an interview on the 9th with Joseph Luns, the Netherlands' Foreign Minister; Gaston Eykens, the Belgian Prime Minister; and Jean Rey, president of the European Committee; and on the 10th with Conrad Ahlers, the German government spokesman.

Consequently, within twenty-four hours, all press dispatches from Holland, Belgium, and Germany carried the same news: "Hostile Reaction to Achenbach Due to Disclosure of His Nazi Past." European newspapers got three dispatches on the same topic on the same day. They decided, with such excitment over the Achenbach affair in three capitals simultaneously, they would give the story some prominence.

Late in the evening of Tuesday, April 7, I landed at Schiphol airport. Television crews and a number of reporters were waiting for me. I talked freely in German about the purpose of my visit, which was to give the Dutch government the facts about Achenbach as well as my personal opinion of him, and I had an opportunity to show the television audience some actual documents. The scene appeared on the late news that night, and on the following day as well.

I spent the night with a couple of reporters in an Amsterdam suburb, and at 9 A.M. I presented myself at the Foreign Ministry. Luns's chief of staff received me. He told me that the Dutch Foreign Minister was having an interview with the son of Tunisian President Habib Bourguiba, but that if I could wait, he would see me. I had no time, however. I had to take the eleven o'clock train for Brussels. Luns, however, was sufficiently impressed by my report to intervene personally a short time later with his German colleague, Scheel.

The Dutch press reported on my television interview, and the Belgian press followed suit. *La Libre Belgique* headlined: "Will There Be an Achenbach Affair?" Its three-column story ended: "Opponents of Achenbach's candidacy find it inconceivable for him to have a seat on the executive level and play a major role in economic, political, and social decisions. To accept Achenbach is equivalent to seating Abetz on the European Committee of the EEC. We definitely share this point of view and hope the Belgian government will react as it should to his candidacy."

Serge had left for Brussels on the same morning to meet EEC officials who wanted to learn more about our report. Arno went with him, for my mother-in-law had no time to take care of him. Of course that had to be the day he had a terrible toothache, and Serge had to interrupt his interviews to rub the boy's gums with honey syrup.

I reached Brussels early in the afternoon and set Serge free. He sat himself down at a photocopier and began reproducing copies of our reports. Arno and I went to the Belgian Prime Minister's. Prime Minister Eykens, after reading our report, told *Der Spiegel:* "This is an unfortunate business."

While I was talking with the Prime Minister's chief of staff, his office staff took care of Arno. I shall never forget the look on their faces when they said: "If you have to put up with him all day long, we don't envy you."

That same evening Serge, Arno, and I left for Bonn.

In addition to my approach to the German government about Achenbach, I was also supposed to fly to the United States as one of the journalists who were accompanying Brandt on his first official trans-Atlantic visit. Rüdiger von Wechmar, deputy to government spokesman Conrad Ahlers, had succeeded in getting me invited. But two days before I was supposed to leave I got a telegram cancelling my trip. The right-wing press thought that it would be extremely discourteous to Kiesinger and cause an inquiry in the Bundestag if the woman who had slapped Kiesinger were to accompany the new Chancellor in an official capacity. Another reason, according to the telegram, was: "The CIA and the U.S. State Department cannot allow Beate Klarsfeld into the

White House for reasons of security." The press interpreted this as meaning that there was fear I would put personal pressure on Brandt about Achenbach.

At any rate, on Thursday the 9th, the international press reacted as we had hoped it would. The Hamburg daily, *Die Welt*, headlined: "Achenbach's Candidacy Attacked in Paris and Brussels— B.K. Touring Europe Again." The Munich *Süddeutsche Zeitung*: "B.K. on the Move to Expose Achenbach's Past." The *Hannoversche Presse*: "B.K. Attacks Achenbach." In Italy, *Il Messagero's* headline on the day after a meeting in Rome between Scheel and Foreign Minister Aldo Moro was: "Astonishment and Anger in Brussels Over a Nazi EEC Candidate." The Brussels *Le Soir* wrote:

> The German Foreign Minister's usual self-confidence, which has so easily and efficiently allayed the hostility of other European countries, seems to have considerably diminished. At any rate, it appears that Achenbach insists there is no difference between Hitler's Europe and the Common Market's, and that he thinks the expertise he acquired in the former is enough to recommend him for the latter.

Instead of flying to Washington, I spent the day in the Bonn Press Building going from one office to another with my data while Arno ran up and down the corridors. I left an exposé with Horst Ehmke, the Chancellery minister who had given me the helpful advice during the 1968 Kiesinger affair: "Don't treat it as a legal matter; make it political."

In the evening we left for Paris and arrived on April 10. We went back to work at once in the CDJC archives. As far as the press and public opinion were concerned, the whole Achenbach case rested on one document: the notorious telegram Achenbach sent on February 15, 1943, to the Foreign Ministry in Berlin. It said:

> On February 13, 1943, about 11:10 P.M., Lieutenant Colonel Winkler and Major Nussbaum, Chief of Staff of the Luftwaffe's Third Division, were shot from behind while walking from their office to their hotel a short distance from the Louvre Bridge over the Seine, which they had just crossed. Winkler was wounded by three bullets; Nussbaum by two. They died the same night. Seven 7.65 mm. cartridges were found near the scene of the crime, and presumably came from the same gun. The whereabouts of the assassins is being investigated. The first reprisal will be the arrest and deportation of 2,000 Jews.
>
> —ACHENBACH

We gave that telegram priority because it seemed to magnify Achenbach's personal responsibility for the reprisals. All Achenbach needed to do to strengthen his position with his government and continue his candidacy was to deny that he had ordered them. Now, we knew enough about the workings of the German authorities in Paris during the occupation to realize that Achenbach would not have sent Berlin a telegram containing a decision he himself had made; in fact, the telegram merely reported the murder and the envisaged reprisals, but not who had ordered them. If Achenbach were now to say that he had not ordered them, he would appear to have been the victim of a cabal.

Fortunately, Achenbach chose to defend himself through sources that had already been made public. The telegram itself had been published in 1953 in the German Jewish weekly *Allgemeine Wochenschrift der Juden in Deutschland*, along with a bitter denunciation of Achenbach. At that time Achenbach, in a ticklish spot owing to his involvement in the Naumann case, explained his conduct in an open letter. Instead of saying: "I was merely making a report," he went so far as to say: "General Heinrich von Stuelpnagel, the military governor of France, wired Berlin about the deportation of Jews just to avoid the execution of hostages in reprisal. I sent the telegram to cover Stuelpnagel." Now Achenbach repeated this explanation to *Der Spiegel* and added: "There had to be a lot of fuss made. As a result, everything turned out fine"—in other words, everything turned out fine for the Jews.

Achenbach chose not to mention me or attribute any moral motive to the campaign. The prominent lawyer who had so glibly explained away the crimes of I. G. Farben and of the German officials in Occupied Belgium had kept quiet until that April 12. But why? After my open letter of April 4, he could have sued me for libel, appealed to an arbitration board of historians, or asked me to produce my documentation. The real reason Achenbach refused to plead his own cause was that he kept running up against the most deadly of accusers: himself.

Achenbach's counterattack was to make the telegram appear to be an act of resistance on his part. But *La Libre Belgique* pointed out:

Achenbach's insistence on this point does not prove very much. To justify himself Achenbach, rather than repeating his 1953 explanation, might have furnished proof that the 2,000 Jews in question had never been arrested or deported.

Requiring the allegedly guilty party to produce proof of his innocence was going a bit too far. That was up to the prosecution. So we had to show that the deportation order Achenbach said he had suggested to Berlin as a bluff was not only planned but carried out.

For three days we researched this point, poring over hundreds of file cards and documents, harassed by the time factor and by necessity. The selection of the hostages to be shot in reprisal for the murders would be made by Abetz and his political counselor Achenbach according to embassy policy established on December 7, 1941. They thought that, in the interest of the German people, they should avoid any mention of the general French repugnance to collaboration. Abetz, therefore, advised taking hostages from among Jews and communists, or at least from among those he called such.

. . . Even then, when it could not be clearly shown that they were French, it was considered wise not to produce such evidence but, considering political interests, to defend the argument that only Jews and agents in the pay of the British and the Russians were involved. In accordance with the above, it would also be helpful not to mention publicly any executions of Frenchmen or hostages, but only reprisals against Jews and agents of the Anglo-Saxon and Soviet secret services.

Any procedures against the material well-being of the French people as a whole do not seem advisable. But heavy fines levied on Jews will have an excellent effect on the opinions of the upper levels of the plutocracy, especially if part of the money so derived is given to French charities.

When the military command informed him that Der Führer had approved the suggested measures, Abetz telephoned that he was very happy his recommendations had been accepted, and said: "These measures coincide with the principles I enunciated in Chapter IV of my report of December 7." Among those measures was the execution of fifty-eight Jewish and communist hostages.

Thereafter the embassy was to edit the text of all communiqués dealing with bloody reprisals, and to wire Berlin about all shootings. I came across a twelve-page report from Achenbach, dated March 17, 1943, in which were listed dozens of names of people who had been shot, some of which I copied:

Housepainter Jean Lecoq, railway worker Felix Bouffay, metal worker Raymond Pottier, undertaker Pierre Vastel, coppersmith Raymond Losserand, interior decorator René Appère, electrician

Collin, peasant Armand Mascret, mechanic André Leclers, chauffeur
Yvon Delare, carpenter Marcel Darnier, printer Jean Bourquard, up-
holsterer Albert Gérard, hairdresser Robert, tax expert Robert Millot,
tailor Marcel Andemar, student Lucien Dupont . . .

Did any of you French people who were tortured at the same
time as those foreign Jewish hostages imagine that one day Achenbach would get the red-carpet treatment in the inner circles of a
French parliament? Or that the members of that parliament, who
today are free thanks to your sacrifices, would be congratulating
that man?

But what happened to the "two thousand Jews" for whom, according to Achenbach, everything turned out fine?

On the day after that telegram, February 16, 1943, the chief of
the Gestapo's Bureau for Jewish Affairs, S.S.-Obersturmführer
Heinz Röthke, wrote in a memorandum:

In a reprisal for the murder on February 13, 1943, of two German
air force officers, 15,000 able-bodied men had to be deported from
France, and thousands of Jews had to make up that quota.

On February 23, 1943, S.S.-Obersturmbannführer Kurt Lishka,
commander of the Paris S.D.-Security Police, informed his Brussels
counterpart that:

The Paris Police Commissioner was told by me that by April 14,
1943, for the sake of reprisals, 2,000 Jews between the ages of sixteen
and sixty-five were to be arrested and shipped to the concentration
camp for Jews at Drancy.

On February 24, Röthke reported to Lishka on a conversation
with Sauts, the chief of staff of Police Commissioner Leguay, about
"the solution of the Jewish problem in France, and the Italians'
attitude toward the Jewish problem":

Sauts replied to me that the arrest of 2,000 Jews by the French
police in the zone formerly and presently occupied in order to effect
the measures of reprisals ordered by the Paris Commander (Kurt
Lishka) was under way. Before February 23, more than 1,500 able-
bodied Jews between the ages of sixteen and sixty-five had already
been interned in the two zones. Lishka had been ordered to see to
it that only stateless Jews be arrested or those whose nationality fitted
our specifications for deportation. . . . I told Sauts that we would
consider the quota of 2,000 filled only if all the Jews arrested did indeed conform to our specifications for deportation.

A report of February-March, from the Federation of Jewish Organizations in France on "Round-ups and Deportation of Foreign Jews," confirms the arrest of Jews between the ages of sixteen and sixty-five in the former Free Zone, their internment in the Gurs camp, and their shipment to Drancy on February 26 and March 2:

Beginning on Saturday, February 20, round-ups of Jews of foreign nationality were made throughout the former Free Zone. Police stations were told to compile lists of persons to be taken either from their home or their place of work.

The operations aimed at a certain number of Jewish men of foreign nationality, between the ages of sixteen and sixty-five, in each precinct. They were found either at liberty (registered addresses or not) or in the reception centers of the Social Service for Foreigners, or even in orphanages such as Château de la Hille in Haute Garonne. Two contingents of one hundred persons were sent from the Noe and Vernet camps directly to Gurs. . . .

From all corners of the old nonoccupied zone persons arrested were sent as swiftly as possible to the camp at Gurs. The total number of newcomers was far from enough, and so a significant number of those already at Gurs had to be included.

FIRST DEPORTATION. The screening for the first deportation, on February 26, was more rapid than careful. Everyone, as his name was called, was earmarked for deportation right away, even the sick and infirm. The only nationalities exempted were Hungarians and Turks. For the first time Belgians, Dutch, Luxemburgers, and Greeks were included. The first convoy consisted of 975 men.

SECOND DEPORTATION. The second deportation took place on the night of March 2–3. It numbered 770. Naturally it included a sizable number of former army volunteers, men who had been wounded in action, and even some who had been decorated.

The number of deportees thus far was 1,745, but the required number was 1,850. Consequently, the quota had to be filled en route. According to some information I have not been able to verify, it appears that four hundred persons who had been rounded up at Nexon were put on the train that left Oloron on March 3. At any rate, it appears that the number of 1,850 was considerably exceeded.

Among the countless testimonies from Jews as to their personal sufferings, we found one from a Hungarian interned at Gurs that confirms the above report:

Deportations began in early February 1943. A large number—about 150—of guards suddenly appeared. They were assigned to the blocks of huts in which were penned internees from other camps, especially from the one at Nexon. The deportation was to include all men of German, Polish, Austrian, and Czech nationality up to the age of sixty-five. At that time I was sixty-four years, nine and a half months old; but fortunately I was able, on the strength of my birth certificate, to pass myself off as Hungarian, and in the general confusion the details were never checked out.

Among the deportees was a large number of Poles and Czechs who had fought in the French army or in the Foreign Legion. These too were handed over to the Germans. The fellow in the bed next to mine, a German rabbi, Dr. Rosenwasser, was to be sixty-five in six days, but he was deported just the same.

The deportations went on for two days. Two guards came after each of the "called" and forced him to pack in five minutes, so impossible a task that many possessions were left behind.

The internees destined for deportation were taken under heavy guard to Block E, each carrying his belongings. Those who were allowed to remain in the hell of Gurs were envied by the deportees as the luckiest of men. All through the night you could hear women weeping in despair, for many had not had time even to say good-by to their sons and husbands. Several could not find out whether their husbands had been deported. My wife did not sleep a wink for two nights for fear that I had been deported.

On the day after the deportations the women were allowed to visit our block, and their shrieks and moans when they saw their husbands' beds empty were frightful.

What happened to the two thousand male Jews of foreign nationality, or of no nationality at all, who were shipped from Gurs to Drancy on February 26 and March 2? The CDJC had a list of deported Jews, itemized by convoy, from which it can be determined that Convoys Nos. 50 and 51 contained only Jewish men aged sixteen to sixty-five and of foreign nationality or stateless. Convoy 51 contained 1,002 Jews, Convoy 50, 1,000. Among the deportees were many intellectuals, such as law professor Georges Himmelochein; lawyers David Isserman, Eugene Himmeler, Julien Frisman, and Erich Danziger; painters Jerzy Aszer, André Basch, Charles Beran, Zalter Fraenkel, Otto Freudlich, and Maurice Hambourg; stage director Paul Haag; writers Bruno Altmann and Lionel **Dunin**; Rabbi Salomon Goldhirsch—all from Paris.

The Auschwitz archives (ZO. No. 4, pp. 81, 82) record the fate of Convoys 50 and 51. As soon as they arrived on March 6 and 8, all the men in them were gassed.

Our research was entirely conclusive. Achenbach had lied. He had tried to pass off as an act of resistance his share in the decision made by Kurt Lischka on the day after the murder of February 13, 1943, that led to the arrest of two thousand Jews, their shipment to Drancy, their deportation to Auschwitz, and the extermination of every single one of them on March 8, 1943. It had taken less than one month to do away with more than two thousand men.

Achenbach admitted his personal participation in that episode, and he tried to disguise it as a bluff that amounted to nothing drastic. It was actually a bloody tragedy in which his role coincided perfectly with his theories about the policy of collaboration. Not only did he send Jews to their death, but he used them as a means of avoiding friction with the French people as a whole.

We rushed the results of our research to Brussels. On April 11, German Commissioner Wilhelm Haferkamp issued a statement in his own name in which he announced that he would resign if Achenbach were appointed.

Arno Scholz, publisher of the *Telegraf*, Berlin's social-democratic daily, helped me get an appointment with Conrad Ahlers, the government spokesman, to deliver the results of our research. Achenbach had to take a stand. "Attacked though I may be," he said, "I cannot withdraw. Scheel has given me his word."

But the coalition was very tactful with Achenbach, and the wheels were well oiled for the fateful day of April 16 so that no irreparable mistake would be made. Ahlers would not get the report of the inquiry, many excerpts from which were to be published in *Der Spiegel* on April 20, until 6 P.M. Brandt had already made a public statement designed to soothe Achenbach and keep him from going over to the Christian Democrats.

That was the end of Achenbach's candidacy. In May, parliamentary Secretary for Foreign Affairs Ralf Dahrendorf was appointed to the EEC. On May 29, when Dahrendorf's appointment was confirmed, the government had to decide who was to succeed him as foreign secretary. Eager for revenge, Achenbach surfaced again, and once more unofficially declared his candidacy.

Fortunately we had kept a spare weapon handy—a document dated February 11, 1943, marked "Secret." The signature on this memorandum to S.S.-Obersturmführer Röthke matched Achenbach's. The document gave the Gestapo the green light for "proceeding against Jews in the newly occupied zone."

The Foreign Ministry has issued the following directives to this embassy: It is required that the aforesaid decisions be executed in the newly occupied zone. In the event that Italian military authorities present any difficulties to the French authorities in the execution of these measures, make a report thereon, describing the exact situation so that those special cases can be reconsidered by the Italian government.

On the morning of May 30 I reached Bonn with one hundred photocopies of that document and an equal number of copies of a release in which I again summed up the matter of the two thousand Jews. I distributed these to the press and wire services, and went straight back to Paris. On June 1, 1970, Karl Mörsch succeeded Dahrendorf.

I have never seen Ernst Achenbach, not even on television.

8

ARREST IN WARSAW AND PRAGUE

I now turned my attention toward the East, for if Brandt were to take his place in history, it would depend on how he dealt with that area. Also, I was distressed by rumbles of anti-Semitism coming from the East.

Once the German elections were over, I telephoned a Polish dipomat named Dmowsky, who a few months earlier had invited me to visit Poland. I told him that I was now ready to accept, because not only did I like to travel, but I also wanted to lecture to young Poles and tell them about the struggle young German anti-fascists were making. I told Dmowsky that I definitely wanted to speak at Auschwitz.

He must have suspected what I would say, for in spite of several more telephone calls the invitation was not renewed.

Some time earlier, on October 5, 1969, I had been invited to East Berlin for the celebration of the German Democratic Republic's twentieth anniversary. Ulbricht shook my hand cordially. Perhaps my persistence was the reason for the attention I now got from that little man who was the embodiment of communist Germany, and who would be remembered in the history of Germany for having transformed the zone he dominated into one of the world's highly industrialized regions. A member of the Central

Committee told me he was present when Ulbricht was informed about my slapping the West German Chancellor.

"It was the anniversary of the Soviet Revolution, November 7. We were having a meeting in Ulbricht's office when a secretary interrupted to whisper to Ulbricht that you had just insulted Kiesinger. I clearly remember his remark: 'She's a brave woman. We ought to support her.' "

The favoritism shown me, more or less to the irritation of the West German Communist Party, was thus due to Ulbricht's attitude.

In the past two years, however, I had become far too used to open defiance to feel completely at ease in any political atmosphere. The compliments, the friendly smiles, and the disarming words addressed to me by the East German officials made me feel good, but they did not alter my conviction that here in the heart of the "Socialist State of the German nation" I represented neither of the two ideologies. So far as I was concerned, the German nation, because of being divided, could find expression only in terms of political morality.

Still, it was a splendid occasion, the kind young girls dream of. Movies were taken of me dancing with a snowy-haired Soviet general—Chuikov, I think—whose uniform was encrusted with gold braid and studded with decorations. The little six-year-old German girl who used to stare in terror at the "Cossacks" invading the village of Sandau, where my mother and I had taken refuge in April 1945, would never have imagined that one day she would be dancing with one of the Red Army chiefs. Total commitment to a cause is impossible; there is always at least one chink through which one contemplates, with a certain mild fascination, one's own adventure.

Toward the end of 1969, I decided to deal with subjects other than French problems in my articles for DVZ. I left for The Hague, where the summit conference of the Six was being held, for I wanted to be present when Brandt made his grand entrance on the European scene to make the Dutch aware that German youth was behind the Chancellor.

The first inter-German summit meeting was to take place on March 19 at Erfurt, in East Germany. I was determined to be present on this unprecedented occasion, but my accreditation from the Press Association for Foreign Affairs in Berlin was late in arriving. Very few foreign journalists were to be permitted to attend this conference. In despair I took a plane to East Berlin at my own expense, insisted, and finally obtained the precious papers. I went to Erfurt in an automobile with two journalists from the Gamma press agency, whom I helped out by getting them through the police checkpoints, for they lacked the magic tickets of admission.

When I stood on the platform of the Erfurt railway station, only a few feet away from Willy Brandt and Willi Stoph, the Prime Minister of the German Democratic Republic, and watched them shake hands like men who admired each other and were being united after a long separation, I felt a kind of exaltation. The Erfurt conference put a *de facto* end to Adenauer's pretensions that Bonn alone represented the interests of Germany as defined by her 1937 boundaries. It was also a point of no return on the road to the *de jure* recognition of East Germany as a sovereign state by Bonn and by the West.

When Brandt came out of the station, I was so close that he saw me, and he allowed a smile to creep over his solemn face. Many of Erfurt's young people were there, a large number of whom had probably come out of curiosity and others because they had been given a holiday to swell the crowd and shout slogans. The spontaneous reaction was very characteristic of the East Germans. When Brandt and Willi Stoph reached the end of the red carpet that stretched between the station and the hotel on the opposite side of the square, the demonstrators could not restrain themselves, but overturned the barriers, shoved aside the security police, and surrounded the two "Willies."

In the afternoon I went to the Buchenwald memorial when Brandt did. It was freezing cold and snowing a little. The monument is on a small rise, and Weimar can be seen from it. Not far away, on the Ettersberg, had stood the concentration camp where more than sixty thousand persons were killed.

Willy Brandt was accompanied by East German Foreign Minister Otto Winzer. They walked to the memorial tower, which was decorated with East German flags, and then visited the crypt. An honor guard of the East German national army and an army band were drawn up before the monument. Brandt walked behind soldiers carrying a wreath, and went down alone into the crypt while the band played—I think for the first time in the Democratic Republic—the Federal Republic anthem. It was a tribute free of ulterior motives that both Brandt and the East German leaders who accompanied him had paid to their countrymen whom Hitler had murdered. For the two Germanys, it was not formal ritual but a true return to their common origin.

When Willy Brandt came out, I took the armful of flowers the East German leaders had given me down into the crypt and laid them beside Brandt's wreath. My eyes fell on the inscription on one of the walls: "Our goal is the destruction of Nazism and its roots."

On May 24, I attended the second summit meeting between West and East Germans in Kassel in the Federal Republic. The change in German relations had not caught me unawares. My reasoning was derived from a simple premise: no great people had long remained divided. The Jewish people had recovered their homeland after two millenniums in spite of persecution and numerical weakness; the German people would regain their oneness.

It was not a utopian notion. To believe the division would last forever is unrealistic. From that point of view I had to bear witness in the East as well as in the West—and not in words alone, but in action—that the Germans in the East as well as in the West are subject to moral imperatives that must take precedence over any commitment to their respective ideologies. After what happened under Nazism, should not Germany as a whole fight against anti-Semitism, labor to get former active Nazis out of high political positions, and oppose the rehabilitation of Nazi criminals?

That is why I would react so strongly when Ernst Achenbach was about to be appointed to the Executive Committee of the EEC in April 1970. In compiling an exposé of his activities under Hitler and stirring up international public opinion against him, I was as powerfully motivated as I was during my campaign against Kiesinger. It was the same when I went to Austria to oppose the appointment of Hans Schirmer as the Federal Republic's ambassador to Vienna.

Hans Schirmer joined the Nazi party as No. 3,143,496 on May 1, 1933. An executive in Goebbel's Propaganda Ministry, he was Kiesinger's superior from 1939 to 1943 as Chief Deputy in the Foreign Ministry's Political Broadcasting Department. In addition, Schirmer was a director of Radio-Mundial, a secret international network that broadcast the idea of a "new Europe" throughout the world.

West German Foreign Minister Scheel had declared: "The Austrians have already completely forgotten the Anschluss." For once he was right. I tried in vain to persuade the Austrian press to question Chancellor Kreisky at his May 14, 1970, press conference. Nothing came of it. Kreisky glibly told me that to refuse to receive an ambassador is a serious gesture of hostility toward the country he represents, and that it is up to the country of which a diplomat is a citizen to check on his acceptability. So far as Austria was concerned, accepting Schirmer was an act of courtesy. I renewed my attack on June 17 at a Congress of the Austrian Socialist Party.

Arno and I were waiting outside the main door for the Congress to open when it began to rain, and we got soaked. To keep Arno quiet, I gave him several pamphlets and told him: "Hand these out and be of some help to your mother." Whereupon he proceeded to frisk about in the rain like a lunatic. Then he began dipping the pamphlets in puddles and molding them into wet balls to throw at the people attending the Congress.

I had hoped the Austrian socialists would take a stand against Schirmer, but just the opposite happened. During the Congress they protested strongly against Simon Wiesenthal, who was reproaching them for protecting former active Nazis in the government. The security force asked me to leave. I was furious.

On August 22, I met Serge at my mother's in Berlin. While I was in Oberhof I had done a lot of thinking. Anti-Semitism had had a noticeable revival in Poland with the blessing of the Polish authorities themselves. More than a year had gone by since I had promised myself to bring the problem of anti-Semitism to the attention of young people in Poland. I had to do that in Poland itself, for thus I would greatly increase the impact of my protest, especially with the young people of East Germany. They had to be aroused against anti-Semitism and told what direction it was taking, and this had to be accomplished not through speeches but by a show of force with the authorities.

In this country it was not the top leadership of the party that was susceptible to anti-Semitism, but the high-level civil servants who were then between forty-five and fifty-five years old and had grown up under Nazism. They had not been in the Red Army like Walter Ulbricht, or in a Nazi prison like Erich Honnecker, or gone into exile in America like Albert Norden, or been interned as a Jew in a French concentration camp like Hermann Axen. I had always observed that these civil servants were silently hostile to me, just like the men of their generation in the Federal Republic.

I had not received honors and congratulations from the East in order to submit to being a narrow-minded anti-fascist who could see injustice only in the Western camp. It was not a question of being anti-Soviet or pointing an accusing finger at the Poles, but of not remaining silent or inactive in the face of disgrace and oppression. I had led my crusade with independence and I intended to maintain that independence.

I was careful to calculate the risks, for I had no desire to be a martyr. As in the incident of the slap, I did everything possible to stay out of jail. The Poles would never believe that I was acting alone. Because of the moral support East Berlin had given me, they would probably think the Democratic Republic had something to do with my raid on Warsaw. The easiest thing for them to do, therefore, would be to kick me out of Poland. That was fine with me—provided the Western press promptly circulated the news of my arrest.

I looked up the names and addresses of the Warsaw correspondents of the Western press to get in touch with them as soon as I got there. Then I wrote a leaflet in German and French, got it translated into Polish, and had two hundred copies printed. Next I had to get a visa. That was hard. The many obstacles I encountered did not augur well for my trip. At the Polish military mission in West Berlin, a clerk made me fill out various forms, and I exchanged my marks for vouchers with which to pay for my hotel in Warsaw. Then, all papers in hand, I went back to the visa window, where the same clerk studied my French passport for a long time.

"You're a journalist?" he asked rather casually. "Come back for your visa in two weeks."

Some young Americans ahead of me had got their entry permit on the spot.

"I don't see why others can get a visa so quickly while I can't. I don't know whether it will be convenient for me to go to Poland two weeks from now."

My persistence got me nowhere. Why not appeal to the Polish Embassy in East Berlin?

I went there the same day. This time I was more subservient, and took the precaution of engaging the clerk, who knew about my activities, in a lengthy conversation to distract him. Nevertheless, he too uttered the fateful words: "So you are a journalist?"

"No. I did some reporting during the electoral campaign, but now I am just a housewife."

"Ah, in that case, just write 'no profession'."

And he granted me my visa.

About 9 p.m. on the evening of August 25, the train began crawling through the suburbs of Berlin. Dare I confess that only then I began to be afraid? The demonstration I intended to make in Warsaw would be quite different from everything I had done in the West. I couldn't get out of my mind that young people had been sent to rot in communist prisons for far less.

After a few minutes a man sat down opposite me. He never took his eyes off me, but not until the train was well under way did he begin to talk. He introduced himself as a counselor in the Democratic Republic's embassy in Warsaw.

What a relief! I began to feel less depressed.

"Do you know Warsaw?" he asked.

"Barely. I thought I'd look around it for two or three days."

"I'd be happy to guide you. My family is in East Berlin, so I'll have plenty of time. I would really like you to have a good look at Poland."

It was a distinctly embarrassing invitation, for if this East German diplomat were to be seen in my company, his career would suffer—beginning tomorrow morning.

We had hardly reached Warsaw early in the morning when my diplomat brought up the subject again: "Let me help you find a hotel."

"I have friends here and I can stay with them. At any rate, I'm going to wander around the city all day. I'll make up my mind later."

Finally I managed to get rid of my attentive diplomat, but I had no luck at the first two hotels I went to. Time was growing short, so I asked for shelter at a youth hostel, which was full at the moment but let me leave my suitcase.

I had only a few hours in which to alert the Western press. I felt very small and vulnerable in the unfamiliar city. My taxi driver kept going around and around the same block, looking for the number of the Agence France Presse correspondent. I finally told him to let me out and I would find it myself. But I couldn't.

The only thing left to do was to telephone. I rang so long I was about to give up. Then someone who did not speak French finally answered. I could not speak a word of Polish. In very halting German the man on the other end of the line said he was just a carpenter who was making some repairs in the AFP office, but at least I found out from him where it was.

After I had waited a full hour, a short, sloppily dressed man came in. He had a very heavy accent. I felt everything tumbling down around me, for the AFP correspondent was apparently a Pole. It would be impossible to tell him what I intended to do.

"I'm a French tourist," I told him. "A friend of my husband who works for AFP in Paris suggested I get in touch with you for information about the city."

He seemed amazed and incredulous. Since I could not continue that line, I took the plunge.

"Are you French?" I asked. "I mean, of French nationality?"

"Yes. But why do you ask?"

"That makes all the difference. I would like to give you some advance notice about something. Can we talk here?"

"No, no, no. It would be safer in my car."

I was somewhat reassured to find that his car had French license plates. I told him what I planned to do about noon that day. He did not seem too happy about it, for censorship was very strict, but he agreed to watch me.

"All I ask you to do," I said, "is just pass by—you don't have to say a word—and send a dispatch to Paris."

I made my final preparations in a restaurant washroom, where I fastened a chain around my waist under my dress and pulled the end of it through a buttonhole of my coat.

In a few minutes the streets were full, for the stroke of noon brought large crowds out on to the Marszalkowska in the heart of Warsaw.

I carefully chose a solid-looking tree near a traffic light at a wide and busy intersection. It would suit my purpose, for more automobiles than I had expected would come to a stop only a few feet away from me. I stationed myself right in the middle of the stream of people approaching the crosswalk. The time was right.

I put my flight bag at my feet. Unobtrusively, and as quickly as possible, I pulled out the chain. It almost slipped out of my hands, for I was trembling. I passed the chain around the tree and snapped the padlock shut. Now what to do with the key?

The crowds were swirling around me. The tiny key in the palm
of my hand felt dreadfully heavy. My first thought was to swallow
it; then I figured that would be stupid. I tried to keep it in my
mouth, but that was very uncomfortable. I looked for a sewer
grating, but there was none near me. Clearly I had not thought of
everything. To throw the key a few feet away would not do much
good, for passers-by would surely see it. The only solution seemed
to be to slip it under the fence around the tree and keep my foot
on it.

Not until I had taken a bunch of leaflets out of my flight bag did
anyone pay any attention to me.

I moved as far from the tree as my chain would permit and
handed out leaflets. The passers-by slowed down and took them. In
less than ten minutes I had got rid of all of them, except for one
that I held against my chest so that newcomers could read it:

Citizens of Poland!

The elimination of Jews taking place in Poland right now has
nothing to do with the suppression of alleged Zionist traitors, but is
anti-Semitism pure and simple. The recent persecution has debased
Poland and socialism in the eyes of the whole world. It is being stimu-
lated by enemies of socialism who want to seize power through
demagoguery.

Hitlerism martyred Poland, but do not forget that while millions
of Polish Jews were being murdered at Auschwitz and Treblinka, the
Polish people as a whole remained passive. It was only the Polish
communists and leftists who made any organized resistance against
that genocide. Follow their example, and demand that your government put an end to a policy that will force the last Polish Jews, among
whom are many patriots and socialists, to leave their country. No
fanatical Zionist, not even a Jewess, is appealing to your sense of
justice, but an anti-fascist German woman.

                    B.K.
                    Recipient of the Lambrakis Medal awarded
                    in 1969 by the World Council for Peace
                    in East Berlin

After I had distributed my leaflets I noticed that the traffic
policeman at the intersection had gone into a telephone booth and
come out again without taking his eyes off me.

Some minutes passed before two policemen got out of a jeep and
grabbed my arm to make me follow them. But we could go no
farther than the length of my chain. There were some good-

1 The Slap, Berlin, 1968.
Chancellor Kiesinger with hand to head; to Kiesinger's right, former
chancellor Ludwig Erhard; Beate seized by secretary general of Christian Democratic party.

2 (*Right*) Kurt Lischka, 1946, in allied camp for war criminals.

3 (*Below*) Sturmbannführer Kurt Lischka: Confidential Memo, 1942.

IV J – SA 225a   Paris, den 15.5.1942

San./Ge.

Dringend! Sofort vorlegen!

An das

Reichssicherheitshauptamt

- IV B 4 -

B e r l i n .

<u>Betrifft:</u> Abstellung von rollendem Material für Judentransporte.

<u>Vorgang:</u> Ohne.

ETRA   Es ist gelungen, zu dem Chef der Eisenbahntransportabteilung

(ETRA), Generalleutnant K o h l, Paris, eine gute Verbindung herzu-

stellen. Generalleutnant Kohl, der absoluter Judengegner ist, hat zuge-

sichert alles für den Abtransport der Juden erforderliche Eisenbahn-

material sowie Lokomotiven zur Verfügung zu stellen. Demnach könnten

schon in nächster Zeit aus Frankreich mindestens 10 Züge rollen.

        Ich bitte unter Bezugnahme auf die verschiedenen Besprechungen

des SS-Hauptsturmführers Dannecker bei der dortigen Dienststelle um

Mitteilung, ob und in welchem Zeitraum eine grössere Anzahl von Juden

abgenommen werden kann und welches Lager für deren Aufnahme in

Frage kommt.

        Da weitere Judenrazzien erforderlich sind, jedoch nur eine

beschränkte Anzahl von Lagern zur Verfügung steht, wäre ich zunächst

für umgehende Abnahme von 5 000 Juden dankbar.

4 (*Above*) Heinrich Illers, 1972, Senatspräsident of the Landessozialgericht of Lower Saxony.

5 (*Right*) Ernst Achenbach, c. 1970, Member of the Bundestag.

6 (*Right*) Klaus Barbie in 1942, Head of Gestapo's Department IV in Lyon.

7 (*Below*) Klaus Altmann [Barbie] at home in Lima, 1972. (*Courtesy Nicole Bonnet—Gamma*)

8   Reopening the Barbie Case.

(*Above*) Protest in Munich, September 14, 1971. Mme. Benguigui
holds photograph of her three sons killed in Auschwitz. (*Courtesy
Fritz Kuhn, Munich*)

9   (*Below*) Protest in La Paz, March 6, 1972. Beate and Mme.
Halaunbrenner, chained to the bench.

10   Protest at Achenbach's office, Essen, June 24, 1971. Arrest of
the seven young LICA members.

11/12   Protest at Lischka's office, Cologne, May 7, 1973. Arrest of Julien Aubert (*above*); Henri Pudeleau (*below*). Both wear their Auschwitz clothing.

13 (*Above*) Protest at Dachau, April 17, 1974. Beate alerts reporter; with her, co-demonstrators Henri Wolff (*left*); Henri Pudeleau (*right*).

14 (*Below*) Inside courthouse, Cologne trial, July 1974. Beate and her Israeli lawyer, Arie Marinsky, confer. (*Courtesy Michel Tessier— Gamma*)

15 Outside courthouse, Cologne. (*Courtesy Michel Tessier—Gamma*)

16   Serge and Beate received by Prime Minister Golda Meir, Jerusalem, March 23, 1974.

17 (*Above*) Presentation of the Medal of the Revolt of the Ghetto by Israeli Minister of Health Victor Shem Tov, Jerusalem, March 24, 1974. (*Courtesy Rochamim Yisraeli, Jerusalem*)

18 (*Below*) Presentation of the Medal of Jerusalem by Mayor Teddy Kollek, July 18, 1974. Serge (*left*), Arie Marinsky (*right*). (*Courtesy Ross Photo, Jerusalem*)

19　The Klarsfeld Family. (Courtesy G. Bosio—France Match)

natured comments from the crowd, and some young people laughed openly. I tried to show the policemen the chain, for they did not seem to have noticed it. Sheepishly one examined the tree, then gestured to me to give him the key.

He repeated the word for *key* five or six times, but it got him nowhere. I remained planted where I was while he went to rummage in the rear of his car. I did not dare take a step for fear of disclosing the key I had been standing on.

The other policeman, who had stayed right beside me, tried to keep the crowd away, but he could not. In a rage he grabbed one young man, who had been attentively reading my leaflet, and took his identity card.

Meanwhile the other policeman had returned with wire cutters, and he cut me loose. While I was waiting, I got several glimpses of the French correspondent.

The jeep drove us past heavy iron gates guarding the entrance to police headquarters. I was dragged into several different offices before a superintendent who could speak German was located. Then began the usual interrogation. The police officers were courteous, but they could not get through their heads what I had been trying to prove by my public demonstration.

"I came to Warsaw," I told them, "for as a German anti-fascist I cannot stand to see anti-Semitism in Poland."

The police wanted an argument. One of them gave me a long explanation of why there was no anti-Semitism in Poland.

"You are mistaken," he said. "You should have asked for a conducted tour. We would have shown you everything. You could have observed our way of life, and then you would have reached the conclusion that there is no anti-Semitism here."

They asked me whether I had any more leaflets.

"Yes," I said, "in the suitcase I left at a youth hostel."

Presently we were on our way there by car. On the way back, still another policeman tried to persuade me that anti-Semitism was no more.

"Just the same," I said, "out of the fifty thousand Jews who once lived in Poland, only five thousand are here now. I have met some of those who used to live here in Germany and in France, and I have found many who are now confirmed communists. You have turned good socialists out of your country."

"They were all Zionists," he replied.

"Even those who have not gone to Israel, but have taken up residence in Western Europe?"

The policeman seemed to have an answer for everything: "Those Jews know how hard life is in Israel, and they would rather have an easier time of it in Germany or France, where they can make lots of money."

The argument continued after we returned to the police station. Then a high-level civil servant took over and told me bluntly:

"What you have done is a very serious matter. You are a foreigner, and yet you have made a protest against a democratic country. You will have to appear before a tribunal. You are likely to get two or three years."

"Do whatever seems right to you."

My resoluteness seemed to embarrass him. He left me to myself for over two hours. When he returned he said:

"We have decided to expel you. We have taken into consideration everything you have done before you made such a mistake today."

I was taken to the airport in a police car. There was a choice of flights to Frankfurt or Paris. I would have preferred to go straight to Germany to meet up with Serge and Arno, but the formalities of getting an exit visa took so long that we missed the plane to Frankfurt.

They took money out of my purse and paid for my ticket to Paris with it. The officer then turned me over to the French pilot. I left Warsaw in the pilot's cabin of a Caravelle.

A few minutes later the crew invited me into the first-class cabin and offered me a glass of champagne in celebration of my lucky expulsion. Serge and Arno reached Orly a few hours after I did, and I therefore could celebrate Arno's birthday in the bosom of my family.

We did not have to wait long for the first reaction from the press. A West German Christian Democratic paper wrote:

This young female globe-trotter in the cause of socialism and anti-fascism is perhaps a little eccentric. It is possible to laugh at this battle-happy amazon, but she is always consistent in her political convictions. She is not narrow-minded; she uncovers flaws in communist countries, and she exposes them.

I went back to Berlin, for I wanted to strike while the iron was hot, convince East German youth, and learn what East Berlin's reaction would be to my performance. I had thought for a while that my mother in West Berlin might change her attitude toward me because the conservative papers were for the first time being more favorable to me. I was wrong, however; her prejudices were as strong as ever, and she was still completely allergic to any kind of public activity.

While I was taking the S-Bahn to the Friedrichstrasse checkpoint, I began to worry that I might not be allowed into East Germany without some difficulties. But everything went as usual. I immediately telephoned one of my friends, a radio executive who had been the first to help me establish contact with East Germany. He and his wife met me the following day in the Hotel Unter-den-Linden.

"I want to show you the leaflet I handed out in Warsaw."

I had thought that might take him by surprise, but he replied that he had already read it carefully. Then he said: "The press service dispatches that descended on the newspapers gave a lot of journalists quite a shock. It certainly made them think, even if they didn't show it."

We arranged to meet again on the following day.

Another telephone call was to an official in the Ministry of the Interior who had helped us in our research on Kiesinger: "I should like to see you. Could Serge and I stop by your office tomorrow?"

He answered me frostily: "I think that is scarcely necessary after what you did in Poland."

"But why shouldn't anti-Semitism in Poland be exposed?"

"You see the matter from the wrong historical perspective," he said.

I wondered whether I might have any better luck with the East Berlin paper, *BZ am Abend,* for which I used to write fairly frequently. When Serge and I went to its offices, we looked up the man in charge of foreign news. I asked him whether he was going to publish the story I had sent in three weeks before.

"We really cannot print any more of your articles," he replied. "We do not approve of your activities, even if it is true that there are shortcomings in the communist countries. Our opinion is that there is no need to expose them, for in doing so you are just furnishing the capitalist camp with ammunition. After this latest performance of yours blows over, we'll see."

I tried one last contact at the Association of East German Anti-Fascists. The conversation was nothing but clichés, for the people

I talked with wanted to avoid discussing what was on my mind. But when I showed them the leaflet I had distributed in Warsaw, the old Resistance people across the table from me changed their tone at once. One of them said in embarrassment:

"Yes, we heard about what you did. Everyone is talking about it in private, but very few wish to discuss it openly. Many of your friends approve of it, because for a long time there has been some uneasiness that became especially apparent after the anniversary ceremonies at Auschwitz and the Warsaw ghetto. Only delegates from the Eastern countries showed up at them. We have tried to remedy the situation through discussions with our Polish friends, but nothing has come of them."

My relations with East Germany got worse and worse. I tried to go back with Serge one more time. We were made to wait at the frontier for two hours and then were told that we could no longer enter East Germany.

I had been ostracized. But a few weeks after my protest, Chancellor Brandt of the Federal Republic also chose concrete action as a means of expression when he visited Poland. He knelt at the memorial to the Warsaw ghetto, thereby greatly displeasing the Poles and many Germans to boot.

Later, when Brandt won the Nobel Peace Prize after negotiating the treaties that restored relations between the Federal Republic and the USSR and Poland, tears I could not repress came to my eyes. Of everything I have undertaken, the one thing that has given me the most joy is that for four years I did my best to get Willy Brandt recognition. For once in my life I had confidence in a politician. Brandt's vigorous and courageous policy toward the East and his easing of human contacts between the West Berliners and the East Germans have already found a place in history.

The sudden change of attitude on the part of the East German authorities did nothing to alter my deep convictions. I continued to think that the final solution of the German problem was recognition of the two states of the German nation. For Germany not to be a member of the United Nations seemed lamentable to me. It was high time for both the Federal Republic and the Democratic Republic to join it simultaneously.

Several weeks later I was to testify to that opinion on the occasion of the twenty-fifth anniversary of the San Francisco Charter, which was celebrated officially on October 23, 1970, at United Nations headquarters in Geneva.

I made up my mind in West Berlin, where I got a telephone call from Michel Lang's mother, who told me of the rumor in German radical circles that I was a CIA agent. I was dumfounded. But when I thought it over I could see the logic of it. The manner in which both the capitalist and the communist systems protect themselves against persons who disapprove of their excesses is the same everywhere. Two years earlier the reactionary press had stated that I was in the pay of Walter Ulbricht. It went on to say that on each of my trips into the Democratic Republic I got instructions straight from him. Now in the liberal West German circles an attempt was being made to discredit me. For the disciplined militants of the communist countries, the mere statement that I was in the employ of the CIA might be enough to convince them without a further examination of the facts, just as they passively accept a number of improbabilities, contradictions, and flagrant deceptions. I was not going to let that slander pass. I would reply in my own way, by a simple, clear, public appeal for support that would prove I had not changed my tune.

To accomplish what I had in mind I needed pamphlets and two big flags—one for each of the two Germanys.

I found the address of a flag manufacturer in the telephone directory, and was considerably surprised when he delivered to me two flags, each about seven feet long by five feet wide. I had intended to tack them to a couple of broomsticks, but I had to abandon that idea and buy six-foot poles. Everything got even more complicated when I boarded the train for Geneva in Berlin the following day, for my long package would not fit upright in the compartment. I had to hold it across my knees, to the considerable discomfort of the other passengers. At the Swiss border a suspicious customs officer wanted to know what was in my cumbersome bundle.

"My country's flags," I told him calmly. "I am going to take part in an international youth congress."

At Basel I had to change trains in the middle of the night. I went to sleep on the platform, my head on my suitcase and my body braced by the enormous package that I would not let go of for one second.

About 6 A.M. my train pulled in, and I hurried aboard so that

I could find a compartment where I might lie down and be warmer than on the cold station platform. Needless to say, I laid my bundle beside me. When I awoke, I saw a young man staring at me from the seat opposite—a Norwegian who was going to Switzerland for two weeks of winter sports. He insisted on talking to me in English, but I was so tired that I went right back to sleep.

In Geneva he helped me off the train with my awkward package, and was utterly astonished to find waiting for me on the platform the several news photographers I had alerted before I left Berlin. Again encumbered with my bundle, I climbed into a taxi that had an open top, and headed straight for United Nations headquarters.

I have no idea who tipped them off, but the security force at the United Nations had been warned of my visit and had been instructed not to let me in. They had been expecting, however, a young woman waving two flags, or perhaps a small army of young people, and so paid no attention to arrivals by taxi. Hence, I got through the main entrance without any trouble.

A number of members just happened to be in the courtyard. Without a moment's hesitation, I unwrapped my two flags. A young man helped me nail them to the wall near the entrance, and I began distributing the two hundred pamphlets I had had printed in West Berlin.

The United Nations security guards lost no time in tearing down first the West German, then the Democratic Republic flag, but the photographers had had time to snap them. What was left of my pamphlets was quickly confiscated, but I was not arrested.

In the fall of 1970, I went to London to protest Rudi Dutschke's expulsion, which had been ordered by British Home Secretary Reginald Maulding. I visited the offices of all the Fleet Street newspapers to argue that Dutschke had been seriously wounded by a fanatic who still believed in Hitler: "The same enemy who tried to invade England now has struck down Dutschke, the first German in politics to be the victim of a postwar assassination attempt. You are degrading yourselves by expelling him."

After reading the news stories, former Prime Minister Harold Wilson promised to intervene. He did so, but to no avail. Dutschke took the path to exile again and went to Denmark.

On the evening of January 7, 1971, Mutualité Hall in Paris was full to overflowing. Three weeks before, two of the five defendants in the Leningrad trials had been sentenced to death. I had marched with thousands of Jews from the place de la Victoire synagogue to La Trinité, and had been at the demonstration in the place de l'Hotel de Ville. The left was making an appeal, and I had been asked to speak. Beside me on the platform were Jean-Paul Sartre; Professor Laurent Schwartz; Daniel Meyer, the president of the League for Human Rights; the writer Vercors; the historian Jacques Madaule, who was also president of Judeo-Christian Relations; and Eli Ben Gal, who represented Israel's Mapam Party in Europe. The many young people present gave me a long round of applause. That truly touched me, for they were cheering me both for what I had accomplished and for the fact that I am German. The means I had taken to bring our two peoples together had won their approval.

In a little while Eli Ben Gal came over to me, shook my hand, and said: "This is the first time in my life that I have taken the hand of a German. Knowing what you have done, I not only can do it, but I know I ought to do it."

Then he wrote on my program: "To Beate, who has brought something unique into my life—hope for an eventual reconciliation between our peoples and, in the meantime, true friendship."

I had traveled a long, rough road since that summer day in 1966 when a young woman in a Galilee kibbutz told me they didn't take in Germans.

A German reporter sent his Hamburg paper a report on the meeting in which he expressed his feelings at seeing a German woman so warmly welcomed by so many Jews. That part of his dispatch, however, was cut; Germans should not be told that my appalling behavior had culminated in what other Germans found hard to attain—respect from the Jews.

That evening I talked with greater fervor than usual, and I could feel my words hitting home. Perhaps it was because my battle was soon to extend to another country of the East: Czechoslovakia.

The expulsion from Poland of many socialist Jews, the insidious persecution of some thousands who would not resign themselves to leaving their country, the second-class citizenship enforced on the majority of Soviet Jews, the obstacles that have prevented them from becoming assimilated and even from emigrating, the Leningrad trials and their horrifying outcome—all this was anti-Semitism. So were the venomous attacks on the Jewish origin of former Czech leaders.

We had to make it clear. All of that was anti-Semitism, and it would grow and be reinforced if the Communist Parties outside the countries of the East, the forces of the left, and the anti-fascists did not throw their weight into the battle against it. In that way, and only in that way, could we assist the people in the USSR, in Poland, and in Czechoslovakia who were taking a stand against anti-Semitism. I warned anti-fascists everywhere not to compare what was happening in the East with Vietnam. That would be too easy a way to salve our conscience and resign us to doing nothing. Our sincerity and our effectiveness would be judged by our fight against an anti-Semitism that some people believed was nonexistent and that was already being called "leftist anti-Semitism."

I spoke several more times on anti-Semitism in the East. Jewish circles sprang to life, and I sensed in the big halls of Paris as well as in stuffy little suburban meeting rooms how much they appreciated a leftist German woman's aligning herself with the Jews of the USSR. Western communists were denying that many Soviet Jews were eager to emigrate to Israel. I was even to see in Brussels, in February 1971, a delegation of Soviet Jews asserting that there was no Jewish problem in the USSR. It was clear, however, that there was indeed a Jewish problem, and denial of its existence was not enough to suppress it. When the Kremlin is finally pressured into allowing a substantial number of Jews to leave for Israel, I would not like to be in the shoes of those communists who will then have to admit the truth of what they once denied.

I could not be content with lecturing or signing petitions. The situation required more than that. Moreover, the East German party paper, *Neues Deutschland*, had just taken a definitely conservative anti-Semitic stand by approving the death sentences handed down in Leningrad. If the East Germans were subjected to such eyewash, I would again have to make a public protest against that detestable policy in such a way that they would have to listen to me.

A number of former Nazis had re-entered the field of propaganda in the German Democratic Republic. They did not hold policy-making positions, but they were able to influence policy. The occupation of Czechoslovakia, the persecution of Jews in the USSR, and the cordial relations between East Germany and the Arab nations were giving them a chance to speak out.

Early in 1971, attacks on Jews increased in Czechoslovakia. The Bratislava *Pravda* had just attacked "intellectual Jews who have succeeded in getting increasingly important positions in Czechoslovakian cultural life." Radio Prague broadcast the conclusions of the Central Committee of the Czechoslovakian Communist Party on December 10, 1970, in which Zionist elements were accused of having played a sizable part in the incidents that provoked Soviet intervention. When a former leader of Jewish origin was mentioned, the radio adopted the usage of following his name with a "born Ben- . . . ," or added such phrases as "an admirer of Lev Davidovitch Bronstein, better known as Trotsky." A trial of twenty-six young Trotskyites, which had been postponed several times, was held on February 8. They were charged with having tried "to overthrow the socialist regime not only in Czechoslovakia, but in other socialist countries, of which the USSR is one." It was a monumental accusation. About half of the defendants were Jews, and their names, which were frequently repeated, gave the people the idea that "deviationists" from the right or the left were being actually encouraged by "Zionist" elements.

I therefore decided to go into action in court on the day the trial opened. I had noticed in *Neues Deutschland* that East German Prime Minister Willi Stoph was leaving on February 7 for a rest cure at Karlovy Vary in Czechoslovakia. There was no doubt that Husak, the First Secretary of the Czech Communist Party, who had met me in East Berlin, the Czechs, and especially the Soviet experts who directed their technical bureaus would look to the East Germans for guidance. I was almost certain that they would not want their young people demonstrating on my behalf if I were found guilty and imprisoned. They would not be able to hide the truth because of the television broadcasts that originated in the Federal Republic. And that truth would incite vigorous protests from young East Germans, especially students, for they were very sensitive to the problem of anti-Semitism.

I figured that as Stoph would be right there, he would have something to say, for I knew from a Dutch reporter that until the Polish incident he had been quite appreciative of my efforts. Whatever happened, he and the other East German leaders would have a conflict of conscience to resolve: whether to let a German woman who was speaking the truth go to jail, or intervene in her behalf in spite of all the trouble she was causing them.

I planned to take along three hundred tracts that I had had translated into Czech by a professional.

Then there was the question of getting a visa. The Czech secretary at the Paris embassy might recognize my name and remember my Warsaw protest, and he might wonder why the same B.K. now wanted a visa for Czechoslovakia. It was important that no one notice my name. So I went to the consulate with Arno, pretending to be a rather snobbish middle-class woman who wanted to take a pleasure trip in an "exotic" country.

Arno, who was often a fiend when I took him anywhere, climbed up on the furniture and the counters and kept throwing forms into the air. I did not stop him, and he continued to behave so atrociously that people began to make remarks. As a result, the secretary tended to me as quickly as possible, gave me a visa there and then, and even reserved a hotel room for me.

I bought a plane ticket Paris-Vienna-Prague-Cologne-Paris.

Parting from my family was difficult. My mother-in-law was wracked with fear, and predicted that I would be drowned in the Moldau as a Jewish leader had been in 1968 through the good offices of the Czech police. Serge could barely conceal his worry. For once Arno was not informed.

I said good-by to Serge at Orly. We kept staring at each other as I moved away. I believed that couples who deliberately live by an ideal and in an atmosphere of danger have a greater chance of seeing their love grow than other couples have. It's not a matter of letting each go his own way, but of living, and really living together.

I reached Vienna by plane on Saturday, February 6. I planned to take a train to Prague: airport police are better briefed than railway guards, and so I would have little chance of passing unnoticed if I got off the plane in Prague. I would certainly be searched, and my tracts discovered.

When I had presented my passport at the Vienna airport, the Austrian customs officers made me wait an hour because I was on the "black list." They had to wait for instructions: an aftermath of the Schirmer affair.

I found a hotel room and telephoned Simon Wiesenthal, who met me that evening in a restaurant. I brought him up to date on my plans, and he gave me some additional information: the trial of the Trotskyites would not begin on February 8 because the Czech authorities were afraid that it might provoke demonstrations from the International Communist Youth Congress that was being held in Bratislava.

Wiesenthal approved of my project, but worried about what might happen to me. "It isn't like other countries," he said. "The police are much stricter there, and you might very well be detained a long time."

I already knew that. One of the defendants in the trial was a twenty-four-year-old West German named Sybille Plogstedt, who had been arrested back in December 1969, for having allegedly brought her Czech friends "subversive" books. She had already been in a Prague jail for fourteen months. More than anything else, I was afraid I might be arrested and "disappear" without anyone hearing about it. Of course I had the addresses of press correspondents in Prague, but I still had to get in touch with them without arousing suspicion. I had told Serge that if I succeeded in reaching any of them by Sunday night, I would wire him in Paris that I was going ahead with my protest on Monday. The code we had agreed on was: "Arrived safely. Lovely city."

So on Sunday I took my train. I hid my three hundred pamphlets, which were printed on thin paper, in the lining of my flight bag, which was filled with food, including a very ripe Camembert cheese that I hoped would be smelly enough to discourage any overconscientious customs officer. I had also brought a big bunch of flowers to distract prying eyes. I did my best to appear frivolous; in a word, I was beyond suspicion.

Everything went well. The young police officer was so busy smiling at me that he hardly looked at my passport. He gave my suitcase a cursory glance and didn't even bother opening my flight bag.

I still had to get rid of an Austrian architect who was determined to show me around Prague and who would run the risk of including a visit to a Czech prison in his tour if he were seen with me.

I took a taxi from the Hotel Flora to the home of the German Press Agency correspondent, who lived quite far from the center of town. It was already growing dark by the time I reached the row of gloomy buildings where his apartment was. I climbed to the fourth floor and rang the bell. No answer. I sat on the staircase to wait. An hour later I left. I couldn't waste any more time because I had to get a release to the press that very evening.

I then went to the Reuters' correspondent, who lived on a wide street in the center of town. He opened the door to me, and I saw how young he was. I told him: "This is what I plan to do to-morrow."

He answered: "I have been in Czechoslovakia only a short while, but I can assure you there is no anti-Semitism in Prague."

Nevertheless, I gave him the time and place of my protest—by then I had settled on the Prague School of Philosophy, in which most of the defendants in the trial were enrolled. He promised that he would cover it, even though he was not in sympathy.

This was not very encouraging, so I also went to see a German reporter who worked for a Cologne broadcasting station. His wife was alone, for he had gone to cover the Communist Youth Congress in Bratislava. She notified a West German cameraman, and we spent the rest of the evening together in a restaurant, where I could speak freely at last, for the woman was obsessed by a fear that her apartment was bugged. When I got back to my hotel about 1 A.M., I sent Serge the telegram and then spent an almost sleepless night.

On Monday I went out about 10 A.M. and walked the streets of Prague for two hours. As in Warsaw, I was sorry not to be able to see this handsome city more thoroughly. By 11:30 I was freezing, so I took refuge in a very busy restaurant to get warm. It was full of young people merrily chatting away, but I felt tense.

At noon I went to the School of Philosophy, which was on a large square, and got out my pamphlets. On one cover was printed in large type: "Fight Re-Stalinization! Fight Repression! Fight Anti-Semitism!" in Czech, and on the reverse the same in both Czech and French. The text was:

Citizens of Czechoslovakia!

This is no Jewess speaking to you, but a German anti-fascist who, in the name of all liberal organizations, led young Germans in a campaign against Kiesinger and was sentenced to a year in prison for having slapped him.

Now in Prague, as in Warsaw on August 26, 1970, I appeal to the citizens of a country in the Eastern bloc to oppose the wave of anti-Semitism that believers in a return to Stalinism are stirring up in socialist countries.

Under the influence of those pro-Stalinists, Czech propaganda has continuously stated that the 1968 crisis was due to the shameful and anti-national activities of "Zionists." Such propaganda always stresses the Jewish origin of liberal leaders because it wants you to be persuaded that there is no difference between a Jew and a Zionist agitator.

That is not anti-Zionism, but it is anti-Semitism, and it is responsible for the evidence in the Slansky trial that was trumped up because some demagogues needed a scapegoat.

Do not permit such anti-Semitism to discredit socialism. The only possible remedy is for broadminded Western anti-fascists to act openly against it and against its proponents in the USSR, where the rights of Jews as citizens have been shamefully abused; in Poland, where that utra-nationalist Moczar has become a member of the Politburo while militant communist Jews have been chased out of their country; and in the German Democratic Republic, where *Neues Deutschland* has dared to approve without reservations the death sentences in the Leningrad trials.

Citizens of Czechoslovakia, do not let yourselves be contaminated. Take a stand against anti-Semitism!

A German-speaking student read my text and then asked me whether I really was Beate Klarsfeld:

"Everyone has heard a lot about you. Everyone knows about your campaign against Kiesinger, and everyone talks about you in class. What you have done is extraordinary, and we have been greatly inspired and encouraged by it. But I am afraid for you now, and I strongly advise you to get out of here right away, because the police in Czechoslovakia are very tough."

He took about twenty of my pamphlets and promised he would give them to his friends.

After a quarter of an hour I went to Wenceslas Square, where a large crowd had already gathered. But everyone was so cautious that I practically had to run after people to get them to take my pamphlet.

A few minutes later a policeman arrived to see what was going on. I gave him a pamphlet at once. He went into a nearby telephone booth, and I could hear him reading it aloud.

A few moments later another policeman grabbed me by the arm, snatched my pamphlets away, and shoved me into a police car. Then, after a long discussion with headquarters by radio, we headed for a large modern building on a narrow street, which must have been the police headquarters. Actually, I never knew where I was.

A forty-five or fifty-year-old police official—stout, with a dark suit and a pleasant enough face—questioned me in a small office. He got tougher with every question he asked me in his reasonably good German. He emptied my flight bag onto his desk and made an inventory of its contents. Then he telephoned for an interpreter, for whom we waited for nearly an hour without saying a word.

The door finally opened and in came a rather thin, sixty-year-old man wearing a dark gray long leather—or imitation leather—coat with a wide belt, just like the Gestapo coats. I got goose flesh. He was a former Austrian, and the official interpreter. Then began a very thorough interrogation that lasted several hours, for the official wanted to know everything. A secretary took it down on the type-writer. Who wrote the pamphlet? Who translated it? Who printed it? Who gave me money? Why were there so many East German visas on my passport? Who were my friends in the Democratic Republic? Did they know about this visit to Prague?

Generally speaking, I only had to tell them the truth, which made my replies easier. I told them about my talk with Husak in Berlin, but I had to invent some of the details because I could no longer remember exactly what he had said.

On the wall was a poster protesting against Angela Davis's im-prisonment, and I had noticed others in the corridor.

Once the first session of my interrogation came to an end, a police inspector and the interpreter took me to the hotel to get my luggage. When we went downstairs we crossed a courtyard lined with barred windows. The effect was so oppressive that I said to the official while we were waiting for a police car: "You know, I feel completely relaxed. I'm not the least bit afraid. You're going to let me go tomorrow, just as they did in Poland, because you can't afford to have a trial on anti-Semitism."

"No, no," he answered. "That could happen in Poland—and, as a matter of fact, I personally agree with you that there is a pro-nounced anti-Semitism in Poland, not official, but endemic with the Poles themselves. But that's not the situation here. You should have come as a tourist and asked to be shown our country so you could have seen that there is no anti-Semitism here. And then you wrote: 'Against repression, and against the return to Stalinism.' If it had not been for Stalin, the Nazis would have won, and the Jews would have been completely wiped out."

I told him: "I'm not saying that anti-Semitism here is the same as anti-Semitism in Poland. I know that the Czech people them-selves are not anti-Semitic, but there is a group in the government, particularly in the propaganda department, that is using the Jews as a scapegoat for all your problems."

"Listen," he replied. "Frankly, the whole thing is unbelievable!

How could you have done the same thing in two countries of the East? You know very well that this repetition of your behavior in Poland is going to be disastrous for you. We will be harder on you, for you have slandered us and you have acted against Czechoslovakia. You may as well expect to spend quite a long time here."

I was really getting worried now. As a foreigner I was helpless. In the West I could have depended on a lawyer, but here in the East what could I depend on?

Another police car was already parked in front of the hotel. I was reimbursed for the two or three days' rent I had paid in advance. Then we went up to my room, while three policemen stood guard in the lobby. The police dumped everything out of my suitcase and my flight bag, rummaged under the mattress and in the blankets. In the closet they found a package of pamphlets I had left there. They even turned back the rug, and they thoroughly searched the bathroom.

All at once the one who was searching my suitcase put his hand inside the lining and fished something out. He seemed terribly excited as he called to his colleague. He had just discovered about ten pieces of microfilm, which they tried to read by the light of a lamp. The films had lists of Czech Jews, and I had brought them for the express purpose of teasing the police. I had cropped enough of them so that their source could not be read. All the names were of Czech Jews whom the Nazis had murdered during the war and to whom the Czech government had awarded posthumous citations. Serge had unearthed them at the Library of Contemporary Jewish Documents. We figured that the police would immediately check on them and would get wise to the trick. As a matter of fact, no one ever mentioned the subject to me again.

I had missed lunch and I was hungry. Delicious aromas were coming from the elegant hotel dining room. Might as well have a decent meal, I murmured. The official agreed. All four of us were seated at a table in the midst of foreign tourists. The policemen just ordered beer, but I selected some expensive and hearty items from the menu, including shashlik and a half-bottle of wine. Everyone at the other tables stared at us, because I was well-dressed and my companions, who were obviously policemen, kept watching me and not eating.

It was after 8 P.M. when we got back to the office we had been in earlier. My escorts had stopped along the way to buy themselves some sandwiches.

An hour later they were in a hurry to go home, so they post-poned the questioning until the next morning. They told me that I would spend the night in a cell, then led me to the basement, through a large barred door, to kind of a filthy cave. I put all my personal effects in a sealed envelope in a small office. The only thing I kept was a handkerchief, which I was later to use as a washcloth. After all that had happened that day, I was glad enough of a chance to rest, and I fully expected to find a bed I could stretch out on, as in Berlin. What a disappointment; I was thrust into a black hole, 12' x 15', where two girls were already asleep on the floor. There was a rolled-up mattress propped against one wall, but it was revolting, and there were no sheets. I was allowed one rough, dark gray blanket, but it too was filthy. I could not actually see the dirt, but I could certainly smell it.

The girls spoke only Czech, but one was pleasant enough and helped me fix up a bed. Like them, I lay down in all my clothes. Their panties and stockings were drying by the window.

One hour later a fat girl, who was weeping hysterically, joined us and began telling her plight to the other two. Even so, I slept better than I had the previous night.

At 6 A.M. there was a rapping on the door. I awoke, but all I wanted was to go back to sleep. One of the girls suddenly started pounding on the wall. Why, I did not know, but after three or four blows water spurted out of a small pipe I had not noticed and dribbled down the wall. The corner served as a toilet, among other things, and it was enclosed by a torn curtain that could not be closed. Beside it was a pail so revolting that I thought it must be a chamber pot. It turned out to be the receptacle for all the water that would be available that day. The girls plunged their hands into it as soon as enough water had collected, but I merely moistened my handkerchief and dabbed at my face. The Czech girls were used to it, however, and they collected every drop, washed their face and brushed their teeth, then used the rest for their laundry. In fact, one of them was so industrious that she dipped a piece of burlap into the remainder of the water and mopped up the entire cell with it. Then we stacked our mattresses against the wall and folded our blankets.

Our guards were all men, who took advantage of a peephole to squint at us. The girls wore rather extreme miniskirts, and the one who mopped up the cell did not put her panties on until she had finished her task. It must have been an interesting scene for the guards.

The cell window opened on the courtyard through which I had passed the previous evening. It could be opened only a crack, and the stench from the corner that contained the hole that was used as a toilet was particularly nauseating. In the center of the cell were a table and some stools. The walls had once been painted gray, and a piece of frayed linoleum half covered the floor. The girls had put a little of the water into an iron jug that sat on the table.

At 6:30 breakfast was served. It consisted of very sweet café-au-lait and a piece of stale black bread.

I waited for someone to come for me. The fat girl was still crying. She was questioned once or twice during the morning. Each time she returned she had a lot to tell the others, who tried to calm her down. The younger one, who had washed the floor, never stopped singing Western popular songs. She would knock on the wall of the next cell, where some men's voices shouted back at her. I would have loved to know how many times they had been in jail before and for what reasons, but it was impossible for me to converse with them. They were in a continual good humor, and from time to time the girls knocked on the door and when the guard would come they would ask him for a cigarette and kid with him until he gave them one. The rest of the time they rolled their own out of butts, breadcrumbs, and a little dust; they would then savor every drag. The good-natured girl made little sculptures out of the bits of bread we had not eaten.

The time passed pleasantly enough. At noon we got some cabbage soup with a morsel of meat swimming in disgusting grease. I sampled it very frugally, for it certainly would not do to get sick to my stomach in that tiny cell.

In the afternoon I began to get a pain in my back from sitting on a stool, so I unrolled my mattress and lay down upon it. A few minutes later the guard opened the door and yelled something at me. I knew what he wanted, but I pretended not to understand. When he came back and saw me still stretched out, he flew into a rage, yanked me up, and stood the mattress up against the wall again. That time I did not pretend not to understand.

I was in agony. The night before, I had been told that I would be questioned again in the morning, yet no one had come for me.

Then, about 6 P.M., the cell door suddenly opened and the guard called my name and took me out. He shoved me into the little office where I had left my personal effects and these were returned to me. In a larger office at the end of the underground corridor one of the policemen was sitting across a table from a bald young man, better dressed than his colleagues, who spoke to me in a German I barely understood.

"Look here," he said. "Contrary to what you were told last night, we have changed our mind and you are going to be expelled from Czechoslovakia at once. Everything is ready. A car is waiting to take you to the nearest Austrian frontier."

I noticed a camera focused on me from a corner, and a tape recorder in operation on a low table.

The young man opened a file and took out a sheet of paper, from which he proceeded to read in Czech. Then he asked me some questions. I told him I could not understand what he was saying, so he repeated the text in German.

All I could gather was that he was talking about my having broken some Czech law or other and that I would not be permitted to enter the country again for four years. He handed me a pen and asked me to sign. Everything he had said was already on tape, and the camera was still focused on me and running continuously.

When I left the office, another young man followed me with a portable movie camera. Apparently he did not like my performance, for I had to repeat my exit three or four times before he was satisfied. Then I was allowed to wash up in a proper bathroom, with a female attendant watching me. My luggage was brought to me, and I could put on my fur coat and hat again. The cameraman followed me down the corridor, his machine whirring all the way.

In front of the building, an unfamiliar-looking big black car—a Tatra, I think—was waiting with a chauffeur and a policeman inside. I climbed into the back seat with the woman who had kept me under surveillance in the bathroom and one other policeman. Again, I had to repeat this scene several times to satisfy the cameraman; either he was a rank amateur or he thought it necessary to get a shot of me from all possible angles.

I was famished, and I persuaded my escorts to stop for an hour at a village inn. Four hours later we came to a small frontier post in the middle of a forest. It was bitter cold, and the ground was covered with deep snow. The car stopped, and as I got out another photographer rushed up to put that scene on film. Then my passport was examined and my luggage searched, and I was sent on my way toward the Austrian frontier with two policemen and a uniformed customs officer.

Suddenly the two policemen stopped without saying a word. There were a few lights along the road for a short distance; beyond them, pitch darkness. The customs officer gave me to understand he could go no farther. Slipping and sliding in the snow, I trudged toward Austria, somewhat relieved but also unpleasantly aware that I had been abandoned in the depths of a forest and that behind me were definitely unfriendly people.

I hurried toward a tiny light I could just make out in the distance. It came from a one-room frontier post. When I entered, two Austrian customs officers stared at me as if I were a ghost.

"Did you come by car?"

"No, on foot."

"Well, where did you come from?"

"I have just been expelled from Czechoslovakia."

"Expelled! You're lucky they didn't make you stay."

It occurred to me that they might be fairly sympathetic, and that I could tell them everything. They could not understand my motives, but they were distinctly anti-communist and consequently willing to help me find a room.

"Listen, Madame," said one of them, "in fifteen minutes—that is, at 12:30—my shift will be over, and I can drive you to the next village. First I'll phone and see if there's a room available at a boardinghouse I know of."

Everything was arranged by the time his relief showed up at about 12:25. After my presence was explained to him, he picked up my passport, which was still on the desk, and began to raise objections:

"She can't be given an entrance visa without authorization from the Vienna police."

He then took the others aside, and I heard him mention Kiesinger's name several times. Obviously he did not approve of my having slapped the Chancellor.

There was, of course, no chance of getting a reply from Vienna until the next day. The customs officer who had offered to drive me to the village could wait no longer. I insisted that they put in an emergency call to Vienna, for I certainly did not want to spend the rest of the night in that hut.

"Why do you need authorization from Vienna?" I asked. "You

can't send me back to Czechoslovakia, because they won't have me there. I don't want to stay in Austria. I just want to get to Vienna so that I can take a plane."

The whole situation reminded me of Charlie Chaplin in "The Pilgrim," with one foot on the American side of the border and a sheriff after him, and his other foot on the Mexican side, where bandits are waiting for him. Here I was, with one foot in each of two camps, wanted by neither, and facing as much trouble from the East as from the West.

At 6 A.M. Vienna replied that I could enter Austria. I reached the capital by bus and train, and telephoned Paris to reassure my mother-in-law, who told me that Serge had gone to Bonn as we had planned. I got a plane to Frankfurt and transferred to another for Cologne, where I found Serge at about 4 P.M. He had had to release the news of my arrest on Monday himself, for the reporters had not been able to get their stories past the censor. Serge had telephoned the Hotel Flora in Prague, but no one there could tell him anything except that I had checked out. Since he knew from my telegram that I had been in touch with the Western press correspondents, he called their Paris branches and asked them to find out from their Prague representatives what had happened to me. That is how he learned of my arrest, and on Tuesday the newspapers carried the story. Perhaps that had some bearing on my being expelled.

A few days later the French Trotskyites demonstrated against the trial of their comrades in Prague by occupying the Czech Consulate and holding a press conference there. The Prague Trotskyites would doubtless have preferred their foreign comrades to express their solidarity on the spot, even at the risk of sharing their fate.

On March 2, in one of his customary local broadcasts, Husak criticized my "bad behavior" in Prague, doubtless because the anticommunist Radio Free Europe had made such a big thing of it and because I had given an interview, broadcast to Czechoslovakia, explaining the reasons for my action.

It is not up to me to entertain, but to tell the truth as forcefully as I can—brutally, if necessary. Forbidden to stay in the German Democratic Republic, I was soon to be arrested in the Federal Republic.

9

ATTEMPT TO KIDNAP KURT LISCHKA

On February 7, 1971, I was in a jail cell in Prague. Two months later I was in another jail cell—this time in Cologne. I had directed a commando operation aimed at kidnapping one of the most prominent Nazi criminals, S.S.-Obersturmbannführer Kurt Lischka.

We had carefully studied the legal aspects of such a kidnapping and relied on the opinion of Colonel Antoine Argoud, leader of the terrorist organization that sought to keep Algeria French, that the manner in which someone who had been tried in absentia was brought back to France would not constitute a major obstacle to his being tried again. *Male captus, bene detentus*—seized illegally, held legally.

Serge approached Marco, his old friend from his School of Political Science days, for help in recruiting an anti-Lischka gang. It ended up with Marco and me as the only non-Jewish members, a photographer named Eli, a doctor named David, and Serge as the Jews.

DVZ furnished the necessary funds, although not intentionally. It had fired me after my escapade in Prague, but I went to Düsseldorf and demanded from Bausch, its political editor who believed the Communist Party right even when it was wrong, the three months' separation pay to which I was entitled. I had to threaten

141

him with a lawsuit that would have shown that the extreme leftist press was more unfair to its employees than the Springer monopoly, but I finally got the money.

I sh..l let Marco tell you the story of the Lischka operation. It could have ended tragically, but it was actually often quite comic.

MARCO'S STORY

In March 1971, Beate and Serge told me all about Lischka, and their plan to kidnap the former top man in the Nazi police in France. I asked them:

"Who is going to help you?"

"That's the problem. We don't have anyone."

I recalled my conversation of a week earlier with a Jewish photographer named Eli, who had warned me that the whole extreme left in France was full of communist cells and that the only organizations that were not communist were the Jewish ones. I suggested to Serge:

"You should get in touch with him and see if he knows anyone who would help."

The three of us met in a pub. Eli's mother had been deported and killed after the Vel d'Hiv round-up ordered by Lischka, but his first reaction was negative. As far as he was concerned, Nazi criminals were hidden in the depths of a virgin forest. It seemed extraordinary and even insane to him that the man who had issued the orders for that round-up could be living openly and peacefully under his own name in Cologne. Then Serge showed him documentary evidence.

It finally got through to Eli that it was not a matter of an imaginary band of avengers executing Beate and Serge's scheme, but that if people like him or me did not do it, Lischka would go on living out a happy life in Cologne.

"Listen," he said to Serge. "I don't like to put the finger on fellows, but basically I'm willing to go along with you."

His decision and his reasoning persuaded me also. I found the project intriguing, almost historic. Going after Lischka could bring to light a number of facts that had not been officially disclosed since the war. I believe there is no distinction between Germans and non-Germans; everyone is more or less to blame. There was no reason why a non-Jewish Frenchman like myself should not take part in such a righteous undertaking.

In the last analysis we were not going to commit a crime, for we had decided to act without anyone running any risks. Lischka was not going to be killed.

We began to get ready by studying the quite professional plans that Beate had made. She had taken moving pictures of Lischka in Cologne, and we watched them at the house of a screenwriter we knew. The operation seemed childishly simple. On the film, the street on which Lischka lived appeared deserted. It would be impossible not to recognize Lischka because of his height. Beate gave us many other details, such as the time Lischka usually left his house and the exact layout of the place.

We perfected our scenario, but we still lacked one partner. Eli thought of an ideal one:

"I know a Jewish doctor who can put our patient to sleep without harming him."

It happened that this fellow, the meekest of the meek, knew judo, as so many meek persons frequently do. We made an appointment with him at the Edmond Fleg Center on rue de l'Eperon, where he practiced.

About 1 or 1:30 in the afternoon, we went to the practice room. The first person we encountered in that place, where normally there are only Jews, was an impressive-looking Japanese judo expert. We watched him enviously and wished we could recruit him. The longer we stayed, the more we wanted to learn judo.

Our new friend, whose name was David, explained that to put someone to sleep one had to act very quickly. He showed us several judo holds, but the first time he put one on Eli it was he who took a fall, perhaps because he weighed less. After that exhausting physical training session, which lasted about a quarter of an hour, we went to lunch. There was no hope, we decided, of anesthetizing Lischka; the only recourse was a blackjack. Eli said he had one and showed it to us, but it seemed ridicuously small.

"You don't know anything about blackjacks," Eli said rather touchily. "With a little one like this you could knock out a mammoth."

Since none of us knew how to use one, we had to agree.

Our arsenal now consisted of two blackjacks. I should add, however, that one soon became useless. At the hotel the night before the kidnapping, Eli was practicing swinging the blackjack, which he had made himself. Its head flew off, miraculously missing a superb mirror on the armoire, and hit the floor of the room with a deafening bang. We all burst out laughing—and not for the last time during that expedition.

We needed a more impressive weapon. Eli had an old pistol from some army or other. We rendered it useless by removing the hammer. It was a way of proving, if anything went wrong, that we meant no harm.

Serge bought a pair of handcuffs that we expected to use on Lischka. Then we all met at the Avis Rent-a-Car office. Thus, the night before we were to leave for Cologne, Serge became an involuntary spectator to a scene straight out of a Grade B movie. He had hardly entered the office when two policemen burst in and without any warning leaped on a young customer, who fought back wildly, all the while trying to pull a revolver out of his belt. The staff ducked, but Serge stayed as close to the action as he could, trying to learn how policemen get handcuffs on an adversary.

Later the clerk explained that the man was part of a gang that rented cars and then sold them—in Belgium or in Germany. It occurred to Serge that he was there for no other reason than to rent a car for an expedition to Germany via Belgium that was, to say the least, scarcely legal.

We left Paris the evening of Saturday, March 20, with me at the wheel. On the way we stopped at a little bistro in a small Belgian mining town. It was there that I realized we had left France. It was a kind of dance hall, so unusual that Eli, the photographer, was furious that we had forbidden him to bring his camera along. We had trouble getting him out of the place; he danced with every one of the girls. We drove all night, and reached Cologne about 3 A.M.

Cologne was very dark, and with its one-way streets and no-passing signs, we had a hard time getting to the apartment that Beate had borrowed. We staked out our bivouac, and tried desperately to convince ourselves that we were really ready for anything. We kept saying over and over: "We've got to get some sleep. We've got to be calm." But we couldn't stop laughing because all we had to do was look at one another to realize that we looked about as much like a commando unit as a council of bishops.

About 9 o'clock on Sunday morning we were up and around. Beate fixed us a fine breakfast to keep up our morale. Hence we were late in calling for the car we had reserved to take us out of Cologne—a four-door Mercedes 220, the most common type of car in Germany. Since we were not on time, Hertz had rented it to someone else.

We tried to get the same model at Avis, but the people there began to quibble and wanted all kinds of identification. They even wanted to telephone Serge's boss to check on us. (Serge had no boss at that time.) So we backed down, trying, if possible, not to attract too much attention. Eli had shaved off his beard in honor of the occasion, and one look at him never failed to make us laugh. Whereas before he had looked like an Old Testament prophet, now he had such pretty, baby-pink cheeks that he couldn't bear to look at himself in the mirror.

We went back to Hertz, where we were given a Mercedes 280, a huge, beige luxury car with an automatic shift. Serge, who hadn't touched a steering wheel in years, rented it in his name, and so he at least had to drive it out of the garage. He started down a one-way street, pursued by the woman in charge screaming at him to go the other way.

At the first intersection I took over and began to get used to the car. The main trouble with it was that it was terribly conspicuous. Furthermore, it had only two doors. The crowning blow was that it had Frankfurt license plates. We had succeeded in assembling three excellent devices to keep us from passing unnoticed.

The next question was how we were going to get a man who was being kidnapped by four other men into a car with only two doors. By adding and dividing we reached the solution that two and a half persons would have to get in by each door. The convenience of such an operation did not escape our notice.

Beate had devised a clever plan and we began to practice the automotive ballet that was to lead to the kidnapping of Lischka. From the spot where we grabbed him we were to drive into some nearby woods that were close to the highway. There we were to transfer Lischka from the Mercedes to the car we had brought from France, an R-16. The place was perfectly situated. It was completely isolated, and we could leave by a lane leading in the opposite direction from the one we entered. It would be easy to see whether we were being followed. Lastly, we would have to drive only about five hundred yards to reach the highway that circled Cologne. That meant we could get from the south of the city, where we were, to the north, and head back to Belgium without passing through the city.

That Sunday we inspected all the sites and practiced our moves. We left the apartment, each car following the other, with David at the wheel of the R-16 and I at the wheel of the Mercedes. Immediately we lost each other in the traffic. A half hour later we met back at the apartment, where we agreed that we had to stop being so nervous, and that the success of the operation depended on our ability to keep cool.

We skipped lunch, which greatly displeased Eli. He had an extraordinary and exasperating ability to be completely at ease and think of nothing but inconsequential matters while the rest of us were gradually coming to acknowledge the seriousness and the considerable risk of what we were about to do. We began to be obsessed by the tiniest details. We decided to prepare ourselves psychologically by having each one foresee, and then continually repeat, every move he had to make—moves that would take only a split second.

Now I have some doubts about the thoroughness of our preparations. When the moment came for us to go into action, everything happened exactly the other way.

That day we went to look over the neighborhood where Lischka lived. We decided on the exact spot for action, but we got a little worried, for there were lots of people around. Beate reassured us and explained that this was due to a minor holiday and that on the next day the place would be almost deserted.

To practice capturing our victim and stuffing him into the trunk of the R-16, we went deep into the magnificent forest that surrounds Cologne. We looked for a deserted spot, for obviously we did not want anyone to see us at this kind of game. David played Lischka. The plan was for only three of us to do the actual kidnapping. One of us would have to stay at the wheel and cover the others' movements. One of the three was to grab Lischka under the arms; the other two by the legs. Everyone played his part superbly, and David found himself locked in the trunk in only a few seconds.

That was when I remembered that the key to the trunk was in his pocket.

At the same moment there came a muffled shout from inside the trunk: "I've got the key in here!"

I had a moment of panic. Thank heaven, however, the trunk could be opened by a device on the instrument panel. It would scarcely have done for us to go roaming through Cologne on a Sunday in search of a locksmith who could open an automobile trunk—and find inside an Orthodox Jew.

That evening we had a quiet dinner in a Yugoslav restaurant. It was impossible to keep Eli from clowning, especially since he had the two blackjacks in his pocket. He never stopped fooling with them and telling jokes. This merry evening did little to allay our apprehension over the following day, however.

A catastrophe awaited us when we got back to the apartment; its owner had just returned, and so we would have to move out and find a hotel where we would not have to give our names. Otherwise the police could track us down.

Beate set out ahead of us into the dark night and found a hotel with some vacant rooms on the Hansaring. We took one with three beds and one with two. It turned out that the young night clerk knew of Beate and sympathized with her cause, and while they were chatting, we slipped in like conspirators without registering. When we got to our room we took out the blackjacks and, for one last time, began fooling around with them again.

We had made up our minds to go to bed early, but that was now out of the question; it was already late. We had hardly fallen asleep when Beate got us up. It was 6 A.M. David said his prayers. Eli complained because it was too early for him to get breakfast and he did not want to undertake the raid on an empty stomach.

It was freezing cold. Eli was wearing a windbreaker; I, a parka; Serge and David, raincoats. At 7 A.M. we got to Lischka's house, separated, and took up our positions along the tree-lined street Lischka would use to get to the Maria-Himmelfahrt-Strasse street-car stop. On one side was a church with a recessed doorway in which Serge—whom Lischka already knew—could hide; on the other were garages in which David could hide. We parked the Mercedes at the curb.

Then we discovered something else to worry about: an enormous number of people took the streetcar at that stop. In our state of mind the presence of those people just a few yards away from us was a huge problem. Serge said there was no reason for us to make so much of it because, after all, the people were not going to move away from the streetcar stop and everything would happen very quickly. But we were still pretty nervous.

First, Eli was to take Lischka by surprise from behind and hold him. I was to pretend to be fussing with the engine of the Mercedes but was really to help Eli while David confronted Lischka face to face and threatened him; Serge was to appear at his side. Beate was to signal that Lischka was coming by taking off her fur hat.

There was continual traffic in the street. Men were waiting at the wheels of their cars for their wives and children to come out. I had left the engine of the Mercedes running. Suddenly Beate took off her hat. A tall man whom we immediately recognized turned the corner and walked toward the Mercedes.

To my surprise, Eli did not budge. Right away I sensed that the whole plot had failed. Lischka kept going on his way. He reached the streetcar stop and then turned around. David emerged from the shrubbery and came toward us. Eli yelled at him to stop. Serge was in a towering rage. It was a moment of total disappointment, and on top of everything else it began to rain.

We got back into the car and headed for the center of Cologne. No one said a word. We couldn't even look at one another. We were despondent that our commando operation had failed. We were also guilty about having let down Serge and Beate.

We parked the car in front of the cathedral and had a big breakfast in the hotel opposite the railway station. Serge tried to raise our spirits. He explained that even if the kidnapping attempt failed, the main thing was to focus public attention on Lischka, to make it known that a sword hung over the head of every Nazi criminal who had dealt ruthlessly with France. Even if we didn't actually bring Lischka back with us, but stirred up a lot of excitement over a serious attempt to kidnap him, that would be success enough, for it would show the world how completely free from retribution his life was.

There was nothing to do, we agreed, but to start all over again. We had not come all this distance to accomplish nothing. We had devoted two days to the expedition, and to go back empty-handed would be too bitter a disappointment.

Beate had observed that Lischka returned home on the 1:25 P.M. trolley. We decided to begin the operation again in the afternoon, hoping that Lischka had not noticed us that morning or had taken us for reporters too shy to approach him. Just the same, we were worried. Lischka might be suspicious and not go back home, or return armed, or with friends or policemen, and, for all we knew, might shoot us and be cleared for having acted in self-defense.

Back we went to the streetcar stop at 12:45, our minds made up to act this time without any thought of discretion or precaution. The car engine was roaring. We stood beside it, chatting like four policemen waiting to arrest a man. In fact, I think we even looked the part. People in the neighborhood were peeping through their window curtains at us, and children were running back and forth.

A streetcar would stop every ten minutes, and hordes of people would get off. We were getting more and more jittery. Would he come or wouldn't he? Suddenly Lischka appeared. He did not walk with the other passengers who got off the streetcar. We had made up our minds that, come what may, we had to do something. I ran up to Lischka, who had walked to within thirty yards of the car, and Serge got to him two seconds later. Each of us took him by an arm, and I shouted: "Come with us! Come with us!"

Mechanically he took two steps toward the car, then realized something was wrong. David and Eli got there by then. Eli snatched Lischka's hat off and hit him on the head with the blackjack, which seemed absurd to us, for he was over six feet tall and weighed about 220 pounds. Eli struck him because there was little chance of our dragging him to the Mercedes. He was discouragingly heavy. Lots of people appeared. Lischka's face was purple with terror as he cried: "Help! Help!"

He must have believed at that moment that we were avengers out to kill him. He stood solid as an elephant while Eli hit him so that there would be cause for legal complaint. But we knew Lischka's one desire was to avoid publicity and that he would certainly not lodge a complaint.

Lischka, more frightened than hurt, finally sank to the ground. By that time we were surrounded, and a German was waving a police badge in our faces. He must have taken us at first for some of his colleagues. Fortunately, he was not armed. We told him in French to go away. It never occurred to me that I had a revolver that at least could have frightened the crowd away. I began to be afraid we would not be able to get to the Mercedes because other cars were stopping and we had left the key in the ignition and no one in the car. All one of the bystanders had to do was to take out the key and we would be trapped.

Serge yelled: "Into the car!"

We ran at top speed, but Eli had kept Lischka's hat, and the little policeman was chasing us, shouting: "Give back the hat, please. The hat!"

Eli did not understand what he wanted. He turned around and the man pointed to the hat. What a relief! Eli gave him the hat and the policeman said: "Thank you."

It was a comic scene; but I was nervous because we had to get out of there as quickly as possible. Lischka was lying on the ground. Beate had her chance to start campaigning against Nazi criminals.

Three minutes later we were in the woods, where we shifted to the other car. We were to meet Beate at the entrance to the highway, but since we could hear police sirens, we did not wait for her. We threw the hypodermic needles and the chloroform capsules out on the roadside. I realized that we had taken the road to Cologne. We couldn't get back on the right road until we were almost to Aix-la-Chapelle. At the frontier no one asked us any questions.

There was to be a sequel to the Lischka operation. But first, let's take a look at his record.

THE LISCHKA RECORD

Paris. October 1940. Sprightly, youthful Dr. Helmuth Knochen felt slightly overwhelmed by his multiple duties. As head of the S.D.-Security Police, he tended to devote himself to political intelligence, his true calling. Furthermore, he was the single high police officer in Hitler's Europe who had not risen from the ranks of the Gestapo.

In Berlin, Reinhard Heydrich, the head of the Central Security Bureau of the Reich (RSHA), was worried that Paris was the weak link in the police chain he was forging in the conquered lands. He consulted Heinrich Müller, the head of the Gestapo, who shared his concern:

"I need someone besides Knochen in Paris—an extremely competent man to dedicate himself specifically to police operations and, above all, to take over the work of the Gestapo."

Müller checked over his best men and came up with the name of S.S.-Sturmbannführer Kurt Lischka.

"But isn't he in charge of the Cologne Gestapo?" Heydrich remembered a blond officer, over six feet tall, a perfect Aryan type.

"Yes. He's an excellent organizer insofar as police work is concerned, and he's on the city council as well as being one of our foremost experts on the Jewish problem. He had just turned thirty. He's a dynamic man."

Müller knew what he was talking about. In 1938, Lischka, at the age of twenty-nine, had directed, among other things, the Gestapo's Jewish Division. It was he who on June 16 ordered the first mass arrest of German Jews—two or three thousand, whom he sent to Buchenwald or Sachsenhausen, where ten percent died within two months. On October 28, 1938, he had supervised the terrible deportation of Jews to the Polish border—twenty thousand who had lived in Germany for generations arrested, piled into trains, left helpless at the frontier. The Poles would admit only Jews who had a valid Polish passport. Many of those who had to stay on the German side of the frontier perished, especially infants. It was this tragic event that induced Herschel Grynszpan, a young Jew whose parents were among the victims, to plan the murder of a Nazi diplomat in Paris. Ernst Achenbach and Ernst von Rath were both on duty. Fate chose Von Rath. The reprisals were terrible. As chief of the Gestapo's Bureau for Jewish Affairs, Lischka was definitely involved in the ruthless pogrom that took place in Germany on the night of November 9–10, 1938, now remembered as the "Week of the Broken Glass."

Lischka was a fastidious man. When his name came up in Nuremberg, someone recalled one of his conferences on the improvement of police interrogations. Lischka had said:

"You should interrogate a political prisoner in extremely polite language. If he does not confess, serve him a meal of salt herring without a drop of water. On the following morning resume the interrogation and give the prisoner a breakfast of salt herring. While you are questioning him, drink cup after cup of coffee. If he still will not talk, send him back to his cell without anything to drink and only salt herring to eat. These tactics are generally effective after a while."

Dr. Kurt Paul Werner Lischka was born in Breslau on August 16, 1909. He became No. 4,538,185 of the Nazi Party, and No. 195,590 in the S.S. He joined the Gestapo in Berlin in 1936. An extremely hard worker, he quickly rose to the top. In 1961 the Israelis asked Adolf Eichmann who had originated and directed Division IV-B-4 of RSHA Jewish Affairs, located at No. 8 Prinz-Albrecht-Strasse. His answer:

"Regierungsrat Kurt Lischka. He was then Theo Dannecker's immediate superior."

It was Dannecker, under Lischka's supervision as chief of the

Gestapo's Bureau of Jewish Affairs in France, who was later to supervise the Final Solution of the Jewish Problem in France.

A document of the S.D. Bureau for Jewish Affairs, dated May 25, 1939, says "Supervision of the Central Bureau for Jewish Emigration had been transferred to a Gestapo officer, Regierungsrat Kurt Lischka, who was entrusted with the direction of all matters concerning the Jewish population."

On November 1, 1940, Kurt Lischka took up his post in Paris. One of the Gestapo leaders in France, Wilhelm Höttl, has described the terms of Lischka's appointment:

Knochen never belonged to Division IV of the Gestapo, nor was he ever trained in any kind of police work. That flaw in his education quickly worked to Knochen's disadvantage with S.S.-Gruppenführer Müller, the head of Division IV in Berlin. Consequently, when Müller was unable to prevent Knochen's appointment as commander of the S.D. security force because Knochen had got such outstanding results from his intelligence work, he insisted that a permanent deputy be assigned to Knochen to make all decisions regarding police matters. This deputy would be in addition to the section chiefs who were also qualified to make such decisions. Insofar as I know, that bureaucratic structure was unique and existed in no other country. Knochen's deputy for the police section was Obersturmbannführer Lischka.

Another member of the S.S., Dr. August Stindt, has verified the nature of Lischka's job as Knochen's permanent deputy:

Dr. Knochen was the only man in the organization who had anything to do with my area of responsibility who had not come from the police force. For that reason he was assigned a special deputy to handle police matters.

Lischka divided his time between two offices: a private house at 72 avenue Foch, where he exercised his functions as head of the police force for France as a whole, and 11 rue des Saussaies, the former headquarters of the French National Criminal Investigation Department, from which Lischka ruled over the Paris area, including Melun and Versailles.

Serge and I began our work in the CDJC archives by identifying Lischka's signature and initials. The initials were important, because the index cards for several documents did not bear the name of the person who had signed them or even of the man who had written them, but did carry the writer's initials at the upper left-hand corner. To identify Lischka's initials, all we had to do was to look in the spot where he usually put them—the space generally marked "For your information" on documents addressed to him. We could thus assign to Lischka documents catalogued under "signature illegible" or attributed to Dannecker, his immediate subordinate in the handling of Jewish matters in Berlin and Paris, who had prepared the directives Lischka signed.

The Paris Gestapo was Lischka. The interrogations at the rue des Saussaies were Lischka. The great round-ups of Jews were Lischka.

The entire German police apparatus in France was in the hands of Kurt Lischka. To these already powerful positions he added the national directorship of the S.D.-Security Police's Division II, which was responsible for police and judicial matters. Among the duties of that extremely important division: the overall supervision of the French police, control of French legislation, personnel demands by the French police, concentration camp police, general measures of internment and detention, the writing and dissemination of ordinances on police matters, and, lastly, reprisal measures.

Lischka was responsible for the men who were shot at Romainville and at Mont-Valerien. More than once when S.S.-General Oberg decided on reprisals, it was Lischka's Gestapo that named the hostages who were to be executed. Lischka, therefore, had the last say on whether hostages were to be shot, on the choice of hostages, and on the execution itself.

At Nuremberg, on June 3, 1946, Knochen confirmed what these documents reveal: "It was my deputy's specific assignment to take charge of executions."

On September 23, 1942, Lischka ordered the following items:

50 coffins to be added to the present supply
150 handcuffs requested by the RSHA
thick curtains for vans taking persons to execution
2,000 liters of fuel oil for burning the corpses of the executed in the Père-Lachaise crematory
refreshments (whiskey, wine, snacks) for the execution squads, preferably to be served in their barracks

On January 13, 1943, he wired all KdR's:

To prevent similar attacks, investigate whether it is necessary to take into protective custody relatives from the age of eighteen up of active communists who have been interned or sentenced. The decision whether or not to take such measures rests with the commandos of the S.D.-Security Police. Such measures should not be published in the newspapers.

On January 1, 1941, Lischka was made Oberregierungsrat. His promotion to S.S.-Obersturmbannführer was to follow in April 1942.

As to torture, the rue des Saussaies Gestapo members testified that "when a prisoner seemed to know a great deal but would not say anything, an authorization for 'in depth' interrogation could be requested from the commander [Lischka] and was always forthcoming."

Starting on January 20, 1941, Lischka exercised a more direct role in dealing with the Jews. On that day a conference took place on the Final Solution of the Jewish Problem, attended by embassy officials, the military, and the S.D.-Security Police. The S.D. was represented by Lischka and Dannecker. Lischka took the floor at once. The minutes record:

S.S.-Sturmbannführer Lischka pointed out that, insofar as new measures for dealing with the Jews were concerned, the goal was to achieve the solution of the Jewish problem in Europe according to the directives the Reich had already issued. To this end, it was proposed that a Central Jewish Office be created in France, or in the occupied zone to begin with, that would be responsible for the following:
1. Handling all police matters relating to Jews (census, index cards, surveillance).
2. Economic control (elimination of Jews from economic life, assistance in transferring Jewish businesses to Aryans).
3. Propaganda (anti-Jewish propaganda among the French).
4. Establishment of an institute of anti-Jewish studies.
A special Jewish division, a precursor of the Central Jewish Office, has already been organized at Paris Police Headquarters. It is advisable to leave the direction of it to the French now, to avoid the French people's reaction against everything of this sort originated by Germans. Germans will restrict themselves to making suggestions.

In 1941, Lischka came within an inch of getting Knochen's job. Knochen had mounted an abortive raid on the synagogues on October 2, 1941, and the military demanded his recall. On November 8, 1941, however, the German military command in France informed Berlin by a secret cable that ". . . although S.S.-Brigade-führer Thomas told us when he left that Dr. Knochen would be transferred on November 14, 1941, and replaced by S.S.-Ober-sturmbannführer Lischka, Dr. Lischka himself, on November 6, 1941, informed us that the transfer would not be made and that Dr. Knochen would remain head of the department."

There are a number of documents that recall Lischka's anti-Semitic activities and the Jewish catastrophe, among which are the following:

February 16, 1942. To the military high command
Subject: Deportation to the East of Bolshevik Jews for forced labor
I have objections involving the police security concerning the liberation of Jews now in Compiègne. Jews designated as unfit for work cannot be set free for just that reason, and they should be transferred to Drancy along with the rest. My objections to the ordinance of the military command of January 22, 1942, providing for the liberation of Jews over fifty-five years of age, are based on the fact that these are for the most part retired Jews or intellectuals who, having spent two months in prison in Compiègne, will certainly generate anti-German propaganda. Besides, most of those Jews will go into the non-occupied zone immediately after their liberation.

February 26, 1942. A telegram to Eichmann in Berlin
SECRET
Subject: Transfer of Jews and young communists to the East
In order to strengthen German authority in the occupied zone, it is now urgent that the 1,000 Jews arrested on December 12, 1941, be transferred as soon as possible. In addition to the fact that the department concerned and the Paris Commander are being besieged by numerous interventions in favor of liberating those Jews, it is certain that the French interpret the delay in the transfer as a sign of weakness on the part of the Germans.

For this reason, I ask you to adopt a special proceeding in this particular case.

Please wire your decision.

Lischka so feared "German weakness" that he turned down, on April 2, 1942, an unusual request from the German Embassy to set free a Jew, Roger Gompel, a friend of a relative of a German diplomat. Lischka refused on the principle that there could be no exceptions made or "the French will think there are no German anti-Semites except the Führer himself."

March 17, 1942. A letter to the military commander, General Hans
  Speidel
Subject: Further deportation of Jews
In accordance with our suggestion, the RSHA has stated that it is
ready to receive 4,000 Jews from France at once, in addition to the
1,000 Jews from Compiègne. This number is about five percent of
the Jews. . . .
A large part of the Jews to be deported can be taken to the Drancy
camp, and the camps near Orléans, Pithiviers, and Beaune-la-Rolande.
It will thus be possible to proceed with replacing the Jews in those
camps and to undertake new round-ups of Jews in order to break open
the ranks of Parisian Jewry.

May 15, 1942. A telegram to Eichmann
Contact has been made with Lieutenant General Kohl, head of the
Department of Railway Transportation. Lieutenant General Kohl, who
hates Jews, has assured us that he will put as many cars and loco-
motives at our disposal as are needed to transport Jews. Consequently,
at least six trains are about to leave France soon. I make reference to
the various talks S.S.-Hauptsturmführer Dannecker has had with the
department concerned, and I would like to be informed if and when
a large quantity of Jews can be received and what camp is designated
to receive them.
Inasmuch as further round-ups of Jews will be necessary, and since
room for them is limited here, I would appreciate it if you would
immediately receive a preliminary shipment of 5,000 Jews.

On May 14, 1942, Lischka informed Eichmann of the "im-
minent introduction of a mark of identification for Jews."

After another discussion about the possibility of making exceptions,
all the departments involved reached an agreement. Consequently,
the eighth ordinance dealing with anti-Jewish measures will read as
follows:
Jews who have completed their sixth year of age are forbidden to
appear in public without a Jewish star.
The Jewish star is a six-pointed one, six inches square, with black
borders. It is made of yellow cloth and bears the word "Jew" in black
letters. It must be worn in plain sight on the left breast and be firmly
sewn to the garment.
Infractions of the ordinance in question will be punished by fine
and/or imprisonment. Police action, such as internment in a concentration camp for Jews, may be added to or substituted for those
penalties.

In his capacity as Commander of the S.D.-Security Police of the Paris district, Lischka gave the orders for the big Vel d'Hiv round-up on July 16–17. On July 18, he signed a report to the military authorities on the results of that extraordinary operation:

A total of 12,884 persons were arrested—3,031 men, 5,802 women, 4,051 children.

Six thousand single men and women, without children, must be shipped to Drancy immediately. Two weeks from now they will be transferred from there to trains containing 1,000 persons each for forced labor in the Reich. The remainder of the arrested Jews, especially women and children, will be kept in the Velodrome d'Hiver. That group will be transferred within a few days to the Jewish concentration camps in Pithiviers and Beaune-la-Rolande.

All those Jews were deported and slaughtered in Auschwitz.

On February 9, 1943, Lischka decreed: "All Jews in Rouen and Amiens must be arrested at once and shipped to the East."

On July 16, 1943, Lischka ordered another large-scale round-up:

To the Chief of Police, Paris

Concerning police procedures to be applied to Jews who have remained stateless now that the law has been published, I have ordered for the Department of Seine, for July 23 and 24, the following:

The operations should proceed in the following sequence:

1. Index cards for Jews of French nationality are, in due time, to be filed in the police headquarters of each ward according to the residence of the Jews.

2. Two thousand policemen are to be detached and divided in proportion to the number of Jews in each ward, and are to be put at the disposal of the police superintendents beginning at 4 A.M., on July 23 and 24.

3. The superintendents are to have the policemen bring to headquarters heads of families or single persons who are to show at once all papers concerning their nationality.

4. The superintendents will thereupon examine in the presence of each Jew in question his identity papers. Should there be no doubt that he was naturalized after August 10, 1927, he is to be put under arrest. Members of his family similarly subject to the law are also to be arrested.

5. Arrested Jews are to be taken to a depot in each ward, from which they are to be shipped to the concentration camp at Drancy as soon as possible.

6. In doubtful cases the police superintendents will request instructions from my office.

7. I request you to do whatever is necessary, and to report to me at 6 P.M. on July 23 the exact number of cases examined, the number of arrests, and separate lists of men, women, and children.

All these memorandums, which were prepared by Dannecker and later by Röthke, the executives of the Bureau for Jewish Affairs, were submitted to Lischka as well as to Knochen and Hagen. They kept in very close touch with the progress of the Final Solution in France, ready to intervene if any obstacle turned up. Lischka was meticulous in his direction of this operation. There are few memorandums or reports dealing with it that are not annotated or initialed with his purple pencil.

On March 23, 1943, Lischka, exasperated by the protective attitude of the Italians toward Jews in their occupation zone, wired Eichmann:

The Italian authorities in regions of France occupied by Italy have forbidden all measures against Jews, whatever their nationality. Consequently, the Italian authorities are protecting not only Jews of Italian nationality, but also French Jews and other foreign Jews. . . .

So long as the Italians maintain that attitude toward the Jewish problem, it cannot be resolved, or at best only incompletely resolved, in the newly occupied French territories. . . .

Consequently, it is absolutely necessary that the Italian military and civilian authorities in the new occupation zone be obliged to alter their stand on the Jewish problem immediately and fundamentally.

Like all other top police executives, Lischka was, of course, informed on the extermination of Jews in the East—perhaps better informed than anyone else, since he had been the top expert on the problem in the entire Reich from 1938 to 1939, and was to become, after his assignment to France, one of the top executives of the Gestapo in the Reich.

Lischka left France on October 23, 1943. When he returned to the RSHA in Berlin, he was promoted to department head in the Reich Gestapo, in charge of Department IV-B and its subdivisions, IV-B-1 and IV-B-2. He was a confidant of Heinrich Müller, whose place he filled when the head of the Reich Gestapo was away from Berlin.

In April 1949, the Czech authorities, who were holding Lischka, informed France that Lischka was in their hands. But, doubtless due to negligence, no request for extradition was made. On August 22, 1950, therefore, they set Lischka free. He announced his intention of going to his wife's house, 13-A Bachstrasse, Dessau, East Germany. But he soon took up residence in Cologne, and, on September 18, 1950, he was convicted in absentia to life imprisonment by a Paris military tribunal. Then France asked Czechoslovakia for his extradition—but it was too late. Fortune smiled more on the executioner than on his countless victims.

10

HARASSING
THE BUNDESTAG

The attempted kidnapping of Lischka took place on March 22, 1971, but it was before my trip to Czechoslovakia that I had become interested in bringing to justice the German war criminals who had abused France. The Brandt government was to sign a new legal convention with France that would place a time limit on the impunity of those criminals.

In January 1971, S.S.-General Hans Lammerding had died. He was the most notorious of the Germans who had been convicted in absentia in France and gone unpunished. Lammerding was responsible for innumerable massacres of civilians in the Soviet Union, and he had used the same tactics in France in June 1944. His division—"Das Reich"—left behind it two names that the French equate with Nazi barbarism: Oradour-sur-Glane and Tulle. Lammerding was made chief of staff to S.S.-Reichsführer Heinrich Himmler, who functioned not only as Minister of the Interior but also as commander in chief of the territorial army. After 1945, Lammerding was to benefit from an unusual situation that also benefited a great majority of the German torturers and assassins who had operated in France. I was enraged that Lammerding had succeeded in staying out of the reach of justice, and so I tried to learn what had prevented and was still preventing the trials of Nazi

160

criminals that all Frenchmen so rightly demanded. My research led to the following:

When the Wehrmacht withdrew from French territory, the German police officers, who would have been the principal defendants in a French trial, withdrew along with the German troops. These included the leaders of the S.D.-Security Police.

The S.D.-Security Police had been modeled on its superior department, the RSHA, which Reinhard Heydrich created and directed until 1942. In Occupied France the S.D.-Security Police included, as did the RSHA, a Department IV, the Gestapo, whose function was the suppression of terrorists and Jews. The Gestapo's sinister reputation spread so rapidly that the French incorrectly applied the name to the entire S.D.-Security Police.

The very few German criminals who were apprehended were tried by a French military tribunal, but others wisely kept out of the French Occupation Zone in Germany, frequently living under a false name. Many had been policemen or intelligence agents before 1939; after 1945 they were protected by their former colleagues who remained in or returned to the postwar German police force.

The new government intelligence bureau in West Germany, the Bundesnachrichtendienst, which, due to the cold war, was concerned with fighting communism, recruited—with the blessing of the United States—as many experts in anti-subversive activities as it could. These experts were by and large former members of the Gestapo and the S.D. That explains why the Gestapo members not only had no need to hide, but also had no trouble getting their jobs back.

Those who went underground in the Soviet Zone flocked into the American Zone where, after 1948, they could as a general rule expect impunity and a job quite in their line. For example, Franz Six, an S.S.-general who had been sentenced to twenty years at hard labor at Nuremberg for massacres of Jews and civilians in the USSR, was soon released from prison. Reinhard Gehlen, the "gray general," whom the Americans installed as chief of West German intelligence, had not forgotten that Franz Six had been one of the S.D.-Security Police chiefs in Russia; he made him one of his principal deputies.

There is a tendency to believe that men like Six were not capable of re-employment after the war because they were too old. They were thought to be old because they had held such high positions; everyone forgot that Nazism banked on the energy of its young people. Franz Six did not reach forty until 1949. Helmut Knochen, his disciple and later his protégé in the S.D. and the RSHA, was only thirty-one years old when Heydrich made him head of the S.D.-Security Police in Occupied France.

Knochen was brought back to Paris in 1947 and tried, along with General Karl Oberg, the top man in the S.S. and the German police force in France. In view of the heinous crimes of which they were accused, the only possible sentence was death. The sooner the trial took place, the more likely the sentence would be carried out.

But Six had become a powerful person again, and he remained loyal to Knochen.

At that time the United States had considerable influence in France, and so Knochen and Oberg were not tried until 1954. They smiled when they heard the death sentence pronounced, confident that it was merely a formality. It was, in fact, commuted to life imprisonment. And in 1962, at the time of the reconciliation between Adenauer and de Gaulle, the Chancellor, among other things, had a chance to oblige the powerful Six. The two S.S. chiefs were pardoned and returned to Germany.

Knochen and Oberg were exceptions; the vast majority of German war criminals were not even arrested. When the Federal Republic became practically independent in 1954, the problem of punishing these criminals became acute. A number of them had been convicted in absentia by a French military tribunal. Preliminary investigations that had been suspended in France were now speeded up so that once the Paris Agreements were signed, there would be no more cases to investigate.

From September 1944 to October 1954, a total of 1,026 Germans were convicted in absentia for war crimes. The French authorities then rightly feared that if the German courts acquired jurisdiction over these war criminals, the courts would prove very lenient. Due to the influence of the numerous Nazi judges still on the bench, a criminal who had been sentenced to death could benefit in Germany from having his case dismissed or from receiving just a token punishment. That is why, in Article 3 of the October 29, 1954, Agreement, France denied German courts access to its non-classified files on German war criminals. Those who had been tried in France, therefore, could not be tried again in the Federal Republic. Once the Agreement was signed, the criminals, of whom Lammerding was the worst, quietly went back home under their real names, were unobtrusively reinstalled in their stratum of German society, and very frequently got excellent jobs.

France was aroused and demanded that the German government extradite those criminals. The Federal Republic replied: "As an occupation power you approved the basic code that serves as our Constitution. Article 16 states that the Federal Republic will not extradite its citizens, a principle that is common to most states."

So it was impossible to bring the criminals back to France except through extradition under international law, but the German government stood firm on that point.

Then France, which had sinned through negligence, demanded that the Germans try the war criminals, an apparent violation of the aforesaid Article 3 of the October 29, 1954, Agreement. Hence there was no prosecution in Germany, and no extradition to France. The 1,026 war criminals who had been tried in absentia were safe.

The French government then tried to extricate itself from this legal tangle. It was motivated first by its own desires, and then by constant pressure from the National Assembly, whose communist members and former Resistance fighters regularly demanded progress reports on the negotiations. In spite of French appeals, the Germans refused to interpret the Agreement as giving them jurisdiction over the criminals.

The French finally discovered a loophole in a decision of the German Supreme Court on February 14, 1966, that provided for a possible special accord between the French government and the German government for the abolition of all impediments to the exercise of justice. Grudgingly the Bonn government finally agreed that the German courts did have jurisdiction over the criminals. All sorts of obstacles greatly delayed the signing of this supplementary agreement. Neither Adenauer nor Erhard nor Kiesinger really wanted to settle the matter until the passage of time had placed the criminals beyond human judgment, as the majority of Germans wished.

The end of the story is that Willy Brandt made the unpopular decision to acknowledge the legitimate claims of the French. During his official visit to Paris in January 1971, I met him at the German Embassy on avenue Franklin Roosevelt, when he held the customary press conference after the conclusion of the Franco-German talks. I raised my hand:

"Herr Chancellor, when will there be an end to the impunity enjoyed by German criminals sentenced by France?"

"Soon, Madame. In a few days the two governments will sign a new agreement that will put an end to the present situation."

The press conference ended. Brandt came over to me. His words went straight to my heart:

"Your courage is refreshing. We talked about you today. We were surprised that you are continuing your activities because we thought they might have stopped with Kiesinger's defeat. Your criticism of both East and West is a good thing."

In fifteen months Brandt had done a great deal of good, especially in the field of foreign relations, in which his personal influence was clearly to be discerned. He had got the Federal Republic out of its rut. In so short a time he had become a great German statesman of European stature. On February 2, 1971, the agreement we had talked about was signed in Bonn.

The ageement was signed, but there was still a problem: it had to be ratified by the Bundestag. Most of the members did not approve of it. There was the danger that it would be watered down if pressure was not put on them. And even if the agreement was ratified, that would be only the beginning. It would then be necessary to conduct an investigation of all those who had been sentenced in France who were still alive. But the German investigators, who are also prosecutors, would conduct their inquiry on the basis of whether or not a particular criminal could be prosecuted under German law. This means they would decide whether he acted out of base personal motives or because he was obeying Nazi doctrine—in racist crimes, for example.

Adalbert Rückerl, the general director of the Central Bureau for the Investigation of German War Criminals in Ludwigsburg, estimates that only 312 of the 1,026 who were sentenced come under the provisions of German law. These are likely to be prosecuted eventually, but the problem is to find out how the investigation will end. The files on the convictions in absentia are very meager, which is quite understandable. Rückerl gives the following example: When the chief of the Saint-Quentin Gestapo was tried in 1947, the Gestapo's crimes were so evident that there was no need to prove his personal involvement. He was given a very severe sentence as a formality, on the condition that the military tribunal would reopen the case when the criminal was caught. But he never was caught, and so his file was never added to.

If he were to be brought to trial in Germany, the German magistrate would ask the French court for the file. Whereas in France a man who had been the head of a criminal organization would have to prove his innocence, in Germany the courts would simply examine the file for evidence of his personal participation. If they found none, the case would be closed for lack of grounds for prosecution.

If there were evidence based on the testimony of Germans interrogated during their imprisonment in France, the German court would call them as witnesses. Rückerl believes that 99 percent of the time—and that's being optimistic—they would retract their testimony because they would be in their own country. Furthermore, they themselves played a part in those crimes, and as witnesses for the prosecution they would be obliged to testify in open court. Germans, they would have to publicly accuse other Germans. If there were French witnesses, they too would have to be interrogated. But many of the witnesses, both French and German, have died since the end of the war. So even if the inquiry did result in a trial, cases in which the evidence was based solely on human testimony would end in an acquittal.

Because the French examining magistrates cannot be expected to resume their inquests—and they can officially transmit to their German counterparts only the file that contains the sentence by default —and because new accusations can only be transmitted "for information," only the worst bureaucratic criminals who signed plenty of directives of a criminal nature can be tried with any chance of receiving a verdict consistent with justice. If they can be tried for the deportation of Jews from France, as they never have been, their trial will have a great impact on history and on justice. It will provide for an understanding of a police system that produced the deportation and death of over a hundred thousand French Jews and will clearly establish who was responsible for it.

The sentencing of those at the top who were responsible for the Nazi crimes committed in France would prevent the rehabilitation in Germany of the thousand criminals who so brutally repressed French resistance. Among them are almost all of the gang that sent so many French Jews to their death. Every investigation that ends with a "no grounds for prosecution," and every trial that ends with acquittal, would naturally cause public opinion in Germany to accuse the French courts of having wrongly sentenced "German patriots." That would be all the more likely as German society does not consider them criminals, because they have been living quietly since 1945. The rehabilitation of these criminals can only disgrace Germany. It is one step more in the direction of an indulgent attitude toward Nazism in Europe as a whole that would distort all spiritual and moral values. There is no reconciliation possible with a totalitarian world. It would result only in an acceptance of Nazi values. German society must be forced into self-examination, however painful that may be.

I told all of this to Yaron London, the Israeli television correspondent in France, when he interviewed me shortly after my return from Prague. He asked:

"Who are the most responsible for Nazi crimes in France who are still unpunished?"

"The two most important are Kurt Lischka and Herbert Hagen."

"Where are they?"

"Living quietly in Germany."

"Where?"

"Lischka, the top police official in France, lives in Cologne. When I was studying his record I found that he had been chief of the Cologne Gestapo from January to November 1940. I thought that if he were still alive he might well have chosen to live in a city where his former employees and associates had found jobs on the police force and in the local government. I asked German telephone information whether there was a Kurt Lischka listed in the Cologne directory. A few minutes later I got the answer: 'Yes, there is a Kurt Lischka. His number is 631–725. His address is 554 Bergisch-Gladbacher Strasse.' "

"So it was as easy as that!"

"Yes. It's only in detective stories that Nazis live a hunted life, quivering in far-off Patagonia every time a door squeaks. Aside from the Eichmann case, which was undertaken and executed by official branches of the Israeli government, there has never been any extralegal action taken against Nazi criminals. Israel acted with a legality that everyone had to acknowledge. In spite of that, there was a flood of protests against the illegality of seizing Eichmann."

"Still, what can private initiative accomplish?"

"The activities of Wiesenthal, Langbein, and anti-fascist organizations in the Federal Republic are leading to trials of the criminals. But don't think these are commandos and Nazi-hunters. They work with records, not with undercover manhunts. They never transgress the law. The most effective Nazi-hunters are the East Germans, who have a great interest in uncovering Nazis, especially if they hold high positions in the Federal Republic. Whatever reasons you may wish to give for East Germany's activities in this respect, the truth is that the East Germans have done an extraordinary and systematic job. They have filed in their famous 'Brown Book' thousands of entries on important Nazis, and on occasion they have circulated numerous individual files.

"West German courts have also collected a great deal of information, but frequently they do not use it. In the case of the criminals who harassed France, the results are in: for twenty-five years they have been living in peace. No one has bothered Lammerding either at work or at play, yet his address is well known.

"Serge has said to me: 'Think of the feeling of power a man like Lischka must have. He caused so many Jews to be killed that he is mentioned in scientific works on genocide. He was sentenced in France, yet he keeps his name in the Cologne telephone book. But who is really interested in the executioners? No one except those who curse them at ceremonies commemorating the Holocaust but do not make the slightest effort to disturb the peace of those S.S. chiefs. I think the Jews have suffered so much at the hand of those S.S. officers that they delude themselves that vengeance has been wrought. Since the Eichmann trial they either believe or want to believe that these criminals have been discreetly eliminated one by one, whereas they are right under their noses and don't even take the trouble to conceal themselves. There must be a reaction against all this—from you, since you are a German, and from me, since I am a Jew.'"

"What do you plan to do?" London asked.

"We would like to focus attention on Lischka and Hagen. That's the first step. We have already prepared a two-page article about them for *Combat*."

"But why don't you make a film about them? We would broadcast it in Israel on the 'Panorama' program."

I was delighted, and I accepted London's suggestion at once. On February 15, Serge wrote the script for the broadcast, which was to last fifteen minutes if we succeeded in filming Lischka and Hagen. On February 19, *Combat* published my article, and on February 21, we went to work in Cologne.

Our cameraman was a freelancer whom we hired without having met him. We learned on the telephone that he was an Israeli named Harry Dreyfus.

At 8 A.M. Sunday, February 21, we parked our car in a small unpaved parking area opposite Lischka's house so that we could watch his windows. He lived on the top floor of a four-story apartment house in Holweide, a suburb of Cologne. We intended to wait until he came out to film him. It was a gloomy, rainy day, and there was no one on the streets. We waited until 2 P.M. with no success whatever. Lischka did not even stick his nose outdoors. We went to lunch. From the restaurant I telephoned Lischka's house to see if there was anyone at home. When his wife answered, I hung up.

We then decided to ring his doorbell, but changed our minds. If he looked out the window and saw a cameraman, he wouldn't answer. So we pushed the doorbells of all the other apartments. A few people came downstairs, and we told them we wanted to see Lischka. They opened the entrance door and told us where he lived.

Lischka must have gathered what was up, for his door was opened. His wife appeared, a still-young-looking woman with well-coifed blonde hair and an icy manner. I told her that we had come to interview her husband for a French television program. She hesitated a moment, then showed us into a small room, probably the dining room, left us there, opened another door, and called: "Kurt, come see what these people want."

Her husband appeared. He almost had to duck to get into the room, he was so tall. I explained that Herr Klarsfeld was a French journalist who had a cameraman with him and wanted an interview. I introduced myself as his interpreter. Lischka prudently asked to see the press card Serge had got in Berlin for *Combat*, and then he asked my name. I told him it was Künzel—my maiden name.

Lischka rose and stood beside his wife. He seemed enormous. Sparse blond hair revealed a baby-pink scalp. He spoke in short, toneless sentences. When I mentioned the name "Klarsfeld," I looked at him closely, but he gave no reaction. Then I translated word for word what Serge said:

"I have come here somewhat as a representative of French public opinion. Since the signing of the Franco-German treaty, I have made a study of Nazi criminals sentenced in absentia in France.

You head the list. But before we start a campaign against you, we want to know whether you have anything to say in your defense."

Lischka replied: "I do not have to account to you. If I eventually have to account for my actions to a German court, I will do so, but only to a German court. I have nothing to say to you, or to a French court."

Serge persisted: "Do you admit to having been chief deputy of the French S.D.-Security Police, chief of the Paris security police, one of the leaders of anti-Jewish persecution in France, and chief of the Jewish Division of the Gestapo in the Reich in 1939?"

Lischka's only reply was icy silence. His expression was stern and hostile. He refused to be filmed, and since he might have broken the camera, we did not insist. In my behalf Serge asked him:

"Would it interest you to see orders that you yourself signed? Perhaps you thought they had been destroyed along with most of the German archives, but they were preserved at the Library of Contemporary Jewish Documents in Paris, and your signature appears at the bottom of them. When the Bundestag ratifies the pending treaty, you will be brought before a tribunal, tried, and, I hope, convicted."

Lischka showed some interest in the documents. I held out to him photocopies of some that were quite compromising.

He took the pages. His wife read them over his shoulder. We distinctly saw Lischka's hand shake. I had given him a sizable stack of papers, and he carefully read one after the other and seemed to be truly stunned. Doubtless he was seeing his past rise up before him—a past that we had been the only ones to reconstruct from our countless hours in the archives.

We left Cologne for Warstein to film Herbert Hagen. But two days later we were back. We arrived in Harry Dreyfus's Mercedes, and parked the car about a hundred yards away from the house. It was 7 A.M., and we were early. It was very cold, and for half an hour we had to keep stamping our feet to keep them warm. At 7:50— later than usual, for it was the day after Carnival—Lischka came out. We were leaning against the fence near the streetcar stop.

Lischka was wearing an overcoat and his coat, hat, glasses, and black briefcase all made him look exactly like a member of the Gestapo. The people waiting for the streetcar kept staring at us because we had a movie camera.

Lischka got closer to the stop and saw the people staring at us.

He turned in another direction and crossed the street so as to put about ten yards between him and us. We ran toward him. Lischka certainly must have been afraid to be photographed in the presence of people who would ask him why on the streetcar. Perhaps he thought we would really harm him. At any rate, he turned down a street perpendicular to the streetcar line, quickening his pace but still keeping his dignity. Then his long legs moved faster, and we had to film him from a distance of several yards. At this moment there occurred the sort of thing one sees in movies. Lischka stopped, then began to zigzag. We kept up with him, the camera turning all the while. He was fleeing just as he had made so many of his victims do.

I felt I was watching a pogrom in which he was the persecuted Jew. Lischka, the once supreme persecutor, was fleeing in his own city and down his own streets; he had suddenly been confronted with his past.

We had filmed a remarkable sequence that was to stir up great excitement when it was shown in Israel.

11

FACE TO FACE WITH HERBERT HAGEN

We were also determined to film Herbert Hagen.

On Sunday evening, after our first interview with Lischka, I telephoned Hagen's house in Warstein and asked his wife whether he would consent to an interview with a French journalist. After a few minutes she came back to the telephone and said: "There's no chance of an interview. Furthermore, my husband does not understand why you want to interview him."

I cut the conversation short, for I knew that people have to leave their house once in a while, and that Monday, February 22, would be Carnival day in Germany's Sauerland.

We left Cologne at 6 A.M. the next day and reached Warstein, 125 miles to the northeast, about 8:30. We went directly to Wilhelmstrasse. It was hard to find a spot from which we could keep watch, but we finally parked a hundred yards from Hagen's house, pointed the car toward it, and settled down to wait. We had driven past the house and noticed that only two families lived in it.

We waited for five hours and were beginning to lose hope when the Carnival music began to blare. I was very hungry and went to a restaurant. Meanwhile Serge and Harry saw a man in a tweed jacket come out of the house and hurry to a spot about two hundred yards away, where a crowd had gathered to watch the parade. Thinking it was Hagen, they ran after him. The cameraman mingled with the crowd and pretended to be filming the parade. But when he got closer, he found he had been following the wrong man.

Disappointed, we all got back into the car and drove toward Hagen's house. Just at that moment the door opened, and out stepped a man wearing glasses and a hat and coat. He came down the short flight of steps and quickly walked to the adjoining garage. There he got into a large Opel. I recognized him at once, although I had never seen Hagen. I had imagined him as a youthful-looking man because his style in the documents we had examined was lively and bespoke a quickness of mind that would not have diminished with age. In the same way I had not been surprised when I saw Lischka, for he too corresponded to the man of his memorandums —exact, meticulous, and cold.

I jumped in front of the car just as it was coming out of the garage and called: "Herr Hagen, is that you?"

He raised his head, nodded, and then saw the cameraman filming him. He stopped the car, opened the door, and ran toward the cameraman and Serge with his arm raised as if to strike them. Then he stopped and got himself under control, probably realizing that if he damaged the camera we would make a complaint to the police and his name would get into the newspapers.

Like Lischka, all he wanted was to live in complete privacy. I went up to him and, pointing to Serge, said: "This gentleman is a French journalist who would like to ask you a few questions."

He made the connection with the telephone call of the night before and got back into his car. I was still standing in front of it. He was waiting for his wife. In better French than mine, he said to Serge indignantly: "Sir, you have no right to film me here in front of my house."

Serge replied: "M. Hagen, there are Germans who have been sentenced to a life of hard labor in France for having done less than take pictures in the street."

"But, sir, I am not in hiding. I have gone back to France more than twenty times since the war."

"It's too bad the French police didn't notice your name. You should have been arrested. All I want is to ask you a few questions and find out whether you recall having had the following jobs:

chief of the Bordeaux Security Police, General Oberg's right-hand man, head of the Security Service's Bureau for Jewish Affairs?"

Hagen took the same tack as Lischka: "Sir, I have nothing to say to you. If you want, you can get in touch with my son. He's a journalist in Cologne."

He had a tight smile on his face, as can be seen in a close-up on our remarkable film sequence. He seemed in control of himself as he kept looking at the steering wheel and taking in what Serge was saying to him, his grim smile pasted on his face. Then he said: "All I want is to live quietly."

Just then Hagen's wife came out of the house. There ensued a kind of ballet, for she started to get into the car, then went back into the house, came out again with her two daughters, a fourteen- and a seventeen-year-old, and one of their girlfriends. Instead of getting into the car, she went off on foot with the three girls. Hagen followed, after bidding Serge a glacial good-by.

The tone of the conversation had been one of confrontation.

That evening in Cologne we recalled what he had said about his son. I called Warstein again.

Frau Hagen answered: "We know who you are, Frau Klarsfeld. Telephone my son and he will tell you what you want to know. He is a radical like you."

And she gave me her son's telephone number.

The first time I telephoned Jens Hagen, the line was busy. His mother was doubtless warning him that I would call. When we met an hour later, I asked him how his mother had known my name. The explanation was simple. Serge had told Hagen he worked for *Combat*; Hagen had called his son and asked him to verify that; Jens Hagen had telephoned some German correspondents in Paris and had happened to find one who had read the *Combat* piece about his father, signed Beate Klarsfeld. So he had been able to tell his father the identity of the woman he had encountered.

We had been a little worried, wondering whether Jens Hagen was going to descend on us with some friends ready for a fight. When he rang the bell, we looked out the window and saw that he was alone.

Jens was about twenty-seven or twenty-eight, tall, thin, long-haired, long-bearded, and informally dressed. He wrote for leftist magazines like *Konkret*, and for DVZ, the weekly that had just fired me. He also wrote theater skits, and hung around with a bunch of young people from good schools.

For Serge's benefit we spoke in English. Jens said: "I understand you took movies of my father. I would certainly like to know what you can say about him. I myself don't know very much, because there are some things he has never told me."

I then took out our file on Hagen and told him the positions his father had held. "Look," I said, "these are his words. These are papers he wrote and signed under the Nazi regime."

Jens began to read. He didn't say a word as he turned the pages. His shoulders were hunched; he seemed completely overwhelmed. You could see by looking at him that his father had not told him the truth. Suddenly he said to us:

"My father was an idealist. He was misled, but he committed no crimes. He did not kill anyone. My father was such an anti-militarist that when he was transferred from France to Yugoslavia, where he was a commanding officer—S.S.-Sturmbannführer—he did not even carry a gun when he led an attack on the Partisans."

Serge replied: "I interpret that exactly the opposite. Your father was such a militarist that he did not carry a gun so that he could show how brave he was and thus get his men to follow him. Without a gun he was far more effective than he would have been with one."

Jens returned to his study of the papers. It would have been impossible to deny the evidence. At one time he even wiped away a few tears, which were not due to eyestrain. That record was pitiless.

THE HAGEN RECORD

Herbert Hagen was born on September 30, 1913. When he was twenty-three years old, in 1936, that brilliant pupil of Professor Franz Six joined the S.D., the S.S. Security Service, created and directed by the masterful hand of Reinhard Heydrich.

Six was then head of the S.D.'s Department II-1, which was concerned with ideological matters and expressly directed against Jews, Freemasons, and the Church. He suggested to young Hagen (S.S. No. 124,273, Party No. 4,583,139) that he assume the direction of Section II-112, the purpose of which was to suppress the Jews. Hagen agreed. His journalistic skills also helped Six, who was director of the Institute for the Study of Foreign Cultures. That Institute was supported by the S.D., and its journal published many articles signed by Six but drafted by Hagen. Works such as "World Jewry: Its Organization, Its Power, Its Policies" and "The Freemasons," published by the Nazi Party under the pseudonym of Dieter Schwartz, were written by Six in collaboration with Hagen. Hagen's predecessors in his post of command against the Jews, von Mildenstein and Schröder, had recruited a nucleus of fanatical Jew-haters. Hagen's subordinates included Dieter Wisliceny, the future liquidator of Hungarian and Czech Jews; Theodor Dannecker, future liquidator of French, Bulgarian, and Italian Jews; and Adolf Eichmann, the future chief executive for the Final Solution of the Jewish Problem.

Hagen followed Six's teachings, and succeeded in bureaucratizing the ideological nature of anti-Semitic operations. It is, therefore, not surprising that the S.D. men were later found to have been more efficient enemies of the Jewish people than the Gestapo, which did not see the problem on the same global scale.

During his trial in Jerusalem, Eichmann was to describe Hagen as follows: "Hagen was a sensible man, broadminded, sophisticated. He could easily grasp the essence of a problem and reduce it to a summary or an article. He was a personal friend of Six, who made Hagen his editor."

As an editor, Hagen was undeniably gifted. Every week he would edit the long reports of II-112 activities and make them remarkably clear and yet detailed. He perfected innumerable memorandums on all aspects of the Jewish problem in Germany and abroad.

I am practically the only person to have consulted those memorandums because of a rather unusual chain of events. In the CDJC in Paris there was a carton full of Hagen's personal records, which had been forgotten since the liberation of Paris and located only after the Eichmann trial. I got research fever again. I checked with Hessel, the librarian: no historian had ever asked to read those pages, on which was written a large part of the preparations for genocide. Hagen was a master spy on the world of Jewry, which he had reduced to index cards. He was a master indoctrinator of anti-Jewish racism. He was the top S.D. lecturer on the Nazi attitude toward Jews to help people and organizations better to fulfill their duties according to Hitler's desires.

For example, during the first half of 1938, Section II-112 conducted twenty-three seminars. Eichmann spoke once on "The Goals and Methods of Solving the Jewish Problem"; Dannecker,

four times on "Legal Aspects of the State of German Jewry";
Hagen, eighteen times on "The Structure of World Jewry" and
on "Practical Methods for Dealing with the Jewish Problem."

Whom was he addressing? One special course, on May 4, 1938,
some months before the Munich agreements, was given for the
benefit of Conrad Heinlein, the Sudeten Führer; another, at the
Peoples Court, for the police and Nazi Party press corps and militants; another, at the War College, for S.S. non-commissioned
officers; another, at the Border Police School, for Nazi Party inspectors; another, at the Security Police School, for Nazi Party
representatives abroad and law students.

Eighteen seminars in six months! And that went on for years.
That is how the internal mechanism of the government and the
Nazi Party were infected. Hagen applied all his judicial and police
talents to a task that seemed impossible to accomplish between
1935 and 1940, but that was achieved between 1940 and 1945 because of the groundwork done by a handful of men, of whom Hagen
was one of the leaders.

Eichmann and Hagen got along wonderfully well. "Dear Adolf"
wrote to his "Dear Herbert," signing himself "Ady." The letters
they exchanged were handwritten and often intimate. On May 2,
1938, Eichmann wrote to Hagen:

> The first issue of *Zionistische Rundschau* [a Jewish newspaper]
> will appear on Friday. I had the copy sent to me and am now in the
> boring process of censoring it. Of course, all of you will get the paper.
> To a certain extent it will be "my paper." I made those gentlemen
> trot, believe me. They are now working very hard indeed.
>
> I expect to become head of the division. . . . Things in Vienna
> are going well toward that end. You know how I truly dislike having
> to leave work that I have enjoyed so much ever since I started, but
> you can also well understand that I don't want to "lag behind" at the
> age of only thirty-two. Our boss [Six] is an excellent one and com-
> pletely understands.

Hagen to Eichmann, June 28, 1938:

> As you requested, I have read very carefully issue 25 of *Stürmer*
> [Julius Streicher's extremely anti-Semitic newspaper] dated June 1938,
> in which Hiemer has written two whole pages without saying anything
> important about his visit to Vienna. Allow me to say that in spite of
> your indisputable eloquence, you have failed to endow *Stürmer* with
> your usual objectivity and give it a new style.

Hiemer, as always, keeps harping on the stench in Jewish offices that he can endure only by keeping a handkerchief over his nose. Consequently, he is far from supplying "objective information." When, for example, he mentions the stench of streets where Jewish offices— the "Israelische Kulturgemeinde" and the "Zionistische Landesverband"—are located, well, that's the city's fault, not the Jews'.

I mention this simply to call to your attention that we have been seriously hampered in our efforts to bring about any change. The most unbelievable statement in his article, it seems to me, is that many Jews in Vienna are returning to Judaism—"a religion that takes the teachings of the Talmud, which advocates crimes against non-Jews, as ultimate authority."

When I hear things like that, I have to hold my head!

You yourself apparently did not notice that Hiemer says the head of the Zionistische Landesverband has "fiery eyes" and that, again according to Hiemer, he said: "Beware. If we get into power we will celebrate a new Purim during which we will sacrifice not 75,000 non-Jews, but 75,000,000. Take heed! Our revenge will be terrible."

The intimacy between Hagen and Eichmann dates from the journey they took to Palestine to broaden their acquaintance with the Jewish world and observe what effect the possible creation of a Jewish state might have on the Reich. Eichmann was to say several times in 1961: "Hagen was my boss. I was Hagen's subordinate."

On September 26, 1937, they left via Poland and Rumania, took the *Rumania* from Constanta, and landed in Haifa on October 3. The next day they went to Cairo to meet their local agents. The watchful British expelled them from Egypt on October 9, and they took the *Palestina* back to Europe via Brindisi.

The trip was the result of clandestine contacts between the S.D. and an agent of Haganah, the army of the Jewish colonists in Palestine, which doubtless wanted to see German immigrants come to that territory. Haganah was slyly feeling out Heydrich's S.S. The meeting between Feivel Polkes, a Jew from Tel Aviv, and Eichmann and Hagen must have been a strange one. The only result of their short visit to the Middle East was their conclusion that the Reich should unalterably oppose the Palestinian Jews. The anti-Jewish persecutions of 1938 put an end to the contacts.

The voluminous report on this trip, dated November 27, 1937, was written principally by Hagen. It gives some interesting indications of his anti-Semitic mentality:

The ways Jews have of distrusting one another is apparently not the determining factor in Palestine's economic chaos. . . . The Jews' complete inability to manage their country's economy is demonstrated by the existence in Jerusalem alone of some forty banks that thrive by swindling their own people.

Another illustration of that mentality is Hagen's refusal, on February 9, 1938, to entrust the Jews of the Fulda-Werra area to S.S. Officer Heinrich: "His youth and his lack of toughness render him unfit to tackle Frankfurt's 20,000 Jews."

By means of carefully thought-out plans, Section II-112, inspired by Hagen and Eichmann, who frequently made tours through Central Europe, made a worldwide study of Jewish organizations and set up a network of spies in Paris, New York, Cairo, Jerusalem, Prague, and Bucharest. Section II-112 also compiled a remarkable set of records and methods that were to be used by the Reich throughout conquered Europe and would allow it to take over various Jewish communities by methods that were so efficient that historians of the Holocaust are still astonished at them.

In October 1938, Hagen went to Vienna and Prague, where he advised the leaders of Czech anti-Semitism that the time was opportune for them to create a general antipathy toward Jews. In May 1939, after the occupation, he went back to Prague. On June 30, he advised: "Show the influence Jews have on politics, culture, and the Czech economy. In that way government leaders who are tolerant of such influence can be spotted—a good chance for getting rid of Czech nationals still in political power. Demonstrate that a converted Jew is still the same as ever."

Section II-112 also saw to it that anti-Jewish measures in Germany were strictly enforced.

Hagen was an expert on France, and spoke French extremely well. In November 1938, Hagen expressed his satisfaction with the way his department had cooperated with the chief of the corresponding department of the Gestapo, Section II-B-4, which Kurt Lischka directed, in the anti-Jewish developments of that month—including the Week of the Broken Glass.

During the early days of the war, Himmler reassigned the directors of his RSHA, which was both a government and an S.S. department. Hagen thereafter directed Section VI-2, devoted to "Judaism and anti-Semitism."

In June 1940, S.S.-Standartenführer Helmut Knochen arrived in

Paris as head of a special commando squad of twenty men, the nucleus of the S.D.-Security Police in France. During his cross-examination at Nuremberg, Knochen said: "Heydrich himself gave me that assignment. With me were S.S.-Hauptsturmführers Hagen and Dietl."

Knochen was soon to give his right-hand man Hagen the important task of setting up the S.D.-Security Police on the Atlantic Coast. Hagen was made commander of the Bordeaux S.D.-Security Police on August 1, and took up temporary quarters on the King of Belgium's yacht, which had been abandoned at the wharf after the debacle of June 1940. On January 8, 1941, the Gironde chief of police wrote François Xavier-Vallat, General Commissioner for Jewish Affairs in Paris:

I have the honor of bringing to your attention the wishes of Commander Hagen, the regional director of the security police, which he expressed during the conference he recently granted the head of the Jewish bureau.

Commander Hagen made known his intention of interning during the present month of January many Jews from countries now occupied by Germany. He did not think the camp in my district, which is at Mérignac-Beaudésert, could be used for his purposes because:

1. Escape from it is easy.
2. It is located in a coastal region.
3. It is necessary to separate Jews from other internees.

Commander Hagen intends to fit out a camp in the Département of Vienne. The necessary funds for doing this are to be furnished by Jews of the region, and an ordinance will very likely be issued for their collection.

Hagen did not even spare children, who were condemned to deportation, as the Grand Rabbi of Bordeaux testified:

In June 1941, the Gestapo, which had sown panic throughout many districts of our city, brought several Jewish families of foreign origin but with French children to Mérignac in the middle of the night. The Gestapo was assisted by Vichy police and the Département police. Headquarters informed me the following day that the Gestapo had decided to place all the children in my care, for only their parents were to be deported. We went right to work and, thanks to the generosity of the people of Gironde, we quickly found good homes for the children. One month later I was again called to headquarters to be told that only those children with close relatives in Gironde could stay there, and that all others were to be deported at once. Fifty percent of those poor little creatures left for destinations unknown, and we have never had any information whatever about them or their parents since then.

On December 8, 1941, Hagen decreed:

In reference to the coastal ordinances, all Jews, no matter what their age, are to be interned. It would be best for the French police to see to the execution of this directive, for that will avoid bringing in German police prematurely and turning the people against them.

On January 13, 1942, Hagen's former deputy, Theodor Dannecker, who had meantime become head of the Gestapo's Bureau for Jewish Affairs in France, wrote a memorandum to S.S.-Sturmbannführer Kurt Lischka:

S.S.-Sturmbannführer Hagen informed me on January 12, 1942, that the internment in concentration camps of Jews from Basses-Pyrénées and Landes was necessary both for military reasons and for expanding anti-Jewish measures.

On January 14, S.S.-Obersturmbannführer Kurt Lischka notified the military command of his decision:

The internment in concentration camps of Jews from Basses-Pyrénées and Landes appears necessary. Apart from reasons of security, there are also military reasons for this action.

German, Austrian, Czech, and Polish Jews must be sent to these camps. There are about three hundred Jewish men who fit this category in the two Départements. I recommend having the French police arrest these Jews, as the Commander of the Bordeaux S.D.-Security Police has advised, and ship them to the Drancy camp. I will appreciate your attending to this matter quickly, and notifying me as soon as it is done.

Hagen extended his zone of activity to Brittany, and arrayed the forces of the S.D.-Security Police in the principal cities of that peninsula in order to prevent or suppress any attempt at opposition from the French and also to arrange for systematic arrests of Jews. He increased his reports and recommendations to Knochen on the Jewish problem. For example, on March 4, 1942, he wrote: "The wearing of a badge will necessarily make Jews stand out, and will prevent any black market in the tight food situation."

On May 5, 1942, Heydrich installed General Kurt Oberg in Paris as the top executive of the S.S. and the German police force in France. Oberg took over all police powers, and acquired as right-hand man an *éminence grise:* Herbert Hagen, who was to be his personal deputy.

This was a dazzling promotion for Hagen, who was not yet thirty. He was also still in charge of Division VI of the S.D.-Security Police, which was devoted to gathering intelligence on foreign countries, the French government, and the French political parties. Along with Section IV it was the best-organized branch of the Gestapo. It had twelve subdivisions. From then on, Hagen was to pull the strings of French politics, and influence upon them was gradually to pass from the military command and the German Embassy to the S.S.

Pétain's ambassador to the German occupation authorities in Paris, Count Fernand de Brinon (who was shot after the Liberation), was well aware of who possessed the power in the splendid, high-windowed house at 57 boulevard Lannes:

General Oberg was a fat Prussian with a shaven head who knew nothing about France or French ways of thought, could not speak our language, was not very intelligent, and was completely dominated by a young S.S. officer, Major Hagen. Hagen had the advantage of speaking French well, but the dreadful disadvantage of hating us and of nursing his resentment of us. He employed spies, and appeared to be General Oberg's chief of staff.

The Gestapo's Bureau for Jewish Affairs, on avenue Foch, was quite near boulevard Lannes. Hagen did not neglect his anti-Semitic activities. He attended all the summit conferences between Germans and between the German and the French authorities, in order to get the program for deportation going and remove all obstacles to effecting the final Solution to the Jewish Problem in France. All documents concerning the measures that were taken about the Jewish problem in France passed through the hands of Hagen as well as of Lischka, Oberg, and Knochen.

Hagen was an example of the "bureaucratic assassin." He never dirtied his own hands or took any pleasure in watching tortures, but he fanatically devoted his keen mind to the service of evil by devising operational procedures. Hagen's memorandums, written in his sunny offices overlooking the Bois de Boulogne, mapped the road that ended for the Jews at the Auschwitz railway station.

Hagen was completely aware of the fate awaiting the Jews. He was kept informed down to the last detail on their arrests and transfers. For example, the following memorandum from S.S.-

Untersturmführer Ahnert, written on September 3, 1942, and directed to S.S.-Brigadeführer Oberg, through S.S.-Sturmbannführer Hagen, showed him:

1. Up to and including September 2, 1942, there have been evacuated:

From the occupied zone	18,069 Jews
From the non-occupied zone	9,000 Jews
Total	27,069 Jews

2. Schedule of evacuation for September and October 1942:
Three trains a week (total 25 trains) with 1,000 Jews in each. Hence, in September and October 1942, will be

evacuated	25,000 Jews
Evacuated up to September 2, 1942	27,069 Jews

Consequently, it is expected that the total by the end of October 1942 will be	52,069 Jews

Hagen kept up his close friendship with Eichmann, whom he saw in Paris in July 1942. His former deputy, Dannecker, was Eichmann's man in Paris. All the members of his former staff divided up enslaved Europe among themselves and turned it into a game preserve in which Jews were hunted from cover and chased into extermination camps.

Oberg was the recipient of memorandums—and he acknowledged receipt of them—such as the following, dated February 27, 1942:

We are trying to purge Ostland of Jews as completely as possible, and there have been executions everywhere, but of such a nature that they have not attracted much attention. The people believe, and so do Jews who are still there, that the Jews have simply been "transferred"!

A number of examples follow, such as:

A purge of Jews is in progress in White Ruthenia. The number of Jews in the part presently under civil administration is about 139,000. Of these, 32,210 have been shot by an Einsatzgruppe of the S.D.-Security Police.

Everything addressed to Oberg passed through Hagen's hands, and so it is impossible to believe that Hagen could not have been involved in the Final Solution of the Jewish Problem that he had been preparing so fanatically for so many years.

On July 17, 1942, Hagen presided over a conference of French and German police officers on the subject of Jewish children arrested since the Vel d'Hiver round-up. In the end the children were deported.

Hagen also participated in numerous talks with French authorities about the Jewish problem. Following are some reports on them that he wrote and signed. The first, dated June 18, 1942, and the most innocuous, exempts "the wife of de Brinon, the wife of the philosopher Bergson, the wife of the writer Jouvenel, and the wife of the writer Caulette" [Hagen apparently thought Colette— "Caulette"—was a man] from wearing the yellow star.

June 26–29. Talks between Oberg, Knochen, Hagen, and Dannecker with Secretary General of the Police Bousquet and his deputies: 22,000 Jews from the occupied zone will be delivered to Dannecker, who will receive Jews from the southern zone whom the French have deemed undesirable.

July 4, 1942. German side: Knochen, Hagen, Schmidt; French side: Bousquet, Darquier de Pellepoix, Wilhelm. Vichy agrees that starting July 13 stateless Jews will be deported from the two zones.

July 4, 1942. Talk between Knochen, Hagen, and Bousquet. Vichy will set up a special police force to deal with Jews, communists, and Freemasons. Its headquarters will have its own budget. Insofar as the arrest of Jews in the occupied zone is concerned, Laval would prefer that the Germans handle it. French police, however, will arrest foreign Jews.

August 1, 1942. Talk between Knochen, Hagen, and Bousquet. Hagen notes: Bousquet assures that the first 3,000 Jews from the southern zone will be handed over to the Germans before August 10. Pétain and Laval would agree to the Germans' demand for the denaturalization of Jews who became French citizens after 1933.

August 3, 1942. Talk between Laval and Bousquet, and Knochen and Hagen. Laval agrees to the principle of depriving Jews of citizenship.

September 2, 1942. Hagen is present at the talk between Laval and Oberg. He notes that Laval will do his best, but cannot promise to deliver Jews "like goods in a Woolworth's." The two parties agree that in the future it will be announced that deported Jews have been sent to forced labor in Poland.

September 20, 1942. Memorandum from Hagen on his talk the previous evening with Bousquet. The authority of the General Commissioner for the Jewish Problem will be increased. Seven thousand Jews have already been arrested in the non-occupied zone, and will soon be turned over to the Germans.

November 19, 1942. Memorandum from Hagen on his talk the previous evening with Bousquet. Once again he called to Bousquet's attention the necessity of settling the Jewish problem once and for all, especially now that the Americans have landed in North Africa.

December 16, 1942. Memorandum from Hagen to Oberg and Knochen: under the title of "Night and Fog" arrange for the arrest of French intellectuals.

January 9, 1943. Memorandum from Hagen to Knochen that Bousquet is running into difficulties in effecting anti-Jewish measures owing to Italian interference.

February 4, 1943. Memorandum from Hagen: The Italians do not want Jews residing in their zone to be treated like French Jews. Achenbach, of the German Embassy, has been informed.

January 23, 1943. Hagen and Oberg direct the destruction of Marseille's Vieux-Port.

March 25, 1943. Bousquet's deputy, Leguay, explains to Hagen Vichy's new reluctance to deport Jews. Hagen comments: "When I complained that such an attitude was surprising, since it had to do with Jews, Leguay explained that without wanting to express a pro-Jewish sentiment both Pétain and Laval, out of humanitarian considerations, could not take the responsibility for shipping Jews to Germany.

"I emphasized to him my personal opinion that this attitude seemed all the more surprising in that the Führer in all his speeches during the last few years—and especially in his speech on the day of commemoration of fallen heroes—had stressed a radical solution of the Jewish problem. I promised him at the end that I would advise S.S.-Brigadeführer Oberg of Laval's decision and inform him at once of the result.

"S.S.-Brigadeführer Oberg decided that shipments are to be made with the help of the German police alone. This decision was transmitted to Leguay as follows: S.S.-Brigadeführer Oberg expressed great surprise that the French government had still not abandoned its 'sentimental' point of view about the Jewish question in spite of the Führer's latest policy statement. He is therefore obliged to handle the shipments himself."

April 12, 1943. Memorandum from Hagen on his talk with Bousquet about the project for denaturalizing French Jews.

June 12, 1943. A conference was held at Hagen's house, at which were present Sturmbannführer Laube, Hauptsturmführer Brunner, and Röthke.

"The following plans were worked out for round-ups: Paris is the hardest place to make arrests because there are still 70,000 Jews there. . . . The Drancy camp for Jews can easily accommodate all the Jews arrested. . . . Jews are to be interned throughout France no later than June 24 and 25, and are to be deported to the East no later than July 15, 1943."

June 16, 1943. Oberg meets with Himmler. As a result, Hagen instructs the anti-Jewish department to deprive Jews of citizenship as quickly as possible, and deport them before July 15, 1943.

June 18, 1943. Knochen and Hagen meet with Menetrel, Pétain's doctor and confidant. Hagen reports that Menetrel said: "You will, of course, understand that in view of his age, the Marshal prefers a humanitarian solution to a radical one. Hence, he does not want to deprive Jews of their livelihood for fear they will starve." Hagen reports: "We explained to Menetrel that experience has always shown that if Jews are permitted to work they will soon drastically hamper economic life and worm themselves into important positions."

August 7, 1943. Knochen and Hagen went once more to Laval's headquarters to speed up anti-Jewish operations. Hagen noted: "In the course of our August 7 meeting Laval told Knochen that he had not signed the denaturalization law. He understood that Jews deprived of citizenship thereby would be deported into Germany, and he had no wish to hunt them down. Knochen protested, saying that since the start of the operation that had been what was intended."

August 18, 1943. Hagen conferred with Lieutenant Malfatti, the Italian liaison officer with the German High Command in France: "I told him that the difference in attitude of the Germans and the Italians was having a very bad effect on the solution of the Jewish problem in France. I asked him to do his best to see that the German point of view, with which the Italian government had agreed up until now, be strictly enforced by the Italians."

August 23, 1943. Various memorandums from Hagen about talks with de Brinon concerning the denaturalization of Jews.

August 28, 1943. De Brinon sends a memorandum to Hagen: "This morning the Marshal himself took up the question of the denaturalization of foreign-born Jews. He ordered the Ministre de la Justice to speed it up. . . . During the week the Marshal will issue one or more reports on the early results. De Brinon will be advised at once, and will then inform Knochen and Hagen."

December 4, 1943. Hagen wrote a telegram for Himmler that he initialed and Oberg signed: "Subsequent to my telegram of November 11, 1943, I wish to report that between November 24 and December 12, 1943, there have been arrested: 1) 1,413 Jews in the south of France, 905 of whom were of foreign nationality, and 524, stateless. 2) A shipment of 1,000 Jews will leave for the East on December 12, 1943. 3) our measures will continue in operation."

Hagen was one of the last criminals sentenced to life imprisonment in absentia: on March 18, 1955, in Paris, by the permanent tribunal of the armed forces.

After examining our data on his father, Jens Hagen recovered his composure. We could see what kind of person we had to deal with as soon as he began to dwell on his parents' personal life.

"My mother is ill," he said.

But we had seen his mother, and she seemed in excellent health.

"My father doesn't earn very much. We live quite simply."

But we had seen his house, which was perfectly adequate, and his car, which was the latest model. Herbert Hagen was the business manager of a big company that manufactured electrical appliances.

Jens had an unpleasant way of dwelling on the Hagens' personal life instead of keeping things on a general level: "Take it easy on my father. Don't start a campaign against him. I have young sisters. . . ."

We could see that he was collecting his thoughts. He very quickly jumped from the subject of other people's sufferings to the problems that his family could have. He emphasized: "My father has changed. He has changed, I tell you. He is not the same man he was then."

I answered: "We are willing to admit that your father may have changed. Everyone can change. But we need proof of his change, and he can easily supply it. The best way would be for your father to give himself up, come to France, and ask to be tried. If he does he will contribute a great deal to history, for he was in at the beginning of the persecution of the Jews. He trained Eichmann, Dannecker, and most of Eichmann's staff. Your father, in fact, effected German policy in Occupied France from 1942 to 1944.

He knows a great deal, and he has great ability as a journalist. That's why we think his appearance before a French court would accomplish a great deal.

"On the moral plane, we believe that if a man leaves his family to surrender to the law and to be tried in another country, then he has truly changed. He can help present-day society understand how he became the Herbert Hagen he was in 1940. We would then defend the case of the Herbert Hagen of 1971 who, under the circumstances, would probably only be sentenced as a formality. It's the Hagen of 1940 who would be sentenced, not the Hagen of 1971, whose actions would prove that he now opposes the S.S. of the old days. On the other hand, if he does not come to France, it is because he has not changed."

Jens replied that he would convey my proposal to his father. Our intensity and our logic seemed to make him agree with our argument. But when he left, Serge and I smiled. We would never get an answer; we were not naive enough to think we would. But as we were sticklers for the law, we had to try everything before going into battle in earnest.

It was interesting to speculate on how a journalist who considered himself a man of the left, the son of one of the worst Nazi criminals, could pass judgment on his father's generation. We had seen how his family loyalty had overshadowed everything else.

He had completely endorsed our campaign against Kiesinger because Kiesinger had continued his career in politics. But, according to him, his father had been out of politics for a long time. Franz Six had come to his house in 1951 to persuade him to return to intelligence work, but Hagen had turned him down.

Six weeks later, after I had been arrested, the newspapers printed a statement from Jens Hagen: "I do not understand B.K. . . . . I told her several times that my father was not a bureaucratic assassin, but that woman is a complete fanatic."

Jens also told us that he had seen pictures of Eichmann and Hagen in Haifa and Cairo in 1937 in his father's photograph album, and that his father was still so interested in the Jewish problem that he had gone to Israel as a tourist a few years before to take another look at the country.

That piece of information struck us as significant, and it confirmed our theory that it is absurd for both Jews and non-Jews to believe that Nazi criminals have been tracked down relentlessly from one end of the world to the other. That's not the way it is. Lischka and Hagen have their names listed in the telephone directory. A man like Hagen can freely go to France more than twenty times to do business. And he can even be a tourist in Israel, although he was one of the most ruthless persecutors of the Jews.

12

JAIL IN COLOGNE

After the abortive kidnapping of Lischka on March 22, I had to get the ball rolling on the Lischka affair because the German police were certainly going to try to hush it up.

So the next morning I telephoned a Cologne newspaper, the *Kölner Stadtanzeiger*, told them I was Frau Schmidt who lived on Bergisch-Gladbacher Strasse, and that I had seen an attempted kidnapping the previous day: "Some young people hit a man with a blackjack. I am amazed. The police came and still there is nothing about it in the papers this morning."

A reporter replied: "Yes, there is. There's a small item at the bottom of page two: 'Four unknown persons attacked a businessman early yesterday afternoon and fled.'"

I realized that I had not been mistaken. There must have been a police report. Lischka surely would have been taken to a hospital for treatment. Plainclothesmen had been there. There were witnesses. And the Cologne police certainly knew Lischka well—they knew him all the better as he was Gestapo chief in Cologne in 1939 and 1940.

I called another newspaper, the *Kölner Rundschau:*

"Hello. My name is Schmidt, and I live at 559 Bergisch-Gladbacher Strasse. Yesterday I witnessed an incident on Maria-Himmelfahrt-Strasse. I can't find anything about it in your paper.

189

All the *Kölner Stadtanzeiger* says is that a businessman was attacked by four unknowns. You shouldn't be so casual about things like that. The muggers were foreigners, and their victim—I know because I live nearby—was formerly chief of the German police in France."

"Very interesting," the reporter said with some enthusiasm. "We did not know about it, but we'll check with the police. If what you say proves true, we'll send you an honorarium. Give me your name and address again."

I telephoned still another newspaper, the *Express*, and told the same story. Then Serge telephoned all the papers and the German press service in Cologne, saying he was a French journalist and that the rumor was going around Paris that the former Paris S.D.-Security Police chief had narrowly missed being kidnapped and that his paper wanted details.

So reporters began besieging the Cologne police, insisting that the French press knew about the incident. When Serge called the *Express* again around 1 P.M., they told him the police had decided to hold a press conference on the matter that afternoon.

Late in the afternoon I called again, this time using my real name. The reporters had talked among themselves, and now they jokingly called me Frau Schmidt. The trick was working. The police had told them that the Mercedes they had recovered had been rented by a native of Bucharest who had come from France. Obviously they meant Serge, but the police did not want to release his name for fear that it would be connected with mine, and that the press would make a big thing out of the affair. The police thought we would keep quiet to avoid trouble. They did not yet realize that our goal, regardless of the risk of being hailed into court, was to bring to the Germans' attention the impunity Lischka and his colleagues were enjoying. I then gave the reporters specific details about the kidnapping and about Lischka. The next day and thereafter there were big headlines in the German papers: "B.K. Tries to Return Former S.S. Chief Lischka to Paris."

The second part of our scheme was to put Hagen into the limelight as much as Lischka and to press for the ratification of the Franco-German treaty.

Forty-eight hours later, while the newspapers were still full of the Lischka affair, I got the Associated Press to release a statement saying that there were still several hundred criminals like Lischka at liberty, and that if the Bundestag did not ratify the treaty, we would take the same measures against the other criminals, whose names and addresses we knew. Our next victim would be Herbert Hagen of Warstein, and we gave details on his Nazi past. Soon his picture was in the German papers along with his curriculum vitae. Thus, the two top men on our list, on whom we had prepared full reports, were brought out of the shadows. Hagen immediately appealed to the police.

If I had merely shown my data around editorial offices, I certainly would not have obtained such results.

During the following days the German press reacted quite strongly to the threat hanging over the head of a considerable number of German citizens. Everyone knew the police could not provide protection for hundreds of people. The entire problem, which up until then had remained in the shadows owing to the impunity those butchers had enjoyed, was now at last exposed in such articles as "Private War Against More than Three Hundred War Criminals," "B.K.: We'll Take Care of the Rest," and "Who's Afraid of B.K.?"

Siegfried Mahran wrote in *Westdeutsche Allgemeine Zeitung*:

The methods of this active little woman, who not only slapped Kiesinger but has staged protests against Stalinism and anti-Semitism in Warsaw and Prague, have at last focused attention on unsettled matters. S.S.-General Lammerding, who was responsible for Oradour, is dead, but he was not the only one to profit from the Allies' mistake.

Wolf Scheller wrote in *Vorwärts*, the Social Democrats' organ:

Since March 22 several middle-aged, well-employed gentlemen have not been able to sleep well in the Federal Republic. They have shut themselves up in their apartments, and won't answer the telephone, or they have whoever does answer it say they are away. They are not at home to anyone.

Some comments were very critical: "We would rather live in a country without law than in one where people take the law into their own hands," or "Whatever Dr. Lischka did, B.K. has no right to abduct a German from Germany to bring pressure to bear on the Bundestag to ratify a treaty."

Rainer Schmitz came to my defense in NRZ:

B.K. says, "I am a completely average citizen, just like other women," but many do not believe her. The Cologne public prosecutor told this mother of a six-year-old boy: "You'd be better off taking care of your child," and, "Why don't you stay in your kitchen?" But B.K. does not want to limit her world to a kitchen and a child. She believes her dedication to Germany's past is only right, and she has taken the consequences. "I will not retreat," she says. That is how she differs from other women. She has staked her whole middle-class security on what she is doing. Her actions have made her name famous and provoked fierce arguments. Such dedication seems as natural to the Klarsfeld family as cooking or bringing up children. That's how they differ from other families.

I resumed my relations with the Cologne reporters, who got in touch with Dr. Bellinghausen, the examining magistrate. I learned then that for the time being no warrant was out for Serge's or my arrest. But *Der Spiegel* had just published quite a long article on the subject.

To intensify the pressure, we decided to send all our data on Lischka and Hagen to the German courts. I asked Ralph Feigelson, a French Resistance fighter who had been sent to Auschwitz, to take the papers to the examining magistrate in Cologne dressed in his concentration-camp uniform with all his decorations pinned to his chest. Ralph's fine physique and impressive beard made him very photogenic. He would be a good subject for the German reporters, and I was counting on this more than on their interest in the data. By photographing him they would give the impression all over Germany that the Resistance and Deportees associations in France were behind me.

Ralph Feigelson was to go to the Press Building in Cologne, and from there reporters who had been alerted by me were to accompany him to the Cologne court. But on the afternoon of March 31, a few hours before he left, I telephoned Cologne and learned that when the reporters had questioned Bellinghausen about why there was no warrant out for my arrest, he had said: "I am under no obligation to believe what I read in the papers."

At that moment I realized that the German courts, which were being hesitant about issuing a warrant because they did not want the scandal to spread, could be caught in a trap. If I were to go in person to Bellinghausen, my provocation could get things moving. There would be a test of strength. If he let me go free, he would prove that the impunity war criminals like Lischka and Hagen enjoy in the Federal Republic is such an outrage that they cannot move against people who take action against them, even when that action is against the law. If he sent me to jail, he would render the whole situation extremely critical. Then not only would the war criminals continue enjoying their impunity, but their accuser, a militant anti-Nazi, would have been imprisoned instead of them.

Serge promised that he would go to any lengths to get me out of jail if I should be arrested, but I was not very optimistic about seeing Paris again in the near future. I chose not to think about that. Ralph and I took the usual night train to Germany and arrived in Cologne at 6:15 A.M. It was April 1, and so when I telephoned the German Press Service to tell them I was there, they thought it was an April Fool's joke.

A little before 11 A.M., a procession consisting of Ralph, me, and several reporters went from the Press Building to the courthouse in Appellhofplaz, a short distance away. There some other reporters, some still photographers, and some motion-picture cameramen were waiting for us. Ralph posed for them in his concentration-camp uniform, which was half covered with decorations. The uniform, however, was now so tight that a reporter had to tear it both front and back so that Ralph could button it. We climbed up to Bellinghausen's office, where we found another fifteen reporters. I introduced myself.

"I know," Bellinghausen said. "Just about five minutes ago I heard you were in Cologne."

"Dr. Bellinghausen," I said, "the first thing I wanted to do was to come here with M. Feigelson to bring you these files. Aside from that I want to assure you that what has appeared in the newspapers is absolutely accurate. I am responsible for the attack on Lischka."

"I have a warrant for your arrest in my desk," the magistrate said. "You are now under arrest."

He allowed me to invite the reporters into his small office, and about forty rushed in. I made a short statement:

"The German police have failed in their efforts to keep this matter quiet and to hush up my campaign against S.S.-Obersturmbannführer Lischka. Our data contain, among other things, documents that prove his cooperation with Hagen and Achenbach in anti-Jewish activities. Hagen has retained Achenbach as his lawyer. Achenbach is now a member of the Bundestag for the liberal FDP party and, of course, has no wish to have his collaboration

with the Gestapo revealed. That explains the obstacles ratification
of the treaty has encountered even in the inner circles of the coalition government."

When Ralph Feigelson got back to Paris, he told the story as
follows:

"Prosecutor Joseph Bellinghausen and his assistant received us
courteously. They seemed pale and embarrassed, but not surprised.
After Beate explained the basic papers in her collection, I demanded the immediate arrest of Lischka. The magistrate, who
said he was too young to know such things, declared himself in-
competent. Beate translated simultaneously, for only having
learned German in Auschwitz I do not understand it well, and I
speak it even less well. So when he mentioned a warrant, for half a
minute I thought he meant for Lischka, but he really meant for
Beate.

"Out of the mass of proof we had brought he wanted to keep
only that which dealt with war crimes. Beate calmly translated my
angry protest. 'They' were very 'proper' as they carried her off before my very eyes. I use that term instead of 'arrest' because it was
not justice but reprisal. Before they took her away, we held a press
conference in Bellinghausen's office at which I said that her arrest
while Lischka was still at liberty was an intolerable provocation
on the part of those who were protesting Nazis, for if that man
who had murdered thousands of Resistance members and Jews
had been in prison, no one would have tried to kidnap him."

I was taken to Ossendorf Prison, a short distance from the center of town, where eight hundred women and several thousand
men were confined. My ground-floor cell looked out on a pretty
courtyard with a lawn and flowerbeds. I had a private cell, rather
like a standard motel room—it was 12′ by 6′ and contained a cot
without a mattress, a wardrobe, a washstand, a toilet, a concrete-
barred window, a table, and a chair. I was allowed to write, to
read three books a week but no newspapers, and to listen to the
radio from 6:30 A.M. to 10 P.M. (A guard was specially detailed to
select radio programs, and would tune in those requested by the
inmates and play records of his own choice.) Everything was proper,
clean—we could take two showers a week—and endurable, except
for the loss of freedom. I thought the food better presented than
it was in Prague but just as unpalatable. I could take two thirty-
minute walks a day. My fellow inmates were almost all common

criminals, except for one female spy who had been in the employ of the Democratic Republic and who took her walks alone. Most of the women were prostitutes. They were even allowed to wear transparent blouses and tight pants. There was a lot of talk during our walks, which allowed them to keep in shape. Plenty of advice on techniques and prices was exchanged.

They also asked me for legal advice. Generally speaking, they were all very nice to me and knew very well who I was. I had slapped the fellow at the top. I had not been afraid to attack the S.S. and, to top it off, I had been in jail before.

The thing that bothered me most was that there was no handle on the cell door. I kept wondering how I would get out if there were a fire. In spite of everything, I felt cut off from the world.

During my first days I had no contact with anyone from the outside except my lawyer, Klaus Himmelreich, a young CDU member whom I had chosen by chance when I was arrested. Horst Mahler, my usual lawyer, could not recommend anyone to me because he himself had been in Berlin's Moabit Prison for six months.

The first time my lawyer visited me, I felt there was little communication between us, for he wanted to submit a colorless brief. He specialized in automobile accident cases, and although he was very dapper and pleasant, he took a dim view of my case. He changed his attitude after he met with Serge—in Belgium, because there was also a warrant out for Serge's arrest. Himmelreich once got a death threat over the telephone with a shouted: "How dare you defend that Klarsfeld woman!"

I had no contact with Serge and really felt a little lost, for I had never been away from Paris for any length of time without telephoning him once a day. Now suddenly here I was, cut off from the rest of the world without any idea of what was going on or if anyone was trying to get me out. I could consider the whole thing a rest cure, and indeed I did relax after so many weeks of tension. But I was afraid I might have to stay in jail for a long time, and I was worried about Arno, whom I had left in Paris with chicken pox.

One or two days after my arrest, I was summoned into court for examination. Facing me sat Bellinghausen and his assistant, Wissborn. Bellinghausen was forty-five years old, short, and very well dressed; Wissborn, who was perhaps thirty-five, was sloppily dressed in a jacket and pants that were much too small for him. Wissborn's chief responsibility was pornography, and he was in charge of reading all the pornographic magazines when they came out. Whenever he looked at me, I always had the impression that he was wondering which magazine he had seen my picture in.

My examination was conducted in a relaxed atmosphere. They brought me coffee and sandwiches, and the prosecutor even made a few jokes. But each of us kept his eyes on the other. I had had experience with German prosecutors before. They try to relax you to make you talk. So they are very polite and try to make you feel you haven't done anything so serious—just to make you talk, to make you say things that usually could be learned only through harsher methods.

My aim was to get into the written record all the positions Lischka had held, but for them Lischka was the victim and they had no desire to take his Nazi past into consideration. They wanted to keep the whole business as coldly legal as possible and to dissociate Lischka's past from the man who had recently been attacked. It was hard for me to get that past down in black and white and to make them understand why I had done what I did. Whenever they mentioned Lischka to me, I always added: "You mean the head of the Gestapo's Bureau for Jewish Affairs." And I stopped talking if I saw that that was not being entered in the record. The next time I would say: "You mean the head of the secret service in France," and again, if that was not taken down, I would shut up. Then I would say "Deputy Chief of the Gestapo in the Reich," and if that position was not recorded I would fold my arms and say nothing further. And so on. By the time the examination was over, the transcript filled two big books and four appendixes—about ten or twelve pounds of paper.

During my sixteen days in jail, Himmelreich twice tried to get the warrant suspended so that I could be free until the trial, which had been set for July. The court turned him down both times.

De Somoskeoy, the president of the tribunal, had already imprudently expressed his own opinion: "The only explanation for behavior like that Klarsfeld woman's is feeble-mindedness." During the court session that ended with the rejection of Himmelreich's plea, de Somoskeoy stated that "Frau Klarsfeld should be examined by a psychiatrist." I protested loudly: "A society that rehabilitates murderers like Lischka is what should be psychoanalyzed."

Before turning down my plea, the president changed his opinion slightly to: "A psychiatrist will be present during your trial and will make a report on his observations of you."

A reporter from the weekly *Die Zeit*, who was covering the hearing, drew the following ironic conclusion from that exchange: "If you don't agree with the president of a German tribunal, you must be crazy."

Neuberger, the Minister of Justice for North Rhine-Westphalia, was a Jew who had emigrated to Israel after the war but had subsequently chosen to make his career in Germany. Needless to say, Neuberger was the last person from whom I could expect anything.

While I was in jail, a biology professor and former S.S. officer, Bruno Berger, was tried in Frankfurt. He had selected eighty-six Jews from Auschwitz in 1943, whose skeletons seemed interesting enough to be added to the collection of Professor Hirt of the Reich University of Strasbourg. Then he saw to it that those eighty-six human beings, those eighty-six Jewish guinea pigs, were sent to Natzweiler, where they were put to death and their flesh boiled from their bones.

His sentence: three years.

My fellow citizens in both the West and the East continue to think that if a man does nothing reprehensible now, the faults of the past can be forgotten.

Meanwhile Serge had stirred up a lively campaign in my behalf. In spite of definite objections to the illegal attempt at kidnapping on the part of some members of the Resistance and Deportee associations, those organizations appealed to the German Embassy in Paris. Their efforts, which I had deliberately wanted to arouse, resulted in my being set free temporarily and the warrant suspended. But in order to save face, the tribunal demanded bail of 30,000 marks. (Bail for S.S. Ludwig Hahn, chief of the Warsaw S.D.-Security Police, had been set at 8,000 marks.)

When I was released, a guard about fifty years old came up to me and shook my hand: "I was worried that you would not be set free. You did well, very well indeed. I hope to see Lischka in your cell someday."

Serge later told me what had happened: "The French press reacted strongly to your imprisonment, and Jean Pierre-Bloch summoned the Resistance and Deportee association executives to his office on rue de Choiseul. It was an extraordinary meeting, for both

communist and non-communist organizations, which had not
gotten together for a long time, found themselves acting together.
At their third meeting they formed a Joint National Committee
for Locating and Punishing War Criminals. So, as a result of your
choosing to go to jail, an active body for prosecuting war criminals
has been created in France.

"Furthermore, I got in touch with some young people. The
Jewish Revolutionary Organization voted to occupy the German
Embassy on April 16, and about twenty young people went to the
embassy on avenue Franklin Roosevelt. As soon as they got inside,
they plastered the walls with stickers: 'Free B.K. Imprison Nazi
Criminals.' Then they shut the embassy gate and chained or hand-
cuffed themselves to it. Some continued to distribute leaflets reading: 'If Germany dares to bring B.K. to trial, then German justice
should be in the defendant's box, for B.K. has stood up for German
honor.'

"When the police got there they cut the chains and kept the
demonstrators in the police station for a few hours. But the whole
affair was a warning shot to the Germans, especially as it had been
filmed for Israeli television.

"The next day you were released on bail."

But that was not the whole story. Raissa had had a telephone
call from a man who said: "My name is Lichtenstein. I left Germany
when I was quite young because of the Nazi persecutions. Every
day I am wiring flowers to Beate in the Cologne jail." Then he
asked how things stood. My mother-in-law told him there was hope
that I would be let out on bail. He told her: "Don't worry. I'll take
care of that." He was not a rich man, but he thought it his duty to
furnish my bail. When Serge telephoned him that it had been set
at 30,000 marks, he immediately went to the Rothschild Bank and
deposited that amount. That's how I had gotten out.

My mother-in-law had come to see me in the Cologne jail and
had brought me an article by the philosopher Wladimir Jankele-
vitch that moved me deeply. Locked into a cell though I was, I
could see that I had moved one step closer to the Jewish people,
toward the most adamant Jews for whom there was no possibility
of forgetting or forgiving what the Germans had done. And now,
because of what I had done, there was "the first great opportunity
for forgiveness." That article was the greatest reward and the finest

justification for all I had done in the name of the German people.
It said:

So it is B.K. who is in prison, and it is Herr Doktor Lischka, S.S.-
Obersturmbannführer, who peacefully continues his business as usual.
B.K. is in prison, but Doctor of Philosophy Knochen, the head of the
Gestapo in France, no doubt continues to pursue his philosophical inquiries and to lead a secure middle-class life with no thought of the
hundreds of thousands of his victims whose bones are rotting in the
earth. For the moment, the pusillanimity of German justice has tri-
umphed over Chancellor Brandt's courage. The Cologne prosecutor is
using the apparent illegality of an act of protest as a cover-up for the
staggering guilt of a war criminal.

The anxiety of German neo-Nazis and their desire to gag B.K. is
understandable. B.K. alone is the conscience of that unconscious country. We can see how prosperity and the "economic miracle" have en-
trapped that country, its captains of industry, its tradespeople, its
tourists, and its soldiers in a deadly failure to realize what is going on.
Should we call it unconscious or good conscience? They think they
owe us nothing, no explanation, no accounting. They don't even understand what we want from them. That is why B.K. is doubly precious to us. . . .

She has fulfilled the promises the judges at Nuremberg made us but
did not keep: to pursue to the ends of the earth the perpetrators of
the greatest crime since time began. Her cause is our cause. Her exemplary perseverance in her battle, clearly stated and at the same time
dedicated, contains the power to rehabilitate German youth.

As a German, she has courageously accepted responsibility for the
terrible crimes that she did not commit. Without being personally
guilty, she has taken upon herself the blood-guilt of her people. Those
crimes, however, were not hers. They were the crimes of the foul, big-
bellied sixty-year-olds who now occupy seats of power in the German
government and in German industry. . . .

In spite of everything, B.K. has not concluded that those crimes do
not concern her. That is noble. . . . B.K. has preferred suffering and
danger. Thus she gives us hope, the chance of reconciliation, the first
great opportunity for pardon. Since she began her crusade, and since
Chancellor Brandt, instead of the guilty, has sought forgiveness from
the martyred, we place all our hope in this effort on the part of the
German elite. For the first time the message of assistance so long
awaited has been spoken. May the Cologne judges soon release this
first chance, this unique opportunity, for pardon.

The response from East Germany also comforted me in my cell.
I learned that Friedrich Kaul, the solicitor general of the Demo-

cratic Republic, had asked to help defend me. Kaul came to see me, and I decided to accept his offer. Lischka's Gestapo had massacred communist Resistance fighters too, and it was, therefore, fitting for me to have a communist lawyer on my side.

Kaul told me: "You can be sure that this trip was not easy. If Honnecker, the new leader of the East German Communist Party, had not ordered me in writing to undertake your defense, I would never have been able to get past the wall of high-level civil servants who are thoroughly opposed to you. I bring you Honnecker's greetings and respects."

I was proud of that acknowledgment, whether it came in spite of or because of Warsaw and Prague and my attacks on East German anti-Semites. It came from a man who had not spent two weeks in a tidy cell like mine, but ten years in Hitler's jails.

I told Kaul that Serge was taking steps to get me an Israeli lawyer who would represent Lischka's Jewish victims at my trial. There is great antagonism between the Democratic Republic and Israel, but Kaul was not offended. Perhaps he thought that Israel would not do anything about it.

At first the news of my arrest did not attract much attention in Israel. Serge had asked the Israeli Embassy in Paris for an Israeli lawyer to undertake my defense, but its answer was slow in coming. He had also telexed an open letter to the principal Israeli journalists. When that was published it elicited opinions much in my favor from Galey-Zahal, the army radio station, and columnists on the two big Israeli papers. *Davar's* Israel Noiman was the first to react in his "Open Letter to a Hardened Criminal—The Silence on the B.K. Case Is a Scandal."

Dear Beate and Serge:
For a long time now my conscience has demanded that I write you this open letter.

I was hoping that persons who are much more important than I would have preceded me with actions that would be much more impressive and useful than this letter. But, to my great surprise, I have waited in vain. That is why I am writing you now. Perhaps this letter will help rouse from their torpor people who should already have taken action by appeals and protests. Young Jews in France have awakened; that makes our silence here in Israel all the more baffling. That silence cannot continue. It is a vicious insult to the victims of the Holocaust. There are many survivors' organizations here, but none has taken the trouble to tell the public that Beate was arrested for revealing that some of the worst criminals are walking around with their heads held high, and sitting in deep, comfortable armchairs although they have been sentenced by the courts. Those organizations are doubtless so busy arranging ceremonies to commemorate the Holocaust that they can't find the time to attend to so unimportant a matter.

Bless you, Beate, for what you have done. You shall not sit alone on the defendant's bench. We will be with you in person or in thought. . . . The State of Israel's voice cannot be absent from the Cologne courtroom, for your trial is ours.

Boaz Evrom echoed Israel Noiman in *Yediot Aharonot:*

Until now I had not read anywhere that any Israeli lawyer, whether a survivor of the Holocaust or one of those who practices in Germany to sue for personal reparations, has come forward to undertake the defense of this woman. Our papers have reported the case with a singularly cold objectivity and lack of enthusiasm. They have written no editorials in support of her. They have not "aroused enlightened public opinion in this country or elsewhere" to her defense. They have not even tried to collect funds to cover the cost of her defense. It is well known that Germany is very sensitive to our attitude and our opinion in matters of this nature. But our silence has been total, as if the case were far in the past and of no concern to us.

Our relations with Germany are not based on diplomatic formalities alone. In matters of this sort we have a right to speak our mind about Germany's internal affairs, and the Germans will find it hard to dispute that contention. It is useless to bring pressure, to "insist"—an Israeli spokesman can show his understanding of this young woman's motives, and express the wish that attention be directed to the unusual nature of her offense, and at the same time discreetly call to mind the fact that men who sent millions of human beings to their death have emerged from German trials with only token penalties.

B.K., who knows all this and understands it as well as we do, will doubtless be astonished there in her jail cell that the Jewish people are so indifferent although they well know how to move heaven and earth when necessary. This article's intention is not only to set forth some of the facts but to avoid any misunderstandings. If you should ask why I think it necessary to tell the Jewish people these facts, my answer would be that B.K. has a privilege enjoyed by few Germans—the right to judge our acts according to moral standards, the right to ask us questions.

Well, Beate, it might be better for you to understand that we do not like some things you have done, and especially that you have rebelled against the established order, even when that order protects the murderers of our people. There is an air of the "new left" about all that, which is much more serious than the purely anti-Semitic reactionary opinions.

One more thing, Beate. After you slapped the Chancellor, you probably thought we would be pleased to know that a former Nazi had lost his job, and that he had been replaced by a longtime militant anti-Nazi, one of the few Germans of that age who can look any one of us straight in the eye without shame. Well, you are wrong. It would have been much easier for us to confer with Kiesinger than with Brandt. Precisely the fact that Kiesinger could not have looked us straight in the eye was one of his better qualities. During our talks with him we regarded him with exaggerated pity, and he squirmed, lowered his eyes, and very politely asked us what we wanted. And he gave it to us without any argument, for he comes of good stock and has good manners. Brandt, on the other hand, is the son of a servant.

It is always easier for us to confer with persons whose past is not beyond reproach. They are ready to pay us handsomely not to remind them of their past. But Brandt can look us in the eye and say: "Gentlemen, that won't do." We cannot remind him of episodes buried deep in his past, for they all do credit to him. That is why it is not contrary to our interest to have former Nazis in high government positions and as masters of industry. Quite the reverse. The more they rise in importance and influence, the more eager they are to have their past forgotten and the more our influence on them increases. We fear the day when a new generation will come into power—a generation that feels no guilt and has no fear of its past being mentioned. The higher that generation climbs, the more German policy will again take the path dictated by its own interests. You, Beate, are of that generation but we cannot fault you. You are perfect. You are magnificent.

This dialogue the Jews of Israel were having with me was really being directed toward the Germans. My acts had made of me a symbol that had meaning for the Jews.

In a telephone interview with Israel Wiener of the army radio station, we learned in May that the National Association of Israeli Lawyers had decided to assume the expense of a lawyer to defend me. Serge then went to Israel to give the Association all the facts of the case.

He needed money for a ticket, for we did not have a penny. My mother-in-law supported us as best she could, but our telephone bills were enormous because we called Germany so often. Serge went to see a director of the Council for the Interests of French Jews and told him: "I have come to you because I think it right for the Jewish community in France to pay my expenses, since

Lischka was the man who actually directed the Final Solution in France."

The director replied: "I agree with you in principle, but our budget won't permit it."

"Do you know," Serge said, "that we are now in a building that the head of the Gestapo's Bureau for Jewish Affairs used to visit frequently? I can assure you that he had a hard time finding trains to ship Jews out of France, but he got them just the same. Just remember that only a week before Paris was liberated, when the German soldiers were retreating in disorder, he succeeded in getting a train for the deportation of a thousand Jews, including hundreds of children."

The matter of the ticket was quickly settled.

In Israel, the Association had in mind an aged lawyer of German birth who could not be expected to mount an energetic attack on German justice. Serge gave several interviews on television and radio and kept insisting that an Israeli lawyer was not needed to defend Beate but to attack Lischka. Thereupon, Shmuel Tamir, a member of the Knesset and a former Irgun commander, volunteered and was appointed by the Association.

Back in 1953, while still quite young, Tamir had taken on the Kastner case. He had defended Michael Greenwald, an Austrian Jew who had written that Rudolf Kastner, the spokesman for the Israeli Ministry of Commerce and Industry, was actually a traitor to Israel for having been an accessory to the Final Solution in Hungary that disposed of a half million Hungarian Jews.

The whole thing seemed unlikely, for Kastner was regarded as a hero for bravely refusing the demands of Eichmann, who had placed him at the head of the Hungarian Jewish community. But after tireless research, Tamir collected documents in Europe and America that proved Kastner's guilt. Kastner lost his suit for libel. In March 1957, he was gunned down on a Tel Aviv street.

13

"THE KLARSFELD GANG"

Shmuel Tamir's involvement in the Kastner case was an interesting coincidence to us, for Serge and I had been involved in another case that was indirectly related—an example of how small and how tight the circles of the former S.S. are.

Kastner had saved S.S.-Standartenführer Kurt Becher, Himmler's special representative in Budapest, from the gallows at Nuremberg through his accommodating testimony. So Kastner was now even with Becher, who had protected him in the past just in case of such an eventuality. Becher knew that Kastner would have to cover up for him or his role in the slaughter of the Hungarian Jews would be disclosed. It would have come to light then how Kastner had continuously persuaded masses of Jews to go quietly to the "work" camp at Auschwitz. Kastner was fully aware of the fate that awaited them there; he also knew that many Hungarian Jews could have saved themselves by going underground or by fleeing to Rumania if he had warned them, at the risk of his life and that of his family.

On February 17, 1958, the Israeli Supreme Court solemnly declared that "Kurt Becher was a war criminal not only in the technical sense of the term but in a still more terrifying sense." Becher had also been guilty of enormous confiscations and extortions of funds from Jews. He had put those sums into a Swiss

204

bank before the end of the war. Once he was free, thanks to Kastner's perjury, he withdrew them and started a grain business in Cologne in 1950. The business grew rapidly, and S.S.-Standartenführer Becher is now living in Bremen, one of the richest men in Germany.

Now, this is what is interesting: when S.S.-Obersturmbannführer Lischka returned to Cologne in 1950, he became the agent for Krücken, also a grain company.

Serge had been connected with Continental Grains, that giant of the grain trade, a year before our adventure in Cologne. Michel Fribourg, an American Jew of French birth, owned that multinational cartel, which controls 25 percent of the world's grain business.

In May 1971, we learned almost simultaneously that Kurt Lischka was in the grain business, and that Kurt Becher, the German cereals king in Bremen, had been one of the most efficient liquidators of Jews. Serge made some inquiries, and found that Continental Grains did a lot of business with Becher's and Lischka's companies. A short while later he sent our data on those criminals to Fribourg's cousin and associate, Maurice Ulmann, and asked him to request the owner of Continental Grains to stop doing business with those German companies. Ulmann told him: "You know how this firm feels. I'm just about the only one who thinks as you do. There's no hope."

He later told Serge that in spite of our reports, Continental Grains would continue doing business with Nazi criminals.

What was to be done about such an attitude? Expose it? No one would have paid any attention. "Business is business." "Money is money." So we chose a different tack. In early November 1971, the international press, all the big grain companies, and the principal subsidiaries of Continental Grains on five continents received two long reports written in English and titled: "Nazi Criminals of the Anti-Jewish Action at the Head of German Grain Companies: No. 1, Kurt Lischka; No. 2, Kurt Becher." Each of the reports consisted of a detailed dossier and was prefaced by a statement purportedly signed by Michel Fribourg:

I was shocked to learn recently that some of the companies with which Continental Grains deals are managed by Nazi criminals who supervised the extermination of the Jews in several European countries. I ordered an investigation. Now I can make available to all companies in this business, and to the international press, data on Kurt Lischka and Kurt Becher, whose impunity is an affront to justice that every honest man resents to the bottom of his heart. Out of respect for the innocent victims of these butchers, I have decided to break off all relations with their firms, and I have no doubt that the business world will do likewise.

That statement was followed by mine:

I acknowledge a debt to Michel Fribourg, who made it possible for me to gather this information. I salute the decision he has made and his sense of responsibility as a Jew, as an American, and as a human being.

Everyone, of course, was fooled, and believed those declarations were genuine. Who could doubt that a Jew and one of the richest men in the world would fail to react as we had made Michel Fribourg react in those reports? Everyone thinks it is obvious that the Jewish world can neither forgive nor forget the Nazi criminals. But that is not always the case. And, as it is hard to go against the current of this belief, it is better to swim with the tide to get results.

They were not long in coming. The subsidiaries of Continental Grains were delighted to have "a boss who dared break off relations with Nazi criminals." Other companies let it be known that they would do the same. Becher was furious at this unexpected blow.

No matter what happened, we would come out ahead in our game with Fribourg. Either he would accept all the congratulations and break with Lischka-Becher or, after everyone had been led to believe that he would sever relations with them, he would go on doing business with them as usual. In such a case everyone would think that he was giving in out of weakness or cowardice.

Fribourg's lawyers came to me to ask me to announce that their client had nothing to do with the whole thing. When I refused, they threatened me with a suit for forgery. There was no case for slander; Fribourg had come off smelling like a rose. And how could a Jew drag a non-Jewish German woman into court and thereby assert his willingness to do business with the murderers of his own people? I held all the trumps.

Fribourg finally backed down. His agents let it be known "that he never made that statement to Mme. Klarsfeld, that the background of the directors of the two German companies had just been brought to his attention, and that his company was, in fact, doing business with the Bremen and Cologne companies."

And then he went on working with Becher.

Henri Bulawko, president of the Association of Jews Deported from France, wrote Fribourg:

I am certain that you did not know what their past history was, but I do think you should have investigated such matters before dealing with Germans of Lischka's and Becher's generation. At any rate, now that you have been informed of the "character" of your German partners, it behooves you to break off all relations with them—and to do so publicly. Please understand that I am not being impulsive by intervening in this sad affair, but my duty compels me to speak up. I shall await your decision which, I hope, will be what the survivors of the death camps expect it to be.

Michel Fribourg never gave an answer to Henri Bulawko or to the Jews of Auschwitz. Those whose ashes served to fertilize the grain fields of Poland did not carry the same weight as Becher and Lischka.

A few days after I got out of the Cologne jail I was invited to the convention of the International League Against Racism and Anti-Semitism (LICA) in Paris.

The LICA had untiringly exposed racist aggression and anti-Semitic persecution. It inspired others, especially the young, with its enthusiasm and energy, and it took concrete and effective action instead of mouthing lofty sentiments that led to nothing. Jean Pierre-Bloch had succeeded in bringing forceful people into the LICA, and also a group of young people whom I found very attractive. They had no pretensions, they liked action, they were braver than many extremists of the right or the left. They themselves paid the costs of their activities, and those who had more money helped the others. I made a speech to them in which I said:

Without the concerted efforts of Resistance and Deportee associations, my activities and those of my friends against Nazi criminals would merely have aroused public opinion against us as agitators, and I would still be in jail today as nothing but a troublemaker. As you all know, I have used sensational methods because all others are worthless, and have been so for a long time.

Today is the national day of commemoration of the deportations. I am going to read you a few lines written in 1943 by a little boy in Drancy. They are from a letter he wrote to God from his prison:

"God, it is You who rule and who see that justice is done. You reward the good and punish the wicked. Believe me, God, because of You I have had such good things. I have had a good mama and such a

good papa. Now, God, I ask for only one thing more: bring back my
parents, my poor parents who are suffering and who are such good
parents. Protect them even more than me, so that I may see them again
as soon as possible. Let them come back just once. I trust You so completely that I thank You in advance."

Friends, that little boy's parents died. The little boy himself took
the train to Auschwitz. Perhaps it is not true that the good are rewarded and the wicked punished. That little boy's letter might have
been from any of those children the Nazis murdered. That is why I
ask you to join me in a common endeavor to seek justice, for without
that there is no true homage to the victims.

The young members of the LICA came to the support of our
cause. On May 11, six of them left for Bonn armed with pamphlets.
Elisabeth Hajdenberg, twenty; René Levy, twenty; Claude Pierre-
Bloch, twenty-eight. They all interrupted debates in the Bundestag
by shouting: "Punish the Nazi war criminals!" and by tossing
around their pamphlets in which was written in both French and
German:

Members of the German Parliament, ratify the February 2, 1971
treaty that Brandt has already signed. Stop letting Nazi criminals like
Lischka live in freedom and respectability.
Brandt has earned the respect of the whole world, but neither the
Bundestag nor German justice has.
Expel Ernst Achenbach, an active participant in the deportation of
Jews from France, from the Bundestag.

The young people were hustled out by the soldiers on guard,
but they were not much hurt, except for Claude Pierre-Bloch, who
got a nasty blow in the solar plexus.

At the same time three other young persons—Gilles Lagassy,
Marc Pudeleau, and Gaby Khalepski—were explaining to reporters in the Bonn Press Building the reasons for the Bundestag
incident.

That sensational protest made a great stir in the Federal Republic, for it was the first demonstration in Germany of French
Jews acting as such. All the daily papers devoted columns to it and
printed their pictures. The great quantity of editorials about it
proved that the young LICA members had touched a sensitive
spot. In a few weeks the Germans had to admit that I was not
alone.

On June 24, 1971, the young LICA members set off for Ger-

many again: this time I went along too. Our purpose: to occupy
Ernst Achenbach's offices in Essen.

I had looked over the place a few days earlier, and I had also
alerted reporters and cameramen. We wanted to prove that Achenbach, the spokesman for the war criminals in the Bundestag and
also Hagen's lawyer, could not sue anyone who accused him of involvement in the deportation of Jews from France. That way we
would prevent him from defending the Nazi criminals again at the
time of the debate on the ratification of the Franco-German treaty.

It was their first trip to Germany for most of the seven young
people: Marc Vitkin, eighteen; Abraham Serfaty, seventeen;
Monique Hajdenberg, eighteen; Didier Kamioner, nineteen; Raphy
Marciano, twenty-two; Francis Lenchener, twenty-two; Serge
Hajdenberg, thirty. They were nervous, and I felt rather like a
mother hen looking after her chicks.

Achenbach's offices were on Goethestrasse, quite near the Essen
police headquarters. When we got there, reporters were waiting.
What a relief! Our performance would not be in vain, for there
would be television coverage. A few minutes later two big Nazi
flags hung from the windows. Passers-by stopped to investigate. It
is a misdemeanor to show a swastika in public. Who could be doing such a thing? Reactionaries or liberals?

Then they read the big streamer pasted across a window: "French
Occupation of Nazi Achenbach's Offices."

Many grabbed a pamphlet as they went by and carried it off
with them to read carefully somewhere else.

After I had led the young people to Achenbach's offices, I left
before the police arrived. This time I did not need to be arrested.
I had been out on bail for two months. If I were arrested again, I
would not get out of jail so quickly. I had already taken a calculated risk in coming at all.

A warrant was issued for me, for I had not gone unnoticed, but
I left on the first train that was going toward Belgium. I changed
trains at Aix-la-Chapelle and got across the border on my French
passport.

After they had held the offices for half an hour, the seven protesters were taken to the Essen Central Police Station. They were
detained for twenty-four hours and questioned at length twice,
and then the four minors were expelled from Germany. The three
adults were thrown into jail until their trial took place six days
later.

I asked the three who were jailed to give me their impressions of their visit to Essen.

Raphy: The official who questioned me was an old man, who began by saying: "Look here, I have never had anything to do with the Nazis."

I answered: "You must allow me to doubt that. I have nothing else to tell you, except that I am a Jew and very tired and hungry."

"Take this sandwich," the official said kindly.

"I don't eat anything that isn't kosher."

The official was annoyed. He reached for a telephone and asked for the president of the Jewish community in Essen. He was obliged to ask him to bring over some kosher food.

The jail itself was like a movie—long corridors and observation posts. A guard took me to the washroom. "Do you want to take a shower?" he asked me.

I snapped at him: "Only if you take one with me. I know what kind of showers you Germans give."

Francis: On Sunday they showed us a Western. I couldn't get over it. At the end, everyone clapped and cheered the sheriff who killed one of the four bandits. My neighbor, a young Italian, whispered in my ear that he had strangled his wife. I moved away.

Serge: The police inspector let me talk a lot about Achenbach and his past, and listened to me carefully without budging from his easy chair. "It's unbelievable," he said at last. "We could not have imagined it." Was he sincere? I think so. While he was taking me away he seemed quite relaxed and chatted with me.

At the hearing, Achenbach's colleague Rudolf Albrecht, a member of the FDP and the mayor of Gladbeck, was the prosecutor. He told the court: "What these people have done is vile." He was confused and excited. He said that it had been impossible to get the streamer off the window because the glue was too thick and had pitted the panes, which would have to be replaced, and that was why he was demanding justice. The prosecutor-general nagged me to tell him the brand of glue Beate had chosen for the purpose, and where it had come from. I lost patience and shouted at him: "I don't know how to dissolve that glue, but I do know one thing, and that is that Achenbach signed papers that led to my family being dissolved in your crematory ovens."

The reaction of the crowd that gathered in front of Achenbach's offices during the twenty-five minutes the occupation lasted was very typical of the clear conscience most German adults have regarding the Nazi past of their country. They could not have missed the point of the demonstration. Still, as the *Frankfurter Rundschau* wrote: "As the police were taking them away, the young people were insulted by many bystanders, who yelled: 'Dope fiends!' They wanted the police to beat them up or send them to work camps." Their sympathies were obvious.

There is no getting around the fact that this is the majority opinion in Germany, where the rehabilitation of "alleged" Nazi criminals is desired. But the German reporters were surprised at the crowd's reaction. They told us that they had reported the incident all the more fully, putting Achenbach in a negative light, because they had been so struck by the negative attitude of the passers-by. In the heat of the moment, the bystanders showed these reporters the true feelings of many of their fellow citizens.

Why didn't the many reporters who wrote stories about the incident condemn it for being illegal? Because its moral legitimacy had immediately been demonstrated by Achenbach's reaction. An innocent man would have appealed to the public and insisted that the data on his activities during the war be made public. He would have brought suit, not for the invasion of his offices, but for libel. He could have sued us for forgery of documents on the Jewish question in which his name appeared. Achenbach did nothing of the sort, just stooped his shoulders.

The trial of the three LICA militants was reported fairly in the German papers. Serge, Francis, and Raphy were sentenced to a choice between twenty days in jail or a fine and one year's banishment from the Federal Republic. They chose the latter.

Some days later, while going through the Achenbach file, I glanced through the list of deportees in the two convoys shipped to the East with Achenbach's collusion. I was moved to find three familiar names on it:

Gilbert Hajdenberg, born January 1, 1911, in Warsaw. Tailor.
Bernard Hajdenberg, born March 15, 1883, in Warsaw.
Lyon Lenczner, born October 14, 1899, in Szeskocin (USSR). Tailor.

They were the uncles of Serge Hajdenberg and Francis Lenchener. That is how, after the Essen demonstration, they learned that Achenbach had played a part in the liquidation of their family.

In July, my Serge went back to Israel to work on my case with Tamir and also to continue our campaign against Achenbach during the visit of Bonn's Foreign Minister Walter Scheel. On television, on radio, and in the papers, Tamir and Serge kept asking Scheel the same question: "How can you retain as parliamentary spokesman for the FDP a man with a past like Achenbach's?" That is the way to undermine the standing and the influence of a German political leader.

Meanwhile the Barbie case had cropped up, but we did not want to interrupt our schedule of attacks on the big criminals such as Lischka and Hagen. We had to invent activities that would be peaceable but still focus a little more attention on those S.S. chiefs.

On January 13, 1972, for example, we left for Warstein, where Herbert Hagen lived, armed with pamphlets summarizing his career, showing his picture, and giving his address and his current positions. On the back was a letter addressed to the citizens of Warstein, asking them to ostracize Adolf Eichmann's former boss.

Aside from André Levy, a former deportee, only young people went to Warstein with me: Elisabeth Lenchener, Jeannot Janower, David Soucot, David Tordjman, and Yossi Kuperholc.

Our journey by train and car was tedious but without incident. Television crews and several reporters, who had been alerted, were on hand to meet us. They accompanied us to Hagen's comfortable house, which we plastered with posters.

The police got there quickly, but although we used the same glue that had scarred the windows in Essen, they did not interfere. The imprisonment and trial of the three young men in Essen had given the LICA prominence in Germany; the police did not want to repeat that mistake.

That afternoon we passed out pamphlets in the city, and held animated discussions with the citizens of Warstein, who now at last knew about Hagen's past. Some of them approved of what we were doing; others did not want "ancient history" brought up.

But Warstein had been aroused over the Hagen case. The deputy mayor of the city received us cordially, carefully avoiding involving himself personally. The demonstration was broadcast that evening on German television and radio, and the newspapers reported it. That is how Hagen was brought out of the shadows by those young people, who are now known in Germany as "the Klarsfeld gang."

With Serge's help I continued my work of collecting documentation on the leaders of the Nazi police apparatus. We collected exhaustive data on twenty of the highest officials of the S.D.-Security Police, and also drew up a list of a hundred and fifty German criminals who had been sentenced by default in France and were now living in the Federal Republic. We had sent our data on Lischka's and Hagen's French trials to the public prosecutor in Cologne, and he sent two assistant prosecutors to the CDJC to verify the authenticity of the documents. Serge returned to Vienna to give the material to Simon Wiesenthal and Herb Langbein, who keep bringing up cases before the German courts. I solicited the help of Frenchmen and Jews living in Germany, and they responded effectively.

To us Germans there was a striking contrast between the French and their emotional tributes at monuments to the dead, and their unwillingness to take action in Germany itself, where both the criminals themselves and the means of bringing them to trial were to be found.

The survivors of the S.S. Division "Das Reich," which was responsible for Oradour, held a reunion at Rosenheim, near Munich, on October 16, 1971. I asked the French to stage a demonstration at it. Even if no more than two people were to show up with signs, it would show the world via television that France was on the side of Germans opposed to Nazism. No one volunteered to go, not even the very victims of the "Das Reich" Division. On the other hand, more than three hundred young Germans clashed with the former S.S. and the Bavarian police, shouting: "Oradour! Tulle!" For these Germans, as for me, it was inconceivable that the worst criminals in all German history should continue to enjoy a shocking impunity while the German people would have to suffer long for what they had done.

Four of us—my mother-in-law, my husband, my son, myself, plus our cat—were still living in a two-room apartment. Our files were stacked to the ceiling, and some had overflowed to the basement. Arno fell asleep late every night on the sofa in Raissa's room, for he was crazy about television. I felt sorry for him in our tight financial situation. But if Serge or I were to give up, who would take any action against the rehabilitation of the war criminals? Morally we were well armed; physically we were young; technically we knew German history and the German language and we had mass-media experience. We just had to rise above the affliction of poverty.

Kaul came to Paris to tell me East Berlin had recognized my Warsaw protest as justifiable. It had been deleted from my record. As to my Prague demonstration, all I needed to do if I wanted to get back into favor and regain the right to enter the Democratic Republic was to write Honnecker that I now had "doubts" as to the timeliness of that protest. Kaul's efforts were in vain.

It was then that the Barbie affair began.

14

KLAUS BARBIE,
BUTCHER OF LYON

My confrontation with Klaus Barbie began on July 25, 1971. I was working at the CDJC to set up an operational chart on the German secret service in Occupied France. M. Mazor, the director of the library, leaned across a box of original Gestapo documents and handed me some papers he had just received, saying: "This will probably interest you."

They were photocopies of the decision Public Prosecutor Rabl had made in Munich on June 22, 1971, disposing of the Barbie case. By July 25, that decision had still not been made public.

Thanks to a procedural maneuver, the Association of German Victims of Nazism had managed, on June 23, 1960, to have an investigation opened on Klaus Barbie for the crimes he had committed in France. As I scanned the ten pages that explained why the Bavarian court had ended the public investigation of the "Butcher of Lyon," that had begun over ten years before, I became aware of the shocking consequences of closing the case. Those ten pages, written in a dry, pedantic style, served to rehabilitate— through Barbie—all the Nazi criminals who had operated in France. The Lyon tribunal, in fact, had twice sentenced Barbie to death in absentia, first on May 16, 1947, and again on November 25, 1954.

The importance of the Barbie case is its indication of what is likely to lie ahead for other Gestapo chiefs who were also tried in absentia and who comprise the 312 cases still capable of being prosecuted according to German law (crimes committed out of base motives or through carrying out Nazi dogma, such as the deportation of Jews).

The Franco-German legislative agreement signed on February 2, 1971, was a warning shot for the criminals and their protectors in German governmental and judicial circles. Back in 1967, the Federal Republic's foreign minister had sent a list of 1,026 Nazis who had been sentenced in France to the German Red Cross, which had hastened to warn each of them: "You have been sentenced in absentia in France. If you enter French territory you will be arrested and tried."

Ratification of that agreement, which was unpopular in the Federal Republic, had been delayed by a pressure group within the inner circles of the three parties represented in the Bundestag. But, sensing the threat that hung over the heads of the condemned, the German courts adopted a bold tactic: to discharge the case against one of the best known, Klaus Barbie, so that that decision could be cited as a precedent by other prosecuting bodies in similar cases. It was also a means of gauging whether the French were really serious.

I immediately realized that the Barbie case was a landmark, and that we would have to fight relentlessly to get the Munich investigation reopened.

That night I translated Rabl's ten pages, which became the first entry in my file. Serge and I decided to launch our campaign on three fronts: to gather and distribute as complete a documentation as possible on the Barbie case; to rouse public opinion in France and the Federal Republic through that documentation and especially through the reactions I would provoke in the Lyon area; and, finally, to attack the Munich court in whatever way might produce the best results.

We went back to the CDJC and assembled basic data designed to show the press and persons likely to react just who Barbie was. The data consisted of documents signed by Barbie that concerned the Jewish problem. Little by little, after painstaking research, we found many more papers in the Gestapo archives to add to our documentation. We also found passages in several books describing Barbie's role in the arrest and torture of Jean Moulin, including Laure Moulin's book about her brother; Henri Michel's *Jean*

Moulin, l'unificateur ("Jean Moulin, Unifier of Resistance"); and Eric Piquet Wicks's *Quatre dans l'ombre* ("Four in the Shadows").

In a few days I had sixty solid pages of data. I now had to get them reproduced. Fortunately Francis Lenchener's father allowed us to use his copying machine. During the following months we spent a lot of time in the Lenchener offices copying those documents and collating them, and eventually we produced about two hundred rather bulky sets for distribution.

Much has been written about Klaus Barbie, including a defensive memoir that he wrote in collaboration with the Brazilian journalist Dantas Ferreira. But what I have added to this literature is the indisputable evidence about his crimes that I discovered in Germany and in records not generally available to the public.

Nikolaus (Klaus) Barbie was born on October 25, 1913, in Bad Godesberg, near Bonn. His mother, Anna Hees, twenty-seven, and his father, Nikolaus Barbie, did not marry until January 30, 1914. The marriage took place in Merzig, in the Saar, the ancestral town of the Barbie family. Klaus's father was first an office worker and later a schoolteacher. He died at the age of forty-five from a neck tumor that resulted from a World War I wound.

Until he was eleven, Klaus went to the elementary school in Udler, where his father taught. Then he entered Friedrich-Wilhelm High School in Trier, from which he was graduated in 1934. Starting on April 1, 1933, Klaus was part of the Hitler Youth. He did not continue his studies at a higher level, but volunteered for work service at Niebull, in Schleswig-Holstein. He stayed there for six months, from April 26 to October 31, 1934. Once his work term was over, Klaus enlisted in the Hitler Youth, and even then he was voluntarily cooperating with the regional branch of the Nazi Party as secretary to the chief of the Trier section.

Early in 1935 he came into contact with the secret service of Reichsführer S.S. Himmler—the S.D. On September 25, 1935, he became S.S. No. 272,284, and was assigned as an assistant in the S.D.'s central office, the IV-D. In October 1937, Klaus Barbie was transferred to the administrative staff of the S.D.

He had joined the Nazi Party as No. 4,583,085 on May 1, 1937. (It is extraordinary that the three principal S.S. members I am attacking had the following party membership cards: Barbie, No. 4,583,085; Hagen, No. 4,583,139; Lischka, No. 4,583,185. There were over eight million Nazis, and these three were of different ages, ranks, and duties.) As an S.D. policeman, Barbie had to do only a short term of military service instead of the regular term. From September 5 to December 3, 1938, he was a private in the 39th Infantry Regiment.

On April 9, 1939, Klaus became engaged to Regina Margareta Maria Willms, twenty-three, daughter of a post-office clerk. She had not completed her secondary education, but had taken a six-month course in cooking. In 1936 she worked as a maid in Berlin, and in 1937 she settled in Düsseldorf, where she took care of children in the day nursery of the Nazi Women's Organization. She too was a member of the Nazi Party, No. 5,429,240.

They were married in Berlin on April 25, 1940. The witnesses were Klaus's associates, S.S.-Obersturmführer Emil Goebel and Paul Neukirchen. Klaus himself, who had been Oberscharführer since September 1, 1939, was promoted five days before his marriage to S.S.-Untersturmführer.

When the Wehrmacht invaded western Europe, the police followed it. On May 25, 1940, Klaus Barbie reached The Hague, where he was assigned to the S.D.-Security Police's Bureau for Jewish Affairs. But game was more plentiful in Amsterdam. The young S.S.-Obersturmführer—Barbie had passed his examination and been promoted on November 9, 1940, and he was awarded the Iron Cross, Second Class, on April 20, 1941—was to work, from early 1941 until March 1, 1942, in the Bureau for Jewish Affairs in the city of Rembrandt and, later, of Anne Frank.

He must have gotten a leave in the fall of 1940, for his daughter was born on June 30, 1941, in Trier.

On May 21, 1942, a new assignment sent Barbie to France, where he was made head of the S.D.-Security Police Exterior Commando Force in Gex, near the Swiss border. In November 1942, he was made head of the Gestapo's Department IV in Lyon.

I have read what two of his associates in Lyon thought about him. To the fanatical Nazi S.S. Alfred Lütjens, Barbie was "a first-class comrade, intelligent and dynamic, the very soul of the Gestapo." To S.S. Kurt Abendroth, "Barbie's excesses were not always reported to Paris. Barbie was the dynamo of the Department." "Soul" and "dynamo"—those two words say what they mean: Barbie was frenzied in his activities.

An S.D.-Security Police secretary, Hedwig Oudra, who was twenty in 1943, says that she considered Barbie to be excessively brutal. He frequently rebuked one of his deputies named Floreck for not being tough enough. After Hollert's death in a bombardment in May 1944, Barbie was to become deputy to the commander of the S.D.-Security Police. Another S.S., Wilhelm Wellnitz, who now lives in Rendsburg, states that "from that time on, Barbie signed all the telegrams."

I shall not retrace here Barbie's actions against the French Resistance, for they were linked to those of the Lyon Gestapo, and Resistance veterans of the region are more qualified than I to give details. I only want to recall some of his crimes while he was posing as a "German soldier and patriot."

It seems that those who have held a grudge against Barbie for having tortured Jean Moulin to death have not been wrong. I offer as proof the following document, dated September 18, 1943, whose reference number is 1–A–16, No. 204,143, of the RSHA. The head of the S.D.-Security Police wrote:

At my suggestion, the S.S.-Reichsführer [Himmler] has, in a personal letter, expressed his gratitude to:
S.S.-Hauptsturmführer Heinz Hollert
S.S.-Obersturmführer Klaus Barbie
Staffelhauptscharführer Alfred Lutjens
S.S.-Hauptscharführer Karl Krull
S.S.-Staffelscharführer Günter Erlers
of the secret police Einsatzkommando for their high efficiency in the pursuit of crime and their indefatigable devotion to the battle against Resistance organizations in France.

Barbie's work was further rewarded, on November 9, 1943, by the Iron Cross, First Class, with sword.

Lastly, here is the opinion of his superiors, stated in a document dated September 14, 1944, from the RSHA, identified as 1–A–56–AS–5,/96. In it S.S.-Sturmbannführer Wanninger recommends another promotion for Barbie:

Barbie is known at headquarters as an S.S. leader who knows what he wants, and is enthusiastic. He has a definite talent for intelligence work and for the pursuit of crime. His most meritorious accomplishment has been the cleaning out of numerous enemy organizations. Reichsführer S.S.-Himmler has expressed his gratitude to Barbie in a personal letter commending his pursuit of crime and his persistent efforts in suppressing Resistance organizations.

From the point of view of ideology and character, Barbie is dependable. Since his training and during his employ in the S.D., Barbie has pursued a regular career as a director of the "superior service," and, providing there is no objection to his promotion, it is recommended that he be advanced, starting November 9, 1944, from S.S.-Obersturm-führer to S.S.-Hauptsturmführer.

The deportation of French civilians from Villeurbanne on March 1, 1943, is a typical example of Barbie's work. Paul Chabert, the mayor of the town, described that tragedy at the trial of Oberg and Knochen:

On March 1, 1943, German troops surrounded a block of houses in Villeurbanne. . . . After classifying its thousand residents, they herded a hundred and fifty of them to a spot near the railway station. I intervened with Commander Hollert and his deputy, Lieutenant Barbie, but we could get nothing from those German officers, and the hundred and fifty Villeurbanne men were loaded into cattle cars bound for Compiègne in the month of March—that is, when temperatures were quite low. . . . We asked Barbie for permission to go to Compiègne to take clothing and food to the unfortunate prisoners, for they had been dragged from their homes almost naked. Barbie finally granted it. . . . The commander of the camp told us: "Lieutenant Barbie did telephone me that you were coming, but he definitely instructed me to forbid you to see the prisoners." Sometime later we learned that the men from Villeurbanne had been deported from Compiègne to Germany. Only thirty came back.

Another example of the summary executions Barbie ordered, one of unimaginable savagery, was described by Superintendent Adrien Richard. Richard was deputy chief of the Lyon police detectives, and he witnessed what went on in the cellar of Barbie's Gestapo:

On January 10, 1944, I learned of a round-up by the Germans on Quai Sainte-Claire following the death of two German policemen who had been killed in circumstances the police did not solve.

About 1 A.M. the following morning, I received a telephone call at my house asking me to accompany my division superintendent to the military hospital that served as Gestapo headquarters, on a mission the purpose of which was not known to me.

At the hospital an officer tried to explain to us the execution of prisoners of the Germans who had allegedly revolted. To set things straight, I should say that we were received by a German officer, not by Barbie, who was head of the department. The officer asked us to follow two non-coms to the cellar to identify the corpses. Two non-coms preceded us and two followed us, all four armed with sub-machine guns, as we went down into the cellar. When we got into the corridor we were overpowered by an unmistakable odor of warm blood. We went farther and came to a puddle of congealed blood in front of a cell door. The door was opened by one of the non-coms and we witnessed a frightful spectacle: corpses were piled up in a corner of the cell and literally swimming in a sea of blood. They were all young men who had been killed by machine guns as they faced the door. They were stuck together or half stretched out, and I remember that the postman, still in uniform, had half-hoisted himself on a seat before being killed. His face bore a frightful rictus grin.

We then realized that the officer's explanation, that these people had been killed while in an act of revolt, was impossible, given the position of the corpses.

Barbie pretended never to have been involved in anti-Jewish measures. He certainly knew that that accusation would weigh most heavily against him if he were eventually to be extradited, since it concerns genocide and children by the hundreds among the thousands of Jews arrested in Lyon for deportation. Until now the only known document to weaken Barbie's assertions is a telegram, dated April 6, 1944, in which he reported the arrest of forty-one Jewish children in Izieu. It should be noted in this connection that the decision to free Barbie from that charge was made by Prosecutor Rabl in 1971, whereas, on October 4, 1969, Dr. Artzt, the prosecutor of the Central Bureau for Research on War Criminals, had written the Munich prosecutor's office:

If Barbie did clear out a camp for Jewish children and had them shipped to Drancy, there is no doubt that he, as an S.S. chief, knew the children would be shipped to Auschwitz to be exterminated there. So, in this one case at least, Barbie was an accessory to murder.

Barbie's telegram about the Jewish camp in Izieu was the only item in his file when he was sentenced to death in absentia in France, and it was not enough to support the charge of genocide. Serge and I found in the CDJC archives a number of documents signed by Barbie that dealt directly with the Jewish problem and demonstrated that, contrary to his statements, he knew about the Gestapo's anti-Jewish activities.

On February 10 and 11, 1943, Barbie sent a telegram and a letter to Röthke, in the Gestapo's Bureau for Jewish Affairs in Paris, concerning the arrest through his efforts of eighty-six UGIF workers on February 9 in their premises at 12 rue Sainte-Catherine, Lyon. He had those Jews shipped to Drancy.

A list dated August 11, 1944, contains the names of the forty-two Jewish prisoners the Gestapo shot between May 28 and

August 17, 1944. Also, on August 11, Barbie sent the last convoy from France direct to Auschwitz, in which were 308 Jews whose names I have.

In addition to these documents, I got statements from Mme. Benguigui, the Halaunbrenners, Dr. Schendel, and M. Geissmann. More about these later.

On November 9, 1944, Barbie was promoted to S.S.-Hauptsturmführer, and on November 20 he was sent back to the S.D. in Dortmund.

The Americans interned him in Oberursel, but soon set him free and put him to work for their secret service.

I have several pieces of evidence that make it difficult to doubt Barbie's work for the American secret service. It is already known that Commissioner Bribe interrogated him three times—on June 4 and 18 and on July 16, 1948—on American army premises about the Hardy affair.

Barbie had not had to give his name to the French Commission of Inquiry, which must certainly have made a deal with the American secret service over the right to interrogate him. I myself can add some new elements:

On April 16, 1961, Carole Bouness, daughter of a friend of Barbie's mother, stated:

In 1948 Barbie and his family were living in Stadtbergen, near Augsburg, in a house the American authorities had requisitioned. They shared it with an American soldier and his family. In 1949, Barbie's mother told mine that the Americans had sent her son and his family abroad. During the summer of 1957, I met Frau Barbie and her two children, who had spent months in Trier, and she told me she was going back to Bolivia. I was to be her mailing address. After reading Barbie's letters I burned them, for I knew that he had been an S.S. chief. I was to forward his mail to Regina Willms—or Müller, or Altmann—at different post office boxes, the numbers of which were indicated in each of Barbie's letters.

On January 20, 1964, the Bavarian police confirmed that the block at 10 Mozartstrasse in Stadtbergen had been requisitioned by the American authorities until 1950, and that Barbie had been registered by the Americans under the names of Spehr, Behrends, Mertens, and Holzer—always with the same first name of Klaus and the same date and place of birth: October 25, 1913, in Bad-

Godesberg. In 1947 or 1948, the Americans had even given him a German identity card bearing one of those names.

On July 16, 1964, Dr. E. Hoffmann of Berlin-Zehlendorf testified that in 1964 Barbie had introduced a Dane, Dr. Zarp, a former journalist and an economics expert for the S.S., into the American secret service in Memmingen. A former colleague of Dr. Hoffmann, Franz Adam Minnich of Stuttgart-Cannstadt, testified in his turn that he had put Barbie in touch with Dr. Hoffmann because Barbie had told him he needed information about Rumania for his work for the Americans.

After the war Barbie's family increased. A son, Klaus-Georg, was born on December 11, 1946, in Kassel (birth certificate No. 3,008, dated December 18 for son of Nikolaus Barbie). Today that son is known as Klaus-Georg Altmann, and he represents his father's company, Transmaritima Boliviana, in Hamburg. His Bolivian passport, dated January 27, 1971, is No. 51/71. He is married to a young French girl.

Klaus Barbie has prospered in Bolivia for many reasons. The German colony there controls sixty percent of the country's economy. The Bolivian army was trained back in the late 1920's by the sinister Roehm, an S.A. leader. On a television program recently broadcast in the Federal Republic, a German magnate of the well-established Gasser family stated: "We are the ones who brought Colonel Hugo Banzer from Argentina, where he had taken refuge. We took up a collection to finance the putsch of August 1971, by which he overthrew General Juan José Torres. We also furnished the arms."

Barbie—or Altmann, as he calls himself—is one of those expert businessmen who saw to the protection of the German community's interests. His name was mentioned in connection with the helicopter crash in which President René Barrientos lost his life in 1969. Barbie had an interest in all kinds of more or less shady businesses in Bolivia: a sawmill, quinine, and even shipping, although Bolivia has no access to the sea. He is a director of Transmaritima Boliviana, a company that buys ships for Bolivia. Barbie has squandered its funds, which had been raised by a national levy. Hence he is in a good position to implicate a number of high government officials in that financial scandal.

On September 20, 1969, the Foreign Minister of the Federal

Republic sent a memorandum to the Minister of Justice, doubtless in reply to a request from him for information about Altmann, whom the prosecutors knew was actually Barbie. Mention was made in it of a secret report about Altmann from the German Embassy in La Paz. That report, which follows, tells a good deal about his status in Bolivia.

He and his family arrived in Bolivia in May 1951, via Argentina. On October 7, 1957, he became a Bolivian citizen. Our investigations could not go much further, for Altmann enjoys extremely cordial relations with the Bolivian authorities. According to unconfirmed rumors, the Barbie family entered Bolivia with foreign (Vatican) passports. His daughter Ute asked us for a residence visa to the Federal Republic to work for the Boehringer Company in Mannheim, which her father represents. She gave her father's previous nationality as "Polish."

We advise your making a very discreet inquiry, for Klaus Altmann is very close to persons in the inner circles of the Bolivian government and to former Nazis now living in South America, such as Fritz Schwend in Lima.

Attached is a photograph of Altmann, showing him in the center of a group, which appeared in a Bolivian newspaper.

It is not at all unlikely that from time to time Barbie also worked for the CIA. He is an integral part of the present oppressive Bolivian fascist regime. General Juan José Torres, former Bolivian Chief of State, who took refuge in Chile, stated:

I am not surprised that the present Bolivian government is protecting that butcher and war criminal Klaus Barbie. It would be logical for them to do so. The same fascism that yesterday tried to reduce the French people to slavery, today wants to do the same to the people of Bolivia. The conditions are different, but the means are identical.

15

REOPENING THE BARBIE CASE

All the international press associations, all the big French and German news syndicates, received the material we had gathered about Barbie. We also distributed it to all the Resistance associations in the Lyon area and to the legal authorities in France and Germany.

The French reaction would have to come from Lyon to have the greatest effect on German opinion. If no vigorous protests against the Munich prosecutor's decision came from the place where Barbie had committed his crimes, the Germans would undoubtedly think the people of Lyon shared Rabl's opinion. I had an idea in mind: The people of Lyon should stage a demonstration in Munich.

The first thing to be done was to alert the Lyon press. On July 27 I went to the Paris office of the Lyon *Progrès* and told reporter André Severac about the various aspects of the case. The next day *Progrès* carried a long story headed: "German Prosecutor Drops Charges against Klaus Barbie, Chief of Lyon Gestapo and Torturer of Jean Moulin."

On July 29 *Progrès* gave a great deal of space to the reaction. The Lyon branch of the LICA asked "all Resistance associations and all citizens of Lyon with a sense of justice to write a letter of protest to the prosecutor."

Dr. Dugoujon, who was arrested at the same time as Jean Moulin, angrily declared: "I have prayed to Heaven to give me the grace never to sit in judgment, but if I were a judge or a member of a jury, I would sentence Klaus Barbie to death."

Alban Vistel, who had fought for the Liberation, said: "We who fought as volunteers in the Resistance firmly believe there should be no time limit on the trials for war crimes."

Also on July 29, I telephoned both Marcel Rivière, a former member of the Resistance and the top reporter on *Progrès*, and the Lyon radio-television station to say that I would be in Lyon in three days. I could already count on the principal newspaper and the television news program of the area to persuade the local people not only to protest but also to fight.

On Sunday evening, August 1, I arrived. I stayed with the parents of Serge Hajdenberg, who had been with us at the Essen protest. On Monday I made a strong bid to the radio-television people, the *Progrès* people, the former Resistance people in Lyon, and Dr. Dugoujon to convince them to organize a group to go to Munich.

Progrès headlined Marcel Rivière's editorial: "The Klaus Barbie Case Must Be Reopened, Says B.K." It went on to say:

Citizens of Lyon, you cannot accept the Munich prosecutor's decision to suspend the prosecution of Klaus Barbie, the former Gestapo chief who caused so much blood and so many tears to flow in your city and your district. A German woman speaks to you. . . .

Her proposal, emotional yet strongly supported by incontrovertible documentary evidence, produced a singularly overwhelming response in Dr. Dugoujon's Caluire villa, where we met her, for it was this house that Klaus Barbie's men brutally raided on June 21, 1943, and, after savagely clubbing them, arrested several members of Jean Moulin's Resistance headquarters.

The papers B.K. has given us speak for themselves. They are photocopies of orders that Klaus Barbie signed or countersigned for the arrest and deportation of hundreds of Jews who had been rounded up in Lyon and its environs, notably in Haute-Savoie. Still other documents deal with arbitrary arrests, tortures, massacres, shootings, and summary executions. . . . But more than these are needed to convince the Munich prosecutor!

Agence France Presse gave my campaign nationwide exposure. I also contributed a full page to *Combat*, in which I said:

Barbie, the chief of the Lyon Gestapo, was born on October 25, 1913, and sentenced to death in absentia on November 22, 1954, by the Lyon military tribunal for participating in 4,342 murders, sending 7,591 Jews to Drancy and the Auschwitz gas chambers, and arresting 14,311 Resistance fighters, often torturing them abominably.

He was in charge of deportations of Jews from the Lyon region. They were arrested on his orders and shipped to Drancy, where they were herded into the death trains. According to Prosecutor Rabl, the Gestapo chiefs were completely in the dark about the "Final Solution." For them it was merely a matter of "evacuation to labor camps in the East." But a telegram dated April 6, 1944, has been found in which Barbie reports the arrest of forty-one children between the ages of three and thirteen from the Izieu camp, and their shipment to Drancy on April 7. In April 1944, even the public no longer believed the explanation about labor in the East; certainly the Gestapo chiefs in France could not have believed it. Moreover, children between the ages of three and thirteen obviously could not have gone to the East to lend a helping hand to the German economy. Even Prosecutor Rabl must concede that. But he surmounts the difficulty by reasoning that is so impertinent that Jews, Frenchmen, and Germans must all be outraged by its total lack of logic, of justice, and of any moral values. Rabl writes:

"The mere fact that on April 6, 1944, the defendant arrested forty-one children who were obviously not destined for the labor camps and had them shipped to the concentration camp at Drancy cannot be interpreted to mean that he knew the eventual destination of those children. At least not one sure proof of this subjective interpretation of his act can be produced."

Prosecutor Rabl has taken no thought of the sufferings of those children or of the abomination itself. It's not his job to have pity on their fate, or to help Germany sincerely rise above her Nazi past. Prosecutor Rabl is only interested in what may not have entered Klaus Barbie's mind: the so-called "subjective interpretation." In discharging the Barbie case, Rabl has condemned those children all over again. If the French people accept today that denial of justice, then each of the Nazi criminals whom France sentenced in absentia will be rehabilitated in his turn, and with them the Nazi police system.

Is there no one who will speak for those young Frenchmen against their executioner? A spokesman with a desire to be effective and not just to make one more of those official statements to the press that are less and less frequently published in France now, and never published on the other side of the Rhine? Are there so few Frenchmen who grasp how relevant to the future of Europe it is that Germany has taken this attitude toward her Nazi past? When can a public demonstration in Munich take place? Will the vacation season take precedence over a time for sorrow and pity even with those who call themselves victims of Nazi barbarism?

My article was deliberately forceful; indeed, some people even found it violent and complained that I was only a child when others were fighting in the Resistance, and so what right had I, etc. . . . Still, weak wills had to be made firm. Otherwise there would be just one result: More criminals would go unpunished or, even worse, be rehabilitated.

Then a wonderful opportunity arose for taking action in Germany: For a whole week the Munich courts were in the limelight because a hold-up had taken place in which the police, on instructions from Prosecutor Schreiber, had opened fire, and a bank clerk had been killed. Germany was horrified. So all that was necessary for us to get some publicity was for a group of us to go to Munich armed with our data, and submit it to the court. Either the Munich judges would be so afraid of an additional scandal that the decision would be revoked, or at least the reporters there would let Germans know the facts about the Barbie case and the stand the French were taking.

Unfortunately, however, the Resistance veterans in Paris whom I talked to slipped away. They belonged to radical associations that were angered by my article, in which I had quoted Deputy Virgile Barel, who was a communist, although I did not know it at the time. Still, I had only talked sense and action. Until I spoke up, not a single German was familiar with the various speeches and appeals Barel had made in the National Assembly. It was not enough for him to demand action from his own government; it would have been just as easy for him to take some action himself. My point was that there had to be unanimous action. Barbie's victims, whether rightists or leftists, Jews, capitalists, or communists, were all up against the Gestapo. It was only fitting that the Gestapo should now be up against all of them.

The leaders of the Nazi police system had not wavered in their repression of the Resistance and of the Jews. Their deceit had helped them overcome many obstacles, for they were fiendishly inventive in the operation of their death machine. Their iron determination and their unremitting efforts were deadly, as the deaths and the misery they caused can testify. What is more, almost all have survived unpunished and full of scorn for their critics, for they have not even bothered to conceal themselves.

How could we fight such an enemy? By making statements that no one would read? By arousing public opinion that would merely expose an unpunished criminal, as in the case of Lammerding, without doing anything concrete about his impunity? By acting like little children dancing around and shouting or pointing fingers at some big bully but never daring to attack him directly? I don't like that kind of game.

In Lyon, with the support of Marcel Rivière, the local LICA, and Dr. Dugoujon, my plan for a demonstration in Munich was taken into consideration. On the morning of August 17, I discussed it with *Le Monde's* experts on Germany, and that afternoon *Le Monde* ran a long story, which ended:

The recent news that the Munich prosecutor has dismissed charges against Klaus Barbie, formerly chief of the Lyon Gestapo, has aroused much protest in France. The LICA has issued a statement that it had learned of the decision with "deep emotion." It is calling on all Resistance associations to stage a big protest demonstration in Lyon on September 3 and 4. A delegation of former Resistance members and deportees is also going to go to Munich in early September. . . ."

The Barbie affair had been launched.

I badgered most of the Paris correspondents of the big German dailies so that each of them would be in a position to write a full story on the subject. These resulted in an enormous number of protests in the Federal Republic. I also telephoned the Munich papers to keep them informed and even more fully supplied with data than the other German papers. As a result, on August 20, *Süddeutsche Zeitung's* Klaus Arnsperger wrote up the Resistance protest expected in Munich in mid-September, and my friend Hans Keppert titled his long story in the *Frankfurter Rundschau*: "German Justice Assailed Again: France Furious Over Barbie's Release." Keppert said:

The Munich public prosecutor can expect a period of agitation. Associations of French Resistance veterans and the LICA intend to make a protest before the court on Munich's Maxburgszrise. They are now sending letters to the Munich public prosecutor's office, and intend to stage a mass demonstration in Lyon on September 3. Both the conservative and the liberal French newspapers are again expressing doubt that West German courts truly want to put an honorable end to a sad chapter in Franco-German relations. . . .

I went back to Lyon on August 31 to spur the organizing of a delegation. September 13 was the date decided upon. The local

LICA, which had polled the Jewish community, assured me that several Resistance veterans would participate.

I took advantage of that trip to visit my son, who was in summer camp at Chambon-sur-Lignon. It was like coming upon an oasis to be with him in the sunny, green countryside. Every one of my campaigns has been a trek across a desert, and where or how it would end I never knew. I was always fearful of defeat, and I knew I would be sick if I did not get results. The story I have been telling gives only a sketchy account of what I did, for there were an infinite number of fruitless endeavors, hours spent in writing up dull but extremely important notes, making telephone calls that were never answered, keeping up files, writing letters, photocopying and classifying documents. There was also the formulating of plans for action. This involved long discussions with Serge that often turned into heated arguments, for he is the more imaginative and I, the more realistic.

On August 24, Serge found at the CDJC a list of the deportation convoy for August 11, 1944, which took the last Jews in Lyon to have escaped deportation from the Montluc concentration camp to Auschwitz. The list bore 308 names, plus the names of forty-two Jews who had been summarily executed in the Gestapo cellars, and the dates of each of these liquidations. Barbie was directly responsible for all of them. *Progrès* published these lists in their entirety.

I went back to Lyon on September 2, and, with Pierre Levy, the president of the local branch of the LICA, saw Mayor Pradel. Pradel assured us of the city's support of the projected delegation. But, alas, his budget allowed him to pay only for the trip of his deputy, Marcel Rivière, who would officially represent the city on the expedition. That evening I spoke on the local television news program.

The delegation somehow or other took shape on September 3 in the course of a meeting of a veterans group. Practical preparations for it brought up matters of organization and financing. The desire to go clashed with the hard realities. I tried to appeal to the veterans' self-esteem, emphasizing that the reverberations of the demonstration might be great enough to influence the Franco-German talks on legal matters in Bonn, in which the French Minister of Justice, René Pleven, would be participating. One of the Resistance veterans rose to address the meeting: "This is a German woman telling you what you ought to do. Wake up, for heaven's sake!"

Finally it was decided that the delegation should go by plane. The LICA, which I was to represent in Munich, paid for my ticket as well as some other delegates'.

In early September we made up twenty-one sets of our data in German for representatives from the Federal Republic to the Congress of the Interparliamentary Union in Paris, and thirty more for distribution to Munich reporters on September 13.

In anticipation of the delegation's arrival in Munich, the spokesman for the prosecutor's court let it be known that if new evidence was forthcoming, the case would be reopened. Proof was essential. The German courts would not be satisfied with motions, statements, or stands. It was not enough for us to go to Munich; there had to be at least sufficient evidence to allow the German courts to renew their investigation. Serge and I tackled this tedious task, and examined innumerable documents at the CDJC in search of a lead to the ones mentioning Barbie.

Among many that led nowhere because of a person's death or disappearance, an important one did turn up. I noticed that the UGIF—that obligatory association that Kurt Lischka had created to represent the Jewish population before the French and the Occupation authorities—had a liaison office with the Gestapo's Bureau for Jewish Affairs. In 1943 and 1944 it was directed by a former lawyer from Berlin, Kurt Schendel, who had emigrated to France because of racial persecutions.

Schendel's task was often dramatic, for he was in direct contact with the two supreme managers of the Final Solution in France: Heinz Röthke, head of the Gestapo's Bureau for Jewish Affairs, and Alois Brunner, one of Eichmann's deputies. Brunner headed a secret service commando squad whose job it was to speed up arrests and deportations, while Röthke took charge of the more administrative duties. Imagine my feelings when I discovered a document dated August 31, 1944, in which Schendel recorded a moving talk he had with S.S.-Hauptsturmführer Alois Brunner on Thursday, July 30, 1944! Brunner showed Schendel a pamphlet, most of which dealt with atrocities committed by the Germans in the Dordogne.

Brunner gave me a full explanation of them. He indicated that he had been present at them in person. A Jewish proprietor of a restaurant or a bakery had lured an automobile full of officers into a Resistance ambush. Brunner told me that to him there was nothing more sacred than the blood of a German soldier, and that he had decided to arrest not only the young people of our communities, but also the children. We had a long discussion, in the course of which I told Brunner everything that was on my mind, paying no attention to the fact that here was I, a Jew, upbraiding a German officer. In any event, I could not see why little children had to be arrested under the guise of reprisals.

I tried in every conceivable way to change Brunner's mind. I appealed to the emotional aspects of the case (the arrest of little children), to the aspect of public opinion (children are especially sacred in France), to the UGIF aspect (this would mean the end of that organization), and finally to my personal point of view. I insisted that this abuse of small children showed lack of courage. I told him that I was a one hundred percent Jew and that I would gladly be deported if only he would leave those children in peace. His only answer was that those children were "future terrorists."

Anyone knows that the most dangerous thing I could do was to try to bring Röthke and Brunner into conflict. Nevertheless, I thought it was my duty to leave no stone unturned in trying to save those children. I was sure before I began that Röthke knew about the situation, but I wanted to try everything even if I risked enraging Brunner. So I telephoned Röthke for an emergency appointment, and got one for the next day, a Sunday, at 11:45 A.M. I also told Röthke everything that was on my mind, and several times he had to request that I get control of myself and not use such offensive expressions. Then the door opened, and in stepped Brunner. Röthke told him we had been talking about the children.

Brunner yelled at me: "You are a liar! You have lied to me!" When I asked him what he meant, he continued shouting that he had questioned all the children and found they were orphans, whereas I had told him a large number of them had parents in Paris. I tried to discuss the matter, but he roared that "he would throw me down the stairs if I said another word." When Brunner left, Röthke told me that he would like me to leave.

In another document at the CDJC, written by a man who had escaped from Drancy, I read what happened to those children, none of whom returned from Auschwitz. Those who survived the trip were immediately thrown into the crematory ovens without having gone through the gas chamber.

Before coming to France Brunner had disposed of Austrian and Greek Jews, and had also directed the liquidation of Jews who had taken refuge in the Italian zone, which cost Serge's father his freedom and his life. After Brunner left France, Eichmann assigned him to deporting Slavic Jews, and he did a good job of that too. In March 1945, he fled from Bratislava. He was sentenced to death in absentia in Paris on May 3, 1954, but at that time Alois Brunner was basking under the blue skies of Egypt. He had returned to Egypt after a long period in the Syrian secret service, where he could still make use of his talent for exterminating Jews. He is now [1971] fifty-nine years old.

Heinz Röthke, who was just as guilty and just as efficient as Brunner, died of natural causes in 1968 in Wolfsburg, West Germany, where he had been a lawyer. Even though he too had been sentenced to death in absentia, he had never spent a minute in prison. Röthke was another one who could smile at tales of Nazi hunts.

I thought that through his contacts with S.S. leaders like Brunner and Röthke, Dr. Schendel might have been able to learn something about Barbie and what knowledge the regional Gestapo chiefs had of the fate of Jews shipped to Auschwitz. Had not Prosecutor Rabl offhandedly and indulgently concluded that there was no proof that Barbie knew about the death of the people he shipped to Drancy and Auschwitz? Luck was with us. There was a "K. Schendel" in the Paris telephone directory. I called his number daily, but no one answered until the evening of September 6. It was indeed the right Schendel. He had been on vacation. He remembered Barbie, although he had never seen him. We met with him, and on September 8 he sent us an affidavit in German, in which he stated that:

Even in official circles the word "deportation" was seldom spoken; rather, it was "fit for work," "evacuation," or "family reuniting." In the course of the frequent meetings I was obliged to have with Röthke and Brunner I soon realized that the word "deportation" had dreadful connotations. On the several occasions when they did not keep an appointment with me, I was told that they were "making reports in Berlin." When they returned to Paris, there were many conferences attended by the executives of IV-B [Bureau for Jewish Affairs], such as the Commander of Paris and the commanders of other regions, with whom Röthke kept in constant touch by telephone.

Over the course of a year my observations of Department IV-B and the numerous talks I had with its employees, as well as with workers in the other German bureaus, completely convinced me that all of them, except perhaps the ones at the very bottom—but at least Röthke, Brunner, and the executives of the regional S.D.-Security Police Bureaus for Jewish Affairs—knew perfectly well what fate awaited the deportees.

I did not know Klaus Barbie personally, but I know that Barbie ordered the arrest of Jews in Lyon, and took part in these arrests himself. I have seen reports stating that Barbie persecuted the Jews with intense zeal. The UGIF branch in Lyon worked independently in the southern zone, and we were constantly in touch with it. Late in 1943 or early in 1944 we called a meeting in Paris of its directors, which I attended. There was a great deal of discussion of the summary executions at Fort Montluc of Jews whom Barbie had arrested. One of the delegates reported that ceaseless attempts had been made at least to keep arrested Jews from being shot, but that Barbie had replied: "Shot or deported, there's no difference."

That remark sticks in my memory because at the time none of us could comprehend what he meant, and our anguish over the fate of the deportees became all the greater. So far as I am concerned, as I have already said, he was beyond a doubt just as aware as Röthke and Brunner of the ultimate fate of the Jews deported from Lyon, which had the second largest Jewish population of all French cities. I might also add that Brunner assigned to several months' duty in Lyon his assistant, S.S.-Oberscharführer Weiszel, who had been a member of Brunner's Secret Commando force in Hungary and at Slonika, and who could give Barbie an eyewitness account of what happened to Jews deported to the East.

That affidavit seemed to us weighty enough to move the Munich prosecutor's court to review the dismissal of the case against Barbie. But the best evidence would be to produce the UGIF director to whom Barbie had said: "Shot or deported, there's no difference." So far, Schendel had provided only hearsay evidence. Serge got the minutes of the UGIF directors' meetings, checked the names of the directors, and telephoned everywhere to locate them. Twenty-eight were dead.

Meanwhile I had learned that the Lyon organizers of the Munich demonstration had gone to the German consul in that city and asked him to apprise the Munich prosecutor of their coming visit. When the consul learned that I was to be there, he advised them to restrict the number of demonstrators to twelve, and to stay away from such a troublemaker as I. The embarrassment in the voice of the Lyon people who telephoned me led me to assume that they had let themselves be persuaded, and were taking a very deferential attitude to the German authorities. But I went ahead and got everything ready in Munich, telephoned all the newspapers and television and radio stations, and notified anti-fascist organizations to meet us at the airport. I knew the Germans were expecting "the French Resistance"—that is, people stoutly demanding an end to the denial of justice to human rights for which they would speak up in Munich.

The Germans were expecting flags, chests covered with decorations, forced entry into the court. They were expecting fighters, not a few dozen Frenchmen no different from other tourists. This new development certainly seemed calculated to ruin the effectiveness of the trip. I also knew that instead of the documents I had collected, the delegation would take only a memorandum. Such a polite request for justice, it seemed to me, would not make much impression on a prosecutor; he would be swayed only by a forceful presentation of completely convincing documents. How could I make such a show of force all by myself?

Once more the CDJC archives were of invaluable help. Among the children Barbie had arrested in the Jewish camp at Izieu were three brothers: Jacques (thirteen years old), Richard (six years old), and Jean-Claude Benguigui (five years old). They had immediately been shipped to Drancy, as Barbie had stated in a telegram to IV-B in Paris, dated April 6, 1944.

I found the names of the Benguigui children on the list of the April 13, 1944, convoy destined for Auschwitz, where they were killed. The brother of some other Izieu children whom Barbie had deported, Alexandre Halaunbrenner, we located through the telephone directory. He knew Mme. Benguigui, the mother of the three little boys, who lived in the Marais at 33 rue des Francs-Bourgeois. I went to see her.

Mme. Benguigui herself had been deported to Auschwitz on May 6, 1943, and was cruelly tortured in Block 10, where medical experiments were conducted. She was seventy-five percent incapacitated, and her only source of income was a meager pension. While she was in the concentration camp, she kept hoping that her children were safe in that underground camp at Izieu, but in the spring of 1944 she recognized her son Jacques' sweater in a pile of clothing that had belonged to recently gassed prisoners.

I told Mme. Benguigui that the man responsible for the death of her children had just been rehabilitated in Germany, and asked her if she felt up to going to Munich to make a protest that would probably be more successful than the delegation's. German public opinion could not fail to be stirred by so martyred a mother. Since

I foresaw that there would be no test of strength with the Munich court now that the delegation had become so biased, we—Mme. Benguigui and I—would have to deliver the necessary blow.

I became even more determined when I received a letter of encouragement from Laure Moulin, sister of Resistance leader Jean Moulin. She wrote:

I don't know how to express my admiration for your unwavering courage in fighting for your country's acknowledgment of its mistakes and of the crimes the Nazis committed, and for sentencing them once and for all.

As I told you over the telephone, I cannot go with you to Munich this month because of my uncertain health, but I want to assure you that I entirely approve of your demonstration. Like you I strongly protest the shameful indulgence German courts, particularly the Munich court, have shown toward Nazi war criminals and toward that abominable Barbie who committed so many atrocities and murders in Lyon from 1942 to 1944.

I hold him personally responsible for the death of my brother Jean Moulin, whom he so maltreated and tortured that he was almost dead by the time Barbie shipped him to Paris on orders from his superiors. Consequently I am wholly and sincerely with you and with all Frenchmen and Germans who support your plan of action.

On Sunday, September 12, the day before the delegation was to leave, I returned to Lyon. That same evening Serge was to put Mme. Benguigui and M. Halaunbrenner on the train for Munich. The LICA was paying their expenses.

Dr. Dugoujon put me up at his house in Caluire, and we had dinner with Lucie Aubrac, the wife of Resistance fighter Raymond Aubrac, who had been arrested and tortured by Barbie at the same time as Jean Moulin. In spite of all I had been through during the past years, I was astonished when Dr. Dugoujon told me:

"Tomorrow you may not go with the delegation to the court in Munich. You must understand our position. The Foreign Minister has asked us not to disturb Franco-German relations in any way, and to behave with dignity and propriety. He has given us to understand that in order to obtain results we should not strike hard, but rather use a diplomatic approach. Also, one of the delegation is the wife of a high official in an international organization who has to be very careful what he does in that capacity, and he has requested that you do not go to court. I am sorry to have to upset you so, for it was you who got everything going."

Just a few minutes earlier, however, Marcel Rivière of *Progrès* had assured me that I could go to the court. Getting angry would only have led to bitterness. I preferred to save my strength for what had to be done.

On Monday, forty-eight of us took off, mostly Resistance veterans and young LICA members. After a stop in Turin, we landed in Munich at eleven A.M. German reporters were at the airport, and also anti-fascists from the Association of German Victims of Nazism, some carrying signs demanding that the German courts stop protecting Nazi criminals.

Mme. Benguigui and M. Halaunbrenner joined us. We drove to the French Consulate on Mühlstrasse, where one of the leaders of the delegation took me aside:

"Please don't go into the consulate. We have already arranged with the consul that you will not, for it would injure Franco-German relations, owing to your having slapped Chancellor Kiesinger."

I replied: "All I have to say to you is that I carry a French passport, that I don't take orders, and that I have as much right as you to enter a French Consulate."

And I did.

I told Vice-Consul Leglaye that I was astonished at what had been arranged. He waved his hand wearily and, since he had been a deportee, apologized for the incident.

Then, as its organizers had planned, we went for a long breakfast in a Bayerstrasse restaurant—even though the more sensible complained that it would have been better to skip a meal this one time, or just pick up a quick snack somewhere.

The names of the twelve "official" delegates were read out and they got up to go to the court. I did not restrain my indignation, for I knew the German reporters would be expecting fifty people.

"It would be a shame for us to stay here," I said. "We must all go together."

At the courthouse on Maxburgstrasse, the twelve "wise men" went into the building while the young people and I managed to lure the others out of the bus and at least mass them in front of the door. The reporters who encircled us were disappointed at the French people's polite behavior and their orderly retreat when the doorman kept them from going into the court.

Everything had been worked out beforehand with the consulate and the German authorities. The demonstration made about one-tenth the stir it could have caused.

Upstairs in the chambers of Public Prosecutor Manfred Ludolph, the delegates submitted to him a "for your immediate attention" memorandum, which "solemnly requested" him to reopen the investigation. Ludolph listened politely, for he was under no real pressure, and he had been given no document capable of causing the original decision to be re-examined. So he promised nothing.

Meanwhile Mme. Benguigui and I had got inside the building, but since I could not get in to see Ludolph, I left him the file of documents Barbie had signed and that we had found at the CDJC, as well as Schendel's affidavit.

The delegation then headed for Dachau, as planned. I had arranged with the Association of German Victims of Nazism to hold a press conference. There was not enough time before the 5:30 P.M. plane to do both. Those who wanted to go to Dachau argued with those, including me, who wanted action to take priority regardless of what happened. The purpose of the delegation still had to be explained to the German public.

One of the Resistance veterans almost came to blows with one of the young people. "What do you mean accusing me of just being a tourist?" he demanded. "I was fighting in the Resistance before you were even born." It was the same old argument, and it showed that the speaker did not believe in the future of the Resistance spirit.

In the end, there was a press conference, and the delegation went back to Lyon, where they were met at the airport as if they were returning Argonauts by the mayor, the local elected officials, a television crew, and many townspeople.

Mme. Benguigui and I were the only ones who stayed behind, ready to act, for the situation demanded it. Two women—one French and one German. Our ammunition: the only picture of her three children Mme. Benguigui had, which I had had enlarged, and two signs I had made in our hotel room. Our plan was simple: on the following day we would stand on the street before the courthouse steps, where Mme. Benguigui would hold up her children's picture and declare that she was beginning a hunger strike. The people of Munich would doubtless respond, and so would the papers and television. Mme. Benguigui and I were going to stage a trial of strength with the prosecutor's court, however laughable our means of doing so.

We were there at nine o'clock the next morning. It was cold and rainy. We stood on crates I had got from a grocery store, and I had bought Mme. Benguigui some heavy shoes and warm stockings. Over her head I held a sign reading: "*I am on a hunger strike for as long as the investigation of Klaus Barbie, who murdered my children, remains closed.*" My own sign read: "*Prosecutor Rabl is rehabilitating war criminals.*"

By five P.M. there was a big crowd. Reporters and photographers turned out en masse. On the next day the German papers ran our pictures and long stories favorable to our effort. Young Germans were shouting: "It's a disgrace to our country for that poor woman to go to such lengths for justice." Women stroked Mme. Benguigui's hair, and people went to buy her blankets. *France-Soir* had sent an urgent telegram to one of its correspondents to notify the French Consulate, and the vice-consul came with a blanket. The police did nothing but warn us that the sign about Rabl might be libelous, but it stayed in plain sight.

At six P.M. Prosecutor Ludolph was still in his chambers, doubtless thinking: "How can I go home and leave that mother, who has been so physically and mentally tortured, behind on the steps? What if she is still there tomorrow? What if she gets sick during the night? If the sensation-hungry television news shows her still there at three A.M., there will be hell to pay over who let her endure such inhuman treatment. A scapegoat will have to be found, and it may turn out to be me. Should I have her arrested? After what she has suffered already, that won't go down too well anywhere." After such a probable analysis of the situation the prosecutor decided to deal with us. The police politely escorted us to Ludolph's office.

Ludolph was about forty years old, beautifully dressed, and extremely cordial. "What do you want?" he asked.

"To have the prosecution of Barbie reopened."

"I have to have conclusive proofs to do that," he said.

"Did you read the data I sent you yesterday?"

"I have not yet had time."

"Well, now is the time to do it."

When the prosecutor reached Schendel's affidavit, he exclaimed: "This is the sort of thing I was talking about. If Dr. Schendel's informer—the man who actually heard what Barbie said—can be produced, and if he confirms what Barbie is reported to have said, I promise you I will reopen the case."

"Will you put that in writing?"

"My secretary has gone for the day."

"That doesn't matter. I was once a stenographer."

I sat down at a typewriter, and Ludolph dictated an official letter in which he confirmed his promise. I gave it to the German reporters who were waiting below.

Dear Mme. Benguigui:

As a result of our talk today I assure you that the material sent me on September 13 by the French delegation, Mme. Klarsfeld, and yourself will be carefully studied. As to Dr. Schendel's affidavit of September 8, it seems to me necessary to locate the witness who told Dr. Schendel that the defendant said: "Shot or deported, there's no difference." If he can be found and will swear to that statement, I will be ready to reopen the prosecution, for that will be proof that the defendant must have at least expected that his Jewish victims would be put to death.

Thank you for your visit. I send you my regards.

I almost dare to say that Mme. Benguigui was happy. For the first time since the death of her children she felt that she had done something for them. She had shown that she could act—better than so many others, who are glib of tongue, but less resolute when it comes to doing battle with law and custom.

Our luck held. Serge found the witness in the telephone directory. His name was Raymond Geissmann, and he was listed as a lawyer in the Court of Appeals, avenue Victor-Hugo. He proved indeed to be the same Raymond Geissmann who had been a director of the Lyon UGIF in 1943–44. When we met him, he told us that he had not been following the Barbie case because he had been on vacation until only a few days ago.

But did he remember Barbie?

He certainly did. It was to him, and him alone, that Barbie made that dreadful remark. Geissmann immediately dictated to his secretary the affidavit that would cause the prosecution to be reopened:

Our branches, whose personnel were known to the officials, had to keep in touch with the Security Police and particularly with the section headed by Barbie.

Some of my colleagues and I were, consequently, summoned to the Gestapo, or went there ourselves, in our efforts to rescue from its clutches a person or family who had been arrested. . . .

Whenever I recall those anxious days thirty years ago I remember that all of us were entirely convinced that the butchers on whom the life or death of our co-religionists depended knew perfectly well the terrible fate that awaited the people they had arrested.

I remember seeing Barbie "froth at the mouth" as he vented his hatred of Jews, and his remark—"Deported or shot, there's no difference"—was truly spoken by him. He said it in front of me and I reported it to my colleagues in Paris.

I immediately telephoned Ludolph to tell him that Pierre-Bloch, the LICA president, and I were coming to Munich to hand him the affidavit. We made an appointment for October 1. To get publicity for this next step, the National Committee for the Pursuit and Punishment of War Criminals called a press conference for September 28. Pierre-Bloch then was authorized to carry out the procedure in the name of the fifty associations that comprised the committee. I notified the German papers, and Geissmann's testimony was printed in Munich. Pierre-Bloch's personality and position impressed the reporters, who were wondering whether the prosecutor would really reopen the case.

When we got off the plane, the press greeted us warmly, and so did the Victims of Nazism and the local chapter of B'nai B'rith. They went with us to Ludolph, who, along with his assistant Steiner, received us politely. Ludolph read Geissmann's affidavit, which I had translated into German, and immediately dictated his decision to his secretary and gave us a carbon copy of it:

Munich, October 1, 1971

File No. 123 Js 5/71
(7 Js 61/65 Sta Augsburg)
Subject: Public prosecutor's penal investigation in the Augsburg Lan-
        desgericht of Klaus Barbie for alleged complicity in murder.
1. The investigation will be reopened as to the charge against the de-
    fendant that he took part in the murders of French citizens of
    Jewish birth by deporting them from France to the East.
2. The decision for reopening the entire investigation will be delayed,
    but is hereby declared without prejudice.

Ludolph said that the Resistance veterans from Lyon had not sent him the depositions on Barbie's repression of the Resistance that they had promised him. He did not conceal from us his private opinion that "the page ought to be turned."

Speaking for the French Resistance, Pierre-Bloch replied that he could not agree, and that the page would not be turned until Barbie had been tried for all the crimes he committed in France.

I can report that Ludolph completely changed his opinion within a few weeks. He took charge of frustrating the Munich court's attempt to legally justify Barbie's impunity and, through him, that of the other criminals whose cases resembled his. Ludolph was obliged to reopen the investigation. I tried to guess what he was up to and what his line of thinking hereafter would be.

Barbie's case was uncommon in that he was one of the few criminals to have expatriated himself from the Federal Republic. The German courts had practically turned the matter of locating him in the country to which he had fled over to the French authorities, who were the only ones to have demanded his extradition, for the German courts would not have jurisdiction over him until the agreement of February 2, 1971, had been ratified. It was far better for France to get Barbie before the treaty was ratified, for afterward the Federal Republic, having acquired jurisdiction, would have to demand the extradition of Barbie from the country in which he had found asylum. By avoiding such hazards the German courts could also test the sincerity of the French government's desire to prosecute German war criminals. If that desire was not sincere, and if France did not want to take the initiative, then why should the Bundestag be in any hurry to ratify the treaty, and even if it did do so, then why should the German courts be severe?

Ludolph gave us two photographs, front and profile, that had been taken of Barbie in 1943, and another of a group of businessmen seated around a table, one of whom looked enough like Barbie as he might be twenty-five years later for the Munich court to assume it was he.

"The picture of the group," the prosecutor told us, "was taken in La Paz, Bolivia, in 1968. That is all I can say at this time. Since you have demonstrated how efficient you are, why don't you help me identify that man?"

16

PURSUING BARBIE
IN PERU AND
BOLIVIA

So we were faced with a challenge. When we got back home, we issued a statement that Barbie was undoubtedly in Bolivia. We had the photographs copied and sent them to Lyon, hoping thereby to uncover some witnesses.

On October 8, Pierre-Bloch met with Foreign Minister Maurice Schumann and asked him to intervene with the Bolivian government for locating Barbie and extraditing him. He also gave Schumann a photocopy of the new German decision and the group picture. Consequently it would have been child's play for the French authorities to get hold of Barbie. All that was needed was to send the picture to the French Embassy in La Paz so that one of the staff—a mere clerk, if need be—could show it to porters and bartenders in La Paz's few hotels. Within a day's time Schumann could have got Barbie's assumed name, and could have proceeded effectively from there on. But nothing was done.

I went to *France-Soir* and gave one of its editors-in-chief a copy of the picture so that it could be published and thus uncover witnesses. It could even be seen in South America, where it would enable people to recognize Barbie and report his current name and address.

A few days later *France-Soir* told me: "Our legal staff has advised us not to run that picture, for if the man supposed to be Barbie is not he, we could get into a great deal of trouble."

One October morning, though I did not have an appointment, I went to the government anthropometric department, explaining that I needed a photograph analyzed. A guard telephoned for a woman to come and help me. My story so astonished her that she took me straight to the head of the department, who proved to be very helpful, for he knew who I was and had himself been in the Resistance.

"I can't give you more than a rather superficial study," he said, "and I can't put it in writing."

That seemed quite enough. For half an hour he scrutinized the three photographs, then, to my great relief, said: "Yes, there is every likelihood that it's the same man. Look at the ears. His earlobes are turned outward, particularly the right one, and that is unusual. The structure of the frontal bone on the left is common to all three pictures, and the folds at the corners of the mouth are absolutely identical." I wrote Ludolph a report of this analysis.

On October 12, Steiner, Ludolph's assistant, wrote me a letter in which was clearly evident a desire for technical cooperation, in that the prosecutor's office in Munich saw in the LICA's activities such energy and coordination that he thought he could get better results from it than from any other association:

As a follow-up to your telephone conversation with Prosecutor Ludolph, may I say that we would be very interested in talking with you in Munich about this case as soon as you have shown the French people the photographs that will allow them to identify the defendant. . . .

In my opinion, the case is so complicated that after actual efforts at identifying Barbie, we should definitely talk about procedural details. We should especially review together the steps you have taken, those the German court has taken, and perhaps even the ones taken by French authorities for penal prosecution.

I will be much obliged for your assistance in this matter. Your expenses for a flight to Munich and return will, of course, be reimbursed as well as your hotel expenses.

Perhaps you could arrange to spend enough time in Munich to give us a whole day. The date will depend upon our receipt of answers

French witnesses make to our requests for identification of the photographs.

Late in October I sent Ludolph various affidavits from people who had met Barbie and recognized him more or less definitely as the man in the La Paz picture.

On November 2, *L'Aurore* ran the picture of Barbie I had given it as well as the anthropometric test, and captioned it: "The Murderer of Jean Moulin." Philippe Bernert wrote that he was amused to see that "for the first time B.K. is leading a crusade with the blessing and support of an important West German judge, even though she is out on bail and under prosecution from the Cologne Attorney General for having tried to kidnap Lischka. A paradoxical situation for Prosecutor Ludolph's new assistant!"

A few weeks later Ludolph asked me if I would get in touch with a German living in Lima, Peru, who thought he could identify Barbie as a businessman who had recently come to La Paz. The German had seen Barbie's 1943 picture in a recent issue of Munich's *Süddeutsche Zeitung* that had come to him in Lima. I agreed.

The German's name was Herbert John, who, as I later learned, was the manager of Editoriales Unidas, a publishing firm owned by the extremely rich Luis Banchero Rossi, Peru's commercial fishing and fishmeal king.

On December 16, Prosecutor Rabl, who had made the decision to dismiss the Barbie case, wrote me:

I acknowledge receipt of your letter of November 19, 1971, containing the very interesting depositions of Mlle. Forest and M. Halaunbrenner. Meanwhile the court has come into possession of recent photographs that may be of Barbie. I have just requested the Anthropological and Ethnographical Institute of Munich University to give me an expert opinion on the question of identity. I hope to have its report by the end of the year. After we receive it, I should be very happy if you could come to Munich to discuss in detail what steps should be taken.

Prosecutor Rabl had been absent from Germany in recent months on a mission to Israel to interrogate witnesses in another case. Furthermore, Rabl was half Jewish; his father, who had been a civil servant in the Berlin patent office, was dismissed when Hitler came into power. He was a young man whose only real interest, he told me, was Oriental art. He had forgotten his family's unpleasant experiences and felt quite comfortable in the inner circles of the

German legal system. "After all," he said, "I did not do anything but apply the law in the Barbie case."

Rabl then put me in touch with Peter Nischk, a Munich friend of Herbert John. When I telephoned Nischk I discovered that John believed the man in the group picture was Theodor Dannecker, the head of the Gestapo's Bureau for Jewish Affairs and one of Eichmann's best assistants.

If John thought the man in the picture was Dannecker, then the actual man must have been known for a long time in La Paz and also in Lima, which he frequently visited, as a Nazi criminal who had been active in France. John managed to get a picture of him, for Barbie had been in Lima since the previous month, October.

On December 28, Nischk sent me Barbie's current name and address: "Klaus Altmann, c/o Fritz Schwend, Santa Clara (via Lima), Casilla No. 1, Carretera Central, km 14."

For several days I had been carefully watching the newspapers for mention of Bolivia and Peru. On the previous evening I had clipped from *Le Monde* the following information:

An official French delegation arrived in Lima on Monday, December 27, headed by Jean Jurgensen, director of political matters on the Quai d'Orsay, and consisting of twelve government officials. On Tuesday and Wednesday, December 28 and 29, it will discuss with the Peruvian government such unresolved problems of the two governments as technical and economic cooperation, Peru's foreign debt, and especially the resumption in 1972 by the French of atomic tests on Mururoa atoll in the South Pacific. The Lima government had threatened to break off relations with France last August, when Paris announced a nuclear explosion for September that was subsequently cancelled. . . . We think the much more intelligent attitude France has taken in the last months in respect to the Peruvian debt accounts for the easing of the political situation.

Consequently, I learned at the same moment that Barbie was in Lima and that France was trying to appease Peru about nuclear testing. The situation was hardly in our favor. Nevertheless, on December 30, Serge telephoned General Bourdis, the Prime Minister's chief of staff, who had been Serge's superior in the Army Ministry in 1961 and 1962, when Serge was doing his military service. Serge gave him all the details we had just received about Barbie and also talked with one of his staff advisers.

Serge told the adviser that he knew of two factors, one of which would help the extradition of Barbie, and the other, not: The first was the emotional response to Pompidou's recent remark about the Resistance. If he were forcefully to demand a swift extradition, the President could put an end to that reaction. The unfavorable factor had to do with the relations between France and Peru, which he felt did constitute an obstacle to the extradition of Barbie. The adviser told him: "One has nothing to do with the other."

Serge was not so sure. "If something isn't done soon," he said, "we'll have to proceed in a different fashion."

Serge repeated that in the circumstances secrecy was not called for. I telephoned Herbert John in Lima. He told me: "Fritz Schwend, Barbie's friend, works for the CIA in Peru. He came here in 1949 under the name of a Yugoslavian, Wenceslas Turi, a Nazi criminal who was sentenced in absentia in Bolzano, Italy, to twenty-one years in prison. He belonged to Department IV of the RSHA in Berlin, and was in charge of the Nazis' celebrated counterfeiting of pounds sterling. He became a chicken farmer, but he actually continued practicing his specialty. He set up postal censorship here, and he has feelers everywhere. If France were to make a request for extradition, Schwend would know about it in five minutes, and so would Barbie."

Therefore it was important that France firmly state that she would prosecute crimes committed by Nazis. In any event, even if everything were done to prevent it, a criminal could manage to flee from Peru.

Later we would be asked: "Why didn't you kill him? You could have taken him unawares."

None of the people who said that would have done it himself. My job was to try to build a fire under legal means for bringing criminals to trial so that public opinion would be aroused, and to prevent the rehabilitation of Nazis who had committed crimes in France. To do that I had to concentrate all my energies on the top criminals—Lischka, Hagen, and Barbie. Only through arguments and the emotion their names aroused would the problem of the insufferable ease those butchers were enjoying be settled one way or another. For if the most egregious of them managed to escape punishment, the cause of justice would suffer a heavy blow from the mass excitement their fate aroused. But if Barbie were to be identified and brought to trial, then people would be truly convinced that the crimes of the Nazis should not be subject to a time limit and were not being minimized and forgotten.

Killing Barbie would not have proved a thing. The papers would only say: "A man suspected of being Klaus Barbie has been found murdered." It would be merely a settling of scores.

On January 12 I received a letter from Rabl telling me that the expert opinion of the Anthropological and Ethnographical Institute had concluded that businessman Klaus Altmann of La Paz, Bolivia, was very likely Klaus Barbie. "Since we possess other evidence to support that opinion," the letter continued, "there can be no doubt of the identity of Barbie and Altmann. I should like very much for you to come to Munich in the near future. The date is up to you."

On January 15 Serge called General Bourdis again. The file was with the Army Ministry, but had not yet reached the court martial, and so nothing had happened. We decided to pressure for a request for extradition. On January 17 we sent *L'Aurore* the new pictures of Barbie that I had received from Munich and our information. *L'Aurore* ran them on January 19, with the headline: "Former Nazi Klaus Barbie Has Just Taken Refuge in Peru After a Long Stay in Bolivia—Is France Going to Demand Him?"

Philippe Bernert's editorial produced the reaction we expected. Resistance veterans and deportees in France demanded that the French government request extradition. In Lima, Altmann fiercely denied that he was Barbie. Many dispatches and stories followed, all containing the question: "Is Altmann Barbie?"

The request for extradition was not forthcoming. It would have to be prodded along by doing away with the question mark both in France and in South America, for there was still no case against Barbie in South America. The whole case could be buried in a few lines—"France claims that Altmann and Barbie are the same"—for want of information, and this had to be prevented.

On the morning of January 21 Ludolph telephoned me to say that he had found proofs in the Registry Office. That afternoon Pierre-Bloch and I held a press conference in Lyon on the current state of the investigation.

Meanwhile I tried to raise enough money for a trip to Lima. Geissmann and some of his friends thought that since they had had the good fortune to survive Barbie's persecutions, they should do something to bring him to account. They offered me a plane ticket. The young LICA members took up a collection and raised 2,500 francs, which was just enough for my other expenses.

On Tuesday, January 25, I reserved a seat on a flight for the following Thursday night. But I had to have written proofs, and Ludolph's information was only verbal. I called his house four or five times that night. His wife was home alone, but she promised to give her husband my message. At two A.M. he called me back and promised to give me an official transcript.

At seven o'clock on Wednesday morning I was at Orly, and at ten I reached Ludolph's house. We worked until seven o'clock that evening. At my request he researched the matter of extradition in volumes on international law, and gave me documentation on the agreements for it between France and Peru in the laws of October 23, 1888, and July 28, 1924. We completed a report establishing the identity of Altmann and Barbie, and the Munich Attorney General signed it. Four essential proofs were included in it:

1. Klaus Altmann's daughter Ute was born on June 30, 1941, in Kassel. The Registry Office had no record of a Ute Altmann. On the other hand, Ute Barbie, daughter of Klaus Barbie, was registered as having been born in Trier on June 30, 1941.

2. Klaus Altmann's son. Klaus-Georg, was born on December 11, 1946 in Kasel, near Leipzig. Unfortunately for Altmann, Ludolph had carefully studied the evidence. There was no district known as Kasel, but, on December 11, 1946, a Klaus-Jörg, son of Klaus Barbie, had been born in Dr. Kuhn's hospital in Kassel.

3. Klaus Altmann's wife was named Regina, and her maiden name was Wilhelms. The succession of extraordinary coincidences continued: Klaus Barbie's wife's name was Regina, née Willms.

4. The anthropometrical examination that Professor Ziegelmayer of the Ethnographical Institute of the University of Munich had made was contained in an exhaustive report sixteen pages long.

My plane landed on Wednesday about eleven P.M. The night was stormy. As usual, Serge was at Orly to meet me, and we spent an hour telephoning London for a reservation on the London-Lima plane the next morning and in getting my ticket adjusted accordingly. All this was due to Serge's having foreseen that I must arrive in Lima on a day—a Friday—when all offices would be open so that I could go into action at once.

Then we went to *France-Soir*, only to find that no one was the least bit interested in our proofs of Altmann's and Barbie's identity. Agence France Presse photocopied the report, but sent out no dispatch. Again I realized how little effect reports have; it's the presentation that counts. On the following day Serge was to give the whole file to the directors of the French military tribunal.

At two A.M., dead tired, I went to bed. It was too late to talk to Arno, and when I left in the morning, it would be too early.

At four A.M. Serge, who was arranging my files, awakened me. The radio had announced that Barbie had left Lima and taken the road toward Bolivia. We figured that he could not reach the border before Friday, by which time I would be in Lima and, if necessary, could follow him to La Paz.

At seven A.M. I spoke on the "Europe No. 1" newscast: "What good is it for French politicians to pay tribute to Jean Moulin in the Panthéon so long as the French government is not doing what is required to bring his murderer to justice?"

An hour later I was in the London airport, where I encountered my first difficulties. The immigration officer looked at my passport, and then consulted a thick volume containing the names of all the people the British were looking for or suspected. He asked for my ticket, took my passport, and disappeared. I was worried that I might miss my plane. I questioned his superior, and he asked: "Why are you going via London and not taking the direct Paris-Lima flight?"

I owed this treatment to my campaign in London against the expulsion from England of Rudi Dutschke.

"Put a policeman alongside of me," I told him, "until the Lima plane leaves. Then you will have nothing to worry about."

At last he let me through. I kept studying the Barbie data, and I slept. The stops—Trinidad and Caracas—vanished behind us, and I landed in Lima at 10 P.M. the same day, thanks to the time difference. I was rather disoriented. It was hot and humid, and I was wearing a winter coat. There were no reporters, for I had made a mistake in my cables by giving Greenwich instead of Lima time. Not even my source of information, Herbert John, whom I had telephoned from Paris, was there to meet me.

I managed to get in touch with Albert Brun, the AFP correspondent, a thin, tanned, fifty-year-old, who came to meet me at the airport in a car with Nicole Bonnet, *Le Figaro*'s correspondent. I got a room at the Hotel Savoy, took a shower, changed my clothes, gathered up my data, and went down to the bar, where reporters congregated for news. I showed the proofs of Altmann's identity while Brun translated for me into Spanish, telling the same story over and over until after 2 A.M., when I could finally get to bed. I found out that Barbie could not possibly have crossed the Bolivian border, and would not be able to do so before the following afternoon.

About 9 A.M. Herbert John met me on the hotel steps. He was not yet forty years old, was very tall, stooped, blond, and had lively blue eyes, but he did not seem at ease, as if he were constantly afraid of something. The way he kept looking over his shoulder made me feel as if we were spies. He promised to put me in touch with the Peruvian police so that I could give them the documents.

Reporters streamed into the AFP offices to examine my data. The press was convinced. That afternoon the Peruvian papers— *La Nueva Crónica, Tercera, La Prensa, Expreso, Ojo, Correo, El Comercio*—ran six-column headlines on their front page: "German Nazi-hunter Proves Altmann is Barbie." "Why Did Peru Let Barbie Escape?"

From various conversations I learned that Peru did not want to be shielding a criminal from either France or Bolivia, and preferred to have Barbie back in Bolivia again. Thanks to "Don Federico," alias Fritz Schwend, Barbie got a lot of help from the Peruvian secret service.

About noon Herbert John sent an emissary to take me to the military police headquarters, where a general received me. I explained the Barbie case to him in English, and asked him to stop Barbie before the criminal could cross the border. He had my data photocopied, and told me he would get it to the proper government minister.

Then I went to the government palace to see the press attaché. I noticed that every one of the civil servants I encountered knew that Barbie intended to cross the frontier. They all studied my data with apparent interest and agreed that Altmann was Barbie, but they did not do the one important thing, namely, close the frontier to him. The press attaché telephoned the Intelligence Bureau, which was across the street from the palace. A colonel there talked to me, photocopied the data, and telephoned the border patrol to ask whether Barbie's car, a Volkswagen with the license plate HH CD 360, registered in Hamburg in his son's name, had crossed the border. The answer was no.

Then I rushed to the French Embassy, where Ambassador

Chambon was expecting me. He was a former deportee and a forceful, extroverted diplomat who embraced me in the presence of the reporters.

I gave Chambon a set of the documents I had had photocopied at the Intelligence Bureau, and immediately he agreed that Altmann and Barbie were the same person. Then the telephone rang. The consul at Puno was calling to say: "Barbie crossed the frontier at noon, accompanied by two Peruvian policemen who turned him over to the Bolivian police."

The request Chambon had just made of General Pedro Richter, the Peruvian Minister of the Interior, to stop Barbie as a precautionary measure until an official demand for his extradition reached Peru, consequently would be fruitless. I went back to the AFP, where I worked until midnight with press and television people. All that effort was very worthwhile because Peruvian newspapers are read in Bolivia. I observed that Peruvian reporters are more prone than French or German ones to report the proofs in a file. Their stories gave in detail all the arguments for the identity of Altmann and Barbie.

I decided to take a plane the following morning, and follow Barbie to La Paz. The weekend would not be lost because Bolivian papers have Sunday editions. To save money, I spent the night with a young Peruvian secretary from the AFP.

On Saturday morning I had to pay an additional $120 for my plane ticket. The only exchange office that was open would not accept my French francs, so I had to trot out all my eloquence for the clerk to take it upon himself to give me what I wanted. I bought a ticket, and then went back to the AFP office for my luggage. Herbert John took me to Jorge Chavez airport. Farewell, Lima!

A two-hour flight over the mountains on the Braniff plane brought me to the La Paz airport, over thirteen thousand feet above sea level. About twenty photographers, television cameramen, and reporters were on the ramp. It was one P.M. They hurried toward the waiting room and into a small office they had appropriated for the occasion but which was really an infirmary. For an hour I held an improvised press conference while a doctor treated a young woman who had been on my plane. Her nose was bleeding because of the altitude, and they put an oxygen mask over her face.

After the reporters left, I went to an office where three plain-clothesmen were waiting for me to fill out the forms necessary for entering the country. I had no visa, and I was not a tourist. Contrary to custom, they kept my passport and promised to return it to me at my hotel. Actually, I did not get it until three days later. The police recommended the Hotel Sucre, and the reporters took me there.

I had been expecting summer weather, but La Paz is chilly, even in summer. On the road down from the airport to the city I glimpsed modern apartment houses in the middle of the valley and Indians' huts on the slopes, but I did not feel too much out of my element seeing all the ponchos, the brightly colored full skirts, the children carried on their mothers' backs, and the stray dogs, for I already had some acquaintance with Latin America owing to my visit to Guatemala in May 1967.

I was maneuvering, however, in a kind of dream landscape, for I had not come to visit the country as a tourist but to achieve a purpose. I let the visual impressions just wash over me, because I was afraid I might get distracted from my mission if I looked around too much.

My ground-floor room opened on the street, and passers-by used my windowsill as a resting place. Behind the Sucre was a stadium from which exciting music blared. That and the altitude gave me a violent headache. The reporters reappeared and came into my room one by one while the others waited in the corridor. I might as well have had a red light outside my door.

I had my room changed. After all, why make it easy for anyone who might want to molest me and would only have to push the window open from the street to do so?

On Sunday, I looked at the papers—*Ultima Hora, Presencia, Hoy, El Diario, Nueva Jornada*—all of which had big headlines: "Altmann Is Barbie," and spread my proofs of their identity over several pages. I went to the hairdresser, for I had had no time for that in Paris, and I got some rest.

In the evening, an employee of the Ministry of the Interior came and wanted me to go to the Ministry with him. Thanks to an American who spoke Spanish, I could ask whether an interpreter would be there. The answer was no. In that event, I said, I'll postpone my visit until tomorrow.

I could understand what was worrying the police. They had

not expected that within an hour of my arrival the press would make of the Barbie case something that La Paz seldom sees: a national issue that put the government up against a wall.

On Monday morning I went to the French Embassy, where one of the staff whom I asked for the ambassador told me he had just come in. Indeed, I had just seen two middle-aged men go by. I waited. Then the consul, whose name was Colombani, came out and said: "The ambassador is not in."

"Do you mean he is not in, or that he does not wish to be in?"

"Take it as you like," he said.

"Has the request for extradition arrived?"

"You'll have to ask the French government Press Division."

I did not press the matter, but went to the Ministry of the Interior, which was next to the French Embassy. A soldier on guard detained me at the entrance and kept saying over and over: "Mañana."

At the hotel the reporters arranged an appointment with the Immigration Minister, Rudolfo Greminger, and tried to get me one with the President, Colonel Banzer. I met Greminger that afternoon, and found him to be about thirty years old, with a European charm. His welcome was a little cool, however, so I just left him my data so that he could have it photocopied.

Ladislas de Hoyos, from the ORTF second network, and his crew had set up their television equipment at the Hotel Sucre. At least one organ of the press had sent a reporter to the place where Barbie, who had made so much ink flow in France, was. It seemed strange to me that newspapers can send reporters to Hong Kong or Australia to cover the drug traffic or a football match, but are quite content to handle something like the Barbie case from Paris or Lyon without letting the French know the real situation in Bolivia.

I still had a headache, and practically no appetite. The hotel food did not help. I made do with an avocado salad and stewed fruit.

Then I went back to work with the reporters, who never stopped telephoning and showing up at my room until late that night, for they wanted to hear everything about my progress during the day. We had long interviews, and I told them all about the Gestapo, Nazism, the Resistance, and the death camps. They were far removed from all those facts. How could we expect to obtain Altmann's extradiction if the Bolivians were not completely convinced that he was Barbie and had been a real criminal who plied his trade from the inner circles of a ruthless police system under a loathsome dictatorship? Such was the task I accomplished in La Paz—an indispensable one regardless of whether or not Barbie would be extradited, and one that others more qualified than I, in that they had fought the Nazis in person, could have accomplished had they seen the purpose of doing so. Moreover, I was quite familiar with the nature of the Banzer government and, by attacking in La Paz the fascism of the past, I was helping the Bolivians make a connection between what had happened under Hitler and what was going on under Banzer.

On Tuesday morning I went back to Greminger, who returned my documents and also my passport. Then he handed me a newspaper in which he had underlined in red pencil some of my statements. He criticized me for speaking so freely to the press since I was only a tourist in Bolivia. Nevertheless, I sensed that he now had more sympathy for me than on the previous evening. He told me that he had been instructed to prepare a report on Barbie for his division, and would send it to the Supreme Court, which would make the final decision. Greminger took Altmann's confiscated passport out of a drawer and showed it to me. I got a glimpse of his birth date—October 25, 1913, like Barbie's, and not October 15, as he had pretended in Lima.

Greminger asked me to go back to Munich and get answers to some questions he had about Barbie's vital statistics and police career. I promised I would do what was necessary. The press also indicated that I was risking expulsion from Bolivia because of my campaigns, about which they had got complete and exact information. In a regime as authoritarian as Bolivia's no one, especially a woman, is supposed to go around saying what she thinks.

When I left Greminger, a policeman approached to take me to the chief of the Bolivian secret service, Major Dito Vargas. Our conversation proceeded through an English-speaking policeman. Smiling sarcastically and speaking dictatorially, he let me know that as a foreign tourist I had no right to make use of the Bolivian press for my crusade. "You will be expelled," he said, "if you continue talking to reporters."

"I don't need to," I replied impertinently, "because I have already seen all of them, and they have let Bolivians know the essence of what I had to tell them."

He must not have been accustomed to talk as an equal with a

woman, for he took me back to my hotel in his brand new big American car.

In the lobby I was paged to the telephone. One of the French Embassy staff wanted to meet me at the hotel but, out of caution, in a room other than mine. The diplomat, who turned out to be Jewish, had kept up with my previous activities. He told me that I had not been received at the Embassy because I had not come on an official mission, but the Embassy was eager to examine my documents. Could I trust him with them? He said he would have them photocopied. So, naturally, I gave them to him.

In the afternoon the radio announced that the French ambassador had just requested extradition. I felt relieved. During the night an American press correspondent woke me up to tell me that I was going to be expelled in the morning for having violated the tourist regulations.

And, indeed, on Wednesday a worried Greminger, whose desk was piled high with all the morning newspaper stories about Barbie, asked me to leave that same day for Paris via Lima. He was being pressured about that, and he himself reserved a seat for me and then told me to come back to see him at 2 P.M. Meanwhile, de Hoyos interviewed me on the road above La Paz. I learned that Colonel Mario Zamorra, the Minister of the Interior, had just announced that I had been expelled from the country, but when I met Greminger that afternoon, he said that news was incorrect.

"You have not been expelled," he told me, "but I need some more documents, and you are the only one who can get them for me. I have decided to work with you, and I have just told the press." Indeed, his statement appeared that afternoon: "Mme. Klarsfeld has left of her own accord."

Two policemen and an automobile were put at my disposal. We stopped at the French Embassy, where I picked up my data, and then at the hotel, where I telephoned several reporters and took away with me the reel of film Ladislas de Hoyos had given me.

Late that afternoon two Lima police inspectors took me to an office. I was not to wander about the city. "We are here to see to your safety," they told me. "You risk being killed by Nazi organizations in Lima that are furious over the campaign you have launched against them in South America."

I reached Herbert John by telephone, and he told me that

Fritz Schwend, at whose house Barbie's wife was staying, had declared that if B.K. came back, "she would be taken care of." But I wanted to sleep in a bed, not on a chair at the airport, which was stifling.

"Give me a revolver," I said, "if you're so scared something will happen to me. I can take care of myself."

The policemen refused, and so I had to spend the night on a bench in a glass-enclosed office next to theirs.

On Friday morning, February 3, in the company of my guardian angels, I boarded an Air France Boeing.

In spite of the early hour—it was barely 7 A.M.—my young friends from the LICA were at Orly to meet me. I allowed myself a few minutes' relaxation with Arno and Serge, then began buzzing around the apartment like a bee, for the problem of keeping my men's clothes clean was in the back of my mind during my trips, as they were sloppy by nature. Probably people have wondered: "What does she think about while she is chasing those ruthless Nazis all over the world?" Perhaps my strength lies in thinking about just such problems of getting home within a week or Arno won't have any clean undershorts, or Serge will go out every day in dirty shoes because I'm not there to shine them, or what can I find for Arno to do next Sunday afternoon, or—oh dear!—I left the laundry ticket under the television set, and Raissa won't be able to find it, etc. Now I could catch up with all those things, and I was overjoyed. Usually I manage to stay away from home for only two or three days, but this time I had been gone for over a week.

I telephoned Ludolph for an appointment, necessary because Greminger needed several pieces of information without delay and wanted me to get them for him. A long time ago I had scheduled a lecture before the Strasbourg B'nai B'rith for Monday night. I could take a 3 A.M. train after it, and be in Munich early Tuesday morning, February 8. Ludolph agreed.

That afternoon Ludolph called me back and told me that the French military tribunal was giving me a respite. The Foreign Ministry in Bonn had asked him to meet with two French magistrates beginning on Monday. We kept our appointment nevertheless, for I had just learned that Barbie had been arrested for fraud; a government development agency claimed he had swindled it out of twenty thousand francs. If only those few Bolivian leaders were hostile to Barbie, we had to make use of them and help them as soon as possible by giving the Bolivian courts as much data as we could that would serve to discomfit Barbie.

French judicial machinery, which at last was beginning to move, is slow and ponderous, for it has to work with diplomats and because Spanish documents would have to be translated, and the La Paz embassy—as I had learned when I was there—had no experts on its staff who could handle such work. These considerations indicated that I would have to go back to La Paz with two trump cards. First, the documents that I could get from the Munich prosecutor that would complete the proof that Altmann was Barbie. These were official documents that I would transmit unofficially because I could represent only the LICA and myself, but these documents would be taken into consideration by the Bolivian authorities and especially by public opinion. Second, I had seen that so far as the Peruvians and the Bolivians were concerned, former Nazis were only political refugees like any others. Scarcely anyone in South America knew about the Gestapo's work of extermination. They had to be shown in a dramatic way that Barbie was not what he said he was: "only a soldier who had done his duty."

Barbie had told a reporter for *Pueblo*: "During the war I acted like any other officer of an army in battle, just like the Bolivian army officers fighting Che Guevara's guerrillas." A great deal of emphasis, therefore, had to be put on the massacres of civilians and the liquidation of Jews.

It occurred to me that Mme. Benguigui would be conclusive proof of those atrocities. The Bolivians had to see something more than documents and photographs. They had to come into direct contact with some of the evils of Nazism by encountering someone whom Barbie himself had caused to suffer. All that was needed was enough money for plane tickets and expenses—plus the individual herself, whom I would have to persuade to go with me.

I spent several hours in Strasbourg on Monday, the day on which I was to lecture. At 3 A.M. I got back on the train, and spent an awful night tripping back and forth between my berth—which, as is always the case at such times, was an upper one—and the toilet at the end of the car. The ORTF crew that met me at the Munich railway station saw emerge from the compartment a mere rag of a woman with but one thought in mind: to lie down in a hotel room. I bought some pills, went to the nearest hotel, fell into bed, and called a doctor. I had no night clothes with me, for I had planned to leave Munich that evening by plane. The doctor charged me forty marks for telling me that I had food poisoning and prescribing the same pills I had just bought.

That afternoon, looking wan and haggard, I went to Ludolph's office and told him that Greminger wanted copies of the birth certificates of the four Barbies, proof that during the war Barbie was officially a police officer and not a soldier, and specimens of Barbie's handwriting.

The French magistrates had not come yet, so we worked until 7 P.M.

Unfortunately, Ludolph was no longer entitled to give me photocopies of the data, for from now on he had to give them to the French military tribunal. Otherwise, I would have been back in La Paz with them on Thursday, February 10, and they would have been of great help to the people who did not want Barbie out of jail. The only official means of getting the documents to La Paz would take ten days at least. Barbie was freed on February 12.

About noon on the following day I translated for Ludolph the questions the French television newscasters wanted him to answer, and his replies. The two magistrates from the military tribunals of Lyon and Paris had spent the morning with him, and he had prepared for each of them two photocopies of selected documents. He had invited me to lunch, and I expected the two judges to join us.

"When I told them that all four of us would lunch together," Ludolph told me, "they declined the invitation." He seemed astonished at their reaction, for, as he himself said, I had done their work for them.

There was a lot of talk in Paris about the Barbie case. Ladislas de Hoyos had managed to interview Barbie in jail, which had cost him a great deal of trouble and cost the ORTF $2,000. The French consul had paid the money over to an executive of the Ministry of the Interior while Barbie and his two lawyers were in an adjoining office.

Now that they could see their abuser on television, Barbie's victims recognized him in spite of the intervening years. What luck! Thereafter, so far as the French were concerned, Altmann was indeed Barbie. I was both happy and furious over that; incontrovertible evidence was hardly taken into consideration, while dubious evidence was believed. Generally I myself am not capable of recognizing a person I met only a day ago unless there is something striking about him, so I tend to question the accuracy of persons who, after twenty-seven years, say they are absolutely certain. The opposite was just as likely; in spite of the fact that Altmann was certainly Barbie and that the Munich prosecutor had stated that he was "one hundred percent sure that any German court whatever would be convinced," it could very well have happened that those witnesses might have proved unable to identify him. In that event, what would have happened? I would have gone rushing around with all my data, and no one would have believed me.

Among the witnesses on the ORTF program was Mme. Simone Lagrange, whom Barbie had interrogated in June 1944, when her name was Simone Kadousche:

I was then thirteen years old. When we reached Gestapo headquarters on place Bellecour, we were put into a room on the fourth floor, where I saw Barbie for the first time. He came toward my parents and me, gently stroking a big gray cat, and without raising his voice he asked my mother whether I was her only child. Mama replied that she had two younger children but she did not know where they were. Then Barbie, who had paid no attention at all to my father, came over to me and politely asked me where my two little brothers were. When I told him I did not know, he gently set his cat on a table, then struck me brutally hard twice, saying he could find them well enough himself.

The German woman who was our keeper advised Mama to tell him where my brothers were if she wanted to escape an interrogation, but Mama and I knew we were going to be sent to a concentration camp where little children were killed.

On June 7 they came to take me to place Bellecour, where Barbie himself was waiting to question me again. He said politely that if I told him where my brothers were he would send all three of us to an old folks' home, where we would be well taken care of and not deported. After I told him again that I did not know, he came over to me, grabbed me by my long hair, and yanked me close to him. Then he struck me over and over again for at least fifteen minutes. I was in great pain, but I did not want to cry. Finally he let me go, and I fell to the floor. He kicked me in the stomach until I got up again. Then he himself took me to jail. He told my mother that she had no heart to allow her daughter to be beaten, and if she would talk now, he would stop interrogating me. Then he struck her several times.

I was taken back to the Gestapo four times, but you can be sure that they got nothing out of me. Then they put me into a different cell. I didn't see Mama again until June 23, 1944, when we were shipped to Drancy before being sent to the Auschwitz concentration camp, where Mama was burned on August 23, 1944. My father was killed on January 19, 1945, as the camp was being evacuated.

Serge met Mme. Lagrange on the day after the television program during a demonstration by Resistance veterans and former deportees in front of the Bolivian Embassy. Mme. Lagrange was immediately interested in going to tell the Bolivians about Barbie and the concentration camps. When I returned from Munich, Serge showed me a story in *Le Monde*, entitled "Troublemakers," which reported the demonstration. It strongly indicated the need for action.

About one hundred and perhaps one hundred fifty people demonstrated on Wednesday in front of the Bolivian Embassy in Paris to demand the extradition of Klaus Altmann.

They waved signs and shouted slogans, but prudently stopped when a police cordon prevented them from proceeding. . . .

It is especially important for automobile traffic on avenue Kleber not to be blocked by a demonstration of Resistance veterans and deportees. A force of three police vans was there to see to it that traffic kept moving. Consequently, there was no traffic jam.

On February 12, Barbie was released from jail, for he had paid his debt. Jean-Martin Chauffier of *Le Figaro* was still hopeful:

There are two groups of hunters on Altmann's trail; one takes the usual route; the other takes short cuts. It may be a long time before Barbie has to face an examining magistrate, but Altmann is already up before the devil. From now on, every hour of the night is that first hour of dawn for which the people whom he sent to the firing squads used to await in anguish.

That story was a mistake, for it actually meant: "Good people, be calm. The criminal will not escape. For a long time yet he will not be able to enjoy his villa, his swimming pool, his chaise longue, and his family. There are, thank God, professionals, the inexorable commando force of justice, that is beginning to get moving. Barbie's score is already settled. Now it is his turn to know nights of hideous nightmares and to be drenched in the cold sweat that once poured from his victims." When people take desires for realities, public opinion is lulled to sleep and led astray, and the hangmen laugh in derision.

In reality, Klaus Barbie regularly frequents the bar at the Crillon,

La Paz's best hotel, downing a few whiskies. Avengers! What avengers? Where are they coming from? The Eichmann case is unique, for his presence in Buenos Aires was an open secret that everyone in Argentina, whether Jew or Nazi, knew about for years. Indeed, he concealed himself so well that he gave interviews and listed his sons under their right name at the German Embassy. When the Bolivian Foreign Minister, Mario Gutiérrez, went to Israel in May 1972, no Israeli authority brought up the Barbie case. International reaction to the abduction of Eichmann so burned the Israelis that they could not or would not hunt for lesser game like Martin Bormann or Heinrich Müller, the head of the national Gestapo. Make no mistake. There is no cleaning fluid for cleansing the world of Nazi criminals. They may issue "contracts," as they say in the United States, for disposing of associates, rivals, partners, or a wife's lover. But no one has ever financed a contract to wipe out mass murderers.

17

STILL IN
PURSUIT

On February 15, I learned that President Pompidou had written Colonel Banzer a "forceful and urgent" letter. Later I heartily endorsed what it said:

Time wipes out many things, but not all. Unless their sense of justice is sadly tarnished, Frenchmen cannot permit crimes and sacrifices to be lumped together and then forgotten through indifference.

The Bolivian government assigned the Barbie case to their Supreme Court. Its justices had been appointed after Colonel Banzer's putsch of August 1971, when their predecessors were removed long before the end of their term.

Mme. Lazurick, the owner of L'Aurore, answered my call for help and got me two plane tickets. Not only did she appreciate my furnishing her paper with so much material, but she was as eager as I to see Barbie brought to trial. But I could not persuade Barbie's victim, Mme. Lagrange, to go with me. She wrote:

I want to assure you that I will be with you in La Paz in spirit, and if I do not go with you, it is because all the associations concerned have asked me to postpone going until the Bolivian government replies to our President's letter. This is not to say that I want to hamper the progress of justice, but to assure you that later on, if positive identification is necessary and can be arranged, I will be ready to go then.

I weathered that blow, and decided to approach Mme. Halaun-brenner, who would soon be sixty-eight years old and whose life had been sad and trying. As with Mme. Benguigui, Barbie had turned her life into one long period of mourning. Her husband, her older son, and two of her daughters had been killed by Barbie. Only one son, Alexandre, and a daughter, Monique, were left.

I got an affidavit from Alexandre:

In 1943, our family consisted of my father Jakob, who was born on July 12, 1905, in Drohobiz, Poland; my mother Itta; my older brother Leon (thirteen); my three sisters, Mina (eight), Claudine (four), and Monique (three).

Between 1941 and 1943 we were interned in several camps in the southern zone (Nexon, Rivesaltes, Gurs). On August 26, 1943, we were put under surveillance in our house in Lyon.

We were living at 14 rue Pierre-Loti, in Villeurbanne, when the Gestapo came to our house at 11 A.M. on October 24, 1943. There were three of them. Two were tall and about forty years old; the third, who was much younger—he seemed to my childish eyes to be about thirty—was plainly in command. He waited impatiently for the arrival of my father's nephew, who must have been betrayed to the Gestapo and who was arrested and killed by them in 1944. While my little sisters were clinging to my father, the younger man pulled out his revolver, terrifying us. His face has been etched on my memory ever since that moment, haunting my dreams and my wakeful nights. When I saw his picture in *Die Weltwoche* for September 10, 1971, I recognized him at once, and so did my mother, who was then with me.

My brother Leon, who was tall for his age, came home about 6 P.M. The three Gestapo men had been at our apartment continuously until then, one of them watching outside the door. When my brother arrived, they searched him, and then took him away along with our father. My mother began to scream in Yiddish for them to let my brother go, and we all wept and howled, but in vain. Barbie shoved my mother aside as she was trying to yank her son and her husband back, took out his revolver again, and beat her hands with it to make her let go. But all was useless. We waited all the next day in the street for the two who had been arrested to return, my sisters clinging to my mother's skirt. Then we saw a German army truck stop in front of our house, probably to take us away. Pretending to be merely passers-by, we moved on down the street, leaving everything behind.

A few weeks later, on December 14, we learned from a Jewish friend that our father had died "in the hospital." I went with my mother through all the hospitals, but we could not locate him. Then I thought of going to the morgue, and there we found my father. "He's been there three weeks," they told us. He had been shot in a summary execution at Gestapo headquarters on rue Marcelin-Berthelot. Seventeen machine-gun bullets were in his neck and chest.

My brother Leon was deported and died of exhaustion from labor in the Polish salt mines after eight months.

My two younger sisters, Mina and Claudine, were put into the Jewish children's camp at Izieu, where we thought they would be safe, but Barbie did not spare them when he liquidated that children's refuge on April 6, 1944. My sisters were deported on June 30, 1944, and were murdered when they reached Auschwitz.

In spite of her age, the altitude of La Paz, and the suspense of waiting to face Barbie, Mme. Halaunbrenner was not afraid. She knew she was going to be useful and that from her mouth the Bolivians would learn how Barbie persecuted innocent people. On Thursday evening, February 17, she told me she would go, and so I set our departure for Sunday.

Since Mme. Halaunbrenner was stateless, Serge had to run around like mad all of Friday to get her a passport. That same evening the Bernard Lazare Club and the Union of French Jewish Societies arranged a meeting at which I answered questions put to me by Henri Bulawko, the president of the Brotherhood of Jews Deported from France. When he asked where I had got the money to go to Bolivia, I said that I had been given the tickets, but that money for our stay and for unforeseen expenses had not yet been forthcoming. At that, the young LICA members pulled off their stunt of jumping up and shouting: "That's shameful. We have to do something about that."

Then someone else said: "That's right. Let's take up a collection. Here's my contribution."

That collection and contributions from friends netted 3,000 francs.

I had asked Ludolph for copies of the pictures of Frau Barbie in 1940 that he had just uncovered, and on the morning after the meeting I flew to Munich. Ludolph gave me the photographs, which were quite conclusive evidence. I also met Peter Nischk, who gave me several documents, one of which, written in English three years earlier, probably by Herbert John, was about Martin Bormann.

Like a businessman I flew from Munich to Paris that evening. It's no problem for businessmen, however, to keep going to South

America to buy and sell things of all varieties. When Serge was working for Continental Grains, one of his associates made two round trips between Paris and Bogota in one week. In spite of all the comings and goings I am accused of, I think it hardly equals that of an ambitious young executive in an international company whose assignments are less imperative than those of the Resistance. I took along the photographs of Frau Barbie, who had scarcely changed in thirty years and who had hardly any wrinkles.

As soon as Serge saw the photos at Orly, he dragged me into a taxi. It was almost midnight when we got to the *L'Aurore* offices. The layout of the paper was changed, and the two photographs and a long story, "The Final Proof," inserted. On Saturday, I got thirty copies made of the two pictures and of the one of the Halaunbrenner family before it was broken up. I intended them for the Bolivian authorities and especially for the Bolivian newspapers so that they could complete their stories as soon as I got there.

We left Paris on Sunday evening, February 20.

Nothing untoward happened on our flight to Lima, where I decided to remain for a day. I was afraid Bolivia might turn us away, and that would be less likely to happen if the Peruvian papers had already run my latest proofs and Mme. Halaunbrenner's story. There was a change in the attitude of the diplomats; the French consul was there along with a group of reporters who almost snatched the pictures of Frau Barbie and the Halaunbrenner family away from me. Mme. Halaunbrenner answered the deluge of questions simply and with dignity, though she was a little at sea. She had not expected such attention from the press nor thought her story would ever create such excitement. Now she recognized how necessary her trip was.

The consul obligingly took us to the Hotel Savoy, and told us that Ambassador Chambron was in Europe. In spite of Schwend's threats, I was not much afraid of any reprisals from the Nazis, for these would only boomerang against them. We talked to reporters all the rest of the evening.

The next day the Lima papers devoted a large part of their front page to our story and pictures. I also talked with a correspondent of an American newspaper who was on his way to La Paz to interview Colonel Banzer.

At eight o'clock on Tuesday morning we were at the airport, where we were made to wait at the baggage check-in. Then we were told that a telegram had come from La Paz denying us permission to enter and instructing us to get in touch with the Bolivian Embassy. The Bolivian consul saw everything that happened at the airport. The American correspondent boarded the plane, saying he was sorry he would not be able to talk to us on the way. We picked up our luggage again and took a taxi straight to the Bolivian Embassy, where the ambassador told us we would have to apply for a visa to the Ministry of the Interior and the Foreign Ministry by means of a telegram with the reply prepaid.

When we got back to the Savoy, I sent the two telegrams, plus one to Greminger to remind him that it was he who had asked us to return. There was nothing to do now but wait, and our hopes sank. Mme. Halaunbrenner was truly in despair over having come so far, only to be kept from entering Bolivia.

We still had close contacts with the newspapers, which started a campaign on the theme: The Bolivians are protecting Barbie by forbidding his accusers the right to demand justice in Bolivia.

I went back alone to the Bolivian consulate as soon as it opened on Wednesday. About 5 P.M. Agence France Presse telephoned me that there had been a dramatic event in La Paz. The Bolivian Minister of the Interior had released a statement saying that Colonel Banzer himself had granted us a visa, that the Altmann papers were actually being studied in the Foreign Ministry (and also in the Ministry of the Interior), and that the legal authorities would reach a decision in good time.

I dashed to the Bolivian consulate with the AFP dispatch, but was told that nothing had come through yet. The consul, Ricardo Ríos, a great friend of Barbie, seemed overjoyed at giving me a negative answer. I was hardly back at the hotel, however, when he called me to say that he had just got our authorization. This time it was I who was overjoyed. I did a pirouette, exclaiming: "Now you see I was right to keep on hoping."

We arrived in La Paz on Thursday at 12:30 P.M. I was worried about how Mme. Halaunbrenner would stand the altitude, but she seemed to take it better than I. As soon as the plane landed, a young man came aboard to tell me that I had to promise not to make any statements to the newspapers or I would be expelled at once.

I played along with him, since I could not do otherwise, but I had no intention of keeping a promise that had been extracted from me. I would have betrayed my cause if I had kept my word.

Albert Brun, the AFP correspondent in Lima, had been in La Paz since Barbie was released from jail. He met us and took us to the Hotel La Paz, where I promised the disappointed reporters that I would see them soon.

I tried to see Greminger, but it appeared that he had had his wrist slapped. "I no longer have anything to do with the Barbie case," he said. "You will have to see Deputy Foreign Minister Jaime Tapia."

Tapia gave me an appointment for 3:30 P.M. on Friday.

Things now seemed all in Barbie's favor. The Presidential spokesman, Alfredo Arce, stated: "There are to be no proceedings for extraditing Klaus Altmann. President Banzer thinks he has enough legal evidence to consider the problem settled."

A few days earlier, Constancio Carrón, Bolivia's leading expert on international law in respect to private citizens, and also a counselor of the Foreign Ministry, had stated:

Bolivia is an inviolable asylum, and all who take refuge in it are sacrosanct. The time limit for the prosecution of major crimes in Bolivia is eight years. Altmann-Barbie's are, therefore, ancient history. The petty deception that Barbie practiced by disguising himself as Altmann is at the most punishable in Bolivia by a small fine.

Carrón was also one of the lawyers who were handling Barbie's defense.

On Friday morning the American correspondent asked me to breakfast at Maxim's, the city's best restaurant. He told me:

"While I was talking with Colonel Banzer on Wednesday, I told him what a bad impression he was making on international opinion by preventing two such brave women from entering Bolivia. That's what made Banzer change his mind, for he is very sensitive to American opinion. The CIA, it appears, pays him seven dollars a day for every prisoner he keeps in confinement for political reasons. That money allows him to pay his army, which is always disgruntled."

In the afternoon we went to Jaime Tapia's office, and I gave him my new proofs. Mme. Halaunbrenner wept as she told him about her family. He patted her kindly on the shoulder and promised that he would try everything, but we knew what that meant. At any rate, we had kept within the law and furnished the proper authorities with data, and so far had not met with the press.

On the previous evening Ambassador Jean-Louis Mandereau had met with the Foreign Minister, and the official request for extradition, in the proper form, had reached La Paz. On the same day Ambassador Mandereau saw us, and we brought him up to date. He let fall a remark that made me wonder whether he really understood the problem: "Because of you, I have had to take all the passion out of this matter and make it entirely a legal one."

"Mister Ambassador," I replied, "Barbie's torture of Jean Moulin was the Passion of the French Resistance."

Without translators (the German Embassy had translated into Spanish the German documents that were in the French dossier), without a press attaché to tell the Bolivian newspapers about the yoke the Nazis had imposed on France, and without energetic leadership, the French Embassy in La Paz hardly seemed in accord with President Pompidou's "forceful and urgent" letter, so well translated into Spanish through the efforts of the French Embassy that the Bolivian authorities are still smiling over it.

On Saturday, February 26, I tactfully sounded out the reporters. They had instructions not to say anything about our presence. Only one concrete happening and they would have a chance to publicize what we had to say and show. My idea of a press conference delighted them, especially since I proposed showing the film of the program on which Barbie's victims identified him from the Ladislas de Hoyos interview, as shown on ORTF television in Paris. Then I had to dash around madly but discreetly to find an adequate projector.

On Sunday, while we were walking on the Prado, Mme. Halaunbrenner suddenly heard two women chatting in Yiddish, and lost no time in introducing herself. Her new friends were already aware of why we were there, and invited us to luncheon and to spend the afternoon in their home.

On Monday morning I summoned all the reporters by telephone to a press conference at 11 A.M. I had to act quickly; if I waited until afternoon, the police might stop everything. At 10:15 half a dozen plainclothesmen entered the hotel. Two came up to me in the lobby and asked me to follow them to police headquarters. I went upstairs to get a few things from my room, and found two policemen standing guard outside it. I telephoned our

Jewish friends to come and comfort Mme. Halaunbrenner, who was terribly worried. I also alerted Brun so that he could explain to the reporters what had happened if I did not return by eleven.

Major Dito Vargas, whom I already knew from my first visit to La Paz, solemnly warned me against holding a press conference and said that if I did, I would be thrown out of the country once and for all.

I went back in a police jeep at 10:50 A.M., and we held our press conference in a large room in the hotel. About thirty reporters attended. I showed the film and handed out photographs and press releases that Serge had prepared. Then Mme. Halaunbrenner took over, and her story of her martyrdom as a woman and a Jewish mother deeply moved the reporters. When she finished speaking at 12:15, the policemen who had been there in the morning came back and took me off to police headquarters again. They shut me up in a filthy little office, and gave me some very salty soup and a plate of something or other. I sweated there until 5 P.M. Then the chief of the "Policia Internacional," Hernán Arteaga, let me go with instructions to keep my mouth shut thereafter. "This is the last warning," he said. "Otherwise you will be arrested."

On Tuesday there was only one topic in the papers—our conference, which had passed censorship. Whole pages were devoted to it, and also to the concentration camps, thus showing readers what the vacuous face of Altmann-Barbie had concealed from them.

When we went out, Bolivians swarmed around us and offered their sympathy to Mme. Halaunbrenner, telling us that they were on our side and that Barbie ought to be extradited.

After breakfast on Tuesday, February 29, two familiar faces suddenly reappeared. I got up to do my turn at police headquarters, telling Mme. Halaunbrenner to go to our Jewish friends.

A dispatch alarmed my family and friends in France: "Two men not identified as policemen have taken B.K. away." Their concern must have made itself felt with the Bolivian government, for during the afternoon the Reuter's correspondent was let into the office where I was being confined to determine that I had not been kidnapped.

I spent the day in that office with the same food as before, which I did not touch, trying in vain to find out why I was being kept there. A police superintendent who spoke a little French got so annoyed at my constant questions that he finally replied in the language of Descartes, but using rather earthy a vocabulary: "You shit on us, so we're going to shit on you and kick your ass out of here."

After that I resigned myself to my fate, and waited patiently until evening, when the office closed and I was released as on the previous day.

Meanwhile, at my instigation, Mandereau made a formal request for a confrontation between Barbie and Mme. Halaunbrenner. Barbie, of course, stubbornly refused, and Tapia told Mandereau on Wednesday morning that it would be impossible to force Barbie to consent. Barbie's refusal was significant. As far as meeting him myself, I did not see what good that would do, any more than I would have benefited from meeting any of my other adversaries.

Consequently, we tried to start a legal action against Barbie, in which Mme. Halaunbrenner would sue him as an individual for the murder of four of her family. The first lawyer we approached, Jaime Mendizabal, had been one of Regis Debray's defense attorneys, but after due consideration he turned us down for political reasons: his brother was in the government (later his brother would be dismissed and he himself would be arrested). The second, Manuel Morales Dávila, agreed, and began proceedings by registering Mme. Halaunbrenner's plea with a notary. Then he told us his fee: $7,000. Since such a charge was clearly an attempt to restrain us, I told the press that "Bolivian justice is too expensive for us." They frequently repeated to me in La Paz the proverb: "Beware of Chilean women, Peruvian friends, and Bolivian justice."

On Saturday we went with our Jewish friends to Lake Titicaca for a rest before undertaking our protest demonstration. That morning I had bought chains and two padlocks.

On Monday morning, March 6, I got our passports in order, procured an exit visa from the Ministry of the Interior, and reserved seats on the 8 P.M. flight to Lima. About noon we fastened the chains around our waist and wrist. We carried two signs in Spanish. Mme. Halaunbrenner's had the picture of her family on it and the message: "*Listen, Bolivians! As a mother I only claim justice. I want Barbie-Altmann, who murdered my husband and three of my children, brought to trial.*" Mine said: "*In the name of the millions of Nazi victims, let Barbie-Altmann be extradited.*" A reporter had translated these texts into Spanish for me.

We headed for the offices of Transmaritima Boliviana, of which

Barbie was a director. We sat down on a bench directly opposite the offices, which were located on the Prado, the busiest street in La Paz. Then we chained ourselves to the bench and began waving our signs. A crowd gathered, and cars slowed down or stopped.

There was a traffic jam. There had not been a demonstration right in the middle of town for some time, and the news was broadcast over the radio. That drew even more people. A police jeep arrived; its occupants read our signs and went away.

At 4 P.M. a small truck drew up, and plainclothesmen jumped out and mingled with the bystanders. Suddenly they leaped on us, snatched our signs, and took to their heels. Some young Bolivians and an Israeli tourist quickly made us new signs.

A Bolivian woman in a poncho and carrying her baby on her back said: "There is no such thing as justice in Bolivia. Kidnap him or kill him."

A reporter held a microphone in front of me and asked me what the chains signified.

"They are the chains that bind Bolivia to Nazism," I said.

It began to rain. Mme. Halaunbrenner, whose courage was extraordinary, could take no more. I, too, was exhausted. We had been on our bench for six hours and seen a good part of the population of La Paz, including the diplomatic corps, file past us. One of the French Embassy staff stopped in front of us to say: "What you are doing won't accomplish anything."

Nevertheless, the reverberations of our protest and our appeal to the Bolivian people would be great and positive in the press and, I thought, also among the public, judging from the sympathy expressed by those who had come to watch us.

That evening we boarded our plane, and spent twenty-four hours in Lima, which was pleasantly warm after La Paz. We had to get Mme. Halaunbrenner back in shape, for she had caught a cold.

We went to a hairdresser, for we wanted to be looking our best before the television cameras that would be waiting for us at Orly, and we also gave the Peruvian press a full account of all we had accomplished. Then we flew to Paris, where we landed on Thursday afternoon, March 9, eighteen days after we had started out.

At Orly, a crowd of friends, reporters, and cameramen rushed up to welcome us home. We did not have Barbie in our luggage, but for a while we had represented the eternal quest for justice. In this myth of a guilty man fleeing to the ends of the earth to escape retribution, two women—one belonging to a murderous people; the other, to its martyrs—had gone to the other side of the globe to find him and demand justice.

Eagerly I searched for Serge in the crowd. Then I saw him, hanging back, smiling at the whole scene. "Make your life a poem. Lift it to the level of an inspiring experience." That's what he had written to the little German girl whom he had just met back in the spring of 1960. Without him by my side, without his complete and tactful involvement, without his everlasting energy, what could I have accomplished? Another man doubtless would have required me to cut myself off from Germany. Serge had helped me to become a real German.

The Barbie case revived serious arguments in France. The crimes committed by the Nazis and their accomplices in Vichy must not have a time limit, or be forgotten, or just chucked into the cesspool of innumerable murders committed since. The battle against fascism must go on, for those who committed crimes are rising to the surface again. It is not surprising that a Darquier de Pellepoix, Xavier Vallat's successor as General Commissioner for Jewish Affairs, should timidly ask to return to France. How many books and articles say that if de Gaulle was the sword, Pétain was the shield, and that deep in their hearts the French hold the two in the same esteem? That is why the Barbie case is a healthy sign. Through one criminal all the crimes committed through a loathsome police system can be remembered, and the need to remember what such a system led to will be kept alive. Of course one can be pessimistic about that, but what good will it do?

An editorial in *Le Monde* said:

The brilliant methods Klaus Barbie used in interrogating victims have since been widely employed elsewhere. In some countries of Latin America torture is a daily occurrence. In Asia, a massacre like My Lai is to some officers merely the purest form of sanction. In France, it took a high military officer to justify the use of the "question" in Algeria. In East Europe, we have known for a long time that confessions are extracted by torture. What's the use of belatedly punishing this man if barbarism such as he practiced can never be eliminated?

How can something that seems to be human nature be changed? I have found my answer to that, the answer of a simple but energetic private citizen determined to be heard. Let no one criticize me for my "dedication" in pursuing Barbie as I was criticized in certain quarters for pursuing Kiesinger. These men stand for prin-

ciples and actions that must be opposed at all costs while there is
yet time.

Pierre Mathias's point of view, expressed in a letter to *Le Monde*,
is a good answer to the attacks and silence of people who say they
are fighting the same battle:

In a world that worships results and where torture is always a means
that justifies the end, is there still room for conscience? Mme. B.K. is
not some Fury stirring up hatred. She is the conscience we seem to
have lost. She strives to remind us that no end justifies crime, and that
crime cannot be forgotten or wiped out.

Many Resistance veterans and Jews helped me. Here are two
examples:

From the Resistance Volunteers of Saint-Die: "Mrs. K. has done
what the Resistance organizations ought to have done, or at least
supported, long ago."

From a dental surgeon in Nice: "Your courage and your determination have made many Jewish men ashamed, and me in particular. We have felt involved in the battle you are waging, but
you, a woman, have done something more. You have acted."

I also regularly received insulting or threatening letters. Some
correspondents needed to think I am Jewish so that they could say:

Dirty Jewess, someday someone will settle accounts with you, and
that's just what should be done. A curse on your whole race!

Or:

Your race has cost so many lives, so much sweat, and so many
miseries, in comparison to which those "extermination" camps of yours
are a joke.

Every time I read one of those letters I feel a stab in my heart,
and then I clench my fists. They hurt, but they bolster my determination even more. Here is another:

Dear Rebecca,

Just a line to tell you we [Nazis] are still around. Even though you
are an Aryan, you married a kike and so, by the rules of our gang, you
are going to be exterminated.

The Fourth Reich is at hand. The Crystal Nights and the Nuremberg Laws will soon be here again! Twelve million slimy toads like you
are going to die this time—and in our new ultra-modern ovens. Half-

Jews too! Children of mixed couples are going to be classed as Jews and sent to the crematories.

Best wishes from an Aryan.

(*signed*) A. HITLER

P.S. My house is infested with termites, and my country with Semites. France is a whore of a nation!

In a television review Jean Dutourd expressed what I resent about the public figure I have become: "This young Spirit of Purity and Justice, who wants to restore Germany's good name by pursuing every war criminal all over the world, is as terrifying in her own way as Barbie is in his. She is pure-white Good incarnate doing battle with jet-black Evil. She is scarcely a woman. She is an ideal and a principle."

I know that the public figure is much bigger than I. I have some of Barbie's or Kiesinger's blackness in me too, and some of the grayness of those who, through indifference or cowardice, are resigned to letting Nazi criminals go unpunished and seeing the Czechs crushed. There is also the "smudged whiteness" of people who are not resigned to all that and to many other excesses just as shocking, but are content with appeasing their troubled conscience by merely signing petitions. What counts is doing something concrete, whether white or black, and choosing values that cannot help but produce action, either white or black. A person can easily be a man of integrity, yet go astray by following principles that lead to black deeds. Once involved, every man's destiny depends on what he does. He becomes white, black, or gray, regardless of what color his soul originally was. As for myself, how long shall I go on being white "Beate"? Shall I someday drift into the blurred background of people who go through life blind, deaf, and dumb?

I did not stop making short trips across the Rhine in order to complete my list of executives of the Nazi police system in France and find out where they are now. Perhaps I overestimated my strength. When I was returning from one of those searches I encountered a general strike in Strasbourg, had to get out of my berth at 2 A.M., and wait for a long time in the cold for a seat in another car. I had hardly got back to Paris when I lost the baby I had been expecting for three months.

Then came, in addition to abusive telephone calls and threatening letters, an attempt on my life. We had spared our adversaries, though we could have killed them without much trouble, since we always found them before they knew what was up. The partisans of those criminals, however, were not so considerate. They had to strike, even blindly. Their objective was to get rid of me or one of my family. On the afternoon of May 10, I left to give a lecture in Cannes for the LICA. Arno went with me, for I wanted to spend a few days with him just resting. That's how we escaped being killed, for this is what happened after we left.

At 5 P.M. our concierge brought up a package addressed to Mme. Beate Klarsfeld that the postman had left. "Probably a nice present," she said.

My mother-in-law set the package on a table, but she was struck by the fact that the postmark, "Paris, May 9, Av. de Wagram, 12:30" did not correspond to the sender's address. The sender was a Samuel Ségal, of "Les Guillerettes, par 34-Gignac." Her suspicions were aroused, but she decided to do nothing until Serge came home. Serge arrived at 6:30 P.M., and removed the outer wrapping of tarred paper, under which he found a soft cardboard box. Inside, well wrapped in tissue paper, was a second box done up in fancy paper and bearing the label of "Marquis" confectioners. Serge removed the paper and found a yellow-orange cylindrical box labeled "Sugar."

"I was astonished," he told me over the telephone. "Who could have been sending us sugar? Yet, do you remember that Mr. Etzold, the former German deportee, who came to the apartment two weeks ago to bring us a present of German black bread? It seemed possible that he might be sending us some sugar now. But when I looked carefully at the wrapping paper, I noticed little black specks like soot. Mama thought it might be black sugar.

"I put a speck on my tongue. It tasted sour. Then I touched a match to a few specks I had spread on the sink. They burst into flame. My suspicions were confirmed.

"I asked Information if she had a number for a Samuel Ségal in Gignac. No. Then I got the number of the Gignac police station. An officer checked it out, then told me he knew of no Ségal or of any place named Les Guillerettes. Then I called 'Marquis.' No, they did not put out boxes of sugar like the one I described. By then I was thoroughly convinced that it was something dangerous.

"I put the whole business into a shopping bag and went to the Auteuil police station. I warned the police there, who were skeptical at first, that it might well be a box of candy, but might also be a bomb. The superintendent immediately put in a call for the fire department. They X-rayed the package in their truck-laboratory. Finding a detonator, the technician had traffic cut off for fifteen minutes at the corner of boulevard Exelmans and rue Chardon-Lagache. Then with a hacksaw he cut into the bottom and the side of the box in order to empty it. Inside were more than a half pound of nails and enough explosive to blow to bits whoever opened the box and anyone near him. I registered a complaint, but there was hardly anything to go on."

And so I got myself ready for my next campaign.

18

OTHER BATTLES IN GERMANY

I wasted no time in again taking the offensive against the German political establishment, which, by repeatedly delaying ratification of the Franco-German judiciary accord of February 2, 1971, was consciously perpetuating the impunity of the Nazi criminals who had operated in France.

I had for a long time been on the trail of Heinrich Illers, S.S-Hauptsturmführer, deputy to Kurt Lischka, head of the Nazi police (S.D.), Paris region. Illers was also head of the Gestapo in Paris. Serge had accumulated a voluminous dossier on Illers who, on August 24, 1944, personally made the decision to dispatch from Compiègne a final deportation convoy from France. The agreement between German General von Choltitz and Swedish Consul Raoul Nordling prohibiting further deportations had already been concluded, but Illers ignored this.

Knowing that Illers was a "Herr Doktor," we were able to locate him as Senatspräsident of the Landessozialgericht of Lower Saxony, and . . . expert in war-victim litigation.

In order to have Illers removed, we had to dramatize our disclosure. We decided to hold a press conference at Bonn in the restaurant Am Tulpenfeld, in the press center. On Tuesday morning October 3, 1972, although there was a warrant for his arrest in Germany, Serge joined Jean Pierre-Bloch and me in

Bonn. He had crossed the border in a sleeping car without incident. We distributed invitations to all the press offices stating that Serge, although under the threat of arrest, would speak. By 2 P.M. the room was filled with journalists. No sooner had Serge entered than three police officers and two warrant officers appeared and declared him under arrest. But by now he had had ample time to declare to the assembled press that "German justice is arresting me just as I am about to reveal what has become of the head of the Gestapo in Paris, the deputy to Kurt Lischka" . . . and amid the general excitement he named the posts currently held by Illers.

Meanwhile I was distributing files of documents signed by Illers, and very eloquent these documents were. For example, on October 11, 1942, Illers mentions that he will suggest 132 persons (for the firing squad); and on October 18, 1942, he notes cynically, referring to the next batch of hostages: "Most are Spanish Reds, but that should be no obstacle to accepting them as hostages. Spain doesn't want them back, and consequently no difficulties are expected to arise from their execution."

Serge had to spend only one hour in jail; he was released on bail and in an odd way: Since he refused to hand over a single mark, the court at Cologne, embarrassed by the case, halved my 30,000-mark bail of April 1971, thus reducing it to 15,000 marks and then attributing the remaining 15,000 marks to Serge's.

The same day, Dr. Illers was retired as of the previous day. The case received much publicity. In an interview Dr. Illers said: "All this is very distasteful; it may result in my losing half my pension." Not the least thought for his victims, who had lost that with which his threatened loss can hardly be compared.

December 1972. Brandt has just won the legislative election by a clear majority. We decide to demand ratification in front of the Bundestag on the day Brandt presents his new government. The association of survivors of Auschwitz send ten delegates, with their chairman, Georges Wellers, in charge. During this project we become acquainted with Julien Aubart, the Jewish resister who had received many awards for his bravery and was deported to Auschwitz at the age of twenty. He brought along two of his friends, Henri Pudeleau and Henri Wolff, escapees from Auschwitz, like himself twenty years old at that time, and after the war militant activists in the Irgun, the clandestine military organization of Jews in Palestine. Thanks to them and them alone, Serge and I had the moral force to fight on; they gave us hope of success, as well as financial support.

On December 15 our demonstration shows signs of success. In the sight of numbers of deputies and journalists who are entering the Bundestag to learn the composition of the new cabinet, the deportees standing erect, Serge and I are surrounded by dozens of policemen and dragged out of the area forbidden to demonstrations. At the police station we are questioned at great length, but what can a police chief do when confronted by deportees who bare their arms branded with their KZ [*Konzentrationslager*—concentration camp] number in reply to the routine question: "Have you ever before been arrested by German police?" Late in the afternoon we are expelled from Germany and escorted to the border by the police.

Klaus Barbie was not the only one in Lyon carrying out the extermination of Jews and resisters undertaken by the Gestapo. Klaus Barbie was head of the Gestapo in Lyon; above him the central command of the S.D. was in the hands of S.S.-Obersturmbannführer Werner Knab, who was killed in 1945, and his deputies. In early 1944 a new deputy arrived from Marseille, where he had fulfilled the same duties in 1943. This was S.S.-Obersturmbannführer August Moritz, born February 11, 1913, in Hanover.

Moritz had been deputy to the head of the S.D. in Orleans. In Marseille, where he is again deputy-chief, Moritz's signature on certain documents testifies to his anti-Jewish activities. On January 10, 1943, Moritz asks Röthke "to which camp should we send the Jews we have arrested." On March 15, 1943, Moritz reports to Röthke in that fine bureaucratic language that speaks of delivery of Jews as of so much merchandise, that he will be shipping him a load of ten Jews for Drancy in two days. On March 18, another invoice for ten Jews. On March 23, again ten Jews. On March 24, Moritz has difficulties in meeting the delivery—a technical incident, twenty-four hours lost! On March 27, Nazi order is restored. Moritz can go back to the usual rhythm of his shipments. On May 7, 1943, Moritz takes precautions, and under the label "Geheim" [secret] he inquires whether the children of the Jews are to be sent to Drancy or placed in the UGIF Center. In May, Moritz reports a shipment of twenty Jews on the 12th, and again on the 14th, 15th, and 16th. Eighty Jews for Drancy in five days; the S.D. of Marseille will bear its share of responsibility for the 100,000 French Jews exterminated at Auschwitz!

According to the testimony of the militia arrested after the murder of Victor Basch and his wife in Lyon, it was Moritz, in charge of S.S. operations against the Maquis of the Ain, who commanded the detachment of S.S. who had come with their French accomplices to arrest the president of the League for the Rights of Man. The S.S. delivered the Basches to the militia, which executed them at the side of a road.

We found a number of August Moritzes in telephone directories of German cities, but not in Hanover, his native city, where I went in October 1972. In Hamburg there were just two. On February 8, 1973, I rang up, saying, "This is the City Register of Hanover. We are working on statistics on the present location of our residents. Is this the same Herr Moritz who was born in Hanover on February 11, 1913?

A woman's voice: "Yes, that is my husband. He's right here."

"Thank you. That is all."

So we have located Moritz. Now we have to go to Hamburg, and without delay. Indeed, Sunday will be a better day to reach Moritz than a weekday; especially this coming Sunday above all others, when Moritz will be celebrating his sixtieth birthday. How many of the Jews he sent to Drancy will live to celebrate their sixtieth birthday? This confrontation with his bloody past will at least spoil the joyful day he is anticipating.

But I cannot go, for early Monday morning I am to take the train to Toulouse where "Presence of Israel" has asked me to speak, as well as at Agen. I find a substitute, Peggy, a Hamburg journalist, the daughter of Polish Jews who died at Auschwitz. Peggy has covered the trials of Nazi war criminals. The commando unit that will leave Paris Saturday evening by train is thus reduced to two: Julien Aubart and Serge.

SERGE'S ACCOUNT

Sunday about noon we arrive in front of the Moritz residence in the middle of the Hamburg equivalent of Pigalle, Sankt Pauli. Our guide is Peggy, accompanied by a photographer friend. Moritz lives on the third floor of a modest building (Talstrasse 27 Tel. 719 32 30). We ring. A woman opens the door a crack. Peggy explains that we are French journalists who wish to question her husband about his police activities in France (where he has been given the death sentence). Moritz makes it known that he refuses to see us. Peggy insists that Frau Moritz take the names of the visitors. I give mine—Serge Klarsfeld. *"Oh nein!"* She brings her hand before her face as if to shield herself from the reality of my name and my presence. Finally she admits us to the parlor. Moritz enters, solid, stocky, his blue eyes cold and crafty. He says aggressively to Peggy: "I know your writings very well. I read your articles. Like you, I am a leftist. In 1948 I helped set up the archives of the VVN in Hamburg; I belong to the DFU [a small extreme-left peace party affiliated with the Communist Party]; I am a friend of so-and-so [and indeed Peggy, stupefied, knows so-and-so well]. M. Klarsfeld, I went to hear your wife in December 1968 at the University of Hamburg, after she slapped Kiesinger."

At that point I exchanged a glance with Julien and, without saying a word, we both understood we had the same thought—we had come upon the ultimate: we were unmasking a Nazi criminal who had fabricated an innocent identity for himself by agitating among the victims of Nazism. I understood the reason for his wife's *Oh nein.* The militant leftist mask was coming off.

"I have suffered for my involvement in peace. From 1952 to 1956 I served four-and-one-half years in prison, sentenced by the Bundesgerichtshof of Karlsruhe, accused of spying for East Germany. And my wife also spent seven months in jail. I was never informed of that death sentence in Lyon. [This was not true, as Moritz had been interrogated about the Barbie case on several instances by the German courts.] I did nothing wrong in France. What's all this about the Basch affair? It's a lie. I wasn't there. I am innocent."

"If you are innocent, come to France and face trial. Your sentence will be dropped automatically. You will have a new trial and your innocence will shine in the light of day."

"Impossible. I have to think of my family, my job, my reputation. I have problems enough as it is."

"Were you involved with the Jews in France?"

"Never! never! I was aware that there were some arrests, but I personally had nothing to do with any of them."

"Do you swear to that?"

"I swear to it, of course."

Then I showed him photocopies of our documents. He could

see his own signature under texts that were irrefutable. A long silence. Then:

"I signed them, but administratively. I never killed anyone."

I answered: "The Jews were conveyed to the gas chambers by a police and administrative machine. Neither Hitler nor Himmler, nor Eichmann, nor you, killed anyone with your own hands, but each of you in his own place helped make the death machine go." After this, no more dialogue was possible.

Immediately following this, Peggy and I questioned the persons named by Moritz. They did indeed know him and had until then looked upon him as a solid and loyal leftist fighter. The last person we interviewed was a woman who was very well known in those circles, the widow of the man responsible for recruiting Moritz in 1946, when he was using a fictitious name. He had admitted to having been a lieutenant in the S.S. but "that will be taken care of, it is not serious." Paying small attention to the moral qualifications of the man or to the accuracy of his statements, and no doubt more concerned with his technical competence as an intelligence agent, the man engaged Moritz.

The Moritz affair scandalized the extreme leftists in Hamburg and they promptly parted company with him. The VVN accused me of having revealed the affair because it was critical of Israel.

Meanwhile, in November 1972, my book was published in France. The advance I received was of great material assistance. A number of Jewish communities invited me to tell them about my work. I did this without pay, but dozens in the audience bought my book. We need this money to live and to carry on our work.

The Jewish social service fund (FSJU) asked Serge in October 1971 to be director of their vacation centers. This was at the time of the Barbie case and was the first concrete instance of Jewish support of our action. There was one condition—that Serge not be seen at public protests, as the purpose of FSJU is social, not political. A few months later, when I was in Bolivia, Serge was the only one in a position to explain the complexities of what was going on to the press, radio, and television. I wasn't there, and he and I were the only ones working on it. Except for Pierre-Bloch and a few youths in LICA, the Jews of France and the resisters were spectators and not actors in this drama.

Adam Loss, the director of FSJU, asked Serge on several occasions to stop speaking in public or FSJU would have to let him go when his six-month trial period ended on April 14, 1972. How could he do this when I was being arrested in La Paz—I, a German, carrying on a struggle that Jews in numbers should have shared and that he alone was doing! Serge refused; once again our work took precedence over all else.

On April 14, 1972, FSJU put an end to Serge's work with them: this cowardly abandonment has left a painful scar. Granted, FSJU has succeeded in creating an indemnity service that regularly sends lawyers to Cologne, Düsseldorf, and Berlin. However, FSJU has not undertaken or encouraged any action to check the rehabilitation of criminals who deported Jews from France. I will give one example. Certain directors of the UGIF, that Union of French Jews established by Lischka, had known Röthke and others who were guilty. But not one of those directors felt the need for FSJU to act against the rehabilitation of the criminals. Röthke, having been sentenced to death in France, died quietly in 1970 in Wolfsburg, where he practiced law. The former directors of UGIF had only to send a few feelers into Germany to locate Röthke and put an end to his career. But that was apparently too much to ask. During this period we moved into a moderate-priced three-room apartment in Paris. I was pregnant; the new baby was expected in August.

On May 7, 1973 we again went to Cologne. The group consisted of me, Julien Aubart and Henri Pudeleau, four young members of the LICA, and a team from Gaumont News who were curious to follow one of our projects. We were putting on another illegal protest to shock public opinion and force the courts to choose between prosecution and acquiescence.

At ten o'clock we went into action. With swollen belly forward, I pushed the bell of Lischka's office. An employee opened the door. The youths pushed past him and entered Lischka's office. He took a pistol out of a drawer and aimed it at the youths who, as always, were unarmed. (We were to learn later that Lischka, former Gestapo chief of Cologne, was routinely entitled to carry a gun.) Only one stood frozen by the threat of the weapon. The other youths joined Julien and Henri, who broke the reinforced windows of the street-floor offices. On the walls they spray-painted S S; that was to be an article in our subsequent indictment.

While hundreds of people left the adjoining buildings or leaned out of windows, police cars appeared. I moved off to avoid being arrested and brought to the hospital a youth who had been cut.

The police finally managed to get the group into their cars. Julien and Henri, in concentration-camp clothing, resisted; they were dragged along the ground. In the car, a policeman sadistically twisted Henri's arm until his colleagues made him stop. They had no sooner arrived at the police station than he fell upon Henri and Julien and punched them in the stomach. What moral courage Julien and Henri displayed in coming back to Germany, only to be beaten by policemen thirty years younger than those who had tortured them at Auschwitz! All this to obtain a hypothetical ratification!

The following day, after a night in a cell, they were tried and practically acquitted. They were penalized only for the actual damage they had caused—a fine of 2000 marks. Once again the judges had bowed.

As for the 2000 marks, they were never paid, nor were any other fines. The firm, Krücken, where Lischka has his power base, demanded that they be paid through the account of a French grain merchant in Lorraine. Julien asked a good friend of his in Metz, Henri Ormont, to inquire into the firm that does business with Lischka's. It turns out that the head of the firm is Jewish and related to Ormont. Ormont lays down the law to his relative, who is somewhat annoyed at having to refuse to accommodate Krücken, a good customer. But he finally writes a polite letter to Krücken that he cannot use his account as requested as he has "learned about the nature of the proposed transaction."

Julien Aubart and Henri Pudeleau belong to the National Union of Deportees, Internees, and War Victims (UNDIVG), whose president is a valorous Basque resister, René Clavel, who fought the enemy in Tunisia and Vercors before being deported to KZ Dora. The UNDIVG is a fraternal organization. Thanks to these friends, the financial burden of our action is lightened. Willy Brandt replied to René Clavel in February 1973: "I hope the accord will be ratified before the parliamentary recess." But more is needed than the good will of Brandt.

On June 13, Julien and Serge went to Bonn. They met with Günther Metzger, vice-chairman of the Social-Democratic parliamentary group and a friend of Israel. They handed him fifty copies of a well-documented dossier covering Achenbach, who was on the foreign affairs committee, which, in cooperation with the judicial affairs committee, was supposed to study the Franco-German accord. These dossiers were to be given to the members of the two committees. A few days later we learned that Achenbach had been named to be the reporter of the foreign affairs committee on the accord. No doubt our dossiers were read, but Achenbach was all-powerful. He represented big industry and he was also head of the lobby for amnesty of war crimes.

While Serge was at the Bundestag, I went to the Knesset in Jerusalem, where I campaigned for Israel to put pressure on Bonn to ratify the accord. Since most of the Jews deported from France were stateless, it seemed only right that Israel should be concerned to honor their memory and keep watch on their murderers.

My lawyer, Shmuel Tamir, obtained a pass for me. But my arrival was delayed two hours by the police because I had a German passport and I had not known I required a visa. I was being met by Akiva Nof and Ehud Olmerd, of Likud, the opposition party, and also by our friend Eli Ben Gal, who had just returned to Israel from France after having represented the Mapam, one of the parties in power. To give my action the greatest weight, I had chosen to come to Israel the day after Brandt had arrived for an official visit. I cannot say I was given the same kind of welcome as that accorded to members of the German delegation. It appeared rather that I was an embarrassment and that I would be prevented from attending any official reception where the German delegation was expected.

In Israel that hot month of June 1973, seven months pregnant, I realize how small is the minority of Germans I represent, even though the battle I am waging is also that of Israel, and even though I am a better friend of Israel than a great number of Herr Brandt's friends.

But there were some who were interested to meet with me: Benjamin Halevi, a member of the Knesset and one of the three judges in the Eichmann trial, became the spokesman for our cause and intervened effectively with Golda Meir and Abba Eban. So did Haika Grossman, member of the Knesset for the Mapam. Menachim Beigin, the former commander of Irgun and now minority leader of the Knesset, invited me to his modest apartment in Tel Aviv and gave me warm assurances of his movement's support for diplomatic intervention with Bonn. The former Resistance and partisans gave a dinner in my honor at Tel Aviv that moved me deeply. Others came spontaneously to offer their help and became good friends: the well-known journalist Yoella Harshafi; Simha Holzberg, known as the comforter to all Israeli war wounded.

I must have been quite a sight, pregnant "up to the neck," buttonholing officials in the handsome locales where the German-Israeli greetings were taking place, urging that Israel put pressure on Bonn for ratification. I held a press conference. I warned the Israelis that the real Germany is not at all like Willy Brandt, that he himself is losing the power to get his way with the Social-Democrat party, most of whose leaders are interested only in one thing—to remain in power, whatever the price. To see Brandt and the Israelis arm-in-arm was impressive and pleasing to both sides, but this beautiful friendship would erode in times of trial; it was too facile, too superficial. Israel has only one trump to play against the German will to follow where self-interest leads (Arab oil, Arab markets, Arab dollars). That trump is to insist that the German people face up to its responsibility regarding the Jewish people. The only hope for Israel to have loyal friends in Germany and western Europe rests on the Germans having the will to assume their responsibilities, which I as an individual am trying to fulfill. It is only by real sacrifice in favor of the Jewish people that Germany will be morally rehabilitated.

This cannot be accomplished so long as Israel muddles along improvising policy day by day, with frequent small victories and grave setbacks, leading from "special relations" to "specific relations" and at last to "normalization" just before becoming bad. Israel must make plain what she expects from Germany and must help change the German people so they stop thinking that not doing harm is the same as doing good. And what a great deal of good must be done when one has done so much evil!

Some months later, during the Yom Kippur War, the Brandt government protested the shipment of American arms to Israel over German territory. Kneel in the ghetto of Warsaw and then refuse arms to the survivors of that very ghetto? And yet it is easier for West Germany than for other countries to resist Arab blackmail. They need only recall the martyrdom inflicted by the German people upon the Jewish people. This moral priority has considerable political power; I believe my whole history proves this. What could I have accomplished alone without it?

August 15. While I let out great cries that belie my reputation for courage, my little Lida-Myriam utters her first roars. Dear God, how happy I am at the birth of this little ball, the best of gifts. All those around me except Serge are thinking: with two babies, no more politicking. They forget that we began our campaign after the birth of Arno. That first birth gave us the sense of collective responsibility. Children are the future; we are struggling not for the past, but for the future.

November 1973. I have been responding to new invitations to lecture on our concern in the principal cities of France, Switzerland, and Belgium. This is not the only work that is being done. Along with Julien and Henri, Serge continues in Germany on the trial of the principal criminals who had operated in France. We build up dossiers for the judiciary phase. Again and again our determination is put to the test. Serge comes back from Israel with a returning French delegation—a group from LICA headed by Jean Pierre-Bloch and some Israelophile members of Parlement. At the Ministry of Foreign Affairs he learns that the Israelis have intervened with Bonn, but are without hope of success. Where to apply pressure now? Serge will take the risk of going to Cologne with an unloaded revolver. His intention is to prove to the German authorities that if we were motivated merely by vengeance we could easily accomplish our goal; we may in fact resort to this, but only if ratification is not approved, or if, after ratification, German justice shows itself to be lenient with Lischka and his accomplices.

Serge opts not for what is easy but for the greater danger. He could take a criminal by surprise who is not yet on guard. But, on the contrary, he decides to confront Lischka, though knowing him to be armed and knowing that he himself is known to Lischka as well as to the Cologne police. Serge arrives in Cologne on December 7, in 4° below. He stands waiting for a long time near Lischka's car. When at 4 P.M. Lischka walks through the snow and opens the car door, Serge rushes out of a doorway and points his gun at Lischka, right between his eyes. Lischka, wide-eyed, falls on the hood of his car screaming. He is staring death in the face, like many of his victims. It is a busy street; dozens of persons look on but do not intervene. Serge fingers the trigger a yard away from Lischka, who is paralyzed with terror. Serge bursts out laughing and runs away toward the station by a roundabout route, and succeeds in crossing the border before an effective alarm is broadcast.

On his return he immediately sends a registered letter to the prosecutor in charge of our case in Cologne, which ends: "To avoid violence there is only one solution—ratify the accord." Unfortunately, this has no effect on the prosecutor. He apparently does not understand that Serge would risk his life for the accomplishment of our aim by peaceful means, while it would have been so easy to shoot and kill Lischka. On December 9 the prosecutor issues a warrant of arrest against Serge and me, his accomplice.

19

WITNESS FOR ISRAEL
IN DAMASCUS

Saturday, January 19, 1974. Orly Airport. I am back from Damascus. Surrounded by my friends, I answer journalists' questions. Many people have been worried about me these last three days, especially in Israel.

"What was the purpose of your dangerous trip?"

Primarily to bear witness to the common cause of a German with the Jewish people; to bear witness in a country where Syrian and Israeli Jews have been persecuted and are in danger; to bear witness not by a written message or in front of an embassy, but right in the lion's mouth. In a message I brought to Syria and that was distributed in French and English by all the press bureaus the evening I arrived in Damascus, I said:

I have come to Damascus to witness to that solidarity the German people must have with the Jewish people as a result of the extermination of six million Jews by Nazi Germany. Wherever Jews are persecuted, it is our duty as Germans to intervene at their side. Here, in addition to the cruel treatment that the Syrian Jewish community has increasingly suffered in recent years, is added the horrible uncertainty about the lives of Israeli prisoners of war. Already dozens of their comrades have been abominably executed after their capture on the Golan Heights. This barbarism and the refusal to publish lists of survivors are not to the credit of Syria. Even if my action appears futile, I must give you this warning, for I come from a people that has deeply dishonored itself by waging a total war on the Jewish people thirty years ago. This blot is difficult to erase even when maximum energy is applied to the task. Let not the crimes of Hitler's Germany be used as a model by the Arab people! I can say this all the more freely as, through the LICA, we are vigorously opposing all signs of anti-Arab racism.

Rather than plot the destruction of a small peaceful state, the state of the descendants of Abraham and of the survivors of Auschwitz, join with Israel in the sincere and patient search for peace and justice for all belligerents.

"What if the lion's mouth closes on you?"

That is a risk I know I am taking. In Warsaw, Cologne, La Paz, Prague, and elsewhere, I have taken risks in engaging in illegal public protests, but I have done this in the conviction that it is my duty as a German to do such acts to rehabilitate my people. This does not at all mean that I am seeking martyrdom. This time more than ever before I am eager to get home safe and sound as Serge and I have a second child.

"How were you able to get a Syrian visa?"

The Syrian Embassy in Paris issued it to me with no difficulty. As I had spoken several times on behalf of the Syrian Jews, I was afraid I would be refused a visitor's visa. But it is the French usage of putting the maiden name "Künzel" on the top line, followed on the second line "épouse Klarsfeld," that made things easier. The visa was issued to Beate Künzel; I made the airplane reservation under that name, and also my reservation in one of Damascus's leading hotels, the Omeyade.

"You got in without difficulties?"

Some technical difficulties en route. On Wednesday, January 16, I stopped over in Geneva to meet with some journalists and give them the text of my message to the Syrian authorities, stipulating an embargo on this news until midnight; by that hour I firmly expected to have arrived in Damascus. I was to take a BOAC at 6:35 P.M. from Zürich, the London-Zürich-Damascus-Singapore plane scheduled to arrive at Damascus at 11:20 P.M. I took the train to Zürich. At the airport a substantial delay is announced, then at 6:30 comes the announcement that passengers on my flight —there were five of us—are to board the BEA plane for London, where the BOAC is being held for us. At 8:15 the BEA plane circles over England as a raging storm beats over the North Sea. At last we land. I am agonizing that in a few hours my whereabouts will become known through the wire services. My message will be broadcast and if the BOAC has left, I'll be stranded in London. In that case, my journey to Damascus will have been short indeed and in the wrong direction. But luck is with us. Our plane is waiting on the runway; we are transferred from one plane to the other without going through the airport. I have time only to ascertain that my suitcase is not among the five passengers' baggage. I have no other clothing than what is on my back. For a moment I am tempted to escape from my responsibilities by taking advantage of this convenient pretext. But no. I'll go to Damascus empty-handed except for my attaché case and my carry-on bag.

"Were you searched on arrival?"

Not at all. The formalities were very brief. They did not examine the papers I was carrying. An hour later I was lying down in the Hotel Omeyade wrapped in a blanket, as I had no nightgown, recovering from my emotions. About 9 A.M. I looked out of my window over a gray muddy city under cold rain. Two hours later I got through to Paris by phone. Serge was anxiously worrying whether the Syrians had allowed me to land, or if between midnight and 3 A.M. they had learned of my mission through the wire services and had ruled to deny me access to Syria. Then I set out to face the Syrian authorities, who were now aware of my arrival and the aim of my visit.

"How did you transmit your message to the Syrian government?"

I had the hotel get me a taxi, as I had a message to deliver to President Assad. Five minutes later I found myself outside the gate of a modest modern office building surrounded by a fence. I spoke to the guards on duty. They did not seem to understand me; fortunately, a man in civilian clothes came and spoke to me in English. I gave him the message, asking him to take it to the president's office and to arrange for me to speak with a member of the president's staff. He disappeared for a few minutes and then told me to return in a few days. All this time I was still standing outside the gate. It began to snow. An old woman who stood waiting near me said in German: "Have patience. I've been coming all week; my husband is in prison." I went next door, to the Ministry of Foreign Affairs, and repeated my action.

"Did you expect to be harassed after that?"

I expected I'd have visitors. And indeed, toward 4 o'clock a Palestinian press correspondent for an American press agency arrived. His Beirut office had appraised him of my "mission." You must remember that there are no Western journalists in Damascus. The rare correspondents of Western agencies are all local people, and thus answerable to Syrian authorities. This correspondent interviewed me in his office, with a second correspondent, a Syrian woman. Of course, they were not carried away with enthusiasm for my action. Back at my hotel I found local correspondents of AFP and Reuters. They were not moderate in their criticism. Later, one of the first correspondents called to tell me that the authorities had censured him for seeing me without their clearance. They had learned of the telegrams sent to Beirut and had issued an order to "kill" all news concerning me. Thus no further news about me went out from Damascus. The censorship had acted effectively.

"How did you spend the night?"

Sobbing into my blanket. I had expected to find sunshine in Damascus when I left Paris. All this time, Serge and our LICA friends were trying to reach me by phone. But I had been effectively isolated. After censoring the press, they cut off my phone. At midnight the hotel operator was telling Paris that I was not expected to return that night. This must have worried my family and friends. I had also tried to phone Paris, but the hotel kept telling me they couldn't get the call through. Early in the morning Serge managed to get an alert through to the French Embassy in Damascus. They immediately called the hotel and asked for me. As if by a miracle I found myself in the lobby where a phone was handed to me. It was a friend, Elisabeth Hajdenberg; I reassured her that I was all right. Apparently the Syrians had reached a decision about their stance toward me during the night. After a visit from the French consul, M. Besson, who had very courteously gone out of his way to come and see me and then telephone Serge in Paris, the Syrian authorities made contact with me.

"Whom did you see first?"

A Syrian woman phoned me as though nothing had happened. The conversation went as follows:

"My name is Colette Khoury. I am a poet. I understand you are a journalist passing through Damascus."

"I am not a journalist. I have come here to protest the treatment of Israeli prisoners."

"May I come and interview you at your hotel?"

She arrived in a few minutes, small, fortyish, long hair, very dark, dressed in pants, holding her car keys. She is an anti-Israel activist and teaches French literature at Damascus University. She was accompanied by Wal Haggar, also a writer. We talked over lunch in the hotel bar. I gave her a copy of my message. At that moment a thin man of about forty-five came to our table. "Madame Klarsfeld, I am Salah Kabany, Director of Information at the Ministry of Foreign Affairs." He handed me a telegram from AFP stating the purpose of my visit and accurately transcribing my message.

"What was the tone of the conversation?"

Courteous. I had the feeling that the Syrians had realized there was concern for me abroad. That was my best protection. If I had not been known and if the foreign press had not taken an interest in me, the Syrian attitude would no doubt have been different. This was the reaction I had hoped for; I preferred a confrontation with politicians to one with police.

"What did you talk about?"

It was a dialogue of the deaf. The abyss between our positions was not to be bridged. For example:

The execution of Israeli prisoners on the Golan Heights—"Pure Zionist propaganda. The papers shown to the press by the Israelis are faked."

The condition of surviving prisoners—"We wish Syrian prisoners in Israel were treated as well as the Israelis in Syria. If you want to observe them, that can be arranged, but it will take some time—two or three weeks."

"Can you give me some assurance that I will see other prisoners than those already seen by the press?"

"No. But in one or two months their situation may be negotiated."

No answer as to the number of prisoners.

As to their physical condition—"If we have not allowed other prisoners to be seen, that's because many of the captured are pilots who were wounded. If we let them be seen in that condition it could be thought that we had mistreated them."

On the recognition of the State of Israel—"Israel may be recognized anywhere, in Guinea, in Alaska, in Germany, but not here."

As for the Palestinians, I reminded them of what happened to Germans who had been repatriated from the Eastern provinces. Answer—"Brandt is a traitor. He has no right to sign treaties in their name with Poland and the USSR. Like the Palestinians, the German refugees have a perfect right to their own homeland."

I answered: "You call yourselves Socialists, but in Germany you would be considered ultrareactionary."

On the Syrian Jewish community—"They are not in any way persecuted. Do you want to meet the richest man in Syria? He is a Jewish businessman." I declined. I had no wish to meet a token Jew who would reassure me, with no guarantee of reliability, about the condition of his co-religionists.

On Israelis—"Colonizers who behave like Nazis."

On my message—"You are very hard, you've been misinformed."

I had no trouble standing firm and answering all their questions, all the while knowing this discussion could lead nowhere. If I were an Israeli, I would mistrust the Syrians; the Syrians are firm in believing that the destruction of the State of Israel is normal and desirable.

The interview with M. Kabany, in which two top officials of the Ministry of Information also took part, followed the same lines as the above conversation. M. Kabany told me he was about to go to Washington in a few days as the personal representative of President Assad. The three gentlemen drove me around Damascus, showing me houses in the center of the city destroyed by Israeli air attacks. The visit lasted until 6 o'clock. Two hours later Colette Khoury came to call for me with the two Information officials. We went to dine at a hotel near the airport, where we continued to share our respective truths. At the end of the dinner, seeing that I still clung unmoved to my opinions, my interlocutors complained that I had only come to protest against them and took no account of their arguments.

Early Saturday morning when I went to pay my hotel bill before leaving for the airport, the clerk said: "You are the guest of the government. Foreign Affairs will take care of your bill."

The two officials accompanied me coldly to the airport. I departed, still minus luggage, with the satisfaction that I had spoken my true thoughts to the implacable adversaries of Israel. I was a surprise to the Syrians. They saw in me a resolute adversary; they can conceive of peace only in terms of the complete annihilation of Israel.

Colette Khoury has described the impression she had of me in the monthly periodical *France-Pays Arabes*. Here are some excerpts:

I had learned through a friend in the Ministry of Foreign Affairs and through the editor of *Al Baas* that she had arrived in Damascus the previous day. They told me she had come to see President Assad and to protest our alleged massacre of Israeli prisoners of war. They said she was pro-Israeli. At least that woman did not conceal her purposes. She received me coldly with a drawn smile. I introduced myself as a writer and journalist and asked if she was not connected with the press.

"Not at all," she answered.

"But I thought you came here to interview our president."

"Sorry," she said, "I'm here to protest."

I was amused by her aggressive response. I asked if she had made an appointment with the Palace.

"I went there yesterday and delivered my protestation."

"Then you do not insist on seeing the president or his deputy? You have come just to deliver a protest?"

"I do want to speak to him. But no responsible person has gotten in touch with me. . . ."

Why did she come, if she is convinced no one would speak to her? To protest? That is becoming a fixation. I said gently: "You are honest and you have sincerely believed the false propaganda that claims we are massacring Israeli prisoners. So you came here to protest. I can understand that."

"I am protesting not only as an individual, but also in the name of the German people."

I felt smothered. This was a being from another planet. "Do you believe the entire German people agrees with you?"

"I don't believe they do," she answered simply. "But being a German I am representative of the German people."

I decided further discussion of this subject would be futile. The conversation turned to her home.

"Oh, the cat and the dog get along very well. And the marmoset is very small. . . . My baby is just five months old. . . ."

Listening to her speak, I thought she is herself a baby, hypnotized, who speaks of reality and ordinary life as if it is a dream, a very distant dream, almost inaccessible. I invited her to lunch. What is this woman? She thinks of herself as young Germany, the daughter of people who lived under Nazism. She began asking political questions and questioning the past. Then she met the man she was to marry, a Jew.

"You can be a Jew without being a Zionist," I said to her.

"That's what you think! It's unimaginable to be a Jew and not be pro-Israel."

"But it is imaginable," I countered slowly, thinking of Jewish friends I love very much.

That my witness was understood by the Israelis is demonstrated by many messages I received, including the following article from *Al Hamishmar* dated January 22, 1974. Serge and I will never be alone again. The Israeli people will always remember the small hand extended to them when their hearts were hurting.

HOMAGE AND THANKS TO BEATE KLARSFELD

Beate Klarsfeld—She did it again! That courageous German woman who married a French Jew, who linked her destiny to that of the Jewish people, and who battles against their foes and detractors, past and present—Beate has gone into the lion's den. She has gone to Damascus, the Damascus of Assad and *Al Baas*, to urge the liberation of Syria's Israeli prisoners.

Beate, audacious Nazi-hunter, does not tilt against windmills. She is as realistic as she is courageous, and clearly knows the limits (sometimes unbreachable) between the possible and the desirable. She is fully aware of the risks—mortal risks—she so often runs. But this awareness does not prevent her from doing what must be done when the time is right, from doing what her conscience dictates.

Beate's battle is not a vogue phenomenon, either in its object—to redress the injustice done to the Jews and assure them of peace and dignity—or in its means. The world lies impressed by the barbarous acts of the Arab terrorists and capitulates to their blackmail. Beate's means are the moral protestation, the passionate claim for justice, the spectacular evidence of the criminal actions and their perpetrators. She exposes herself not only to the vengeance of her desperate enemies, but she must also combat the indifference and bad faith of others. Yet, in the face of this indifference and cowardly defeatism, her action will prevail.

In these dark days, bereft of ideals and moral enthusiasm, that bold and resolute action will succeed in stamping itself on men's consciences. Beate seems alone, almost unique, in her generation—but we are convinced she will become an example to many.

Beate, our sister, you have come to us from far away. The admiration and the gratitude of the Jewish people will accompany you on all your future paths and all your future deeds.

While I was campaigning in Paris, Strasbourg, and Bordeaux to mobilize public opinion on the side of the prisoners in Syria, we had problems on the German "front." Our trial in Cologne was set for February 5. Serge had been requesting a postponement since December, as that was the day he was to take his law examination. The court, which had moved so slowly that the trial date was set three years after the incident, refused to postpone the hearing even a few days. In that case we would stay in France. We told our attorney, Shmuel Tamir, not to bother to come from Israel. The only ones, then, to appear on February 5 were the lawyers Kaul and Gregorius; the latter was the one who was attorney for the LICA youths at Essen. Kaul violently accused the bench of prejudice, and quarreled with Chairman de Somoskoey. Our lawyers departed, all but slamming the door.

The same day, a thirty-one-year-old German Jew, Sam Maedge, whose father died in Auschwitz, distributed tracts in front of the courthouse, demanding punishment of Nazi criminals. He had come to see us spontaneously in Paris two weeks earlier and expressed his wish to do something in support of our protest. That morning in the street he was struck by a man who had just read his tract, which bore his signature and his address. The next morning, just as he started his Opel, four shots were fired and pierced his car. One bullet shattered the front left window and glanced his head. Two others made holes in the front left door, the fourth in the rear left door.

His complaint was taken down at the police station. An inquiry established that the shot was fired with intent to kill. But late in February the inquiry was closed because the perpetrator of the attack could not be traced. The German press gave only a few lines to this case. A long article was prepared by the staff of *Der Spiegel* in Düsseldorf, but it was never published. Why? Simply because it seemed advisable not to let the outside world know that Germany is a country where a Jew, the son of a deportee, who protests the impunity of Nazi criminals, runs the risk of being gunned down. Incidents like this attempt cloud the image Germany wants to see when she looks into the mirror of her conscience.

March 1974. Back in Israel with Serge as part of a delegation of French Jewish intellectuals. I am greeted with flowers by relatives of the prisoners in Syria. We are received on March 23 by Golda Meir in the Prime Minister's office and have a warm meeting. The whole visit is comforting. After the Yom Kippur War and the prisoners held in Damascus, the Israelis know who their few friends are.

On March 24, Victor Shem Tov, the Minister of Health, awards me the Medal of the Revolt of the Ghetto, saying:

"This is a particularly symbolic event. Here in Jerusalem, the capital of the State of Israel, in the presence of delegates of French Jewry, an Israeli minister decorates a young German woman to commemorate, thirty years after the end of World War II, the terrible hecatomb of European Jewry.

"This ceremony symbolizes the fact that the Jewish people will never forget, nor will non-Jewish people forget, thirty years after the end of the war, the horrors of Nazism, which, known to the younger generation only through books, might be forgotten in criminal neglect if we do not renew our memories. This event also symbolizes that in spite of evidence to the contrary, there is a universal conscience sensitized to the destiny of the Jewish people and the State of Israel.

"You, Madame Klarsfeld, are a living example of both these aspects. You have not forgotten the horrors of the past, and you are sensitive to the present condition of the Jewish people, as you have proven by going to Damascus to act on behalf of our imprisoned soldiers.

"Madame Klarsfeld, as I greet you here today, allow me to pay homage to a daughter of the German people who has been campaigning tirelessly year after year to bring Nazi criminals before man's judgment, who has unceasingly borne witness to her solidarity with the Jewish people in the whole tragedy that envelops our generation.

"Madame Klarsfeld, allow me, as I award you this Medal of Courage symbolizing the resistance of the ghettos, to thank you, now after the difficult trials we have just gone through, for having again launched a campaign for the Jewish people and ultimately for the honor of the German people."

20

ARREST AT DACHAU

The award of this medal, in recognition of the solidarity I feel toward Israel, has encouraged me to attempt once more a difficult test of strength to obtain ratification. But the road ahead is a long one, for ratification will only be the achievement of the political phase: the consent of the German Parliament that the German courts are competent in regard to Nazi criminals. Next will come an equally arduous phase, the judiciary one. But we must face one step at a time. If I thought only about the innumerable obstacles between me and my objective, I would be demoralized.

We work out a plan. Each of our actions must include people or places that have strong symbolic meaning. Such meaning must be present in order that any single and generally peaceful demonstration may generate unforeseen power, an activating shock that will make those to whom the demonstration is addressed aware of their responsibilities. Tomorrow the symbol will be Dachau and my arrest there. We must set a trap for the German police since, if I am arrested outside the compound, the desired effect will be lost and I might rot in prison. Yet we know that no policeman feels that entering a compound where tens of thousands of anti-Nazis were assassinated will lead to a confrontation with his conscience. That is one of the problems of the German conscience: the absence of reflection and comprehension, on both the individual and institutional level, of the lessons to be learned from the Hitlerian tragedy. There are all too few persons who experience any obligation or responsibility for true justice or for helping the Jewish people.

So I am going to get myself arrested. I don't know for how long. My release will depend on the volume and intensity of the reaction to my arrest. This time I am depending upon the reaction in Israel, where I have been so warmly welcomed. But in this cruel world I know it is not easy to arouse a tide of moral indignation strong enough to wear down the dike of German law, with its severity toward those who attack the established order. I am sometimes compared to Antigone. But the task of pitting the unwritten law against the written law is better suited to unmarried persons than to young mothers. It is always a painful wrench to go away from Arno and little Lida, who is now only eight months old, and in spite of the deep concern that makes me go, it always leaves me with a tinge of bad conscience. Katia, the little marmoset perched on my shoulder, rubs her head against my neck. Petia, the good cocker spaniel, licks me. All the responsibility for the family falls once more on that true heroine, my mother-in-law. Serge, who will have to orchestrate the campaign to get me out of jail, is worried. Oh! to have to leave all these dear ones! I will be understood by all those who have experienced separations in time of war. I will be understood in Israel.

I leave Paris Tuesday evening, April 16, with two faithful companions, Henri Pudeleau and Henri Wolff. This is not Pudeleau's first expedition with me, but it is Wolff's. Like Pudeleau, he is forty-nine, and was sent from France to Auschwitz after eighteen months' imprisonment in France in the camp at Gurs. Like the other Henri, like Julien Aubart, he too was active in the Irgun from 1945 to 1948 after his release from the camp. They are here with me as a sign of the solidarity of deportees, to demonstrate the connection between yesterday's battle and the one we are waging today.

We arrive in Munich in the morning. We have some difficulty in rounding up journalists, as the United States Secretary of Defense, James R. Schlesinger, is in Bavaria today. At last we reach someone at the Associated Press. I tell him what we plan to do and have him tip off the police and get them to come to Dachau. We arrive before the police. There are tourists, the museum is open.

In Israel this day is being dedicated to the memory of the deportees. Now, at Dachau, two police cars and a bus filled with police arrive. They stop in front of the camp. In spite of the extra-territorial status of the former death camp, three plainclothes po-licemen cross into the compound and approach our group—I, my two friends in their KZ coats, and a few journalists. They tell me I am under arrest and take me away without outward violence, but with that sinister legal manner that tends, even unwittingly, to strike terror into the hearts of the Nazis' victims. I am taken to the state prison of Bavaria. Early the next morning four police take me in a car from Munich to Cologne, to Ossendorf prison, in which I had been confined in 1971.

The next day there is a demonstration in Tel Aviv before the German Embassy. They chant, "Nazis in, Beate out!" Serge is in daily contact with Tel Aviv; an office and telephone have gener-ously been contributed to our cause by the parents of our friend, Francis Lenchener. Akiva Nof, Yoella Harshafi, Simha Holzberg, Bronia Klibansky, Myriam Meyouhas, and Haika Grossman do their best in Tel Aviv to rouse public opinion. Benjamin Halevi, the member of the Knesset and former member of the Supreme Court of Israel, personally goes to the German Embassy on April 20 and requests that I be released, making himself responsible for my appearance at the trial.

But the German press prints practically nothing about these events in Israel, nor of any in France. On April 23 there is a demonstration in front of the German Embassy on the Champs-Elysées. Numerous reports are wired to Bonn, but the German press does not carry the story, nor does it mention the acerb com-ments in the French press criticizing the "tactlessness" of the Bavarian police. At the end of the first week, Serge, who has been in constant telephone contact with our supporters, comes to the conclusion that public reaction has not been strong enough. We must increase the pressure or I may be kept in jail until my trial, which is set for June. That is not too long to wait, or to cause our friends to relax their efforts. But in June the Germans can postpone the trial until the fall. By that time I will already have spent five or six months in jail. The court need only sentence me to time already served, thus satisfying the German public that the "trouble-maker" has paid her debt.

And it is true that I will have paid. Six months in prison is wearing. And what a disaster for my family! And how exasperating to be locked up when I am convinced I am acting for the honor of my country, while the criminals I accuse with ample documentation enjoy total impunity. It's all very well to have good morale, but it doesn't help to be locked up with a young woman who, jealous of her husband's love for their little daughter, whom he could "eat up," served her to him for dinner in the form of meat balls. Or another who had mowed down her fiancé with a scythe. Or with Hermine Braunsteiner, the concentration-camp guard extradited from the United States, who confessed she used to set dogs on the Jews, but whom I used to see here during recess daintily lift earthworms off the pavement and set them down on the grass, all the while grumbling against the American judges ("all Jews") responsible for her extradition. Moreover, Gregorius, my lawyer from Essen, is so pessimistic and negative that little by little my morale weakens. Gregorius is probably influenced by Professor Kaul of East Berlin. Kaul has written Serge a violently critical letter, blaming him for my "childish" action and declaring that France and especially Israel will never do anything to help me. Serge sends this letter and other news to me through friends, who keep up their struggle against German bureaucracy and manage to get in to see me every other day in spite of regulations—an Israeli couple traveling in Germany, my mother-in-law, Julien, the two Henris and still another Henri, Henri Hajdenberg, a young lawyer (brother of Serge and Monique who had been arrested at Essen, and of Elisabeth, who had demonstrated at the Bundestag), and a delegation of Israeli journalists who are touring Germany as guests of the German government. Serge and I decide to get rid of our two lawyers, Kaul and Gregorius, as we have lost confidence in them.

A number of delegations of former Maquis and deportees picket the German Embassy in Paris. The UNDIVG charters a bus for forty-five of its members. The bus arrives in Bonn on the morning of May 2 with Julien Aubart in charge. The resisters are all wearing their decorations, their deportee shirts. Serge has prepared a number of posters and banners. The delegation goes to press headquarters, near the Bundestag, trespassing on territory supposed to be kept cleared. The journalists have been alerted; they flock to the scene. So do the police—more than two hundred, helmeted and armed with clubs. After several ineffective warnings, the police prepare to charge. The German reporters succeed in dissuading them, warning them of what a disastrous impression it would make on the international press to see French Resistance heroes beaten by German police.

Early in the afternoon the bus brings the delegation to my prison, in defiance of the ruling forbidding them to come. Followed by three buses loaded with police, my friends arrive at Ossendorf. Each has a tricolor bouquet, and presently, in full view of the press, the prison guards, and growing crowds of citizens, forty-five tricolor bouquets are laid at the door of the prison while banners are raised. Julien, the two Henris, and my mother-in-law come in to see me. The jail staff is very much impressed by this unprecedented demonstration for a prisoner. For my part, I do what I can to impress the staff that my attitude is worthy of the cause I champion. While girls belonging to the anarchist league, Baader-Meinhof, destroy property, yell, swear, and attack the guards, I keep everything scrupulously clean and stay aloof from the guards, but polite.

Brandt has just been ousted as a result of the Guillaume espionage scandal, and the new chancellor is Helmuth Schmidt. I wonder how that will affect my situation. The wife of Guillaume has been arrested and is in prison at Ossendorf. They give her my cell, which I have cleaned so thoroughly, and transfer me to another. I start cleaning again.

May 2. The interim president of the Republic, Alain Poher, publicly expresses through the press his "deep emotion" over my imprisonment.

In Israel, the youth organizations issue a petition that rapidly lists some hundred thousand names. There are frequent demonstrations of small groups before the German Embassy. The young deputy Akiva Nof chains herself to the fence of the Embassy. A young mother, Pamela Klein, comes up from Beersheba and begins a hunger strike at the Wailing Wall. I receive hundreds of letters from Israelis and am moved by such thoughts as:

"You are our justice fighter."

"A Jewish tradition says that in every generation there are thirty-six righteous people; because of them the world exists. I'm sure you are one of them."

"I was deeply shocked and profoundly pained when I learned of the arrest of the only true representative of conscience in Germany."

"All the Jews of the world are behind you in your continuing struggle."

"I wish all the people in the world were like you."

"I am a young student in Israel and I wish to thank you for giving me faith that there is still hope for mankind. You are great."

"Such courage as yours is today a symbol for Israel; a small woman against great power is like little Israel against enormous powers."

"Be assured you are not alone. You are in the hearts of all the members of an ancient people—the Jewish people."

"Especially now that all the world is against us, it is heartwarming that you, Beate, come to our aid; we are so in need of friends."

I learn in my cell that Arie Dulzin, president of the Jewish Agency, has protested to the German government, calling me "the friend and ally of the Jewish people." How these words comfort me!

Admiral Limon writes to me in a poem:

> The chimneys of the death-oven no longer smoke,
> There is no open grave,
> The sky is filled with stars:
> The eyes of little children
> Fill with sadness and suffering. They behold
> This world crawling with murderers;
> They see your prison and your cell.
> How can it be that you are behind those bars—you!

> Blessings upon you,
> You in the shadow,
> You sparkling with hope
> That the human race may continue to live.

I learn that the association of Israeli journalists refuses to attend a talk by German Ambassador Jesco von Puttkamer. On May 6 I also learn that, in spite of the arrival of Henry Kissinger in Jerusalem on May 2, a special session of the Knesset is called that same day to consider my case, after thirty deputies have signed a proposed resolution drafted by Akiva Nof. This reads:

Beate Klarsfeld, a young German woman, a child of post-war Germany, of rich and self-satisfied Germany. She is the wife of a loving and successful husband, the mother of two children, the youngest of whom is only eight months old; a woman filled with love of life, optimism, beauty; a woman of sturdy spirit; a woman whom nothing should have bothered; and yet, there arose within her a fiery opposition to one man's hate for another, a thirst for justice, morality, and humanity, a yearning to atone for the sins of her nation.

She binds herself in chains in Prague and Warsaw to demonstrate against anti-Semitism in these two states. She is a Socialist in her views, she does not consider justice and injustice according to who perpetrates it. She considers only the matter itself, and when she is convinced that Czechoslovakia, a nation built on principles close to her own social views, shows anti-Semitic behavior, she doesn't hesitate to denounce it.

This friend of the Jewish people endangers her life and goes to Damascus, the center of barbarity, in an effort to ease the suffering of the Israeli prisoners there.

And she continues untiringly to spare no effort, in Europe and in South America, to bring Nazi criminals of war to trial and to justice. Not out of a spirit of revenge, but, as she has told me more than once, in order to create a balanced world that includes reward and punishment, in order to prevent a repetition of Nazism and its effects, in order to bring sanity back to the world.

Beate Klarsfeld carries out all her activities in the manner of setting a personal example, and not only by exhortation as to what should be done. She does this without any establishment behind her, without power, with the courage of her convictions alone. And I deliberately omit the word "passion" from this description of her belief in order to stress the fact that there is within Beate Klarsfeld so much faith, and so little fanaticism.

Today Beate Klarsfeld is in prison. And thus, while the murderer Lischka roams free after his trial, Beate Klarsfeld, the voice of morality, is in prison awaiting trial. The arrest of Beate Klarsfeld is the personal arrest of every upright and honest person in the world. Every lover of humanity feels as though he were in prison with Beate Klarsfeld today.

In a declaration she published before her arrest, Beate Klarsfeld wrote: "Today once more we are forced to see how Jewish children are murdered, this time by Palestinians. These people draw inspiration from the crimes of the S.S., and they draw encouragement from the immunity given to these criminals. From the time of Hitler and the mass murder, the Germans owe a special debt to the Jewish people. It is not enough to mourn the victims or to plant trees in Israel—we must keep up an intensive struggle against anti-Semitism in all its forms."

Today, when we demand the immediate release of this fighter for morality from the German authorities, we demand her release from an administrative imprisonment, an imprisonment that is entirely under the control of the executive authority. But more than this, we deliberately ignore completely all questions of legal formalities, of who is eligible to appeal and who is empowered to release. We turn to the German governmental authorities and public representatives as the authorized representatives of the Jewish people, the victims of Nazism, on the highest plane of morality: Do justice, and in the words of the prophet Isaiah—"Your hands are filled with blood, wash yourselves, remove the evil of your deeds, refrain from evil, learn to do good, seek justice."

The Jewish people shows its gratitude to its benefactors today. It is to the honor of the Knesset that members from all branches of the House, without reference to factional ideology, have united together, even amid the turmoil of current serious events that occupy us today, to stop and think a bit, thanks to Beate Klarsfeld, about from where we came and what are the principles of justice, morality, and humanism that we carry with us, and together—members of many factions—we presented the motion to hold this special discussion. It is to the honor of the Knesset and of public-mindedness in Israel that one of its members, former Supreme Court Judge Benjamin Halevi, offered his personal guarantee for Beate Klarsfeld to the German authorities. It is to our honor that one of our members, the lawyer Shmuel Tamir, dedicatedly took her defense upon himself. It is to the honor of all of us that the Speaker of the Knesset, Yisrael Yeshayahu, accepted our suggestion without delay and scheduled the immediate opening of this special session.

CONCLUSION OF THE SPECIAL SESSION OF THE KNESSET

The Foreign Affairs and Defense Committee of the Knesset met today to discuss the motion for the Agenda proposed by Member of Knesset Akiva Nof, concerning the arrest of Beate Klarsfeld in Germany. At the conclusion of the meeting, the Committee sent the following telegram to the German Bundestag:

"The Knesset held a special meeting on May 2, 1974, concerning the arrest of Beate Klarsfeld, and passed the matter on to the Foreign Affairs and Defense Committee for further consideration. The Committee decided at its meeting to appeal to the Bundestag of the Federal Republic of Germany in order to procure the immediate release from prison of Mrs. Klarsfeld and the ratification of the agreement between the Federal Republic of Germany and France concerning judgment of Nazi criminals. The Committee considers that it is the moral duty of the Federal Republic of Germany to sign and ratify similar agreements concerning the trial of Nazi criminals with other nations who were among the victims of Nazism. As a result of the non-signing and non-ratification of such agreements thousands of Nazi criminals are free today—among them over a thousand who were already convicted in absentia, in France, for sending a hundred thousand Jews to the gas chambers. This situation is intolerable to human society."

Because of his political obligations and the situation in Israel, Shmuel Tamir cannot leave his country to represent me at my trial, which may be a long one. He asks his friend Arie Marinsky, an eminent lawyer, to take his place and represent me at Cologne at the request of the Israeli Bar and of the Association of Invalid Victims of Nazism. Marinsky will be assisted by Jürgen Stange, a lawyer from West Berlin. Arie Marinsky immediately accepts. He takes the next plane to Paris and with Serge's help prepares for his coming confrontation with the Cologne court.

In Paris, *Le Monde* prints a petition with a long list of signatories in support of my action and demanding that I be released and ratification approved. Outstanding Jews were among the signers: many leaders of the Resistance, political men like Mitterand (then in the midst of the presidential campaign), writers, journalists, lawyers.

In Cologne, Arie Marinsky and Stange fight inch by inch with Victor de Somoskoey, chairman of the court, a stern, intransigent man who desires to limit the trial to the simple fact of a violation of the law. In his eyes I am merely a delinquent in a civil case and he does not understand or wish to understand the public excitement over my arrest. At the end of eight hours of discussion, Marinsky obtains my release in the personal custody of Benjamin Halevi and my promise to appear at my trial. At the same time the 30,000 marks bail paid three years ago by Mr. Lichtenstein is refunded by him. De Somoskoey seems to have gained the impression that Marinsky will not speak at my trial and only Stange will be responsible for my defense, so there will be no confrontation with the Israeli lawyer. But before long he will realize that this was a misapprehension. For Marinsky had clear insight into the true nature of most German magistrates, as represented by de Somoskoey. He confesses his apprehensions in the *Jerusalem Post*:

Mrs. Klarsfeld is in real danger. The German legal machine may be inflexible to a point that we may not even imagine. It may seem totally unthinkable to us that an idealist like Mrs. Klarsfeld should be incarcerated while some of the world's most ruthless murderers like Lischka stay free and unpunished. But it is quite possible that this is just what may happen. The German philosophy of "Ordnung muss sein" (there must be order) is fanatically stressed to the point of absurdity. Such things as motives, justice, and right are forgotten and all that remains is a pedantic adherence to the letter of the law. While the Germans are not too outraged by Arab terrorist atrocities, they are incensed at the fact that a native Berliner should deviate even slightly from the straight and narrow path, if only for the sake of justice. They feel that they have paid for all the atrocities with reparation money and that they have now earned peace of mind. This is the predominant mentality. That a German should remind them of all they want to forget is to them unthinkable. There is a conspiracy of silence. The fact that the Israeli Parliament took a step unprecedented in the history of parliaments anywhere in the world when it called on a foreign court to release a *détenu* was completely ignored by the German press.

Meanwhile, Marinsky and Stange have come to escort me out of jail. Before de Somoskoey I reiterated my declaration. I sensed he was reluctant to release me. He almost made a reversal, but I suppose that he and his superiors in the Department of Justice also wished to blunt the effect of the wave of indignation coming from Israel and France.

I arrived at Orly on May 9. Many friends were there to welcome us. The first to rush at me and cover me with kisses were Arno and Petia. I am back in my family after three weeks' absence. Back to the vacuum cleaner, the washing machine, the kitchen, the supermarket. This may be disappointing to members of Women's Lib, but if they only knew how I savor all these domestic chores each time I leave and when I return from an action. That is where I draw my energy, attending to those indispensable daily chores, in the bosom of my family where I love and am loved, just as Antaeus renewed his strength by touching the earth, his mother, with his shoulders.

We prepare our defense methodically. Our files pile up. On June 10 I go to Israel for a week to work on my defense. This time I bring Lida along. There is an official reception for me at Yad Vashem, the memorial to the martyrs of genocide, whose director Yithzak Arad awards me a medal. Yisrael Yeshayahu, President of the Knesset, also awards me its medal. Thanks to Myriam Meyouhas and Teddy Kollek, the Mayor of Jerusalem, our family will be the guests of the city of Jerusalem for one week and the Dalia kibbutz invites us to spend the rest of the summer there. This is an exciting prospect, as we would not have the money for a family vacation—provided I am still at liberty this summer and not back in a sinister cell, which this time, if I am given an unequivocal prison sentence, would be in the decrepit prison of Essen. Achenbach is that town's deputy.

Arie Marinsky (who is about to leave for Paris to check all details with Serge) and I work out our tactic. He now has all the dossiers in his hands and has put great effort into assimilating in so short a time all the historical facts about the war criminals. On June 20 Marinsky leaves Paris for Cologne, where he informs Presiding Judge de Somoskoey that he firmly intends to plead my case in English. De Somoskoey refuses. Marinsky says that in that case I (Beate) will withdraw counsel and remain silent if my chief lawyer is not permitted to speak. De Somoskoey does not wish to yield. The case is scheduled to come up Tuesday, June 25. Saturday, June 22, de Somoskoey reverses himself: he agrees to allow Marinsky to defend me as my principal lawyer, and in English. But in fear that I may dismiss my lawyers and refuse to speak if I am displeased with their conduct of the trial, he appoints on his own an additional lawyer to defend me, Herr Jochum of Cologne, with whom, of course, I shall have to deal at some future date.

In spite of all the research and documentation he has undertaken to win our case, Serge, who had decided in the course of our experiences that he should enter an independent profession, had begun his law studies in February 1973. With his degree in history from the Sorbonne and as a graduate of the Institute of Political Studies in Paris, he was admitted as a third-year student to the Law School of the University of Paris, and after a few months passed the examinations to enter the fourth year. Now, in June 1974, he faces his finals. But at the same time he is bearing the full weight of the preparation for the trial. He says: "You were released from jail because of the pressure from Israel, but to win the trial we need strong public reaction in France." So he is putting all his energy into building up this reaction, while taking—and passing—his law examinations. Our tactic is to play up the true nature of the conflict and refute the heavy legalistic collar with which the court intends to constrict the trial. It will be a clash of wills at the end of which one of the two antagonists will necessarily lose and the other will win.

21

AN EXTRAORDINARY
TRIAL IN COLOGNE

On the first day of the trial, Le Monde prints an article that spells out for the ruling circles in France the basis of the problem I, the accused, am trying to resolve. After that article we are in good shape to combat German justice: the French understand why we are fighting. The administrative assistant of Prime Minister Chirac receives Serge and assures him that France wants to prevent my going to jail, even though they are skeptical about ratification—all French overtures on the subject have been repulsed by German inertia.

I will sum up the details of the trial:

First session, June 25, 1974. I am not alone. Many of my supporters have come from Paris. Judge de Somoskoey has still not said whether he will admit witnesses for the defense. He has said he himself does not consider them necessary in order to inform the court of my motivation. Yet many French persons have performed illegal acts with me on several occasions in Germany, and it is obvious that their testimony would introduce some interesting elements, as would the testimony in German of the historian Joseph Billig on Lischka's career. But the judge does not want to listen to this. His move has been to call in a renowned psychiatrist to listen to the proceedings and give his opinion of me.

At the entrance to the court there is a silent demonstration of German women, members of the VVN. Each carries a poster protesting my trial and demanding that Lischka be placed on trial instead. The judge tries to provoke me. He reproaches me: "You have duties toward Germany and not only toward humanity." I answer, "All that I do I am doing for Germany." The audience applauds spontaneously. There is an interminable recital of events. The judge produces a translation he has had made of the chapter of my book describing the attempt to kidnap Lischka. The translation is read; certain points are highlighted. I had forgotten the name of a street. The judge berates me for this lapse of memory, saying, "Now, *I* wouldn't have forgotten." I answer: "I'll make a note of that and next time I'll ask you to join my team." De Somoskoey is speechless. The next morning he threatens to put me in jail for insolence. Marinsky, incensed, jumps up and says: "You said you would have the chapter read, don't stop with this episode, but continue with the dossier on Lischka, which follows." Trapped, the prosecuting attorney is obliged to require a reading—lasting several hours—of the pages of my book devoted to the career of Lischka in the Gestapo, along with the documents quoted therein.

Second session, Thursday, June 27. De Somoskoey attacks: "In the course of the previous session Herr Marinsky received two notes from two people in the room. We understand that Jerusalem is very much interested in this trial, but Herr Marinsky can wait until the end of the session to receive instructions. Who are these persons and what was the content of those messages? Should I not include them in the minutes?"

Marinsky, very courteously: "I apologize for my ignorance of German procedure; I had noticed notes passing between the judges and I thought this was permissible. The first person was Yehuda Milo, First Secretary of the Israeli Embassy. I asked him: 'Is there any mail for me?' as I have given the Embassy address to my friends in Israel. The second person was Alfred Wolman, the representative of the newspaper *Yediot Aharonot*, whom I asked: 'Can you go out and get me some aspirin?'" Continuing in a louder voice: "But I have not finished my explanations. You all have eyes to see my messages, but none of you of course noticed that your clerk was laughing and sending notes to the usher while you were reading with evident boredom how Lischka was putting Jews to death. That's a very old story, isn't it? In your opinion the dust of thirty years ago should long ago have been swept out of the way. I was about to protest, but Herr Stange stopped me. If this happens again, my client and I will have to leave the court. As for alleged instructions from Jerusalem, I perceive you do not understand the situation of Israeli lawyers. I received my instructions thirty years ago when I learned that my entire family had been killed by the German Nazis at Bialystok." The judge withdrew into his shell.

The trial drags on with the twenty-one witnesses for the prosecution, which has its nose stuck tight in facts and dares not raise its eyes to look into causes. This trial needs dynamite. The resister René Clavel makes an appointment for June 27 with a member of Giscard d'Estaing's cabinet. He informs the minister that he is determined to make himself heard by fair means or foul at the trial where the presiding judge refuses to hear the testimony of the muzzled French witnesses. Informed of this, the President of the Republic intervenes in an extraordinary fashion the next day, June 28. Through diplomatic channels he sends a message to the German Minister of Foreign Affairs declaring that he is concerned about my trial, demanding that the French witnesses be allowed to testify, and reminding His Excellency that the Bundestag has still not ratified the accord. On Saturday, June 29, de Somoskoey reverses himself: the court will hear the French witnesses.

Third session, Monday, July 1. My faithful team, Jean Pierre-Bloch, and René Clavel, along with youths of the Jewish Student Front are present. It is Lischka's turn to testify. All my friends have put on their medals; the associations have sent flag-bearers. I enter the court between two rows of French flags that honor the Germany I represent. A storm breaks. De Somoskoey protests against the letter from Giscard d'Estaing. "I cannot take this letter into consideration. This is an intrusion on the independence of the court." He makes it known that the Minister of Justice has replied to this intervention on the part of the President of the Republic that "In Germany the judges are independent and subject only to the law."

The same day there is an editorial in the Israeli paper *Maariv* saying: "This intervention was highly necessary for public morality, but it is certainly without precedent in the history of international relations. The step taken by M. Giscard d'Estaing was intended to demonstrate with what gravity France looks upon the situation. The intervention of the French head of state has communicated in no uncertain terms to the German court that is trying Beate Klarsfeld, and to the entire judicial establishment in Germany that they are answerable to the court of world public opinion where they are on trial."

When Lischka is called to the witness stand, the French witnesses seated on benches in the corridor, taking their cue from Julien Aubart, refuse to stand up to make room for the colossal Gestapo chief to pass. The police fear the witnesses may attack him. After arguing for an hour, the police take Lischka into the courtroom by an unused side entrance. It has been agreed that I will give a discreet signal to start a riot, but only after Marinsky has interrogated Lischka. The cross-examination begins:

MARINSKY: "Have you any sentiments about the number 195590?"
LISCHKA: "I don't know what this number means."
MARINSKY: "Surely you remember your personal number in the S.S.?"
LISCHKA: "I don't remember it at all any more."
MARINSKY: "Perhaps you remember your Nazi Party number?"
LISCHKA: "No."
MARINSKY: "Why don't you want to talk about the years from 1936 to 1945? Are you ashamed?"
LISCHKA: (Referring to his right to refuse testimony that might incriminate him) "I refuse to answer this question."

The lawyer, seeking to show that Lischka lived a respected existence in Germany since the war's end, then tried a different approach:

MARINSKY: "How long have you lived in Cologne?"
LISCHKA: "Since 1950."
MARINSKY: "For twenty-one consecutive years, is that correct? Is that correct?"
LISCHKA: "Yes."
MARINSKY: "Nobody attacked you in these years, until these people [referring to Beate Klarsfeld and her group]?"
LISCHKA: "No."
MARINSKY: "Not a finger was pointed at you and nobody called you a killer?"

The judge protests: Counsel, you are trying to say that the inhabitants of Cologne have voluntarily integrated Lischka. I cannot permit such question.

MARINSKY: "It is you who said that, Your Honor." To Lischka: "Your hands are trembling now; they did not tremble thirty years ago."

The court explodes. Our friends have risen and start up the *Marseillaise*. There are shouts of "Assassin! Nazi!" Jean Pierre-Bloch, a former cabinet member under General de Gaulle, is seized by the throat and beaten by a guard. Police enter the courtroom in numbers. The session dissolves in total disarray. In France, and even in Germany, the press reaction is extraordinary. Now all eyes are on the trial.

Fourth session, Tuesday, July 2. Lischka completes his testimony. Marinsky recalls how Lischka reacted when we demonstrated in his office in May 1973. "Just like the good old days, Obersturmbannführer, you with a pistol and a Jew with his face to the wall."

JUDGE: "I must warn you once more that you must address the witness with all the respect due to the court. No more questions like that."
MARINSKY: "Yes, I forgot myself. . . . I have to keep remembering that people here don't like to be reminded of the good old days."

In a calmer atmosphere two French witnesses, Georges Wellers and Joseph Billig, are called to the stand. De Somoskoey, more cautious after reading the morning papers, exhibits the patience of an angel. These two witnesses are very important. In the course of three years Wellers saw tens of thousands of Jews transferred from Drancy, the anteroom of Death, to the gas chambers of Auschwitz. He tells how thousands of children were led lamentably to an atrocious death.

Joseph Billig gives a masterly presentation of Lischka's career. Of course, since there are no noisy incidents, practically none of these essential depositions are reported in the German press. We will have to stir up some commotion tomorrow to break this silence.

Fifth session, Wednesday, July 3. The climax of the trial is reached. Returning to the intervention of Giscard d'Estaing, the judge terms it intolerable. The lawyer appointed by the court to defend me suddenly rises and stigmatizes the gesture of the President of the Republic, "a pressure tactic reminiscent of the Nazi era." I rise and protest: "Herr Jochum is not my attorney, he is Herr de Somoskoey's," and I praise the intervention of Giscard d'Estaing as desired and approved by so many Frenchmen.

The first witness of the day is René Clavel. He will turn out to be the last of my witnesses. For more than an hour, impetuously and relentlessly, he puts the trial on trial. With his pitiless dis-

agreeable truths he irritates de Somoskoey to the point that the
latter imagines he sees René Clavel at the conclusion of his deposition parody the Nazi salute. To everyone's astonishment de
Somoskoey furiously accuses Clavel of mocking the court; decides
to admit no more French witnesses and declares a recess. The
other witnesses want to come in; there is shoving and pushing.
Henri Pudeleau is beaten by a guard so badly that he suffers broken
ribs. Julien Aubart cries out in a voice so anguished it brings tears
to the women's eyes; "You are trying to finish the job you began
at Auschwitz!" Pierre-Bloch is mobbed. These incidents have great
repercussions, especially so as Achenbach, the deputy to whom I
had alluded at several points during the trial, that day lost his
patience. In a radio interview in Cologne he revealed himself: "We
demand a general amnesty for humanitarian and Christian reasons.
As reporter to the Bundestag for my committee I shall scrutinize
the ratification proposal with care, and that will take a long time,
a very long time." Now public attention is turned on Achenbach.
From all sides we receive requests for his dossier. The Achenbach
affair is about to hatch.

Meanwhile Serge, who cannot cross into German territory under
pain of arrest, meets me in Liège on Thursday, July 4. We work
together on the draft of my final statement.

Sixth session, Friday, July 5. De Somoskoey announces this will be
a closed session because of Wednesday's disorders. I rise and say:
"Your Honor, those incidents took place because of the inhuman
way you are conducting this trial; you completely fail to take into
account the feelings of the victims of Nazism." After these words,
which are the only part of the trial to be reported that day because
of the closed session, I try to leave the courtroom. They force me
back. A scandal. De Somoskoey wishes to clap a prison sentence
on me immediately on the grounds that I have insulted the court.
The journalists, shut out of the trial, are on my side. Things calm
down. But the journalists refuse to accept their news at second
hand, through a few approved reporters, and file a complaint against
the judge. The court is emptied. The French consul-general at
Bonn is authorized to remain, while the Israeli diplomat is asked
to leave. But the French consul expresses his solidarity with his
Israeli colleague and departs with him.

The courtroom is thus empty when Prosecutor Gehrling (who
will have the special duty of prosecuting the Nazi criminals if the

accord is ratified) requests a sentence of six months, to be suspended. The psychiatrist gives his deposition. To my great satisfaction, he considers that I am perfectly normal and act as I do for the very reasons I state.

Marinsky then makes a vibrant and remarkable plea in English. It was published by the Israeli Bureau several weeks later. Here are some extracts:

Mr. Chairman, Honorable Judges, in a wider sense, in a cardinal sense, transcending every legal-technical criterion—an attorney from my country has not only the moral right but a moral duty of the highest order to plead the case of Beate Klarsfeld. Because, Mr. Chairman, Honorable Judges, for my country and its people, the one hundred thousand men, women, and children whom S.S.-Obersturmbannführer Lischka sent to their death are far more than faceless numerical statistics. They are our brothers and sisters, our mothers and fathers. Theirs is a living memory. A memory that compels us to rally to the defense of this woman, who has sacrificed her liberty and well-being in order to expose the mass-killers still at large and demand that they be brought to justice. . . .

My country, Mr. Chairman, Honorable Judges, is afflicted by strife and bloodshed. We have to preserve every ounce of energy, emotion, and will power in order to face immediate and mortal perils lurking just beyond our borders. We certainly have neither reason nor desire to antagonize German public opinion, to interfere with your internal politics, or to impair whatever goodwill exists in this country for Israel.

And yet, all this is completely nonexistent and fades away in face of a hallowed, deeply rooted commitment to the memory of our kith and kin—a commitment that does not allow for compromise.

We are committed, Mr. Chairman, Honorable Judges, to make every effort in order to ensure that Germany bring the Lischkas still at large to justice. We believe that Beate Klarsfeld and her friends are basically moved by the same purpose. We know that Beate Klarsfeld has, at considerable risk to herself, campaigned against anti-Semitism in every part of the globe. She has literally risked her life in Syria demanding humane treatment of Israeli war prisoners. She has demonstrated in the streets of Warsaw and Prague against anti-Semitic policies. She has gone to distant places such as South America in order to track down Nazi war criminals. We feel that a sincere desire to atone for the past has moved Beate Klarsfeld to act in this manner. We therefore admire her and salute her courage. That, Mr. Chairman, Honorable Judges, is the reason why an Israeli lawyer is here to defend her and plead her case. . . .

Beate Klarsfeld is not Jewish, Beate Klarsfeld is German. Please note,

Mr. Chairman, Honorable Judges, German, not anti-German. She is merely anti-Nazi. Categorically anti-Nazi. And this, Mr. Chairman, Honorable Judges, is the true and basic motive underlying her activities. *For Beate Klarsfeld and her friends, more than any other national public or individual factor, have shattered the impasse and complacency existing in this country and its legislative body. It is they who have planted the black flag of protest on the soil of Germany: It is they and their activities that focus public opinion on the remnants of a malignant cancer that spread throughout this nation's lifeblood only one generation ago.*

And I respectfully submit to this Court that in assessing motivation and punishment, if any, the outstanding issue in question is not one of individual personality or personal frailties. No, Mr. Chairman, Honorable Judges, these are but minor considerations in the scheme of things that confronts us. It is the acts of Beate Klarsfeld, her overt acts, as related to the obvious aim of remedying a terrible and deadly wrong—it is this act and its implication that deserve the Court's foremost attention and scrutiny. . . .

Mr. Chairman, Honorable Judges, an absolute acquittal or symbolic punishment in this case means much more than deciding the fate of Beate Klarsfeld. For much more than the liberty of Beate Klarsfeld is at stake in this trial. For here, you as judges of post-war Germany have a unique opportunity to proclaim a juridical and formal protest against the perpetuation of this deadly lacuna, which has turned your country into a law-protected haven for mass-killers. Here, for the first time, you have the opportunity to voice your legitimate protest by employing concise words deploring the state of affairs to which your legal framework has exposed you. You can, of course, avoid this issue, you can deal harshly with Beate Klarsfeld. You can also mitigate the punishment on grounds of Beate Klarsfeld's personality and background. You, of course, are entitled, in a legal sense, to confine yourselves to the dry facts of the charge sheet. But that, Mr. Chairman, Honorable Judges, would not be a mere evasion of the cardinal issue, but, in a way, a mute consent to and compliance with the existing state of affairs.

Mr. Chairman, Honorable Judges, when a doctor is summoned to treat a patient suffering from a light disease and encounters next to him a man in need of immediate cure in order to remedy a serious and deadly illness, the doctor, if he is true to his oath, will not disregard the man whose life is in danger—on the formal pretext that he has been summoned to deal with another case. Your position, Mr. Chairman, Honorable Judges, is somewhat similar. You have been called by the legal apparatus of this country to set down facts and apply the law specified in the charge sheet. But you have next to you, Mr. Chairman, Honorable Judges, on the very doorstep of these proceedings, ample proof of a poison that has permeated the pores of your legal system. I want to believe, I sincerely want to believe that you will not shirk this responsibility and that from this Court, the "Erste Grosse Strafkammer of Cologne," will come the "Erste Grosser Juristischer Protest" against this state of affairs.

. . . For this, Mr. Chairman, Honorable Judges, is not a purely Jewish or a French problem, it is primarily a German problem, and my appeal is an appeal to the conscience of the new Germany and its judges to solve it in an honorable way. We all know, Mr. Chairman, Honorable Judges, that the legislature is but an instrument of public opinion. The man in the street elects the Bundestag. Public opinion, the legislature, the judiciary and the Government are, in a way, interdependent in coping with the issue. But you, the judges of the new Germany, more than any other individual group or factor, represent the face and image of Justice and Law. Your word and opinion, your moral philosophy, your protest, carry or should carry tremendous weight and influence.

Mr. Chairman, Honorable Judges, I have already noted that two Arab terrorists armed with a bomb have shattered your entire legal framework into thousands of pieces. I, Mr. Chairman, Honorable Judges, come to you from Israel unarmed and alone. My only weapon is a deeply rooted moral conviction and the support of a country and a people whose claim to justice in this case cannot be refuted or denied.

I pray and plead not only for the sake of Israel or France, not only for the sake of Beate Klarsfeld, but also in the hope that a new Germany has indeed taken root, and that this plea for justice will be heeded.

When my turn comes, I say in conclusion:

If you limit this trial to acts of civil disobedience I have committed, without going into the grave problem that triggered them, you will surely find me guilty and sentence me with or without time off. But you will not be doing your duty. You have an opportunity to show the Bundestag it is its duty to ratify the accord and strengthen the sense of justice in this country.

For my friends and myself it has not been easy to break laws in order to obtain justice. For you also it would not be easy to acquit me when you know I have done an illegal act. But if you do, you will bring something valuable into German justice, by not adhering to the letter of the law as so many other German judges have unfortunately done before you. What I am asking of you is a courageous decision.

As for me, I have been struggling for a long time in the name of the brave men and women who faced torture, the ax, or the firing squad. You may be sure I do not fear your verdict. No, it is not fear that moves me at this moment, but hope—less for myself than for you and the FRG, the hope that you will decide to acquit me. If you do so, you will help the ratification of the Franco-German treaty and you will bring respect for German justice, which it surely needs."

The verdict is to be announced Tuesday, July 9. Meanwhile two events give a great boost to our cause. On July 7 the Knesset in special session unanimously approves a protestation against my trial, and blames the court for the incidents that victimized the former deportees. All parties collaborated in rushing through the formalities, so that the debate took place and the motion was approved the same day. Ygal Allon, the Minister of Foreign Affairs, Haika Grossman, Meir Palik (Moked), and Ehud Olmerd (Free Center) each made a speech.

Monday, July 8. There is a summit meeting in Bonn between Schmidt, the new chancellor, and Giscard d'Estaing. That evening Schmidt announces, to the amazement of Germany: "I have resolved before the President of the French Republic that the agreement will be ratified before the end of the year." The summit was expected to deal with economics; it opened with the agreement.

The French press carries the story of my trial on the front pages every day. An article by Maurice Delarue, chief of the diplomatic section of *Le Monde*, puts great pressure on Bonn. "The European Union is not only a matter of trade, factories, grains, and currency. It is also a matter of men. It is not with the Germany of Lischka and the judges of Cologne that the French wish to shape the European Union; it is with the Germany of Willy Brandt and Beate Klarsfeld."

Monday, July 9. There are many of us at Bonn. We have come in a bus chartered by LICA. In the morning we lay flowers on the monument to the German anti-Nazis, and we read the text of the epistle of Thomas Mann, "To the Germans," written during the war. Then we take flowers to the prison in Cologne where countless members of the French Resistance were executed. M. Katzman, cantor of the Synagogue on rue Copernic in Paris, reads the last and magnificent letter written by Abbé Deroy, who was guillotined here in 1943.

Then at 2 P.M. comes the verdict. To the astonishment of almost everyone, but not mine, as I had sensed de Somoskoey's rage, the sentence is: two months in prison without obligation to serve the time already passed in preventive jail (37 days—16 in 1971 and 21 in 1974) and without obligation to serve immediately the time remaining (23 days), as my case had to be submitted in revision to the Federal Court of Karlsruhe.

In the courtroom, crowded with reporters from all over the world as well as resisters and deportees, there are sounds of protest. They start singing the *Marseillaise*. The verdict has heightened the effect of the trial. There is general indignation.

Wednesday, July 10, Paris. At a huge demonstration before the German Embassy I am surrounded by a delirious crowd. Thousands of people demand ratification and declare their support of me. Our apartment is besieged by French and foreign press. I don't get a chance to stop talking, answering questions—especially about Achenbach, who is on his way to becoming the scapegoat of the bad conscience of the Germans. In fact, in Germany it was immediately recognized in political circles that the verdict was a disaster for the Federal government, which is celebrating its twenty-fifth anniversary. The young democrats of Achenbach's Liberal party come to see us in Paris and take back with them two thousand photocopies of documents in our files. They hold a press conference in Bonn; they are going to demand that Achenbach resign as reporter of his committee to the Bundestag on the agreement. On July 22, this is accomplished. Achenbach resigns. The ratification will be approved.

But by this time I have left Paris. So have Serge, Arno, Lida, and Petia; all five of us are in Israel. We are honored in Jerusalem. Gradually the turmoil of the trial, which has more than fulfilled our hopes, is stilled.

In Germany public opinion, except for the extreme right, is changing in my favor. A Liberal deputy nominates me for the Theodor Heuss Prize "for having awakened the German conscience." I am also nominated by the "Christian-Political" movement for the Bundesverdienstkreuz, the legion of honor. Perhaps someday I may even be a prophet in my own country.

22

RABAT AND THE MIDDLE EAST

While waiting for that distant day to come, we are enjoying life for a few weeks at the swimming pool of the Dalia kibbutz. But all too soon Serge must return to Paris to study for his bar examination, which he will take in October. What a joy this vacation has been in the kibbutz, punctuated by lectures all over the country! What a lot of friends we now have in Israel!

The energetic Myriam Meyouhas, member of the city council of Jerusalem, has undertaken to form a committee to support my action. This idea is most welcome at a time when LICA, which has underwritten a large part of the expense of our work, has exhausted its resources. It will take some time to build up this committee, but by November it will be a going concern. Its co-chairmen are deputies Haika Grossman of Mapam, and Benjamin Halevi of Likud.

Serge passes the bar examination. He is now a lawyer. Only 250 out of the 850 who took the examination passed. He had prepared for his orals in October in Israel while making a 55-minute program on the Irgun for French television. The film will show how brave men fought against the English for the independence of Israel. This struggle is fairly unknown, while people accept almost as gospel Arafat's allegations of collusion between Zionism and British imperialism.

As for me, a few days before the Arab summit meeting in Rabat I decide to try to go there and make a public protest against the Arab policy against Israel, and to speak some truths I feel need to be spoken. Of course I know in advance that the Moroccans will not read what I write, but I know the international press will broadcast my protest and my message if I get a chance to give it. Moreover, it would be a witness of solidarity that would bolster the morale of the Israelis in these difficult times of isolation. All summer the Israelis have seen me among them with my family and they know I am not a fanatic with a martyr complex, but a normal woman deeply aware of the exceptional situation of Israel and of the special responsibility the Germans have toward the Jewish people.

Serge and I draft a statement:

I have come to Rabat because there must be at least one voice to protest here, at the summit of the Arab countries, against a policy whose goal is the destruction of the State of Israel.

Thirty years ago, Hitler's Germany exterminated six million Jews amid general indifference.

As a German woman, it is my duty to tell the Arab people not to take as their example the crime of which my country is guilty.

Let the Jewish state live in peace: a country and a refuge for the survivors of Nazi extermination, for Jews expelled by Communist states and oppressed in the Soviet Union, and for the Jews who have been obliged to leave the Arab countries in greater numbers than the Palestinians who were exiled in 1948.

Israel is also the land of Jews who never left the country of their ancestors and who have maintained the age-old and inviolable rights of the Jewish people throughout various invasions.

Thanks to an anti-Semitism that has been transformed into anti-Zionism and thanks to oil, you have in the West and the East allies and clients. You and they pretend that Israel is an imperialist state: this is not true! From 1944 to 1948 it was the Jewish people who dared liberate Palestine from colonial British power. Since then the Jews have asked only to live in peace, which you persist in denying them.

You pretend that Israel is not a Socialist state: this is not true! Moreover, it is among your states that one can find feudal structures antithetical to any person of the left. Such a one is Jordan, which is, as much as Israel and Cisjordan, part—and the biggest part—of Palestine. More Palestinian blood has been shed by the weapons of Hussein than by those of the Israelis.

In the Palestine of the Balfour Declaration, approving a national territory for the Jewish people, there is room for the State of Israel (now 27,000 square kilometers of the 111,000 square kilometers of the 1917 Palestine) and for a Palestinian state.

Your problems, those of Egypt, of Syria, of Iraq, of the Maghreb, are problems of development and social progress. The huge amount of money belonging to the least populated Arab countries should be used to help you solve these problems, instead of financing war against Israel, scapegoat of the real problems of the Arab masses.

Everyone knows that Eastern Prussia is not Russian, but there is not a single German Democrat who would defend a policy of revenge. These lost territories are the price of an unfair and devastating war that was started and brought into the east by Germany. And the Federal Republic of West Germany has integrated nine million refugees, the German Democratic Republic three million.

In 1948, the Arab countries also started an unfair war against a state of Israel that had accepted the 1947 partition decided upon by the international community.

You will buy or seduce consciences for more or less time, but you will not make anybody believe that three million Israelis are perpetually the aggressors against one hundred million Arabs.

I have no lesson to suggest to you other than the one of the German experience, which unfortunately has a link with Kiryat Shmoneh and Maalot: do not try to find the final solution for Israel in the way Hitler sought the final solution of the Jewish problem.

This time I do not go alone. Through the press we are aware that the Moroccans have taken extraordinary security measures. A large number of Palestinians suspected of intending to assault Hussein and the King of Morocco have been arrested. I do not envy their situation. As I am carrying 250 copies of my statement at the bottom of a traveling bag filled with food and trifles, this can be discovered when we land in Morocco, and I could be whisked away by the Moroccan police without anyone being apprised of my arrest. Police who are confident they can work on a prisoner without outside interference easily slip into brutality. Our friend Marco, who was a member of the team that went after Lischka in Cologne, volunteers for this assignment. Having lived in Morocco for more than a year, he knows his way around, and is better equipped than any other of our friends to deal with any sensitive situation that might arise. He is aware of the risk he is running, but he is a courageous boy.

Saturday, October 26, 1974. 2 P.M. I kiss the babies good-by. Raissa, my mother-in-law, will supervise the baby-sitter whom I have engaged until, God willing, I return Monday at noon. Marco leaves behind his wife who is pregnant and has to stay in bed for a few weeks. Our tickets read Paris-Casablanca-Paris. The airport at Rabat is closed because of the Arab summit meeting. We have telephoned a half-dozen hotels in Rabat; all are filled. We decide to spend the night in Casablanca and go by taxi tomorrow morning to Rabat. There we will get in touch with reporters and arrange a busy place for them to come and watch my distribution of the leaflets until my probable rapid arrest.

In Paris, Serge, Julien, and Elisabeth have secured three Moroccan telephone numbers: those of the Ministries of the Interior and of Information, and the Information Desk of the Hilton Hotel where the summit is being held, and which is practically out-of-bounds for journalists—they have just been brutally ejected from the opening session.

Marco and I pretend to be strangers during the flight. In Casablanca I show my French passport. The officer stamps the Moroccan entry visa right on the same page on which six Israeli visas interlace. They go through my baggage carefully. But it is obvious that they are looking for guns, not tracts. The inspector puts her hand into my bag, pulls out various objects, feels around the bottom, but doesn't take out a single tract. Ooh! That was a close one!

We each take a room at a big hotel. I am nervous and don't sleep well. At 7 A.M. we take a taxi. It would have been more cautious to have taken two taxis, but in such circumstances one feels as if one is in a whirlpool. One is drawn toward the center that is the moment of action, and one tends to be less and less cautious as the moment of truth approaches. As we leave the city, there is a police barrier. "Your passports." They take down our names but do not search us. Just in case, I had previously shoved the thick envelope of leaflets under the seat. Between Casa and Rabat we are stopped by police at six checkpoints. In the hotels the journalists are not yet up. I make an appointment to meet a few of them in front of the Ministry of Information at 12 noon exactly. There, on time, I begin handing out my leaflets. Some passers-by accept them, no doubt expecting the familiar party line. Then there is a double take. Two women turn back to me and say: "Slob, go do this in your own country."

Fortunately, two officials accept my tract and hasten into the Ministry. They come back with two guards who pull me inside the building, then come out once more to get two photographers. A few minutes later we are put into police cars and taken to head-quarters. The inspectors confiscate the journalists' film. The Chief of Police, Foreign Section, a little man some forty years old, begins a long interrogation. He is looking for, hoping for, a conspiracy. He would have wished the tracts to have been printed in Morocco. I tell him how I got them into the country. Examining my passport where Moroccan, Israeli, even Syrian visas are juxtaposed, he cannot conceal his anger at the laxity of the airport police. "Are you alone?" "Yes." By the end of a half hour his courtesy is giving way to rage. He has received reports from the checkpoints between Casa and Rabat. "You lied to me. You are not alone. Who is this Marc P——? He's your lover, your accomplice . . ." and I hear him telephone an order for Marc's arrest. I hope Marc gets away! The interrogation goes on, but I've been through this before. I always tell the truth. I have nothing to hide. They take me to the criminal police; line-up photographs, fingerprints, new interrogation. Back to the Foreign Section police. Hours go by.

As for Marc, as soon as he saw I was being arrested, he ran to the post office, got Serge on the telephone, and, dejected and in his blue jeans jumped into a bus and got away. He spends the night in a flophouse in Tangiers and in the morning, unnoticed by the border police, enters Spanish Morocco in the midst of a crowd of natives. Then by ferry to Spain, by train to Madrid, by plane to Paris.

In Paris, Serge and our friends immediately telephone the Moroccan ministries for information about "the Klarsfeld affair"; they introduce themselves as West European journalists. The incident has been broadcast on the radio. At 8 P.M. my policeman informs me: "They are worrying a lot about you in Europe." Those words are a comfort to me. A few minutes later he says: "You are going to be expelled. There is a plane at 2 A.M." Thank God! A car comes for me with three police officers. How often have I already taken a ride with three policemen! Berlin, Cologne, Munich, Warsaw, Prague, La Paz; sometimes on my way to jail, sometimes going to the border and freedom. At Casablanca there is no 2 A.M. plane. I stretch out on a bench between two police-men who watch over my slumbers.

At 9:30 A.M. I get on the plane, the very one on which I had a reservation, and arrive at Orly at noon. There is no one to meet me, as the Moroccans chose not to reveal they were expelling me before I was back in Paris. You can imagine the joy of my family when I telephoned! I am promptly surrounded by the press, so again I have the opportunity to explain the meaning of my actions for the cause of Israel.

My schedule for October–December: lectures, all unpaid. A sampling: October 21, Geneva one hour, live, on television. October 30, Paris, the Freemasons. November 7, Geneva. November 11–15, five lectures in Israel. November 25, Paris, the Synagogue. November 26, Pau. November 27, Toulouse, the Jewish Agency. December 1, Cercle Bernard Lazare, Paris. December 4, Avignon. December 6, Montpellier. December 7, Aix-en-Provence. December 8, Nîmes. December 10, Antwerp. December 13, Metz. December 17, Lycée Chateau-Thierry. December 18, ORT, Villiers-le-Bel. December 19, B'nai-B'rith, Vincennes.

At the conclusion of my lectures I autograph my book, whose sales provide some of the money we need to go on working and living. The halls are always filled. I say this not in vanity; people like to see an activist. I often appear on radio and television. My lectures typically end up with something like this:

In conclusion, I can only repeat what I consider essential. Anti-Zionism today is the main branch of that same sturdy old tree, anti-Semitism. For centuries the cry against the Jewish people during pogroms was, "Go back to your own country." But at that time they didn't have a country. So one day the Jews started on the road to the Land of Israel and they rebuilt the Jewish homeland.

Later, when the Nazis undertook the systematic destruction of the Jewish people, with many active collaborators in most of the European nations, they forbade the Jews to return to their country, Palestine, where their brothers awaited them. Then we saw ships, overladen with Jews forced back from Palestine, go down at sea and go down, too, into the bored indifference of the belligerents. This must not happen again.

And yet today, when the Jewish people have their own land to protect them, anti-Semitism is striving relentlessly to destroy this protection. The anti-Semites are nostalgic for the forties. How easy it was then in the Ukraine to club Jews to death, how easy in Lithuania to make them undress and dig mass graves before being shot in them, how easy in Poland to make rabbis crawl on all fours or burn their beards; how easy for the Germans to build huge gas chambers, for the Austrians to put Jews to scrubbing the streets of Vienna with toothbrushes; how easy it was for Vichy to "aryanize" Jewish property and deliver to the Germans thousands of foreign Jews who had trustingly come to France thinking the French would protect them.

Today, now that there is an Israel, such things are impossible, and that is why the destruction of the State of Israel is and will remain the first priority of anti-Semitism. Auschwitz was the negation of the Jewish people. Israel is the negation of Auschwitz. One of the chief battlefields on which this war is being waged is in Europe.

Jews and non-Jews, you have not the right to remain indifferent or inactive. We must and we can act.

Serge is assisting Joseph Billig in putting together a detailed in-depth study of the contributions made by Achenbach to the "final solution" in France. We hope this study will put an end to Achenbach's career in the Bundestag. Achenbach is one of the German deputies who has joined with representatives from other countries in sponsoring a parliamentary association for European-Arab cooperation, a cooperation that will, of course, suffocate Israel. Serge is also issuing a paper that we intend to distribute selectively in Germany. It reproduces, among others, a document proving that Lischka and the High Command of the Gestapo knew what was to be done at Auschwitz to the Jews who were arrested in France and deported. This document will dispose of the principal argument of the defense. If our pressure is great enough, Lischka and Hagen will be found guilty. In order that this trial of the agents of the final solution in France succeed, that it be a fitting memorial to the 100,000 victims, that it obstruct the rehabilitation of Nazi criminals in Germany and Vichy collaborationists in France, that it compel the Germans and the French to face up to their heavy responsibility toward the Jewish people, we need to mobilize much energy, much effort, much support from our friends, and a good dose of luck. I deeply hope we will succeed, I deeply hope to bring effective assistance to Israel, and I hope that after next summer we can return to the Dalia kibbutz, which we love as if it were our home. I hope that those who have placed their confidence in us will continue to hold us in their esteem.

Monday, January 13, 1975. Bonn. I hold a press conference and hand out the special number of the periodical *Le Monde Juif*. Its contents include a study of Achenbach and the Final Solution of the Jewish problem in France; and the paper that refutes the principal argument Lischka and his associates intend to use in their defense. These two documents (which we have financed) will be delivered to each of the 500 deputies of the Bundestag. I also make public a list of the 950 Germans who committed war crimes in France. Serge was given this list by the French Military Court.

This press conference is critical, as I have been informed that on Wednesday the last step will be taken in committee that could bring ratification of the French-German agreement before the Bundestag. This is the Committee of Foreign Affairs of which Achenbach is a member. I know that the Christian Democrats on the committee plan to vote against ratification on a legal technicality. Achenbach will also vote against. If he can persuade two members of the Social-Liberal coalition to go along with him, the committee can table the accord for a long, long time. I must therefore attack Achenbach, isolate him by exposing his opposition as based on self-protection, and thus demonstrate the real need to bring to trial the perpetrators of the final solution by revealing to the press and to the deputies glaring evidence of Lischka's guilt. The young liberal faction of Achenbach's party is at my side during the press conference, and will insist on Achenbach's resignation from the Bundestag.

On Wednesday the agreement clears the hurdle of the committee; as I had foreseen, the CDU and Achenbach voted no, but Achenbach had not succeeded in making a single convert among the FDP and SPD.

Tuesday I went to Frankfurt and told the press corps I was leaving at 3:30 for Cairo, with the intention of transmitting the following message to the National Assembly of Egypt:

I have come to Cairo first of all to ask the Egyptian parliamentarians to remove Ernst Achenbach, the Liberal German deputy, from the Parliamentary Association for European-Arab Cooperation.

This Association was created in Paris on March 23, 1974, by thirty-five of the several thousand parliamentarians of Western Europe. Ernst Achenbach was one of the thirty-five, one of the four Germans M.P.s who were then in Paris.

Today I have brought to Cairo the thorough study done by Professor Joseph Billig of the role of Achenbach in the Final Solution of the Jewish question in France from 1940 to 1943. During that time, Achenbach, head of the political section of Hitler's embassy, cooperated actively with the Gestapo to annihilate the Jews of France, of whom 100,000 were killed in the death camps.

The presence of Achenbach—an accomplice in the genocide of which the Jewish people were victims—is inadmissible within a body representing European-Arab cooperation. If he is not removed as soon as possible, it would mean that this cooperation is plunging its roots into a criminal past.

One of the people in Achenbach's law office, his former client Horst Wagner, was liaison between Ribbentrop and Himmler. It was Wagner and the Grand Mufti of Jerusalem who, in 1943–1944, sent to death thousands of Jewish children rather than let them go to Palestine.

There you have an example of German-Arab cooperation that we would not care to see again.

This is why those people in Germany who have the courage to assume their responsibility as Germans in regard to the Jewish people are also asking the Arab world, through me, to change its unjustly aggressive policy toward the State of Israel, and to admit the sovereign existence of Israel within secure and recognized frontiers.

This is why we are also asking Egypt to influence the Syrians and Iraqi authorities, so that the living conditions of the Jewish communities in Syria and Iraq may be improved. The lot of those Jews signifies, to the entire world, the lot suffered by Jews in Arab territory.

It is my intention to do the same in Damascus, Baghdad, and Beirut. But this time I have no visas. It would have been a waste of time to try and get them. As I check in at the Egyptian Airline, the Reuter correspondent informs me that a visa will be ready for me in Cairo. Some hours later I land in Egypt; I have no trouble the first night. The following morning, on the advice of the press corps, I report to the Ministry of Information, near the Nile. I am received courteously by Dr. Metwalli, chief of the Foreign Press section. I explain the purpose of my visit. He telephones to the office of the National Assembly and asks to see my dossiers (they also include copies of anti-Jewish correspondence between the Mufti and Nazi officials), in order that he may inform the President of the Assembly, as the latter cannot see me personally.

Thursday morning, before boarding the plane for Damascus at the Cairo airport, I have a televised interview with CBS in which I explain the major reasons for my Mideast tour. I am the only European on the plane, and I am aware of stares of curiosity. At the airport at Damascus the police keep me waiting a half hour and then say I am not authorized to receive a visa. It is now close to noon. They tell me I can return to Cairo or proceed to Beirut. Of course I choose Beirut, but I have to wait until next morning. So I spend eighteen hours in the icy drafts of the transit area, with nothing to do but observe the comings and goings of a handful of planes, most of them from Arabia and Kuwait, carrying picturesque passengers, veiled women, motley baggage, many prayer rugs. As at Rabat I spend the night on a hard bench.

Friday morning I leave for Beirut, where the police give me a 48-hour visa. I take a room at the St. George Hotel and try to persuade the local press to get me into the Lebanon Assembly. A typical response is that of Edouard Saab, editor-in-chief of *Jour* and correspondent of *Le Monde*. "Oh, you're the lady who was at Damascus. I can't do anything for you . . ." and he hangs up. They all know that my message has nothing in it for those to whom it is addressed. They are very much afraid of compromising themselves.

At six o'clock two German journalists and one from the Associated Press look me up. A few minutes later five agents of the Lebanese Security break into my room, followed by the manager of the hotel and a couple of employees who pack my belongings. Three cars bring us to the security office. Several commissioners interrogate me. The chief says, "I was in Lyon at the time of the Barbie affair. You conducted yourself very well."

"Then why do you object to what I am doing in this place today? The reasons that bring me here are the same as those that made me go to La Paz."

"No, it's not the same thing. You should be concerned about the poor Lebanese in the south who are bombed every day."

"If you think it's all right for terrorists in the south to go into Israel and kill children . . ." It becomes another dialogue of the deaf.

Commissioner Antoine Baroud takes my very succinct deposition and tells me I will be expelled and will leave for Rome at 2 A.M. I put two armchairs together, borrow a blanket, and try to get some rest, thinking of room 327 at the St. George where my money was spent for nothing.

At 2 A.M. three police officers, mustachioed and reeking of garlic, escort me to the airport, bypassing the check-in. Inside Japan Airlines they try to examine the contents of my handbag (perhaps fearing I was about to hi-jack the plane and force it to Tel Aviv. Why do they not do the same for the terrorists who are based in Lebanon?). The plane captain requests that they do this on the runway, not on Japanese territory.

The plane leaves. The mission is concluded. No doubt there will be others to come.

23

RESOLUTION

At Bonn, on January 30, 1975, the Christian Democrats see to it that I am refused admission to the Bundestag. They do not wish me to be present for the vote on ratification—that ratification they persistently oppose and for which I have worked so hard. Achenbach, defeated, has not come to see his more liberal colleagues join with the Social Democrats to ratify the Franco-German judiciary accord. The long-sought victory is celebrated in France and Israel.

However, I am off to Jerusalem on February 4 and take with me little Lida whom I cannot leave in Paris. Thanks to my supporting committee, I hold a press conference in Jerusalem the following day revealing that Hans Schirmer, the former Nazi propagandist, has been entrusted with the preparation for the European-Arab talks at the Ministry of Foreign Affairs in Bonn. Schirmer is that German ambassador whom I opposed in vain in 1970 in Vienna, when he was appointed to represent the Federal Republic there. And now here he is, entrusted with the preparation of the European-Arab talks for Bonn when he, a Nazi, was the associate director, from 1939 to 1943, of the vast radio apparatus for sending Hitlerian propaganda abroad. The political line of the vilely anti-Jewish propaganda broadcast to the Near East is unmistakable: "The Jews are the mortal enemies of the Arabs. . . . Your salvation can be attained only with the forces of the Axis; they stand ready to deliver you from the Jewish pestilence." (Shortly thereafter Schirmer went on leave for "reasons of health.")

Some days later, on February 17, I am in Strasbourg to witness the vote in the European Parliament—unanimous except for the German CSU of the extreme right—on a resolution condemning all amnesty for the war criminals and demanding their punishment. It is through such processes that the political morality common to the countries of Western Europe is expressed. Achenbach has always proposed general amnesty. Through our action, and that of all our friends, such an amnesty has not only been denied but also solemnly condemned. Achenbach, having already been forced to resign his post as president of the European Parliament's Commission for Development and Cooperation, has not shown himself in Strasbourg. Serge, Julien Aubart, Francis Lenchener, and I have been distributing to each member of the Parliament a copy of our study on him.

On February 21, the other German House, the Bundesrat, votes unanimously for ratification of the agreement. The Christian Democrats, who are in the majority there, realize that a negative vote risks deterioration of Franco-German relations anew. In consequence they are obliged to take the position contrary to the one they adopted three weeks earlier in the Bundestag. This time ratification is wholly won.

An enormous weariness weighs upon me . . . all that work, all those financial problems. But I look at my little family, so close-knit, and confidence springs up again—and courage, too.

BEATE KLARSFELD

230, avenue de Versailles
75016 Paris, France
Telephone: 288.91.37

SOURCES

KURT-GEORG KIESINGER

The documents from which I have quoted are in the archives of the Foreign Ministry and the Propaganda Ministry of the Third Reich; the National Archives, Washington, D.C.; the Central State Archives, Potsdam; and the Library of Contemporary Jewish Documents (CDJC), Paris.

Schnabel, R. *Missbrauchte Mikrophone* ("Misused Microphones").
    Vienna: Europa Verlag, 1967.
Kiesinger Dokumente. Munich: Verlag Politisches Archiv, 1967.
Billig, Joseph and Klarsfeld, Beate. *Kiesinger ou le fascisme subtil*
    ("Kiesinger or Subtle Fascism"). Hamburg, 1969.
Klarsfeld, Beate. *Kiesinger-Dokumentation.* Preface by Heinrich Böll.
    Darmstadt: Melzer Verlag, 1969.

The Kiesinger file may be consulted upon request in the CDJC, 17 rue Geoffroy-l'Asnier, Paris IV.

ERNST ACHENBACH

Political career. See in particular in the CDJC: NG 3628, 5470, 5627. LXXI–4, 30. XCVI–93. CCCXCV–5.

Achenbach's preface to Otto Abetz's *Das offene Problem* ("The Unsolved Problem"). Bonn: Greven Verlag, 1951.

The Naumann Plot. London: Wiener Library, 1953.

Grimm. *Unrecht in Rechtsstaat* ("Injustice in the Constitutional State"). Tübingen: Verlag der Deutschen Hochschullehrer, 1957. Pp. 70–71, 178, 201–221.

Clermont, Julien. *L'homme qu'il fallait tuer, Pierre Laval* ("Pierre Laval, the Man Who Had To Be Killed"). Paris: Ch. de Jonquières, 1949.

Du Moulin de Labarthète, H. *Le temps des illusions* ("The Years of Illusion"). Geneva: Editions à l'enseigne du cheval ailé, 1946.

Wesemann, Fried. *Die Totengräber sind unter uns* ("The Grave-diggers are Underneath Us"). In *Frankfurter Rundschau*, June 9–13, 1953.

The part Achenbach and the German Embassy in Paris played in the Final Solution of the Jewish Problem. V 8, 59, 61, 62, 63, 64, 83. VI 142, 143. XXV 37, 42, 44, 46–52a. XXVb 14, 15, 144. XLVIIIa 13. XLIXa 41. XCVI 80 (p. 60). CXXVIa 87. CCII 2.

Achenbach's February 15, 1943, telegram and the deportation of 2,000 Jews. CXXXVIa 92. XXVC 207. XLVIIIa 3. XXVa 277. CCXIX 49a. CCXVIII 23. XXVc 214. XXVa 272, 274a. 275. XLIX 62. XXVc 211, 215.

KURT LISCHKA

His positions. CDJC: CCCL 34. CCCLXIII 127. CCCLXIV 2 (pp. 39–43), 5 (p. 23), 6 (p. 32). CCCXCV 1, 23. CDXXXIV 13, 17. CDXXXVII 25. Nuremberg: R 108. Central Archives, Potsdam: 2919 A 6009 (685), 4054 A 9171, 2917 A 1220 (928), 2425 A 6392, 7631, 7680, 1174 A 2673 (684). Eichmann Interrogation: Band 4 (S3, p. 129).

His anti-Jewish measures. CDJC: I 41. IV 168, 187, 199. VI 142. XXI 4, 5, 7. XXIV 13, 27. XXV 46, 50, 51a. XXVa 274a, 275, 276, 278, 281, 282a, 294. XXVb 1, 5, 7–13, 15, 18, 27–32, 41, 45, 49a, 55, 60, 68, 80, 96, 105, 115, 118, 127, 132, 134, 147. XXVc 175, 177, 224, 228, 247, 253. XXVI 4, 6, 12, 14–18, 29, 31, 33, 37, 38, 40, 49, 58, 59, 63, 69, 80. XXVII 7–11, 24, 26–33. XLI 2, 6. XLVI 1. XLVIIIa 3, 9. XLIX 19, 43, 43a, 67. XLIXa 4, 11, 13–22, 45, 48, 50, 55–61. LXV 2, 5, 7, 9, 12. LXXVI 14. CDXXXIV 13, 18. CDXXXVII 25.

His measures of reprisal. CDJC: VII 2, 9. XLI 41. XLV 42, 44, 49, 68. XLVa 42, 43, 47a, 48, 49, 55, 59. XLIX 68, 70. CCCLXIV 2 (pp. 40–43), 4 (p. 237), 5 (p. 23).

HERBERT HAGEN

CDJC: VII 3. XXVa 238, 252a, 253, 261, 283, 287, 296, 318. XXVb 1, 9, 30, 37–44, 49, 49a, 112, 127, 132, 147, 172, 174. XXVc 232. XXVI 33–36, 40, 54–56, 63, 66a, 68b. XXVII 4, 17, 24, 33, 35, 39. XLI 5. XLVa 57. XLIX 42–47. XLIXa 90a, 91b, 110. LXV 1–4, 8, 15. CCXXXIV 2, 3, 4, 10–12. CCCVIII 7 (pp. 1192, 1221, 1229). CCCXCV 1, 2, 3. CDXXXVII 1–30. CDLXXX 8, 9, 17, 19, 23.

KLAUS BARBIE

Anti-Jewish measures. CDJC: XLVI (Folder A8). XXVa 139, 331. XLIX 1. VII 10. Transport list of August 8, 1944.

Barbie file in the Munich Public Prosecutor's Office and in the Library of American Documents in West Berlin.

INDEX